TABLE OF CONTENTS

THE FEDERAL WATER POLLUTION CONTROL ACT, AS AMENDED 63

INTRODUCTION TO THE 2ND EDITION

The basic structure of the 1972 Clean Water Act has lasted for fifteen years. During that time, however, the programs created have changed significantly as experience with and perceptions of water quality problems changed. Each of the major amendments to the 1972 Act significantly adjusted these programs. The law, its amendments, and the programs derived from the statute constitute a national water quality policy for the United States of America. That policy has evolved over time and that evolution has been strongly influenced by various factors and events. WPCF's "user's guide" to this edition of the Act interprets that evolutionary process.

The Federal Water Pollution Control Act Amendments of 1972--as the Clean Water Act is officially titled--was enacted October 18, 1972. It was the 500th public law passed by the 92nd Congress, hence its short title, PL 92-500. Congress intended the far-reaching set of national programs created in PL 92-500 to address almost every type of water pollution control problem. While not the first federal statute on this subject, PL 92-500 was, a distinct break with the philosophy underpinning previous statutes. Local, state, and national water quality programs since 1972 have been more firmly shaped by the assumptions in PL 92-500 than by any other law. In more ways than most people realize, Congress changed "business as usual" when it passed PL 92-500.

For the past 15 years, United States water quality policy has been built upon the four precepts set down on page 1 of the original 1972 Act.

One: no one has a right to pollute the navigable waters of the United States. Anyone wishing to discharge pollutants must obtain a permit to do so.

Two: permits shall limit the composition of a discharge and the concentrations of the pollutants in it. Anyone violating the conditions of a permit is subject to fines and imprisonment.

Three: some permit conditions require the best controls technology can produce, regardless of the receiving water's ability to purify itself naturally. In essence, Congress decreed that certain levels of control are--de facto--worth their cost.

Four: any limits or control higher than the minimum federal requirements must be based on receiving water quality. The only way to impose higher standards than those PL 92-500 called for was to demonstrate that continued protection of the receiving water demanded such limits.

The statute has been amended 12 times since 1972. Most of those amendments have been minor. Three of them, however, represent different phases in the Act's evolution. One phase was anticipated in 1972 and executed in 1977. The second phase, in 1981, was a major shift in the elements of the municipal construction grants program intended to resolve some serious differences between the Administration and both Houses of Congress. The third, adopted in

1987, extended the Act through 1994. It also brought the municipal construction grants program full circle, supplementing it with the type of state loan program discarded in the 1972 Act. Finally, the 1987 amendments extended the requirements for industrial dischargers of pollutants in toxic amounts starting a third round of effluent limit based on water quality considerations.

Two authorizing committees of Congress created the Act. One was the House Committee on Public Works and Transportation, chaired in 1972 by Congressman John Blatnik (D-MN). The other was the Senate Committee on Environment and Public Works, then chaired by Senator Jennings Randolph (D-WV). In addition to the strong influence of these two legislators, Congressman Bob Jones (D-AL) and Senator Edmond Muskie (D-ME) made critical contributions.

Although all of these legislators has since left Congress, and control of the Senate has passed from the Democrats to the Republicans and back again, the philosophical positions held by the House and Senate committees 15 years ago have changed very little. House leaders on recent amendments include Congressmen James Howard (D-NJ), Robert Roe (D-NJ), Gene Snyder (R-KY), and Arlan Stangeland (R-MN). With their House colleagues on the full committee, these Representatives continued to advance the interests of their predecessors. The same is true in the Senate, where Quentin Burdick (D-ND), George Mitchell (D-ME), Robrt Stafford (R-NH) and John Chafee (R-RI) held to thephilosophical assumptions presented by the Senate negotiators in 1972. Those contrasting positions of the two bodies, more than any partisan differences between Republicans and Democrats, created tensions that persist even today between the letter of the law and the intent of the lawmakers.

* * * * * * * *

HOW TO GET THE MOST VALUE FROM THIS EDITION OF THE CLEAN WATER ACT

To mark the tenth anniversary of the Act, WPCF published its first edition of the Act and its amendments in 1982. To mark its fifteenth anniversary, WPCF releases its second edition of the statute as amended. Because the 1987 amendments are the last major adjustment in the Act, this edition examines PL 92-500's precursors, as well as its programs. All of the features of the first edition have been retained. Additionally, our analysis of the statute, its amendments, the political circumstances at certain times, and the scientific and administrative issues has been extended through February 1987. The following user's guide has two parts.

Part I is a short history of water pollution control policy in the United States as it is reflected in national legislation. Historical analysis alternates between the legislation of a particular period and evaluations of the pollution control programs affected by that legislation. Alternating reveals an underlying cycle to U.S. water quality policy: legislate; implement; evaluate; then legislate again. This cycle is powered largely by the different answers made to a question: Do we control water pollution primarily by managing receiving water quality, or by managing effluent quality?

Part II has several elements. The first element is a summary of the Act's major feature, with an emphasis on changes made by the 1987 amendments. Use the summary of main features if your are already familiar with the basic statute but need an update on the latest changes. The second element is a section-by-section summary of the Act. Use this if you want a comprehensive review of the complete statute, or if you need to find a particular section but do not know its actual number.

Following the sectional summary of sections are synopses of four appendices with additional legislative provisions that related to the Act but which do not actually amend it. References throughout Parts I and II direct you to specific sections if you need detailed information at that point in your reading.

Do we control water pollution primarily by managing water quality, or by managing effluent quality?

* * * * * * * *

USER'S GUIDE, PART I

HOW IT ALL STARTED: U.S. CLEAN WATER PROGRAMS BEFORE 1972

1948-1956: Limited Federal Interest

Goals

The Water Pollution Control Act of 1948 (PL 80-845) was the first comprehensive statement of federal interest in clean water programs. PL 80-845 was also the first statute to provide state and local governments with some of the funds needed to solve their water pollution problems. Its primary sponsor was a former science teacher from Minnesota, Congressman John Blatnik. In the words of the statute, it was "...the policy of Congress to recognize, preserve, and protect the primary responsibilities and rights of the states in controlling water pollution". There were no federally required goals, objectives, limits, or even guidelines. There were no mandatory indicators of whether pollution was indeed occurring. Nevertheless, the U.S. Surgeon General was charged with developing comprehensive programs to eliminate or reduce the pollution of interstate waters.

Municipal Dischargers

PL 80-845 provided the trickle of federal aid to municipal wastewater treatment authorities that was later to become a torrent in PL 92-500. A five-year grants program was created to assist local governments by defraying the costs of preliminary planning and design work. The annual authorization was $1.0 million. Loans for construction were authorized for $250,000 or one-third the cost of construction, whichever was less. The only costs considered eligible for such loans were those of the plant itself and such major appurtenances as interceptors. This, too, was a five-year program with annual authorizations of $22.5 million.

Industrial Dischargers

To encourage the control of industrial water pollution, PL 80-845 created a five-year, $5.0 million study fund. The money was to be appropriated at $1.0 million annually and to be "...allocated equitably..." among the states. In addition to the municipal and industrial programs, the Act also authorized spending $800,000 a year for five years on a national water pollution control research facility in Cincinnati, Ohio. Later named the Robert A. Taft Engineering Center, this facility was the focus of federal clean water research for many years.

Compliance & Enforcement

Federal involvement was most strictly limited when it came to enforcement. The 80th Congress was very careful to respect that part of the Constitution that reserved to the states all authority not expressly given to the national government. Enforcement under PL 80-845 applied only to a pollution problem involving "interstate waters...which endangers the health or welfare of persons in a state other than that in which the discharge originates, and is...declared to be a public nuisance." Together with state authorities, the U.S. Surgeon General was empowered to investigate the quality of interstate waters in search of such problems.

Upon finding a public nuisance, the Surgeon General was required to give formal notice of the problem to the state and the discharger creating the problem. After a reasonable period of time he could give a second notice if no corrections were made. Should the second notice not produce a solution, again within a reasonable period of time, a public hearing could be called on the problem. Finally, after an investigation, two notices, and a public hearing, the U.S. Attorney General could be requested to bring suit against the discharger on behalf of the United States...but only with the consent of the state in which the discharge originated.

The federal program had no definition of a "reasonable" period of time to allow for each step in the process. Nor was there any mention of the civil or criminal penalties to apply in the event of an actual suit. To further limit enforcement, the statute specifically required the court to take account of "the practicability and...the physical and economic feasibility of securing abatement..." prior to passing judgment in a case. Obviously Congress intended state enforcement programs to take precedence over any national effort in all but the most unusual of cases.

1956-1969: A Growing Need For More Action

Goals

During the latter half of the 1950s and well into the 1960s, water pollution control programs were shaped by four statutes: the Federal Water Pollution Control Act of 1956 (PL 84-660); the 1961 amendments to that Act (PL 87-88); the Water Quality Act of 1965 (PL 89-234); and the Clean Water Restoration Act of 1966 (PL 89-753). All of these statutes dealt largely with federal assistance to municipal dischargers and with federal enforcement programs for all dischargers.

Municipal Dischargers

With each successive statute, federal assistance to municipal treatment agencies increased. The amount of funding authorized went up; the percent of total costs covered by federal assistance was raised; and the types of project costs that were deemed grant-eligible were multiplied. Yearly authorizations rose from $50 million in Fiscal Year 1961 to $1.25 billion in Fiscal Year 1971. The federal share went from a flat 30% to 30%, 40%, or 55%, depending upon the level of a state's matching grant. Grant eligibility was expanded to include feasibility planning, preparation of design and specifications, and actual construction. Only the definition of "treatment works" remained unchanged from the 1948 statute. In comparison to the 1972 law, however, legislation during this period allowed grants to be made only after all of the planning and design work had been approved by state and federal authorities. By 1972, more than 13,000 grants had been started in about 10,000 treatment jurisdictions.

Industrial Dischargers

There were very few direct provisions affecting industrial dischargers in the 1950s and 1960s. When industrial interests were mentioned, the provisions usually addressed such matters as industrial involvement in preparing comprehensive programs to eliminate or reduce the pollution of interstate waters.

Compliance & Enforcement

Changes in the federal enforcement authority came slowly. If anything, the state role was strengthened in the 1956 law by a provision encouraging state and interstate abatement actions. The notification and public hearing requirements of the 1948 Act were retained and clarified by defining a "reasonable time" for action as at least six months. Federal intervention was still limited to cases involving interstate waters. The laboratory in Cincinnati became home to mobile teams of engineers, chemists, biologists, and microbiologists used to investigate pollution problems. Enforcement conferences were still jointly run by federal and state authorities. And any remedial actions were largely the result of negotiated agreements, state agency pressures, or the force of local public opinion. The 1961 Act did little to change this pattern. PL 87-88 did permit, however, suits for abatement action on behalf of citizens in the state in which a problem originated -- though only with the written consent of the Governor.

Water quality standards become a prominent feature of the law with the passage of PL 89-234, the Water Quality Act of 1965. That law created the Federal Water Pollution Control Administration (FWPCA) and required the development of state water quality standards for interstate waters. Such standards were to be used in determinations of actual pollution. If a state failed to set standards in one year, the Administrator of the FWPCA was empowered to do so. The actual enforcement process remained unchanged and court action was taken only once during the period. Suit was filed against the City of St. Joseph, Missouri...but only after negotiations running from 1957 until 1973 broke down.

Any action against a discharger had to be based on a showing that its waste discharge reduced the quality of the receiving waters below established standards, or that it endangered health and welfare. Allocating waste loads among all dischargers within a stream segment was an immense technical exercise and a regulatory nightmare. In most instances the scientific basis for such allocations was questionable. When the allocations were finally made and the dischargers in violation identified, the questions weren't long in coming. It became very difficult to enforce the law.

Overall, enforcement actions were seriously hampered by four factors. First, there was a heavy dependence by the enforcing authority on the dischargers themselves to supply the data needed. Second, in many cases general water quality standards had not been written, much less specific effluent standards. Third, the burden of proof lay with the enforcing agency to demonstrate that a particular discharger was violating a stream standard or endangering the public health and welfare. And fourth, the chances of securing a meaningful judgment against a violator were reduced by the lack of civil and criminal penalties and by the statutory requirement that the court consider the cost of cleaning up the problem. A widespread perception that the water quality standards approach was flawed and the enforcement procedures were too time-consuming fed a growing conviction that a tougher set of standards and enforcement procedures had to be developed. The stage was being set for the 1972 Act.

1969-1972: Politics, Economics, and Ecology

Background

All through the 1960s and into the early 1970s this country experienced a period of sustained economic growth. But perceptions of growing national wealth were matched by an uneasy sense that the quality of life was declining. Clean air and water were no longer perceived as inexhaustible and unchanging. Nevertheless, it was a time of burgeoning technological prowess, convincing many that all problems could be solved by the creation of new products and processes. As a society, Americans were concerned but they were confident that the application of money and mindpower would provide short-order answers.

In the area of water pollution control policy there was mounting frustration over the slow pace of clean-up efforts and a suspicion that control technologies were being developed but not applied to the problems. A steady stream of investigations and reports issued from Congress probing the dimensions of the clean water problem and the inadequacies of existing programs. A sampler of six such documents illustrates this phenomenon. In 1968 Congress published the "Joint House-Senate Colloquium To Discuss A National Policy For The Environment" and "Waste Management and Environmental Quality Management." In 1970 came the "National Estuarine Pollution Study." The year 1971 saw the release of "Red Tape - Inquiring Into Delays And Excessive Paperwork In Administration Of Public Works Programs" and "National Environmental Quality Laboratories." And in 1972 Congress published "Toward A National Growth And Development Policy."

In 1970 Richard M. Nixon was President and, as any incumbent facing re-election would, was seeking some way to respond to the public's insistence that something more be done about pollution. The Administration's solution was to resurrect the Refuse Act of 1899, empowering the Corps of Engineers to issue discharge permits from the national level. There were problems with this initiative, however. The 1899 law had no provision for criteria or standards on which to base such permits, for example. But the move had considerable appeal within the Administration. It would take a cadre of highly skilled technical people and direct their energies into an area of high public visibility. It would respond to a growing number of critics of the Corp's existing mission: water resources development and maintenance. It also put the

Administration at the head of the vanguard favoring a new federal campaign for clean water.

Thus it was that the first national permit program was put into place during the three-year period from 1969 to 1971. But the Administration's bold stroke carried a political pricetag. Reviving the 1899 Act without congressional authorization, a clear legal basis, a legislative record, or consultation with key policymakers in Congress gave the House and Senate strong reasons to override their traditional differences and fashion a program of their own. Legislators felt Congress's prerogative to set policy was at stake.

In The House: A Matter Of Economics

House leaders, although concerned about guarding the legislature's prerogative to make law, were willing to work with the statutory elements at hand -- the 1899 Refuse Act and the water quality standards concepts of the 1965 Act. They wanted to tailor these basic materials to fit the needs of the day, fashioning an enforcement program based on criteria for water quality and effluent limits for discharge quality. House members recognized the importance of economics in any dramatic expansion of the national program. They sought ways to balance the costs of clean-up with the benefits, as well as clarification and preservation of the role of the states in any new plan. The major players on this side of the Hill viewed any new statute as dynamic: what was needed was an improved approach, time to gain experience in carrying that approach through, and then an evaluation before legislating further improvements.

In The Senate: A Matter Of Ecology

Senate leaders, on the other hand, adopted the guiding principle that restoring water quality and protecting public health should be the touchstones for new legislation. At issue was whether the goals and requirements should be based on economic or ecological principles. The Senate wanted ecological principles to dominate. Growing out of this viewpoint was the notion that pollution control technology could be forced, through a combination of statutory deadlines and ambitious requirements, to provide a much higher level of pollutant removal than had been the case up until that time. Set the deadlines and the standards, Senate thinking went, and municipal and industrial dischargers would install and refine more economical treatment systems in their own self-interest.

Compromise: Effluent Limits And Water Quality

It took nearly 18 months to arrive at a common position to resolve the differences created by these two philosophies. Even then, under the intensifying pressure of producing a bill to respond to the Administration's initiative, all of the major disagreements were not completely reconciled and it was left to administrative interpretation to settle the remaining issues.

At the start of the negotiations between the two sides Fate intervened and removed one of the key players, Congressman John Blatnik (D-MN). Blatnik was chairman of the House Public Works

Committee during the period when there was tremendous loyalty to committee heads and strict adherence to the seniority system. Known informally in the House as the "father of the Federal Water Pollution Control Act," Blatnik's influence pervaded every piece of clean water legislation since the 1948 Act. Recognizing the general preference of the Committee for public works programs, he knew that tensions ran high and that some serious compromising was in order. A serious heart attack prevented him from guiding his colleagues, however, and the mantle of leadership passed to Alabama Democrat Robert E. Jones as the next senior member. While Jones did necessarily not agree with Blatnik's philosophical position in every respect, he called the committee staff and the members together and gave orders that the panel would produce a water pollution control bill Blatnik could be proud of.

In the Senate, meantime, Senator Edmund Muskie of Maine emerged as the spokesman for a bill founded on ecological rather than economic principles. No doubt Muskie's presidential aspirations played an important role in his decision to adopt the issue of environmental protection as his own. Pollution abatement was important, but water quality restoration was fundamental. Thus it was that the questions of cost and affordability came to dominate the legislative conferences between the two chambers.

Yet throughout the negotiations a mutual regard for the constitutional role of the legislative branch kept the two sides working together. Congress should make laws and write them as clearly as possible for the Executive Branch to implement. A mutually acceptable bill had to emerge because the alternative was to give ground before the Administration's permit program, something neither side considered acceptable.

A NEW CHAPTER IS WRITTEN

The Federal Water Pollution Control Act Amendments of 1972

Goals

On October 18, 1972, Congress overrode a presidential veto to enact the Federal Water Pollution Control Act Amendments of 1972 (PL 92-500). In spite of its title, the new statute did not continue the basic components of previous laws as much as it set up new ones. On the basis of the Act's new provisions, the Federal Government, through EPA, assumed the dominant role in directing and defining water pollution control programs across the country. For better or for worse, that dominance has been maintained for the past ten years.

Section 101, "Declaration of Goals and Policy," concisely summarized the new order. Section 101(a) stated, "The objective of this Act is to restore and maintain the chemical, physical, and biological integrity of the Nation's waters." This was the clearest expression of the Senate's position that ecological concerns should be placed ahead of economic concerns. Elaborating on that position, the same Section set down two "national goals": (1) eliminating the discharge of pollutants into navigable waters by 1985, and (2) achieving an interim water quality level that would protect fish, shellfish, and wildlife while providing for recreation in and on the water wherever attainable. Section 101(b) made it congressional policy to recognize and preserve the states' primary responsibility to meet those goals.

Section 101(a) also contained four "national policies," each connected to specific provisions in other titles of the statute authorizing the creation of programs to fulfill those policies. Section 101(a)(3) made it national policy to prohibit the discharge of toxic pollutants in toxic amounts. Section 307 of Title III establishes the programs designed to accomplish this policy. Section 502(13) provides the working definition for "toxic substances in toxic amounts."

Section 101(a)(4) made it national policy to assist publicly owned treatment works (or POTWs as they become known) with federal grants. Practically all of Title II expands upon this policy. Section 101(a)(5) made it national policy -- for the first time -- to support area-wide waste treatment management planning at federal expense. Section 208 of Title II laid out the system for creating, funding, and evaluating such planning operations. Section 101(a)(6) called for a major research and demonstration effort to develop the technology that would be needed to "...eliminate the discharge of pollutants into the navigable waters, waters of the contiguous zone, and the oceans." The majority of provisions in Title I created the programs through which Congress expected this policy to be implemented.

Municipal Dischargers

PL 92-500 dramatically increased federal support for POTWs. In the year before the Act was passed the total federal contribution was $1.25 billion, a level that took ten years to reach. Section 207 of the Act authorized $5.0 billion for Fiscal Year 1973, $6.0 billion for Fiscal Year 1974, and $7.0 billion for Fiscal Year 1975. Perhaps as stunning as the amounts to be spent was the way in which they were to be made. Congress conferred upon the municipal construction grants program the status of contract authority, eliminating the need for prior appropriation action each year. The funds were to be automatically available for allotment and obligation at the start of each fiscal year. The heavy infusion of federal money carried with it an important deadline for POTWs. Section 301(b)(1)(B) required all treatment facilities existing on July 1, 1977 or approved for construction under Section 203 of the Act before June 30, 1974 to achieve secondary treatment as defined in Section 304(d)(1). Section 301(b)(2)(B) set an additional deadline of July 1, 1983 for a level of treatment described in Section 201(g)(2)(A) as "best practicable wastewater treatment."

Other incentives to reach the deadlines were built into the Act. Section 202 raised the federal share to a flat 75% whether states had matching grants programs or not. Section 205 expanded the period during which allotted funds were to remain available for obligation. States had two full fiscal years to obligate each year's allotment, compared to the 18 months allowed under the 1965 statute. Section 206 authorized $2.6 billion to reimburse treatment authorities that had built treatment facilities under earlier laws but had received less than the maximum federal share of 50% or 55%. And finally, the definition of "treatment works" eligible to receive new grants was expanded in Sections 212(2)(A) and (B) to cover almost every phase of wastewater treatment, effluent discharge, solids management, and stormwater control. Expanding the set of eligible needs meant expanding the national estimate of how much it would cost to meet those needs. PL 92-500 addressed this point in Section 516(b) by requiring the Environmental Protection Agency to make a biennial estimate of the total needs remaining to be met.

A comprehensive planning scheme was established through four interconnected provisions in the law. Section 201, often referred to as "facilities planning," set out the requirements for a specific plant. Section 208 set up an ongoing regional or "area-wide" waste treatment management process intended to embrace all industrial, municipal and non-point sources. Section 303(3) provided for basin planning within a state and Section 209 authorized interstate river basin planning. Separate appropriations were provided for Sections 208, 209, and 303(e).

In return for these incentives, however, the Federal Government expected municipal treatment authorities to accept certain conditions that directly affected their operations. Grants were made in three steps: feasibility planning; facility planning; and construction. At nearly every point in the planning, construction, and management of a treatment facility the Federal Government required POTWs to do more than they had in the past. For example, Section 201(g)(2) required any POTW or "grantee" to study alternative waste management techniques before settling on conventional technology. Section 201(g)(3) required the grantee to eliminate "excessive" infiltration and inflow from his system so that the works built with federal money would be treating wastewater and not groundwater. Section 204(a)(1) required a facilities plan to conform to the work done under area-wide waste management agencies funded by Section 208. Section 203(a)(5) limited the amount of reserve capacity a grantee could claim as eligible and Section 204(a)(6) required grantees to accept "two brand names or equal" when writing the specifications for plant components.

Section 204(b) contained two provisions that were to result in problems later on: one required grantees to institute user charge systems that made each user pay his "proportionate share" of the costs of treatment; the other required industrial and commercial customers to pay back their individual shares of the federal grant that was judged to be providing industrial rather than domestic capacity. Finally, Section 307(b) mandated the creation of "pretreatment" systems for controlling industrial discharges that would harm a treatment plant, interfere with the works, or pass through it to pollute receiving waters. These conditions, coupled with the three-step grant making process, created a much more complex relationship among all of the parties involved than had existed previously. It took several years for each party to learn its part in the new arrangement.

Industrial Dischargers

Direct industrial dischargers were, like their municipal counterparts, given two statutory deadlines to meet. It was generally accepted that these deadlines would apply to the control of conventional pollutants. First, Section 301(b)(1)(A) set July 1, 1977 as the date for meeting effluent standards written by the U.S. EPA. Those effluent limits were to be designed to apply the "...best practicable control technology currently available..." and became known as "BPT limits." Whenever a state's own water quality standards required an even higher level of treatment, that target had to be met by the July 1977 deadline. Second, direct dischargers also had a July 1, 1983 deadline set. Section 301(b)(2)(A) called upon them to install "...best available technology economically achievable..." that would bring them even further towards the national goal of eliminating all pollutant discharges by 1985. These became known as "BAT limits." The BPT requirement, coupled with BAT, was the legislative embodiment of the Senate's desire for a "technology-forcing" program.

But the statute did not stop at these two deadlines for conventional pollutants. There was an additional concern among the authors of the bill: toxic pollutants. Section 307(a) provided that the EPA Administrator must publish a list of toxic pollutants for which effluent standards must be written. Six months after publishing the list the Administrator was to publish a proposed effluent standard for each substance, taking into account its toxicity, the organisms it affected, and the importance of those organisms. If necessary, the Administrator could require zero discharge of a pollutant on the list. Generally, EPA was expected to publish final effluent standards six months after proposing them.

Section 307 reflected the Senate's underlying principle of ecology over economy. The test for putting a pollutant on the toxics list did not rest on human health consequences and did not take account of economic or technological limitations on control or treatment. Section 307(a)(6) required all dischargers covered by a toxic pollutant effluent standard to comply with it no more than one year after final publication.

In general, the provisions of PL 92-500 that applied to industrial dischargers were restrictive in nature, unlike the inducements of the Title II programs for POTWs. Industries, the reasoning went, could raise the money they needed to meet the new standards while municipal treatment agencies could not. Therefore grants were not an appropriate way for the Federal Government to secure improved treatment from the private sector. But, whether industry or municipality, all dischargers faced a radically different enforcement outlook than they had under any of the previous statutes.

Compliance & Enforcement

Title III of the Act provided the basic vehicles for compliance: effluent limits backed by water quality standards. Section 301(a) succinctly says that all discharges were to henceforth be illegal unless in compliance with Titles III and IV of the Act. Everyone wishing to discharge pollutants through a "point source" had to obtain a permit from either EPA or an authorized state agency. Section 510 of the Act preserved the authority of any state to set its own standards, where they were more stringent than those developed nationally. The permit system to enforce the new discharge controls was laid down in Section 402.

Together with the prohibitions in Section 301(a), the programs of Title IV gave EPA the authority to issue permits to every point source discharger in the country...and required it to do so by December 31, 1974, barely two years after the passage of the Act. Section 309 contained the penalties to be applied if a discharger failed to obtain a permit by the last day of 1974.

Previous enforcement provisions were vastly streamlined by the provisions in Section 309. If, on the basis of "...any information available to him..." the Administrator learned of a violation, he was able to immediately notify both the state and the discharger involved. State enforcement authorities had 30 days to act. If they did not act within one month, the Administrator was free to issue an administrative order requiring compliance or to initiate a civil suit against the discharger. Gone were the multiple notifications, the hearing, and the enforcement conferences. According to Section 309(c), any willful or negligent violator could be fined no less than $2,500 and no more than $25,000 per day of violation. A violator was also subject to possible imprisonment of not more than one year in addition or in place of any fines. Repeated violators could find themselves facing maximum fines of $50,000 per day or up to two years in prison or both. Nonwillful violators could be subjected to fines of $10,000 per day, as could any person knowingly making a false statement or representation regarding his discharge.

Mid-Course Correction

Congress was fully aware of the implications of the more stringent second-level, requirements called for by 1983. As a result, Section 315 was included in the Act as a way to re-evaluate the need for these requirements before they were implemented. The Section established a national study commission to make a complete investigation of "...all the technological aspects of achieving, and all aspects of the total economic, social, and environmental effects of not achieving, the effluent limitations and goals set forth for 1983." The commission was to be composed of five Senators, five Congressmen, and five members of the public. Three years were allowed for the report.

Implementation of PL 92-500

Goals

As various levels of government moved to implement the programs of the new law -- and Congress began its oversight of their actions -- controversy arose over the "true" meaning of the 1985 zero discharge goal. This provision was one of the key points in PL 92-500, but it meant different things to different lawmakers. Each stated his personal view in the legislative history, leaving EPA to select the interpretation it preferred.

In the House, for example, John Blatnik (D-MN), William Harsha (R-OH), and Bob Jones (D-AL) all made floor statements referring to the goal as a target, not a legally binding requirement. In the words of Chairman Blatnik:

> "...the direction from Congress is there. Increase the level of research. Initiate demonstration programs. Stimulate change. Provide the basis for calculation. Proceed in an informed manner."

On the Senate side, however, there was the notion of forcing technology and industrial process changes to actually achieve a zero discharge goal. To illustrate: Senator Muskie stated, "These policies simply mean that streams and rivers are no longer to be considered part of the waste treatment process. This fact in turn means that advanced treatment, a level of treatment not generally required under existing law, will be required for every community in the Nation...What we need to produce the technology required by the bill is a national commitment to what we want to achieve -- come up with modern technology, new and changed; it may not cost more. It may cost less to achieve."

Informed observers and affected industries took pains to point out the pitfalls of a literal interpretation as the effluent limits were written by EPA. And the agency, for its part, often used the strict interpretation of the 1985 goal as justification for proposing zero discharge limits for a number of industrial categories based on the BAT requirements of Section 301(b)(2)(A). Zero discharge of process wastewater has been proposed or required for BPT and BAT in several categories. Some are pesticide manufacturing, glass manufacturing, and certain subcategories of the inorganic chemical industry. Representatives from municipal and industrial dischargers also expressed concern about zero discharge, pointing to the ecological truism that pollutants removed from one medium were only transferred to another.

Municipal Dischargers

As with any new grants program, the municipal construction grants program required some time to reach the level of operation comtemplated by Congress. Had the availability of the first $18 billion gone as Congress intended, federal, state, and local officials would have had a difficult enough time coordinating their various responsibilities. As events turned out, the sustained influx of funds never occurred. President Nixon impounded $9.0 billion of the $18.0 billion total as soon as the Act was passed. The impoundment also withheld initial funds for the area-wide planning program of Section 208, leaving the facilities planning process of Section 201 and the basin planning of Section 303(e) to move ahead. The grants program received $2.0 billion in Fiscal Year 1973, $3.0 billion in Fiscal Year 1974, and $4.0 billion in Fiscal Year 1975 instead of the $5.0, $6.0, and $7.0 billion sums intended.

Section 516(b) required a Needs Survey every two years to adjust the allotment formula by which grant funds were divided among the states. Not surprisingly, states used the Survey as a way to keep their share of the allotment as high as possible. Section 510 of the Act made it possible for states to do so fairly easily, since it allowed them to set higher standards than the national requirement of secondary treatment and, some argued, committed the Federal Government to pay 75% of those needs.

From an initial estimate of $63 billion in 1972, the survey figure went to a high of $342 billion in 1974, dropped to $96 billion in 1976, rose to $106 billion in 1978, then hit $120 billion in 1980. In the beginning, state estimators tended to calculate their needs generously. It was difficult such estimates because of the imprecision with which some of the needs, such as combined sewer overflow correction and stormwater control, could be assessed. The 1980 needs survey represented perhaps the best evaluation to date, relying as it did on compilations of actual projects rather than broad estimates for metropolitan areas.

Between 1972 and 1977, congressional oversight hearings focused on EPA's administration of the grants program. The House Public Works and Transportation's oversight subcommittee was particularly active in this area. Several problems emerged as perennial obstacles to smooth implementation. Secondary treatment, called for in Section 304(d)(1), was rigidly defined by EPA, some critics charged. Less expensive treatment processes that removed slightly less than the 85% removal standard called for could not be used. High state water quality standards (often imposed in the rush to meet the Act's tight deadlines and urged upon the states by EPA) required advanced wastewater treatment in areas where the benefits of such treatment were only marginally better than secondary and certainly more expensive to the consumer. Small communities on relatively clean streams or at the headwaters of streams were particularly vulnerable to this problem.

As the 1970s wore on, the errosive effects of inflation took an increasing toll in the value of the grant dollars, hitting as high as 20% per year in some communities. The "two brand name or equal" requirement of Section 204(a)(6) limited the professional judgment of engineering firms and was cited as a factor in the filing of nuisance suits when a low bidder wanted to protest the selection of a higher bidder. A complex set of regulations and guidance was drawn up for the grants program, stretching the time it took to prepare grant applications as well as to approve them. Duplicate reviews of grant documents at the state and federal level lengthened the time even more. Hearings in the late 1970's revealed that the average time needed to design and build a treatment plant under the grants program was nearly twice as long as that required under the "old law."

As a final complicating factor, the Supreme Court ruled in 1975 that the Administration had acted improperly in impounding $9.0 billion of the $18.0 billion initially available for the grants program. The Court ordered the impounded funds released, leading to an injection of $9.0 billion in Fiscal Year 1976 -- literally twice as much as had been available for the preceding three years. Congress responded to the unlawful impoundment by enacting the Congressional Budget and Impoundment Act of 1974, in which the benefits of contract authority were eliminated and the grants program was placed on the traditional cycle of authorization, appropriation, and obligation.

Industries discharging to municipal treatment authorities found that the problems with the construction grants program affected their pollution control decisions, too. Three questions became increasingly important as the first statutory deadline approached. Would the POTW be on-line in time for its industrial customers to tie in before the July 1, 1977 date? Would the industrial cost recovery (ICR) payments required under Section 204(b)(1)(B) make it cheaper for an industry to become a direct discharger? What were the pretreatment requirements going to be?

As early as 1973, industrial plants in metropolitan areas had to start guessing whether their POTW was going to get the grants it needed to build the plants that business wanted to tie into. If the chances were good, then the 1977 deadline would probably be met and the costs of ICR and pretreatment became the next important questions. If the chances were not good, then each industry had to calculate its own chances of becoming a direct discharger and having BPT in place by the 1977 target.

Once the initial set of ICR regulations was drafted by EPA, many of the major metropolitan treatment authorities joined their industrial customers in arguing that the cost of implementing an ICR program was prohibitive, especially in cities where there were thousands on industrial and commercial customers, each requiring a separate calculation of how much grant money was owed to the Federal Government. ICR programs were not needed until a plant was completed. Thus, for the five-year period between 1972 and 1977 there was very little implementation of the ICR provisions in Section 204(b)(1)(B) because very few facilities requiring ICR were finished during that time.

With regard to pretreatment, the statute required EPA to publish mandatory pretreatment standards for each industrial category. Like BPT standards, pretreatment standards were to be technology-based. EPA's first pretreatment standards proposed limits that were equivalent to BPT limits for direct dischargers in the same category. Industries and municipalities were both dissatisfied with this approach, yet resolution of the practical problems engendered by a pretreatment program (as with ICR) were delayed by the fact that most POTWs were not far enough along in their construction programs to implement pretreatment. The issue simmered on the back burner while other questions, notably those for direct industrial dischargers, boiled away.

Industrial Dischargers

Theoretically, BPT and BAT standards were to be applied in successive 5-year stages roughly equal to amortization periods. When determining BPT under Section 304(b), the Administrator was to consider the total cost of the technology in relation to the effluent reduction benefits to be achieved. Factors to be examined included: the age of the industrial plant; the process used; the engineering aspects of the control technologies; and non-environmental factors such as energy requirements. The House conferees, in the legislative history of PL 92-500, went several steps further and specified that the term "total cost of application of technology" was to include both the internal costs of the industrial discharger and the external costs to the community such as potential unemployment, dislocation, and effect on the development of rural areas.

It came as no surprise, therefore, that industrial dischargers were quick to contest the scope and content of the effluent standards being proposed and the degree to which economic and social considerations had been incorporated into the standard-setting exercise. But cases involving BPT or BAT limits were largely technical in nature. For example, the key questions litigated were whether the Act required the imposition of nationally uniform standards, a single fixed number, or a range of numbers. Although courts upheld EPA's right to issue nationally uniform numbers, they also required the agency to build an extremely detailed record for each exercise in order to give the courts enough information to rule on the appropriateness of the particular numbers chosen. In American Meat Institute v. EPA, for example, the court said, "Since we...lack the expertise necessary to make such a judgment and the record is barren on the point...we are unable to uphold EPA." Legal opinions of this type contributed to the agency extending the time it took to set a standard, in turn delaying publication.

While these differences about interpreting the BPT requirements were being hammered out in court, there was general agreement that BPT itself was to be used to control conventional pollutants, i.e., biological oxygen demand (BOD), suspended solids (SS), and acidity factors (pH). Consensus was harder to achieve on the subject of toxicity control.

Section 307 uses phrases such as "preponderance of evidence," "ample margin of safety," and "the importance of affected organisms" to connote properly selected toxic pollutants and properly developed standards. These are subjective phrases that ultimately required value judgments, no matter how much data was on hand. Section 307 instruct EPA to first identify toxic pollutants based on their effects on organisms and then to issue effluent standards. Unfortunately, the toxicological and epidemiological knowledge of the 1970s was inadequate. There were too many gaps in the record on most substances with suspected toxic effects to permit prompt production of control standards for them.

During the 5-year period immediately following PL 92-500, EPA managed to propose effluent standards for only six toxic pollutants. Several public interest groups found this rate of progress unacceptable, considering that the law called for publishing a list of the substances only 90 days after enactment and the proposal of effluent standards for all such substances six months later.

In 1975 the Environmental Defense Fund (EDF) and the Natural Resources Defense Council (NRDC) filed suit against the EPA

Administrator under Section 505 of the Act, charging him with failure to perform a mandatory action by omitting certain substances from the list. By June 1976 EPA and the plaintiffs had entered into a consent decree that became the controlling element of EPA's development of toxic standards. The agreement opened a new avenue for implementing the law: consent decrees laying out court-ordered schedules of work.

Often referred to as the "toxics consent decree," this document required EPA to upgrade BAT effluent guidelines, industrial pretreatment standards, and new source performance standards. Revised standards for all of the substances and industrial categories covered by the decree had to be issued no later than December 31, 1980. This deadline was intended to give industrial dischargers at least two and a half years to comply with the 1983 BAT deadline. Under the terms of the decree, EPA was to make a full-scale regulatory push for 65 "priority pollutants" and their compounds...a total of 129 substances. The BAT standards to be produced from this effort were to be incorporated into the permits of some 14,000 dischargers divided into 21 industrial categories and further subdivided into 399 subcategories. In addition, the agency was to develop water quality criteria for each pollutant by June 30, 1978.

To over-simplify, the consent decree gave EPA 42 months to become roughly ten times as productive as it had been in the first three years of toxic regulatory action. Looking back, an outside observer might question the wisdom of entering into such an agreement, given the agency's past performance record. In fact, the task turned out to be beyond the resources at hand. EPA lacked the technical experts, the money, and the time to put together the package it negotiated in 1976.

Compliance & Enforcement

The period following enactment of PL 92-500 was devoted to starting the NPDES permit program. As described in Section 402, the program was EPA's principal way of carrying out BPT, BAT, secondary treatment, and the other enforceable requirements of the Act. In theory, every discharger had to obtain a permit or cease discharging effluents by December 31, 1974...just 26 months after the Act was passed. The EPA Administrator could delegate permitting authority to the states, thereby reducing its own workload, but every state, whether delegated or not, was required to review and certify each permit written for a discharger in its jurisdiction. So the need for two reviews -- one at the federal, one at the state level -- had to be included in the 26-month schedule.

Compelled by the statute to write permits for each of at least 60,000 municipal and industrial dischargers, the Agency quickly turned to outside contractors for the help it needed in gathering data on the hundreds of industrial categories to be covered in the program. Millions of dollars were spent on data collection and analysis. But the results were uneven: some work produced sound standards; other studies did not. Some industrial effluent limits were successfully challenged in court and remanded to EPA for more work. At least one standard was withdrawn after being proposed because the agency found the rule's foundation too flawed to withstand serious criticism. EPA was caught on the horns of a dilemma. It had a very short period of time to complete a large number of sophisticated studies that were subjected to very careful scrutiny by affected industries.

To cope with the problem, agency officials exercised their "best professional judgment" -- a mixture of the best data at hand, sound engineering, and common sense -- in some 57,000 cases involving industrial dischargers. But "BPJ" did not guarantee that all dischargers in an industrial category would be treated equally, so the idea of "uniform national standards" was not fully realized. State and federal permit writers managed to issue approximately 44,690 permits by the 1973 deadline. Out of that total, 3,808 were considered "major" sources in terms of the volume of their effluents. By the July 1, 1977 BPT deadline, nearly 90% of the major sources were believed to be on schedule with the installation of their pollution control facilities. Unfortunately, relatively few of the permits issued during this "first round" of the NPDES permit program were able to address the control of toxic pollutants in addition to the more conventional ones of BOD, SS, and pH. Because of the start-up time required for the municipal construction grants program and the initial impoundment of grant funds, only 30% of the municipalities were able to meet the 1977 deadline for secondary treatment.

The National Commission on Water Quality: Divided Over Direction

During the time that EPA was struggling with its toxic pollutant control program, the National Commission on Water Quality (NCWQ) was working to finish a comprehensive report on all phases of the Act. The concept of an outside review group grew out of the House position that PL 92-500 was a dynamic statute and Congress needed the benefit of an independent assessment before making any changes to it. In the original House position, the study required by Section 315 was to focus on the consequences of meeting the 1983 deadlines. Should the study validate the need for those standards and Congress act on that conclusion, then and only then would the 1983 requirements go into effect. In legislative conference, House members had to give up this idea of a "trigger mechanism" on the 1983 requirements in order to save the study commission concept.

Section 315(b) required the Commission to be composed of five members of the House Public Works Committee, five members of the Senate Environment and Public Works Committee, and five members of the public appointed by the President. The mandated composition of the Commission guaranteed that the philosophical and practical differences that dominated the House-Senate conference on the bill would be considered in the study. Since the statutory charge of the NCWQ was to examine the technological, economic, social, and environmental consequences of meeting or not meeting the 1983 goals and requirements, the Commissioners found themselves in the same quandary that the conferees had in 1972.

Because they were unable to reach unanimous agreement on a single set of recommendations, the Commissioners decided to publish a set of recommendations accompanied by a series of separate statements by the Commissioners. NCWQ chairman Nelson Rockefeller, then Vice President and formerly governor of New York, made a revealing statement in his opinion. "The data on which the recommendations were based," Rockefeller wrote, "are so comprehensive that arguments can be found for any position...but the Commission and its staff came to their conclusions on the basis of value judgments." (Emphasis added.) The Vice President also pointed out that an analysis of the 1983 requirement could not be made without first assessing the progress made in meeting the 1977 requirements.

Senator Muskie stated that the recommendations were "...a disservice to an otherwise excellent analysis..." and disassociated himself from them. Congressmen Jones, Harsha, and Cleveland gave qualified endorsement to the recommendations. At the heart of the differences among the Commissioners were these points. First, did the water quality benefits of the technological standards justify the expenditures? Second, to what degree should economic factors be taken into account when developing the 1977 and 1983 requirements? Third, was there a need for extensions or waivers regarding some requirements? And fourth, what were the appropriate methods for achieving toxic pollutant control?

As general recommendations, the Commission came up with the following:

1. Redefine the zero discharge goal to stress conservation and reuse.
2. Decentralize the construction grants program to emphasize state responsibilities and stabilize federal funding.
3. Retain the 1977 secondary and BPT requirements for municipalities and industries, but provide for time extensions and waivers.
4. Postpone application of the 1983 BAT requirements for five to ten years and meet the 1983 goal by applying the 1977 requirements.
5. Begin immediately to develop "...effluent limitations for the elimination of the discharge of toxic pollutants in toxic amounts."

MID-COURSE CORRECTIONS

The Clean Water Act of 1977

Goals

In December 1977 Congress completed its first major revision of PL 92-500. These amendments, known formally as the "Clean Water Act" due to a parenthetical revision in Section 518, were the result of four factors. First, the July 1, 1977 deadline passed, leaving 85% of major industrial dischargers in compliance with their BPT requirements but only 30% of major municipalities complying with the secondary treatment requirement. Second, there was a need to act on the recommendations of the National Commission on Water Quality, especially those dealing with the 1983 standards. Third, there was concern about the effect that the 1976 consent decree on toxics would have on the overall direction of the program. Fourth, political pressure was building for corrections to and multi-year appropriations for the construction grants program.

The new law, PL 95-217, endorsed the policy directions set in PL 92-500. The 1985 "zero discharge" goal and the 1983 "fishable, swimmable" goal remained intact. To realize the goals Congress chose to focus on revisions to Section 301 regarding BPT and BAT and to Section 307 regarding toxic pollutants. Section 301(b) was clarified to make it congressional policy that states manage the construction grants program, the NPDES permit program of Section 402, and the "dredge and fill" permit program of Section 404. As in the 1972 statute, this amendment to Title I was complemented by substantive revisions to Section 205(g) for the grants program, to Sections 402(d), (h), and (1) for the NPDES program, and a substantially modified Section 404.

Municipal Dischargers

The construction grants program received new authorizations for Fiscal Years 1977 through 1982. An authorization of $5.0 billion was approved for each of the last three fiscal years in that 5-year period. These sums were substantially below the levels in the 1972 Act, a recognition that the $7.0 billion level of 1975 was not realistic. A new element to the grants program was added when Congress decided to reserve or "set aside" certain percentages of each state's allotment for specific types of projects. The first of these was "innovative and alternative" (I&A) technology, as set forth in Section 205(i) and other related Sections in Title II. Congressman Don Clausen (R-CA) sponsored the I&A concept. Each state was required to set aside three percent of its allotment for projects using innovative or alternative treatment technology. One half of one percent was to be reserved exclusively for innovative products and processes. Section 205(h) contained a second set aside, this one for states with sizable rural populations. Four percent of the state's allotment was reserved for alternative projects in small communities. The term "rural" was defined in the Act; slightly more than 30 states qualified for the set aside under that definition. Rural set asides were the creation of Senator Robert Stafford (R-VT).

In another revision that modified the scope of PL 92-500, the wide range of eligible needs was narrowed. A direct restriction was imposed by the amendment of Section 211(c) removing pollution control for separate storm sewer discharges from eligiblity. An indirect restriction was applied by adding Section 216 giving states the authority to set their own priorities among the different categories of needs. Section 216 also gave the Federal Government the authority to challenge the placement of specific projects on a state's priority list. EPA wanted such authority to combat what it saw as a tendency among some states to fund lower priority projects, such as collector sewers, that were easier to move to construction than treatment plants. The agency's ability to challenge a particular project was tied to the enforceable requirements of

Section 301. Congressman Robert Roe (D-NJ) managed to temper this amendment somewhat by adding language identifying seven grant-eligible categories and specifying that no less than 25% of any state's allotment could be spent on projects in the so-called "pipe-related" categories.

The recommendation of the National Commission on Water Quality that states should be given more authority to administer the programs of PL 92-500 appeared as a new Section 205(g). It gave states up to two percent or $400,000 of their annual allotments to administer the construction grants program, whichever was greater. "State delegation" was a high priority amendment to Representatives James Cleveland (R-NH) and James Wright (D-TX), but delegation was not total. EPA still retained important approval authority throughout the grant-making process. Significantly, even with "total delegation" to a state, only the Administrator could make a grant award and only the Administrator could make judgments on fulfillment of the National Environmental Policy Act.

In several revisions to Section 301, Congress turned to the pressing question of how to deal with POTWs that had not met the July 1, 1977 secondary treatment deadline. To start with, PL 95-217 allowed for case-by-case administrative time extensions in Section 301(i) whenever the Administrator found that a municipality's failure to meet the deadline was caused by a lack of federal grant funds. PL 92-500 made no direct connection between the availability of grant funds available and the responsibility of meeting the deadline. In a more controversial move, Congress also created a waiver of the secondary treatment requirements by adding Section 301(h). Through it coastal communities might be allowed to discharge effluent of less than secondary quality. This amendment was the first chink in the concept of minimum national standards based on technology in the 1972 law.

Two other changes increased the chances that POTWs would be able to increase the speed with which they completed new facilities. During the preceding three years metropolitan treatment authorities had lobbied persistently for revisions in the user charge and ICR requirements of PL 92-500. A strict interpretation of Section 204(b) would have forced many authorities to re-calculate their systems of sewer and water charges...usually with the unpleasent consequence that most customers would have to pay more for their wastewater treatment. A move to raise public service charges was always unpopular at the local political level. Many treatment agencies felt their own systems were sufficient. The House was generally sympathetic to the point of view that local governments should have the freedom to develop their own administrative and financial systems. Thus, Section 204 amended to allow limited use of ad valorem tax systems in place of strict user charges.

House members were also concerned about the growing problem of implementing industrial cost recovery programs. To meet their concern, Section 204 was further amended to put a floor on the size of the industrial and commercial interests that had to pay ICR charges. In addition, Section 75 was written to require EPA to study the consequences of implementing ICR systems, since Congress had received repeated testimony that ICR systems would cost more to administer than they would recover. While the studying was being conducted, Section 75 required a moratorium on the collection of ICR charges.

Finally, Congress responded to the problems arising from EPA's initial efforts to vigorously implement the pretreatment requirements of Section 307 by completely rewriting most of Section 307(a) in a way that recognized the POTWs' capability to remove some of the substances in a pretreatment program. The idea was a simple one: industrial users of municipal systems would be allowed modifications of the uniform national standards that reflected the removals normally obtained at the municipal plant they discharged to. "Removal credits," as these modifications became known, seemed fairly straightforward, but EPA's subsequent implementation of the idea did not improve the pretreatment program.

Industrial Dischargers

Direct industrial dischargers also received extensions on the BPT deadlines, although the extensions were shorter and more limited because the vast majority of the major industrial plants had met the 1977 deadline. Municipal extensions went until July 1, 1983; industrial dischargers were allowed up to April 1, 1979. Municipal extensions depend on a finding that grant funds would not be available in time to complete construction before the deadline was reached. An industrial extension required findings of good faith - 22 - and a commitment of the resources needed to meet the April 1979 date; of no adverse effect on another discharger requiring installation of additional controls; an NPDES permit application on file dated no later than December 31, 1974; and construction underway on the facilities needed to meet the extension. Extensions aside, the basic BPT requirements of PL 92-500 were not changed by PL 95-217.

Major revisions for industrial concerns were made to the BAT requirements of the Act. The concept of BAT controls was clarified and expanded to include toxic pollutants under Section 307. While remaining one of the goals in Title I, the 1983 deadline was no longer considered directly enforceable with the establishment of new requirements and dates. Three distinct classes of pollutants were created and there was a renewed emphasis on controlling toxic substances.

Under the new law, EPA was to develop lists of conventional, nonconventional, and toxic pollutants. A group of conventional pollutants was the easiest to create because they were the most familiar. Biochemical oxygen demand (BOD), suspended solids (SS), acidity factors (pH), and fecal coliforms were classed as conventional pollutants under Sections 301(b)(2)(E) and 304(b)(2)(F). EPA had to set Best Conventional Control Technology standards for these substances and industry had to comply with those standards by July 1, 1984. Section 304(b)(3) required EPA to take into account the same factors that Congress had stipulated for BAT under PL 92-500, with the important addition that the agency must make a comparison between such standards and those developed for POTWs as a ceiling on the costs and the level of reduction to be required of direct dischargers.

Nonconventional pollutants are all those substances not defined as either conventional or toxic. Conceived as a catch-all category for such substances as phosphorous, nitrogen, and ammonia, nonconventionals would still require BAT standards. Consideration is to be given to cost and technology limitations when industries complied with those standards, but in no case could compliance be delayed beyond July 1, 1987. Statutory variances from effluent standards are to be allowed only for nonconventionals, based on economic hardship as covered in Section 301(c) or environmental considerations as covered in Section 301(g). The terms of Section 301(g) allows EPA to waive -- with state concurrence -- BAT requirements for nonconventionals where an industrial discharger bore the burden of proof to show compliance with BPT, water quality standards, and the 1983 goal.

The toxic pollutant category reflected the understanding reached in the consent decree between EPA, NRDC, and EDF. All of the 129 "priority pollutants" identified in that document were included in the category. By July 1, 1984, industry had to comply with effluent limits for all 129, according to changes in Section 301(b)(2)(C). For any substance added to the list, compliance was generally required one to three years after promulgation of the final standard. EPA was directed to use the criteria for setting standards contained in the 1972 Act and to publish standards no later than July 1, 1980.

Toxic pollutant revisions in PL 95-217 recognized the fact that EPA had failed to publish the vast majority of the effluent standards called for in PL 92-500 due to a general lack of sound scientific information about the pollutants, very few control technologies, protracted litigation sparked by industry's concern for the economic consequences of overly strict limits, and limited EPA resources. Congress intended the amendments to improve toxic pollution control and to free EPA's effluent standards process from the federal court direction, as stipulated in the consent decree of 1975.

Implementation of PL 95-217

Goals

The years 1977 through 1981 saw a gradual maturation of the national water pollution control program. "Mid-course corrections" in PL 95-217 contributed to this development. But so did some more mundane factors. People involved with the various programs created by PL 92-500 or PL 95-217 understood the complexities of their assignments more completely. The different levels of government learned to coordinate their responsibilities more efficiently. Industrial and municipal dischargers alike had the experience of operating under an NPDES permit or an administrative compliance schedule that took the place of such a permit.

Municipal Dischargers

Many states began using the innovative/alternative and the rural set-aside programs in the 1977 amendments. By the end of March 1981, 675 projects were using alternative technologies; 140 were using some form of innovative technology. The total value of facilities built under these programs was approximately $800 million. However, 17 states, six Territories, and the District of Columbia did not fund any innovative projects. Failure to take advantage of the set-asides was attributed to the reluctance to invest too much time and energy in a small portion of each state's total grants program. New programs required learning new ropes. By September 30, 1980, 32 states stood to lose all or part of their Fiscal Year 1979 set-asides. Congress agreed to give them more time to do so by passing PL 96-483, allowing them an extra fiscal year to obligate the money.

While the 1977 amendments on categorical eligibilities and state project priority lists were accepted as part of the program, state agencies found the delegation provisions a bit harder apply. Basically, each delegation agreement was a contract between the state agency and EPA setting forth a schedule by which the state would assume certain responsibilities from EPA. A pattern of progressive delegation emerged. States started by taking technical activities first, followed by administrative responsibilities for initial planning actions, and finally review of grant applications. While a relatively small number of states were able to complete agreements to take all of the responsibilities that EPA could legally transfer, most states were well on their way to delegation by the end of the decade.

Unstable federal appropriations continued to plague the construction grant program. The amounts appropriated each year between 1977 and 1980 varied significantly as Congress became increasingly concerned about the growing backlog of unobligated money in the system. In the spring of 1980, President Reagan attempted to defer the obligation of some construction grant funds, but Congress rejected the deferral and the money was released. One year later, the President had more success. In June 1981, Congress agreed to a recission of $1.7 billion, throwing a new uncertainty factor into the calculations of state and local grant managers attempting to meet the statutory deadlines.

Predictably, the biennial needs survey estimates continued to fluctuate. In the 1978 survey the total reached $106 billion; in 1980 it was $120 billion. Congressional supporters of the program became dismayed that the one-time, "catch-up" plan they initiated in 1972 was getting out of hand. Ever-changing needs were of special concern when viewed in light of the inflation rate in the construction industry and the absolute decline in annual appropriations. The needs grew and the dollars shrank. Despite ballooning costs, the construction grants program had reduced the actual treatment needs of the country significantly since 1972, but the progress was hard to measure.

Between 1977 and 1980, the practical problems of creating local pretreatment plans caught up with the grants program. Pretreatment standards for most pollutants had not been written. Local treatment authorities criticized the administrative requirements as being unrealistic. Industrial customers complained about the lack of consideration for removals at the POTW.

EPA responded with two studies. The first began in April 1981 and looked at the kinds of pollutant loads being contributed by industrial customers at 2,000 POTWs discharging more than 5.0 million gallons a day. Investigators found that industries accounted for 82% of the heavy metals going into a treatment plant. The second, commonly called the "forty city survey," showed that well-operated secondary treatment facilities removed significant amounts of heavy metals and complex organics. Armed with evidence that industrial customers were a major source of pollutants to be regulated through the pretreatment program and that POTWs could remove large amounts of those pollutants, EPA suspended the detailed regulations it had proposed and decided to seek legislative amendments on the issue.

Industrial Dischargers

Most of the amendments in PL 95-217 that affected industrial dischargers involved the toxic pollutant control program. Congress intended to take matters of scientific analysis and publication of effluent standards for toxics out of the courts and return them to EPA. Less than one year after the 1977 amendments were passed, however, the court again exercised its jurisdiction and ordered the initial decrees modified to change the deadlines a second time. EPA had not been able to meet them.

Representatives of the agency, defended its failure to fulfill the terms of the original decree by citing many of the same problems that had hampered earlier standard-setting efforts: lack of funds; insufficient time; inadequate data; and unproven analytical methodologies. At the insistence of the court, the parties to the original decree came to a new agreement. The list of affected industries was to be expanded and a new schedule for setting toxic effluent limitations was drawn up. Thirty-four industrial categories (and some 700 subcategories) were covered in the revised decree agreed to on March 9, 1979. In December 1979 the court extended the deadline for issuing final effluent limits to March 1981. In October 1980, water quality criteria for 64 of the 65 toxic pollutants were published. By the end of 1981, however, agency officials found themselves unable to meet the promulgation deadline in the revised agreement, once again throwing into doubt industry's ability to meet the July 1, 1984 treatment deadline of Section 310(b)(2)(C).

Compliance & Enforcement

During the 1977-1980 period many of the "first round" NPDES permits issued under the 1972 Act came up for revision. Because secondary treatment was required of all POTWs by July 1, 1977, all "second round" permits required immediate compliance with the secondary treatment goal unless EPA issued extensions pursuant to

Section 301(i). Many POTWs received such extensions because they could not receive enough construction grants money to complete their projects by the deadline. The extensions granted were good until the middle of 1983.

Section 301(b)(2)(B) of the Act required municipalities to install the best practicable wastewater treatment technology (BPT) by July 1, 1983. Since EPA decided to define secondary treatment as BPT for POTWs, the problem of meeting secondary for the July 1977 deadline and some other level of treatment for the July 1983 deadline was avoided. Thus second round permits for municipal authorities focused on proper operation and maintenance to ensure continued compliance with the effluent limits set in the first round.

By 1980 municipal treatment plants were removing approximately 32 million pounds of BOD and 38 million pounds of suspended solids daily. These figures represented a 57% increase over 1973 levels and was due in part to a significant increase in the number of POTWs capable of providing secondary treatment. One survey of the time showed that compliance with secondary treatment went from 40% in 1975 to over 75% in 1980.

MAJOR CHANGES IN THE CONSTRUCTION GRANTS PROGRAM

The Construction Grant Amendments of 1981

Goals

In 1981 Congress dramatically revised the municipal construction grants program. PL 97-117 brought the national program almost full circle. After critical reviews by EPA's Inspector General, the General Accounting Office, and House and Senate oversight and authorizing committees, Congress decided to act. The new law was designed to cut down on the time it takes to go through the grants program. It also focused more attention on creating a sound financial basis for POTW operations so that the plants built would meet their treatment capabilities.

After ten years of effort, the lion's share of municipal discharges had yet to be cleaned up. More than half of the country's 20,000 municipal dischargers, including 106 of the larger urban areas, were still unable to comply with the July 1977 secondary treatment goal. Thousands of construction grants projects had been started, approximately $26.6 billion in federal funds obligated, but only 2,223 projects worth $2.8 billion had been completed. Most of the completed projects were small, relatively simple facilities; projects for the larger treatment authorities had to be divided into phases or segments requiring many years' worth of regular grants.

Escalating costs explained some of the delay. Controlling the inflation that drove costs was beyond the scope of the Act. But congressional leaders felt other factors could be adjusted. Some of the more important were the stop-and-go federal funding; too much paperwork; serious understaffing of state and federal agencies; and the requirement to comply with over 54 other federal statutes and

Executive Orders. Projects that would have taken two or three years under "the old law" (i.e., PL 84-660 and its amendments before 1972) now took seven to nine years.

The Administration responded to these concerns by proposing a number of legislative reforms in the spring of 1981. EPA Administrator Anne Gorsuch presented the new president's program before House and Senate authorizing committeess. Deputy Administrator John Hernandez coordinated EPA's campaign to win congressional approval for Gorsuch during the rest of the year. EPA officials wanted to limit the types of eligibilities so that the long-term federal commitment could be kept down. By focusing on existing rather than future needs, they wanted to fund only treatment plants and interceptor sewers for the current population. To impress congressional leaders with how important the changes were, President Reagan stated that he would not ask for new money for the program in FY 1982 unless his legislative package was accepted. Congress adopted most of the revisions President Reagan requested. In return, the President signed PL 97-117 on December 29, 1981.

Municipal Dischargers

The provisions of the new law were tightly interconnected. To begin with, the range of eligible needs was to be reduced in a series of steps until only treatment works, interceptors, major appurtenances such as pumping stations, and infiltration/inflow would be grant-eligible. Section 201(g) was rewritten to say that grants could only be made for projects in these categories after October 1, 1984. Exceptions would be allowed in a few carefully described situations. Under Section 201(n) a Governor could set aside 20% of his annual state's allotment for projects in the other categories after October 1, 1984 if he wished. He could also use grant funds for projects designed to correct combined sewer overflows (CSO) if that need was a major priority for his state. A separate national fund of $200 million annually for CSO control in marine bays and estuaries was authorized. These exceptions aside, the beginning of Fiscal Year 1985 saw a return to federal support for the categories that were originally eligible in PL 84-660.

Fiscal Year 1985 was also the first year in which the federal share of eligible projects dropped from 75% to 55%. Section 202(a) mandated this return to the same percentage originally called for in PL 89-234, the 1965 law. As with eligibilities, however, some exceptions were allowed. Section 202(a) as amended also contained a "grandfather" clause for any primary, secondary, or advanced treatment facility, related interceptors, or any infiltration-inflow correction projects that received a grant for construction by October 1, 1984. Such projects could continue with 75% federal grants even if only one phase or segment of a multi-staged system made the October 1st deadline.

Section 204(a)(5) was revised to limit the amount of reserve capacity that would be eligible. Beginning with Fiscal Year 1985, grant awards were limited to that capacity needed to serve the population existing at the time the award was made. In no case could such population totals go beyond the figure applicable on

October 1, 1990. As with Section 202(a), treatment plant and interceptor projects awarded grants before the end of Fiscal Year 1984 remained eligible for a 20-year reserve capacity.

A fourth major change became effective immediately. As of December 29, 1981, Step 1 planning and Step 2 design work were not grant-eligible, except for projects that had combined Step 2 and Step 3 activities. Under Section 201(1), grants for Step 3 construction continued. At the time of a Step 3 award, grantees also received an allowance for their Step 1 and 2 work. Thus a grantee to pay the full cost of these activities before getting any grants. Allowances were based on the average historical cost of work done on projects of the same type and size, rather than on a particular project's own design and specification costs.

Even this change was not ironclad, however. Section 201(1)(2) directed states to set aside up to 10% of their yearly allotments in order to make advances to small POTWs that could not pay for the necessary planning and design work before receiving a Step 3 grant. In states with delegated management authority, the chances of a grantee receiving a Step 3 award and an allowance for his Step 1 and 2 work were increased by the addition of Section 219 to Title II. That provision gave the EPA Administrator 45 days to act on any Step 3 grant application submitted for award by that state. Failure to act in 45 days meant the state could consider the application approved.

Congress's concern for proper operation of grant-funded POTWs was formalized in a new section on engineering performance. Section 204(d) requires the engineering firm supervising construction or providing architect-engineering services during that period to continue working with the grantee for at least one year after construction is completed. The firm must oversee the operation of the new facility and, at the end of the year, the owner and operator must certify to the EPA Administrator whether the plant meets its design specifications and effluent standards. If it does not, the problems are to be corrected by the owner and operator at their expense.

Costs incurred by the engineering firm during its supervisory period are considered grant-eligible as part of the construction grant. A separate amendment to Section 201 reinforces this interest in proper operation by calling for EPA to encourage and assist grantees in the development of capital financing plans that look ten years into the future, project new improvements that might be needed, and set down how the grantee can finance such improvements.

Many smaller treatment authorities in rural areas found their needs eased somewhat by an addition to Section 304(d). Oxidation ponds, lagoons, ditches, and trickling filters are deemed to be equal to secondary treatment, provided water quality will not be adversely affected by such treatment. This redefintion of secondary treatment allows such communities to meet the July 1, 1977 deadline of the Act without building facilities that are too complicated or too expensive for them to operate.

Larger POTWs also received some relief from the pressure of meeting deadlines without reliable federal appropriations. PL 97-117 changed Section 301(i) to allow POTWs until July 1, 1988 to meet the national goal of secondary treatment. They could request an extension of their existing schedules (which did not go beyond July 1, 1983) in good faith, but had to demonstrate that federal funds were not available to them in time to meet the 1983 date.

Section 25 of the 1981 law called for a new Needs Survey. Congress required the survey by December 31, 1982, directing that it estimate the total cost and the amount of federal funds needed to fulfill the needs unmet so far. To do this, EPA had to isolate all current and potential phased or segmented projects from all other projects, since the former could still receive the 75% federal share for all of their eligible categories. In earlier surveys, phased and segmented projects had been informally estimated to comprise $8.0 billion in additional federal support.

Congress realized that existing water quality standards were driving up the cost of treatment in some places. To encourage more reasonable standards, it added Section 24 to the statute, directing states to review, revise, and promulgate new standards by the end of 1984. No construction grants could be made after 1984 where a state had not, at a minimum, reviewed the applicable standards.

Despite the mixed results of the 208 area-wide planning program created by PL 92-500, Congress remained committed to the concept of long-term water pollution control planning. In an addition to Section 205, the EPA Administrator is directed to reserve 1% or $100,000 of a state's construction grant allotment for water quality management planning. States had considerable flexibility in how they could use the funds. They could, for example, use them to revising water quality standards as called for in Section 24, described above.

Finally, Congress decided to clarify its wishes regarding the use of marine discharge waivers pursuant to Section 301(h). Revisions to that section opened the eligibility for such waivers to any coastal POTW, not just those with discharges as of 1977. Section 301(j) was amended at the same time to open the application period for one year after enacting PL 97-117, giving any new applicants from December 29, 1981 until December 29, 1982 to submit their requests for a modification of the secondary treatment requirement.

Implementation of PL 97-117

Goals

The 1981 amendments recognized that the construction grants program needed a thorough reform. EPA had actually started such a reform eight months before the Act was passed. Thus it is not surprising that the changes Congress ordered came quickly after enactment. The Administration was eager to provide local governments with more leeway in meeting the basic requirements of the grants program It also wanted to give state agencies more direct program management authority. In fact, these two goals were also uppermost in the minds of the House and Senate supporters of the program. The House Public Works and Transportation's oversight subcommittee set a 25% reduction in the time needed to go through the grants process as its benchmark for evaluating the success of legislative and regulatory reform.

Municipal Dischargers

EPA began its advance reform process by tackling the volumes of regulations and guidance created for the grants program since 1972. In April 1981 the regulatory reform effort started. It shifted into high gear by July and a streamlined set of proposed regulations was published in the Federal Register on November 1st. Congress agreed with most of the proposals and incorporated almost all of them into the 1981 law. Subsequent to the law's adoption, EPA reviewed its proposals and published interim final regulation in May. To complement that effort, a revised set of procurement regulations for all EPA grant-assisted projects was proposed in the Federal Register at the same time.

Agency policy makers continued to have difficulties working out an effective set of pretreatment regulations. By 1982, only a handfull of the pretreatment standards needed had been proposed. EPA's development of the removal credit concept was so cumbersome that major treatment authorities declared they could not use it, much to the dismay of their industrial customers. Yet work continued at the local level to develop programs that would meet the general pretreatment requirements still in force. At the time, EPA estimated that 80% of the larger POTWs and 39% of the smaller ones were working on such programs. Furthermore, the agency estimated that 65% of the heavy metals and 37% of the toxic organics from industrial customers were being removed through local programs. EPA's most important pretreatment objective was to issue pretreatment standards for some 34 industrial categories thought to be major sources of toxics discharged to municipal systems.

Industrial Dischargers

EPA continued to wrestle with the problem of promulgating BAT effluent standards. Initially industrial dischargers were to have up to four years to meet a given standard. But the longer it took EPA to issue the standards, the shorter the time industries will had to meet them before the BAT compliance date of July 1, 1984. By 1982, final BAT standards had yet to be issued for 26 industrial categories. The court-ordered schedule that EPA worked under required it to issue final regulations for the most important BAT and BCT standards no later than July 1, 1984...the same deadline that industrial dischargers to actually comply with the standards.

The court's schedule proved impossible to meet. Scientific knowledge about the pollutants to be controlled, about the methods used to analyze them, and about the treatment technologies to remove them was too limited. EPA faced the challenge of building build large and reliable data bases for substances about which very little is known, using techniques that are still being refined. During the late 1970s, for example, the agency used almost all of its laboratory capacity for toxic pollutant studies, but progress was slow in coming. It was as if EPA were given the task of building a bridge ...cross it at the same time.

Compliance & Enforcement

Enforcement activities for both municipal and industrial dischargers centered on revising national permits. On the municipal side, 3,371 "major" POTWs (i.e., plants handling one million gallons or more a day) had NPDES permits by 1982. Of this total, 2,956 were second-round permits, 775 were first-round permits. Some 2,805 of the second-round permits contained final limits requiring secondary treatment or better; 553 of those contained limits on toxic pollutants. In addition, EPA and the states re-issued approximately 50% of the permits originally written for 12,208 "minor" POTWs.

On the industrial side was judged in terms of meeting the 1977 BPT deadline. Approximately 81% of the major industrial dischargers met that deadline on time. In 1982, 96% of industrial dischargers had installed the necessary treatment equipment or were on compliance schedules to install it. These facilities reduce BOD by 69%; suspended solids by 80%; oil and grease by 71%; and dissolved solids by 52% of the amounts discharged in 1972. Monitoring data available showed that BOD reductions often yield significant reductions of toxic organic pollutants as well. BPT treatment also resulted in the incidental removal of heavy metals.

LEGISLATION TO IMPROVE IMPLEMENTATION, 1982-1986

Administration Bills HR 6670 and S 2652

Goals

In 1982 EPA announced a new set of amendments designed to deal primarily with the 1983 requirements for industrial dischargers. Because some of the proposed revisions were controversial and Congress had a full legislative calendar without this bill, House and Senate versions of the Administration's bill were carried over to the 99th Congress. Subcommittee and full committee action on them set the stage for alternative measures that became the basis for the 1977 amendments.

Municipal Dischargers

EPA proposed expanding scope of Section 301(i)(1) to allow more POTWs facing construction delays or lacking federal funds one year after the passage of the 1982 bill to apply for extensions up to July 1, 1988. Under the 1977 Act, POTWs could apply for extensions of the 1977 secondary treatment deadline for as long as July 1, 1983. Congress provided an additional 5-year extension for qualifying POTWs in the 1981 amendments. POTWs not eligible for the first extension could not apply for the second one. By 1982, however, some communities found they needed the extra time provided in the 1981 amendments.

EPA also proposed rewriting the national pretreatment provisions of the law. Agency officials requested three major changes in a renewed effort to create a national program that would meet the criticisms of POTWs, industrial customers, and concerned public interest groups. First, they wanted to clarify the removal credit concept. Second, they proposed to eliminate the reporting requirements of Section 402(b)(8). And third, they suggested Congress allow local pretreatment standards in place of the national categorical standards where appropriate.

Several other amendments dealt with continued authorizations, administrative fees for permit modifications, and state delegation. Sepcifically, EPA proposed five year reauthorizations for the research, demonstration, and development programs funded by Section 104(u)(1), the state program management provisions of Section 106(a), and the general authorizations in Section 517. The agency also advanced the idea of charging application fees of anyone wishing to modify certain permits. Finally, EPA proposed to amend the state delegation process in Section 402 by requiring a state to be fully delegated five years after the first delegation agreement was signed. The delegation amendment also required any state wishing to return delegated authority to give back all such power, rather than turn back a portion of its responsibilities.

Industrial Dischargers

By 1982, agency officials realized they would not be able to meet the promulgation schedules for BAT and BCT effluent standards set under the revised consent decree. Accordingly, many of the revisions proposed in the 1982 legislative package dealt with promulgation and compliance deadlines for these standards. Section 304(b), for example, gave the Administrator until July 1, 1984 to publish BAT and BCT effluent limitations. EPA also had until the same date to publish new source performance standards for the 27 industrial categories listed in Section 306(b)(1)(A) and for the toxic pollutants listed in Section 307(a)(1). Section 301(b)(2)(C) would be amended to give industrial dischargers four years (until July 1, 1988) to meet the toxic effluent standards EPA published. BCT compliance could be pushed back to the same date.

Compliance & Enforcement

Several changes in EPA's 1982 legislative proposal would have changed the course of federal enforcement programs. To begin with, the agency wanted to stretch the federal and state permit renewal workload by extending the period of NPDES permits from five years to ten years through a revision to Section 402(b)(1)(B). It also sought to create a new set of administrative penalties of up to $10,000 per day or a total of $75,000 for violations of Sections 301, 302, 306, 307, 308, and 405. That amendment -- a revision of Section 309(g) -- would apply identical administrative sanctions to any violation of the permit conditions or limitations of Sections 402 and 404.

Felony sanctions were toughened by several changes. A revised Section 309(c) changed "willful and negligent" violations of the section mentioned above to "negligent" violations only. Fines for such violations were set between $2,500 and $25,000 per day, one year in prison, or both. A second change to Section 309(c) penalized "knowing" violations with fines between $5,000 and $50,000 per day, two years in prison, or both.

Knowing falsifications of statements, records, plans, and monitoring devices, were punishable with fines up to $10,000, two years in prison, or both. Complementing these felony sanctions was an amendment to Section 502(5) that the definition of "person" was to include any responsible corporate officer. Lastly, Section 309(c) was enlarged with a definition of "hazardous substance" to explain how the new felony provisions applied to such pollutants.

The Pressure Mounts for New Amendments to the Act

The 98th Congress passed without further changes in the statute. During the first session in 1983, nearly everyone's attention was focused on the oversight investigations of alledged mismanagement in Superfund. Hearings led to resignation of President Reagan's first EPA Administrator, Anne Gorsuch Burford in the spring of that year. Several other high-ranking political appointees decided to leave as well. In May, William Ruckelshaus, EPA's first Administrator, agreed to return and pull the badly shaken organization back into shape. Congress welcomed Mr. Ruckelshaus's return, and that of the new group of Assistant Adminstrators he presented to the Senate.

In 1984, both chambers of Congress moved ahead with their own clean water changes. Each side went beyond the scope of anything the President would accept without a fight. House clean water leaders of the Public Works Committee pushed HR 3282 and 4037. Their measures contained a $3.4 billion annual reauthorization of the construction grants program, a $1.6 billion per year program of state revolving loans for wastewater treatment, and nonpoint source controls. This passed the House floor on June 26, 1984 but went no further. The Senate Environment & Public Works Committee offered S 431 which set strict deadlines for reaching industrial discharge limits and created a narrowly focused clean-up program from toxic "hot spots." It also launched S 2006, calling for new controls on urban runoff and rural nonpoint sources.

By the summer of 1985, the 99th Congress passed new versions of the 1984 measures. On June 13th, the Senate passed S 1128 by a vote of 94-0. Five weeks later, on July 23rd, the House passed HR 8 by a vote of 340-83. With the two versions reade for a legislative conference, Members turned away from clean water to concentrate on reauthorizing Superfund and on water resources. But something more than Superfund made it seem prudent to delay a legislative conference on the two bills until late 1985, or even 1986. Concern over the budget deficit had reached the point of panic. Congress felt a radical change in the mechanics of budget-making had to be made. Consequently, it passed the Gramm-Rudman-Hollings deficit reduction bill. The bill called for automatic cuts in the FY 87 budgets of EPA and other agencies if no other way was found to limit the deficit that fiscal year to $144 billion. To come anywhere close to a $144 billion deficit, Congress had to drop at least $50 billion from the total federal budget for FY 87.

Thus the second session of the 99th Congress opened in January 1986 with every agency and every interest group looking to protect the funding levels of favored programs. Authorizing new programs without cutting back on old ones seemed foolhardy. Construction grants looked particularly vulnerable, given the backlog of unobligated money among the states. Nevertheless, House and Senate conferees on HR 8 and S 1128 met twice that spring. They cleared away some of the minor differences between the two bills, but postponed work on construction grant authorizations, nonpoint sources, "anti-backsliding", and waivers for industrial dischargers.

Summer 1986 was spent in informal negotiations, work on a supplemental appropriations bills for EPA, and Superfund reauthorization meetings. Not until the final weeks of September were the conferees able to meet again for formal negotiations. Superfund, water resources authorization, clean water, and a budget reconciliation bill crowded the top of Congress's agenda as the legislature went into overtime in early October. Despite the pressure of off-year elections, House and Senate leaders kept their colleagues on the Hill until October 16th, less than one month before the elections of November 4th.

Clean water conferees resolved their final differences in the first two weeks of October. On October 15th, the House approved the conference report on a $20 billion extension of the Clean Water Act by a vote of 408-0. The next day, the Senate did the same with an equally impressive count of 96-0. Two days after the elections were over, on November 6th, President Reagan vetoed the bill. Because Congress had adjourned, there was no opportunity to override the veto. Reauthorizing the Act would have to wait until 1987.

Reagan's veto involved more than saying no to a bill that proposed to spend three times what the President had requested in 1985. While Reagan pondered his choices on the Clean Water Act, two other equally controversial pieces of legislation had been passed by Congress. One was a multibillion dollar extension of Superfund; the other the first water resources project authorizations in more than fifteen years.

Amid the pressures of Congress to adjourn for the upcoming off-year election, threats to stay in session to override potential veto of all three pieces of legislation, and pressures on the White House by incumbent Republicans asserting the election-related importance of supporting environmental legislation, it was widely-rumored that a deal was struck. Superfund would not be vetoed. House and Senate conferees on the water resources bill accepted certain cost-sharing reforms; and, the Clean Water Act would be vetoed after Congress had adjourned thereby allowing the Administration to take a public stand on fiscal issues while avoiding a politically-damaging confrontation between a Republican President and a Republican Senate.

Confrontation and Climax

President Reagan's pocket veto of the 1986 amendments did not deter congressional leaders from pressing the issue in the opening hours of the 100th Congress. The veto was a delay, but certainly not a defeat, from the legislators' point of view. The 1986 Amendments were quickly reintroduced in the as H.R. 1 and S. 1. They were approved and brought to the floor for vote without going through the regular committee procedures. On January 6th, the House overwhelmingly approved HR 1, 406-8. The Senate substituted HR 1 for S 1 to set up a vote on the same bill, considered and rejected by a vote of 17-82 an Administration alternative, and passed HR 1 93-6 on the afternoon of January 21st.

President Reagan steadfastly refused to accept the measure. He vetoed the amendment for the second time on January 30th, noting that the real issue at hand was not clean water but "...the federal deficit -- and the pork-barrel and spending boondoggles that increase it." Reagan referred to the $18 billion reauthorization of the construction grants program as "a classic example of how well-intentioned, short-term programs balloon into open-ended, long-term commitments costing billions of dollars more than anticipated or needed." He stated that treatment works funding "...is a matter that historically and properly was the responsibility of state and local government."

In retrospect, it is ironic that the 1972 Act also carried an $18 billion price tag and was also vetoed by a Republican president. In 1972, however, Congress assumed the original $18 billion program was enough to fully fund known treatment works needs. Fifteen years and $52 billion in federal aid later, Congress proposed a final $18 billion program, a portion of which would re-establish the states' responsibility for supporting wastewater treatment.

The House overrode the President's veto on February 3, 1987; the Senate on February 4, 1987. With the enactment of PL 100-4, the Water Quality Act of 1987, support for municipal wastewater treatment came full circle, returning to pre-1972 program elements; emphasizing technology-based standards for industrial dischargers; enhancing enforcement authority with increased civil, criminal, and administrative penalties; and recognizing the critical pollution problems of non-point sources.

EXTENDED AUTHORIZATIONS

The Water Quality Act of 1987

Goals

The 1987 amendments contained in PL 100-4 address the issues raised by the Reagan Administration's 1982 bills. They also return to the problems of the municipal construction grants program in what may be its final reform. No radical changes were made in the goals and objectives of Title I. Yet the way in which future progress towards those objectives will proceed resembles the arrangement of programs and responsbilities that existed before the 1972 Act was passed. Implicitly and explicitly, states are recognized as the level of government primarily responsible for making the federal program succeed.

Municipal Dischargers

PL 100-4 extends the authorizations for the construction grants program through FY 1990. Phasing out the grants program overlaps phasing in a revolving loan fund program for states so they can continue to support municipal wastewater treatment. The revolving loan fund program continues through FY 1994, at which time federal assistance for wastewater treatment will end. Together, these two programs are authorized at a total of $18 billion.

Congress encourages states to begin capitalizing their revolving loan funds immediately if they wish. Provisions in the 1987 amendments authorize states to deposit up to 50% of their FY 87 construction grant allotment in a revolving fund. That figure rises to 75% in FY 88 and 100% in FY 89 and 90. States must use the fund to make low-interest loans to communities in need of sewage treatment systems. A state fund "revolves" as the monies loaned out are returned, with interest, over time. The more money a state uses to capitalize its fund, the more long term construction it can support.

The overlapping of community construction grants and state capitalization grants is illustrated by the annual authorizations for each mechanism:

Construction Grants		Capitalization Grants	
1987	$2.4 billion	1987	-0-
1988	$2.4 "	1988	-0-
1989	$1.2 "	1989	$1.2 billion
1990	$1.2 "	1990	$1.2 "
1991	-0-	1991	$2.4 "
1992	-0-	1992	$1.8 "
1993	-0-	1993	$1.2 "
1994	-0-	1994	$0.6 "

A state revolving fund may be used for purposes other than wastewater treatment construction. The 1987 amendments permit a state to use monies from the fund to carry out the state-wide non-point source management plans authorized by Section 319. States may also use the fund to develop and implement an estuary conservation and management plan as authorized by Section 320.

There are several ways a state can use its revolving fund to support municipal construction. It may, for example, purchase or refinance local debt obligations. It can guarantee local obligations or purchase insurance for them. Or it can use the fund as collateral for state-issued wastewater bonds. States can even use their funds to guarantee "mini-funds" established on the local level. Finally, a state may use up to 4% of the fund to offset the fund's operating costs.

Congress extended the construction grants program and created a revolving loan program because it wanted to help municipalities meet the secondary treatment requirements of the Act. Congress could have extended the July 1, 1988 deadline set in 1981 at the same time it extended federal funding. Yet it chose to keep the

July 1st deadline, despite evidence that many communities would not meet the secondary treatment requirement at that time. It is noteworthy that Congress chose to not address this issue in the 1987 Amendments. At a minimum, this provides a handle for Congressional scrutiny of the construction grants and revolving fund programs, as well as state and federal enforcement activity in 1988.

Increased Congressional concern for toxics is reflected in new amendments to Section 406. These changes require EPA to identify toxics in sewage sludge and to establish numerical limits for maximum concentrations of these toxics. EPA must also develop sludge management practices geared to the protection of health and the environment from any reasonably anticipated adverse effect of each toxic pollutant. The management practices must enable a POTW to achieve the numerical criteria for each toxic no later than 12 months after they are published.

To ensure the implementation of these regulations, the NPDES (Section 402) permit for each publicly owned treatment works must be modified to include sludge management requirements which implement the toxic pollutant technical sludge regulations. Also, Section 406 makes it unlawful for any person to dispose of sludge from a municipal treatment works which is not in compliance with EPA's technical sludge regulations to further implementation of these regulations, EPA is required to develop and publish procedures for the approval of state sludge control programs.

New provisions to permit stormwater from separate storm sewers affects both municipal and industrial dischargers. Originally, the 1972 Act required EPA to issue a Section 402 NPDES permit for all point sources of pollution. The agency interpretted that requirement so that it could issue areawide permits for separate storm sewers, rather than each stormwater outfall. Subsequent court rulings held that stormwater outfalls, regardless of whether wastewater was discharged through separate storm sewers, also required individual permits.

Section 405 phases in stormwater permits. EPA is to publish regulations governing large municipalities those serving a population of 250,000 or more -- by February 1989 with permit applications due by February 1990, permits to be issued by February 1991. For municipalities serving between 100,000 and 250,000 people, EPA is to publish regulations by February 1991 with permit applications due by February 1992 and permits issued by February 1993.

EPA and the states with NPDES permitting authority have some flexibility in that they can issue permits on a system-wide or jurisdiction-wide basis. This means that an entire city or municipal service area could be covered by a single stormwater permit instead of permits for each individual outfall. Also, in contrast to the technology-driven treatment requirements of the Act, municipalities are to be held to a new "treatment" requirements of reducing the discharge to the maximum extent practicable.

Industrial Dischargers

Industrial dischargers remain more dependent on advances in technology for new limits and requirements than do municipalities. Unlike POTWs, industrial dischargers do not have a federal grants program to influence their rate of compliance. To a significant degree, industrial noncompliance results from EPA's inability to meet tight, back-to-back schedules to publish complex effluent standards.

These schedules were established by statute in some cases, and by settlement agreement with environmental activist organizations in others. The 1987 Act amends Section 301 to give industrial dischargers additional time to meet BAT and BCT effluent limitations. Compliance with each limitation is to be as expeditious as possible, not to exceed three years from the publication of the limitations on March 31, 1989.

EPA's flexibility in negotiating permit limitations on any one facility is restricted by Sections 306 and 404 of the 1987 amendments. Section 306 gives EPA statutory authority, with the state's approval, to set alternative BAT and pretreatment standards for an existing facility based on the existence of fundamentally different factors. These alternatives are known as "FDF variances".

Section 306 requires anyone applying for an FDF variances to prove that: (1) the facility is fundamentally different, on factors other than cost, from those factors considered in the effluent limitation or pretreatment standard; (2) the application is based solely on either information already submitted to EPA during the rulemaking which raised the fundamentally different issue, or information that the applicant did not have a reasonable opportunity to submit during the rulemaking; (3) the alternative requirement is no less stringent than justified by the fundamental differences; and (4) there will be no resultant non-water quality environmental impact markedly more adverse than those considered by EPA in developing the limitation or standard.

The anti-backsliding requirement is established by Section 404. The statute, in a new Section 402(o), provides that an existing permit may not be modified to require effluent limitations less stringent than those already written.

The Act provides that permits not based on published effluent limitations, so-called "best professional judgement" or "BPJ" permits, may be issued to relax permit limitations where: (1) material and substantial alterations which justify a less stringent limit were made to the facility after the permit was issued; (2) new information is available justifying less stringent limitations, or technical mistakes or errors of law were made when the original permit was issued; (3) a lesser limit is necessary because of events beyond the applicant's control; (4) the applicant has received a variance or modification before; or, (5) the applicant has installed and properly operated treatment equipment necessary to meet the permit requirements, but is unable to meet the limits.

No limit less stringent may be issued if it would lead to violating a water quality standard. Also, no BPJ permit may be renewed or modified to include a limit less stringent than an effluent guideline applicable at the time the permit is renewed.

In regard to stormwater discharges, industrial sources are still subject to BAT and BCT requirements. Compliance with permit requirements is to be as expeditious as practicable but no later than three years after the permit is issued therefore, stormwater permits are not subject to the 1989 BAT, BCT, and BPT deadline.

In regard to stormwater associated with industrial activity for which permits are required, there is some legislative history indicating that such a discharge is one directly related to manufacturing processing or raw materials storage. Discharges outside this definition could include discharges from parking lots and administrative buildings. Like municipalities, industrial owners of separate storm sewers are subject to a phased or tiered permit program. EPA must establish permit requirements by February 1989. Industries must file permit applications by February 1990. And the NPDES permit authority must act on the application by February 1991.

Compliance and Enforcement

Section 309(g) provides for a two-tier administrative penalty, modelled after that of the 1986 Superfund amendments. In Tier I, EPA may assess a penalty not to exceed $10,000 per violation up to a maximum of $25,000. The maximum is to apply regardless of the number of violations or number of days violation. There is an opportunity for an informal hearing. In Tier II, the penalty may not exceed $10,000 per day of violation with a maximum of $125,000. As with Tier I, there is opportunity for a formal hearing as provided by the Administrative Procedure Act.

EPA's new authority to assess civil penalties applies to violations of Sections 301 (BAT, BCT, water quality standards), 302 (water quality related effluent limitations), 306 (new source standards), 307 (toxics and pretreatment standards), 308 (inspections and monitoring), 318 (aquaculture permits), or 405 (sludge regulations). Before EPA issues an order assessing an administrative penalty, there must be public notice and opportunity for comment.

Section 309 was amended to provide more stringent civil and criminal judicial penalties. Negligent acts subject to a fine of $2,500 to $25,000 per day of violation, one year imprisonment, or both are defined to include: (1) negligent violation of Sections 301, 302, 306, 307, 308, 318, 405 or any pretreatment program (Sections 402(a), 402(b) or 404); or (2) negligent introduction into a public sewer system of any pollutant or hazardous substance which the person knew or reasonably should have known could cause injury to health or property, where such discharge was not compliance with applicable limitations or permits.

Where there is a knowing violation of the Act's requirements, the fine is between $5,000 and $50,000 per day, three years imprisonment, or both. For cases of knowing endangerment, the Act provides for a fine of $250,000, imprisonment for a maximum of 15 years, or both.

It is worth noting that the term "hazardous substance" in Section 309 was expanded to include four other environmental statutes: the Resource Conservation and Recovery Act (RCRA), Superfund (CERCLA), the Solid Waste Act (RCRA), and the Toxic Substances Control Act (TSCA). Thus a "hazardous substance" under the Clean Water ACt is any of the following: (1) a substance so designated under Section 311 of the Act; (2) any toxic pollutant listed under Section 307 of the Act; (3) any substance so designated pursuant to Section 102 of CERCLA; (4) any hazardous waste with characteristics identified under or listed pursuant to Section 3001 of RCRA; or (5) any toxic pollutant listed under Section 307 of the CWA.

State Role

The 1987 Act emphasizes state responsiblity for daily implementation more than any other amendment to the 1972 statute. For example, states can now create and manage self-sustaining revolving loan funds for municipal construction. Additionally, states have gained important new authority to manage and control toxic discharges and nonpoint sources of pollution.

For nonpoint sources, Section 316 requires each state to assess nonpoint sources of pollution within its boundaries. State investigations must identify nonpoint sources of pollution that contribute to water quality problems, as well as waters or stream segments unlikely to meet water quality standards without additional nonpoint source controls. State management programs must: (1) run for four years; (2) identify the nonpoint source controls necessary; (3) specify the programs which will apply the controls; (4) certify that the state has adequate authority to implement these measures; (5) all sources of funding for these programs; and (6) a schedule for implementation.

Four million dollars is authorized over four fiscal years for grants to states to implement the program. Also, funds are available under Title VI, the state revolving fund program to aid in implementation. To some degree this program resembles the groundwater wellhead protection program created by the Safe Drinking Water Act Amendments of 1986 reflecting an increasing trend to return program decisions to the state and local levels.

Similarly, the new toxics program created in Section 304(1) emphasizes the role of the states. By November 1987, EPA must publish guidance to assist states in identifying water bodies that will not meet water quality standards, after implementation of BAT and BCT, because of point source toxic discharges. By February 1989, each state must submit its list to the agency. The list will include the specific point sources of concern,plus strategies for controlling each source. Each strategy must be designed to reduce toxic discharges in tandem with the technology-based limits, so that water quality standards will be met. Water quality must come up to standard three years after the strategy is put into operation.

In some way, this program mimics the Clean Act's state implementation plan process in that EPA sets the air standards but it is left up to each state to develop its own implementation program. In the event that no state plan is submitted or EPA and the state are unable to agree on an approvable plan, EPA may develop and implement a federal implementation plan.

The similarities between state responsibilities after 1987 and state responsibilities before 1972 illustrate how important aspects of the overall national program have come full circle. Before 1972 discharge requirements were water quality-based. After 1987 discharge limits for many stream segments will again be water quality-based. Before 1972 states had much discretion how the water quality standards could be met. After 1987 must of that latitude is restored. Before 1972 states had project-level control over wastewater treatment construction. After 1987 the transfer of such control from the federal to the state level will accelerate. The parallels are significant, but it is important to remember that the changes made in 1981 and 1987 to create these similarities are based on what was learned and accomplished during the 15-year period in which federal control predominated.

CONCLUSION

Much has been accomplished since 1972, yet much remains to be done. Experience implementing the programs created by Act in the public and private sectors reveals the inherent limitations of basing those programs solely on water quality or technology considerations. Gradually, U.S. policy-makers are adjusting the law and the regulations to combine the two approaches. Congress's original 1972 decision to set minimum requirements using technology-based standards remains firm. But it has also created ways to effectively include water quality factors in subsequent standard-setting activities. Examples of this type of integration include marine discharge waivers; secondary treatment redefinition; best conventional control technology and the individual toxics control strategy are examples of this.

Fifteen years ago the differences between a water quality-based program and a technology-based one were seen as a question of ecology versus economy. That difference is real; it remains with us. But much of the antagonism created between the adherents of the two approaches has disappered. Disagreements have become much more specific. They now involve matters of practice, not matters of principle.

Today, the political and economic context surrounding Clean Water Act amendment and implementation is driven by increasing competition for decreasing funds. In 1985 and 1986, Congress had to adjust the pace of pollution control programs in the Act within that context. For that reason, perhaps the most revealing way to view the the 1987 amendments is to consider how they change the pace of national water quality improvements called for in 1972.

Speed and timing depend heavily on the factors discussed in this analysis. Federal assistance for municipal treatment will end in 1994. Municipal wastewater construction must meet the enforceable requirements of the Act. At the same time, the July 1, 1988 secondary treatment deadline remains in effect. Major program decisions will return to the states. Administrative and judicial enforcement programs are strengthened. The net effect of these adjustments is a deeper commitment to clean water.

* * * * * * * *

USER'S GUIDE, PART II

MAJOR FEATURES IN THE CLEAN WATER ACT TODAY

TITLE I - Research & Related Programs

Title I states the ultimate objective of the Act, namely "...to restore and maintain the chemical, physical, and biological integrity of the Nation's water." Two national goals support the objective: elimination of all pollutant discharges to navigable waters by 1985 and achievement of fishable and swimmable waters wherever attainable by 1983. Four national policies support these goals. Each policy is elaborated upon in the programs authorized within the Act.

For example, Sections 104 and 105 authorize major research and demonstration programs to implement the national policy of Section 101(a)(6). Title I also recognizes that the states have primary responsibility for controlling pollution within their borders and for managing the municipal construction and permit programs of the Act.

Title I also establishes several other programs. Section 117, for instance, authorizes the Chesapeake Bay Program, funds for maintaining the program, and funds for 50% matching grants.

TITLE II Grants for Construction of Treatment Works

Title II provides the necessary funding, eligibilities, and requirements for federal grants to construct publicly-owned treatment works (POTWs). It also encourages basin planning, area-wide planning, and annual surveys by the EPA Administrator of treatment plant operations. Title II contains the general order of priorities to be followed when making grants.

Funding & eligibilities. Section 207 of the Act authorizes 4 years of grants, at $2.4 billion annually in Fiscal Years 1987 and 1988, and $1.2 billion in Fiscal Years 1989 and 1990. The Act also retroactively authorizes $2.4 billion in appropriations for Fiscal Year 1986 (Section 207). Funds are allocated among the states and Territories according to a new Congressional allotment formula (Section 205(c).)

Grants are available to cover 55% of the cost of treatment plants, interceptors and major appurtenances, and correction of infiltration/inflow (Section 202(a)(1)). If, prior to the beginning of Fiscal Year 1985, a 75% grant was made for the actual construction of a segment or phase of one of these three project types, then the federal share for such projects remains at 75% (Section 202(a)(1)).

Design/build projects are eligible for grants, as long as the estimated cost does not exceed $8 million, and the project contains one of the allowable types of treatment systems. Design/build projects cannot exceed 20% of the total of the construction grants funds alloted to any state in Section 205(c). (Section 203(f)).

The Governor of a state may set aside up to 20% of the state's annual allotment to be used for any of the categories which would otherwise not be eligible for federal grant assistance (Section 201(g)(1)). Additionally, the Governor may choose to direct some portion of the general construction grants funds to correct high priority CSO problems (Section 201(n)).

Reserve capacity. Construction grants may be used to fund only the capacity needed to serve the population existing at the time the grant is made. (Section 204(a)(5)). If a grant was made for construction of a segment or phase of a plant or interceptor before Fiscal Year 1985, then all segments and phases of such a facility will be funded for reserve capacity on the basis of 20-year population projections. (Section 204(c)).

Project planning. As of December 29, 1981, grants were made only for actual construction, not feasibility planning or for detailed plans and specifications. At the time a construction grant is awarded, the grantee will receive an allowance to offset some of the costs of planning (Section 201 (1)). A state is required to reserve up to 10% of its allotment for planning loans to small communities if they would be unable to finance planning and design work otherwise. Any such advances are to be subtracted from the grantee's available allowance (Section 201(1)(2)).

Set-asides. Grants to states for water quality management planning are authorized at not more than 1% or $100,000 of a state's annual construction grant allotment (Section 205(j)). Of this amount, 40% must go for comprehensive planning by appropriate regional and interstate organizations. If such organizations are found not to be assisting in development and implementation of such planning, this 40% may be reduced by the Administrator with the agreement of the Governor. If a state is fully delegated, however, its management grants rise to 2% or $400,000 of its allotment (Section 205(g)). To ensure prompt attention to a delegated state's recommendation for approval of a grant application, the agency must act within 45 days or the application is deemed approved (Section 219).

States are also required to set aside from 4% to 7 1/2% of their allotment to fund innovative and alternative technologies (Section 205(i)). A separate 4% to 7 1/2% set-aside for alternative technologies in rural communities must also be created (Section 205(h)).

Marine Combined Sewer Overflows (CSO) and Estuaries. Beginning in Fiscal Year 1987, funds are reserved before being alloted to states to address water quality problems in marine bays and estuaries. The amount reserved is 1% of the total funds appropriated Fiscal Years 1987 and 1988, and 1.5% of the total funds appropriated for Fiscal Years 1989 and 1990 (Section 205)(1).

Two-thirds of the reserved monies are to be used to address water quality problems in marine bays and estuaries impacted by stormwater and sanitary sewer overflows discharges. The other third of reserved monies shall be used for the implementation of the National Estuary Program, authorized under Title III. The National

Estuary Program calls for comprehensive management plans to be developed and implemented for estuaries of national significance.

Project Performance Certification. Architect-engineer firms hired by the grantee are required to remain associated with a completed facility for one year after completion. During that year the engineer is to supervise the plant's operation and to train personnel. All of the costs for such follow-up services are grant-eligible, except corrections to the facility. At the end of the year the owner must certify to the permitting authority whether the plant is meeting design specifications and effluent limitations (Section 204(d)).

Comprehensive Planning. General planning activities are provided for in five sections of the Act. These are Section 201 for treatment facilities; Section 205(j) for state-wide planning; Section 208 for area-wide planning, Section 209 for interstate river basin planning, and Section 303(e) for basin planning within a state. For practical purposes the most active programs are those in Sections 201, 205(j), and 303(e).

TITLE III - Standards & Enforcement

Title III of the Act provides for the establishment of technology-based effluent limitations for municipalities and industries (Section 301(b)). States are required to establish water quality standards (Section 303). Technology-based limitations prescribe minimum standards of performance for municipal and industrial dischargers without regard to the quality of receiving waters (Section 304(b)). In contrast, water quality standards identify intended uses and set the biological and chemical conditions necessary to sustain those uses (Section 303 and 304(a)).

Generally, technology-based standards set minimum control requirements that dischargers must meet. Where those limitations are not adequate to achieve a particular designated use, then state water quality-based standards come into play and prescribe the additional controls necessary to meet the designated use (Section 303(d)).

Municipal dischargers. By July 1, 1977 municipalities should comply with secondary treatment (Section 301(b)(1)). Currently EPA may extend the time for compliance until July 1, 1988 (Section 301(i)). Oxidation ponds, lagoons, ditches, and trickling filters are recognized in law as the equivalent of secondary treatment (Section 304(d)(4)).

Industries discharging to municipal treatment works must comply with pretreatment standards. Uniform national standards are to be developed by EPA for any pollutant that would otherwise pass through or interfere with the operation of a facility. EPA may grant "removal credits" where municipal facilities have demonstrated their ability to remove significant amounts of such pollutants (Section 307(b)).

Industrial dischargers. Industrial dischargers must control three classes of pollutants: conventionals; toxics; and non-conventionals.

For conventional pollutants, "best conventional technology" or BCT must be met by three years after effluent guidelines are published but not later than March 31, 1989. (Sections 301(b)(2)(E) and 304(a)(4)).

For toxics, the Act refers to a list of 65 "priority pollutants" and requires industries to install the best available control technology achievable or "BAT" three years after effluent guidelines are published, and in no case later than March 31, 1989. Industries have one to three years to comply with standards set on any pollutant added to the priority pollutant list (Sections 301(b)(2)(C) and (D)).

Any pollutant that is not classified as conventional or toxic is considered non-conventional. Industries have until three years after effluent guidelines are published but not later than March 31, 1989 to install BAT for non-conventional pollutants (Section 301(b)(2)(F)). When developing BAT and BCT standards, EPA must take into account a range of economic and technological considerations (Sections 304(b)(2) and (4)). Variances from BAT and BCT standards may be granted under certain circumstances (Section 302).

Toxic Pollutants. Title III also establishes a program to identify those water bodies not achieving water quality standards because of toxic pollutants discharges and point source implementation of specific measures to reduce these discharges. The states must assess and identify affected water bodies and by February 1989, set specific effluent limitations for these discharges in NPDES permits. These individual control strategies must assure water quality standards are attained. States must also expand and revise their standards to include all Section 307(a) toxic pollutants where EPA has set standards and where discharge of these pollutants can reasonably be expected to interfere with designated uses.

Among other duties, EPA must publish information on methods for establishing and measuring water quality criteria for toxic pollutants. It must look at biological monitoring and assessment, as well as other methods that do not set pollutant-by-pollutant criteria.

Enforcement. Section 309 has two types of penalties: administrative and judicial. Administrative penalties are divided into two tiers: Class I, specifying a certain dollar amount and an informal hearing, and Class II, specifying a certain dollar amount and a formal hearing after certain requirements of the Administrative Procedures Act (APA) have been observed.

Judicial penalties are divided into civil and criminal categories. For criminal penalties, there are four types of violation:

Negligent violations - fines of not less than $2500, but not more than $25,000 per day of violation, or imprisonment for up to one year, or both;

Knowing violations - fines of not less than $5000 and not more than $50,000, or imprisonment for up to 3 years, or both

Knowing endangerment - fines of not more than $250,000 or imprisonment for up to 15 years, or both;

False statements - fines of not more than $10,000 or imprisonment for not more than 2 years, or both (Section 309(c)).

Civil, criminal and administrative penalties were strengthened by the 1987 amendments. Section 313 of PL 100-4 raises civil penalties in Section 309 from $10,000 per day to $25,000 per day for each violation, and authorizes civil penalties for violations of any requirement imposed in an approved pretreatment program.

The EPA Administrator or his authorized representative is granted certain powers of inspection, monitoring, and entry onto private property for the purposes of enforcing the Act (Section 308).

Variances for "Fundamentally Different Factors". EPA has the discretion to modify permit requirements where a facility owner can demonstrate that the facility is fundamentally different with respect to factors other than cost. Section 301(n) of the Act establishes specific statutory authority for the Administrator, with the concurrence of the state, to establish alternative effluent limitations for BAT and pretreatment standards for existing sources for a facility based on FDF factors. There are four criteria that must be satisfied before an FDF variance can be granted (Section 301(n)).

TITLE IV - Permits & Licenses

Title IV establishes the National Pollutant Discharge Elimination System (NPDES) permit program that is the heart of the Act. NPDES permits are the key to enforcing the effluent limitations and water quality standards of the Act. Every point source discharger must obtain a permit from either EPA or an authorized state. Allowances are made, however, for additional pretreatment of conventional pollutants and the establishment of a partial permit program for discharges into navigable waters (Section 402).

NPDES permits are required on a phased basis for municipal and industrial stormwater point sources. Generally, industry and large cities are required to obtain a permit by 1991, small cities have until February 1992. This section also defines categories of dischargers. Best available treatment (BAT) and best conventional treatment (BCT) will be required for industrial stormwater sources. Municipal sources will be required to reduce discharges "to the maximum extent practicable" (Section 402(p).

Unless in compliance with a permit, all dischargers are considered unlawful and are subject to the civil and criminal penalties in Sections 301(a) and 309. Anti-backsliding prohibitions prohibit renewal, reissue, or modification of permits where effluent limitations are less stringent than those in the previous permit except in certain defined situations (Section 404).

Title IV also sets criteria for the granting of ocean discharge permits. (Section 403). A separate program for permitting the disposal of dredged or fill material from or in navigable waters appears in Section 404.

Section 405 provides general directions on the disposal of sewage sludge from municipal treatment authorities. Section 405(d)(2) requires that EPA promulgate regulations to identify toxic pollutants present in sewage sludge and specify acceptable management practices for each such pollutant. Initial sludge regulations must be issued by August 31, 1987. Additional regulations must be published by June 15, 1988.

TITLE V - General Provisions

Title V embraces a diverse set of programs, authorities, and responsibilities. Administrative procedures and judicial review provisions appear here. Some key elements of the title are: Section 502 on definitions in the Act; Section 505 on citizen suits to compel compliance with the Act; Section 510 declaring a state's prerogative to require more stringent effluent or water quality standards; and Section 517 with general authorizations for EPA's programs.

TITLE VI - State Water Pollution Control Revolving Funds

Title VI establishes a system of federal grants to capitalize state-operated water pollution control revolving funds (SRFs). SRFs may be used to finance POTW design and construction and (eventually) for projects under the nonpoint source and estuary programs. States must provide a 20% match, and must make binding commitments to provide assistance equal to 120% of the grant payment within one year.

Funds from SRFs must first be used to assist projects that will assure progress toward compliance with the enforceable requirements of the Act, including the municipal compliance deadline. Once the enforceable requirements are met, any other treatment works, nonpoint source, or estuary project can be funded. Assistance can be in the form of loans, loan guarantees, or security on debt.

Over six fiscal years, $8.4 billion is authorized, beginning in 1989. SRF funds are to be alloted according to the formula for grant funds contained in Section 205(c). States may choose to direct 50% of their 1987 Title II allotments, 75% of their 1988 allotments, and 100% of their subsequent allotments toward revolving funds.

PART II

THE CLEAN WATER ACT SUMMARIZED, BY SECTION

TITLE I - Research & Related Programs

Title I declares the ultimate objective of the Act is "...to restore and maintain the chemical, physical, and biologicical integrity of the Nation's water." Two national goals support that objective. First, eliminate all pollutant discharges to navigable waters by 1985. Second, achieve fishable and swimmable waters wherever attainable by 1983.

Four national policies support the goals. They are: (1) prohibit the discharge of toxic pollutants; (2) provide financial assistances for publicly owned wastewater treatment plant construction; (3) implement areawide waste treatment management processes; and (4) make a major effort to develop the technology needed for completely eliminating pollutant discharges.

The Act's ultimate objective is an ideal state that all ofits practical aspects should contribute to in some way. But neither the objective nor the two goals supporting it are legally enforceable requirements. Only the four national policies contain programs and deadlines that can be enforced through the judicial process.

After stating the objectives, goals, and policies of the statute, the remaining sections of Title I describe a variety of coordinated research efforts intended to further the purposes of the Act. Section 102 discusses coordination between U.S. EPA and other federal agencies, and EPA and state agencies. Section 103 encourages multi-state compacts for pollution control. A long list of research, investigations, training, and information programs are authorized in Section 104. Section 105 focuses tightly on research efforts designed to advance various facets of wastewater treatment technology.

State pollution control programs are supported in Section 106. Acid drainage from mines can be fought with the demonstration programs in Section 107, as can pollution problems of the Great Lakes in Section 108. Sections 109, 110, 111, and 112 outline a federal investment in operator training programs run by state agencies and institutions of higher learning.

Specific programs considered especially important when the Act was originally passed or amended appear in the remaining six sections of Title I. Section 117 and 118 are the latest additions to this collection. The Chesapeake Bay Program, in existence since 1972, is formally incorporated into the statute through Section 117, while a Great Lakes National Program Office is created at EPA by Section 118. Section 118 also recognizes U.S. commitments with Canada forged in the Great Lakes Water Quality Agreement of 1978.

TITLE II - Grants For Construction Of Treatment Works (See also Title VI)

Title II creates a federal grant program to support construction of publicly-owned treatment works (POTWs). Its provisions authorize funding, define eligible projects, and set requirements for state and local participation in the grant program. It also creates four of the five comprehensive pollution control planning programs called for in the Act, the fifth program appears in Title III. The Title II programs are POTW facility planning in Section 201, statewide planning in Section 205, areawide planning in Section 208, and interstate river basin planning in Section 209. Of the programs created under this title, those in Sections 201 and 205 are the most active now.

Section 201 explains the specific purposes the grant program is designed to promote. Section 202 describes how different types of POTW construction qualify for different amounts of federal assistance. The necessary plans, specifications, and cost estimates for any grant project are set down in Section 203. Section 204 lists the conditions that a proposed project must meet before it can be approved. Noteworthy for the controversy they created during implementation are the limits on reserve capacity at POTWs, "two brand names or equal" clauses in any contracts let under a grant-funded project, and user charge mechanisms such as ad valorem taxes.

Section 205 is one of the most politically sensitive provisions in the law. It includes the allotment formula EPA must use to divide construction grant funds among the states and territories. Limits are set on how long states may keep allotted funds before they must earmark them for particular grants or return unobligated money to the U.S. Treasury for re-allotment among the remaining states. Small percentages of a state's annual allotment must be set aside for specific types of projects and for the state's own water quality management program.

Section 206 directs the federal government to partially reimburse POTWs that raised their treatment capabilities to the levels required by the Act prior to 1973. The amount of reimbursement for advance construction varies with the date of the improvements.

Section 207 contains the yearly authorizations for the construction grant program. For fiscal years 1982 through 1985, the federal government is authorized to appropriate $2.4 billion annually. Authorization expired in 1986 until the Act's 1987 amendments were finally adopted. Those changes authorize four more years of grants: $2.4 billion annually for fiscal 1987 and 1988, $1.2 billion annually for fiscal 1989 and 1990. The 1987 amendments retroactively authorize $2.4 billion for fiscal 1986.

Section 208 creates the areawide waste treatment program. Congress wanted areawide plans to address point- and nonpoint source pollution within areas delineated by a state or group of communities. Plans were produced through the 1970s, but no funds have been appropriated for this provision since 1980. Section 209 directs the President to prepare "Level B" plans for all river basins in the United States, as outlined in the Water Resources Planning Act.

Section 210 requires EPA's administrator to annually survey the efficiency of POTWs built or improved through the grant program in Section 201. Section 211 prohibits Title II grants to sewage collection systems (other than major interceptors) except in two types of projects. The various construction programs of Title II are limited by the definitions of "construction," "treatment works," and "replacement" appearing in Section 212.

Section 213 establishes a loan guarantee program for POTW construction. Through it the EPA Administrator guarantees loans issued by state and local governments to the Federal Financing Bank exclusively. A guarantee is only available if, without one, the originator cannot find enough credit on reasonable terms in the private market. The Secretary of the U.S. Treasury determines whether credit is available on reasonable terms. This section of the Act has not been used once since 1972.

Section 214 directs the EPA Administrator to create an ongoing public education program about recycling and reusing wastewater, land treatment for effluents, and wastewater reduction methods. The "Buy America" requirement for anyone receiving a grant under Title II appears in Section 215. Deciding the relative priority of one type of grant project, compared to any other type, is a prerogative of state agencies, subject to the conditions set down in Section 216.

Sections 217 and 218 detail the cost-effective considerations that all participants in the grant program must fulfill. "Life-cycle" cost analysis and "value engineering" are two of the better known requirements covered in these sections.

Section 219 is the final provision in Title II. It gives the EPA Administrator 45 days to act on grant applications that a state certifies as meeting all relevant requirements in the Clean Water Act. If the Administrator does not act within 45 days, the application is automatically approved.

TITLE III - Standards and Enforcement

Title III contains the standards and standard-setting procedures that must be used in the National Pollutant Discharge Elimination System (NPDES). Some Title III sections explain how to develop and apply "technology-based" effluent limits. Others outline the process for creating "water quality-based" effluent limits.

Technology-based limits prescribe minimum standards of pollution control for municipal and industrial dischargers without regard for the quality of the receiving waters. In contrast, water quality-based standards identify an intended use for the receiving waters and prescribe the biological and chemical conditions that must be met to sustain that use.

Permitting authorities (EPA or the states) use technology-based standards to set minimum control requirements for all dischargers to a body of water. In some cases, however, technology-based standards are not enough. If water quality does not support the designated use even after every discharger meets his technology-based standards, additional controls must be applied. Water quality-based standards are the basis for such restrictions.

Section 301 makes any discharge of pollutants unlawful unless it complies with this section and Sections 302, 306, 307, 318, 402, and 404. The limitations set forth in this section are the technology-based limits called for by the Act. Some of the substances controlled by technology-based limits are known as "priority pollutants" because they appear on the Priority Pollutant List created by Congress in the 1977 amendments to the Act. Several deadlines for meeting the various limits are built into Section 301. The most important are:

July 1, 1977 - the date by which industrial dischargers must apply "best practicable control technology" or "BPT" to their effluents.

July 1, 1977 - the date by which industrial customers of municipal treatment systems must comply with local pretreatment requirements and the conditions in Section 307.

July 1, 1977 - the date by which POTWs must meet effluent limitations based upon "secondary treatment", or more stringent limits if required by the state.

July 1, 1988 - the date by which POTWs, unable to meet the 1977 deadlines because they could not finance needed construction, must complete their improvements and attain secondary treatment.

"Promulgation + 3 years" - a date three years from the day an effluent limit is promulgated by which industrial dischargers must meet that limit for for toxic pollutants, for other pollutants, and "best conventional pollutant control technology" or "BCT."

March 31, 1989 - the latest possible date by which industrial dischargers must meet BCT, "best available technology" or "BAT" , and any other effluent limits required by the Act.

Section 301 also contains several subsections that describe exceptions to the deadlines just listed. For example, coastal municipalities that discharge to the ocean can apply for waivers from the secondary treatment requirement in situations carefully circumscribed by the provisions in 301(h). Industrial dischargers can seek waivers based on "fundamentally different factors" under 301(n). Such waivers are known as "FDF variances." EPA may charge application fees for some of the waivers and variances contained in this section.

Finally, Section 301 describes the authority that the EPA Administrator has to add or remove substances from the list of priority pollutants. It outlines a set of procedures that must be followed whenever a substance is moved on or off the list.

Section 302 requires "water quality-based" limits wherever meeting the technology-based standards in Section 301 fails to achieve or maintain the water quality called for in the river or stream. Public involvement in setting water quality-based standards for a particular body of water is required, and provisions are made to waive such standards for any discharger who can prove that meeting it is not worth the social and economic costs in his case.

Section 303 provides for a transition to the water quality standards required by the Act if states were in the process of setting their own standards immediately prior to the Act's adoption in 1972. It also details the way in which such standards are reviewed and modified by states. Section 303 also requires states to identify the waters within their boundaries that cannot meet water quality even after all dischargers apply technology-based limits. It then lays out a process to develop and apply the water quality-based limits called for in Section 302.

Since Sections 302 and 303 deal with the extremely complex matter of setting water quality standards, Section 304 mandates a long term program of research and analysis to produce the information needed to create such limits. The standards must be based on ideal limits call "water quality criteria," tailored to the designated uses of the water body in question. Section 304 also tells U.S. EPA what it must do to adopt or revise the technology-based standards of Section 301.

Section 304 applies to programs in Title II as well. For example, it directs EPA to issue guidelines on identifying and controlling nonpoint sources of pollution. To fulfill its mission in this area, EPA investigates a range of activities that cause diffuse, intermittant flows of pollutants. Runoff from fields and forests, mining activities, construction, underground injection, and salt water intrusion are examples of nonpoint sources. Programs under the jurisdiction of the Secretaries of Agriculture, Interior, and the Army are affected by EPA's actions under Section 304, so the provision involves their departments in 304 programs, too.

Section 305 requires EPA and the states to prepare a nationwide inventory of point source dischargers and of water quality in all navigable waters. The report must be presented to Congress by January 1, 1974, and updated every two years thereafter.

Section 306 establishes a list of particular industrial dischargers, arranged according to their activities, for which controls called "performance standards" must be set. These dischargers are termed "sources". The Act orders EPA to set performance standards for "new sources" which start discharging after PL 92-500 is passed. New source performance standards require an industry to adopt the best pollution control technology and methods available at the time it begins discharging.

Section 307 returns to the Priority Pollutant List mentioned in Section 301. This section describes the factors that EPA must consider when setting effluent standards for priority pollutants. It requires public consideration of those standards before they are finalized and orders all standards reviewed every three years. There are two types of standards for priority pollutants. One group applies to industries that discharge their effluents directly to receiving waters. The other group applies to industries that must pretreat their effluents before releasing them to public sewers.

Section 308 invests EPA with the authority needed to require all dischargers to maintain adequate monitoring and record-keeping facilities. It also prescribes how EPA and its authorized representatives can inspect a dischargers facilities or its records and monitoring stations.

Continuing with the theme of enforcement, Section 309 sketches the boundaries for federal enforcement programs. Under it, EPA has the authority to seek administrative, civil, or criminal penalties against violators. It may: issue administrative orders requiring a discharger to comply with its NPDES permit; take civil action against someone; or seek criminal penalties for negligent violations, knowing violations, or false statements in any of the documents required under the Act. This section also describes various forms of judicial review available to anyone assessed a civil penalty under the Act.

Section 310 acknowledges the international implications of national water pollution control. EPA has authority to locate U.S. sources of international pollution and then involve the states where such discharges reside in negotations that are designed to reduce pollution endangering people in a foreign country. Negotiations must also include the Secretary of State or his representatives.

Pollution control moves offshore in Section 311. This section declares a U.S. policy prohibiting the discharge of oil or hazardous substances to navigable waters, waters in the "contiguous zone", or waters of the Outer Continental Shelf. At the heart of Section 311's requirements is the National Contingency Plan for removing oil and hazardous substances. The National Contingency Plan and related programs are capitalized by a federal deposit of $35 million, with supplemental appropriations considered by Congress whenever the balance drops below $12 million. Section 311 authorizes the federal and state governments to recover the costs of pollution control and of damages caused by violations, depositing them in the Plan's account.

Section 312 addresses the use of marine sanitation devices. Programs and procedures created by Section 312 are intended to prevent the discharge of untreated or inadequated treated wastewater from vessels. Companies producing such devices must comply with certain provisions in the section; marina owners and vessel owners with other provisions.

Section 313 deals with the need to control water pollution from federal facilities. Military bases, national parks, and a myriad of other federal installations must obey the Clean Water Act as much as any nonfederal discharger. Waivers and exceptions to the Act's requirements can be obtained under certain circumstances.

The desire to protect water quality in publicly owned lakes is contained in Section 314. A "Clean Lakes" program is created in this section, through which states can survey their lakes and apply for federal assistance to improve the water quality in some of their more seriously degraded ones. Specific lakes are named as demonstration sites for pollution control and restoration techniques.

Section 315 creates a 15-member National Study Commission to investigate the technical, economic, and social aspects of meeting the requirements of Section 301. The Commission's report and any recommendations for improving the programs created by PL 92-500 were presented to Congress in 1976, some three years after the Act was passed.

Section 315 creates a 15-member National Study Commission to investigate the technical, economic, and social aspects of meeting the requirements of Section 301. The Commission's report and any recommendations for improving the programs created by PL 92-500 were presented to Congress in 1976, some three years after the Act was passed.

Section 316 tackles the phenomenon of thermal pollution in receiving waters. The effluent standards presented in Section 301 include standards for controlling the temperature of discharges to receiving waters, since water temperature strongly influences the biological and chemical activities within a stream. Power plants are most directly affected by the requirements of this section.

In Section 317, Congress directs the EPA Administrator to study alternatives to the municipal construction grants program in Title II. The possibility of using a pollution abatement trust fund, analogous perhaps to the national Highway Trust Fund, is specifically mentioned as such an alternative. As directed by this section, EPA delivered a study to Congress in 1974 and recommended that the grants program be continued.

Aquaculture is granted special consideration under Section 318. In it, EPA is authorized to set special discharge requirements under controlled conditions for any aquaculture project approved under Section 402.

Section 319 is one of the 1987 amendments to the Act. It encapsulates much of what has been learned about nonpoint sources and their control in the last 15 years. States are directed to inventory waters within their jurisdiction that fail to meet water quality standards because of nonpoint source pollution. Then they present EPA with a plan for controlling nonpoint sources and a schedule for doing so. Once the inventory of affected waters and a plan for controlling them have been presented to EPA, the agency is authorized to make grants to any state that implements such a plan.

A second major 1987 addition is the National Estuary Program in Section 320. Through it, state governors can single out an estuary and ask EPA to convene a "management conference" to produce an overall plan for controlling water quality in the estuary. Eleven estuaries are given top priority. Among them are Long Island

Sound, Narragansett Bay, Puget Sound, Delaware Bay, Galveston Bay, and San Francisco Bay.

TITLE IV - Permits & Licenses

Title IV is the heart of the Clean Water Act. It contains the National Pollutant Discharge Elimination System (NPDES) that limits discharges to the navigable waters of the United States. Every point source discharger must receive a permit from either EPA or an authorized state. Thus, the permit system is the key to enforcing the effluent limitations and water quality standards of the Act. Allowances are made, however, for additional pretreatment of conventional pollutants and the establishment of a partial permit program for discharges into navigable waters. Permits for separate storm sewers are required, as are permits for dredging and disposal of dredge spoils.

Dischargers without permits or in violation of their permits are considered unlawful and are subject to the civil and criminal penalties in Sections 301 and 309. Permit limitations are reviewed and changed as needed. But "anti-backsliding" provisions prevent renewal, re-issue, or modification of permits where effluent limitations are less stringent than those in the previous permit except in certain defined situations. Since wastewater treatment produces sludges composed of the solids removed from the waste stream, Title IV includes directions for managing the disposal or recycling of such sludges.

Section 401 requires everyone planning a pollution discharge to certify that they will comply with all limitations placed on that discharge under the provisions of Title III. The certification procedure allows for public comment on the proposed discharge, interstate negotations if an adjacent state objects to the discharge, and review of the discharger's operations to verify they can meet the limits. No discharger can receive an NPDES permit without certification.

After being certified, a discharger must comply with the provisions in Section 402. This section describes in great detail what must be done by each involved party when an NPDES permit is issued. It also spells out the authorities that a state must have if it wants to take over permit-writing responsibilities from the U.S. EPA. Partial assumption is possible, and provisions are made for returning authority to EPA, if necessary.

Some exemptions to the permit requirement are allowed. These are listed in Section 402, along with certain types of waivers from other permit requirements, cross-referenced to provisions in Title III. "Anti-backsliding" safeguards appear in Section 402, as do requirements for permitting separate storm sewer discharges.

Section 403 addresses the problem of issuing permits for ocean discharge. The Act prohibits discharges in marine waters unless they comply with guidelines EPA issues under this section. If the information on a proposed discharge and its effects is insufficient to make a reasonable judgment under the guidelines, no permit can be issued.

Section 404 authorizes a special permit program to control dredge and fill operations. It makes the Secretary of the Army responsible for issuing such permits. But the Secretary and the EPA Administrator are jointly responsible for setting the guidelines by which permits are to be judged. EPA is involved in the 404 permit program in other important ways, too. For example, EPA controls what areas can be listed as suitable disposal sites and can prohibit certain materials from being discharged at an approved site on certain grounds. Permits issued under Section 404 expire at the end of five years.

Section 405 brings the management of wastewater treatment sludge under the NPDES permit program. It requires EPA to identify by November 30, 1986, those substances whose toxicity and persistence can render a sludge hazardous to public health. By August 31, 1987, the Agency must publish a final set of regulations for the proper disposal of such sludges. A July 31, 1987 deadline is set for identifying a second set of sludge contaminants with final regulations for their control due by June 15, 1988. Finally, Section 405 allows a sludge management agency to meet its permit obligations in this area by complying with alternative sludge disposal provisions in a permit issued under the Solid Waste Disposal Act, the Safe Drinking Water Act, the Marine Protection, Research & Sanctuaries Act, the Clean Air Act, or an EPA-approved state permit program.

TITLE V - General Provisions

Title V embraces a diverse set of programs, authorities, and responsibilities. Administrative procedures and judicial review provisions appear here. Specific terms whose exact definitions are important to understanding the scope of PL 92-500 programs are defined in this title. Important powers that are reserved to state governments, plus a citizen's right to sue under this statute fall under Title V's purview.

Section 501 gives the EPA Administrator the basic authority to carry out other sections of the law. Section 502 defines such key terms as "person", "pollutant", "navigable waters", and "discharge of pollutant", among others. Section 503 establishes a Water Pollution Control Advisory Board within EPA to advise the Administrator on policy matters arising under the implementaton of the Act. Section 504 allows the Administrator to move swiftly through the U.S. district courts to restrain any discharge that threatens public health or the livelihood of people such as shellfish harvesters.

Section 505 allows any citizen to take civil action on his or her own behalf against someone else who violates provisions in the law. Courts are allowed to award such a plaintiff the costs of their litigation if they prevail or "...substantially prevail..." in a civil suit. Section 505 also allows the Governor of a state to initiate action against the federal government in the person of the EPA Administrator if EPA fails to enforce the standards and limits in the Act, causing harm within that state.

Section 506 requires the U.S. Attorney General to represent the United States in any civil or criminal action in which the EPA Administrator is a party. However, the section permits EPA attorneys to represent the United States in civil actions when the Attorney General chooses not to do so.

Section 507 protects any employee who files or supports the filing of an enforcement action under the Clean Water Act. Employees can not be fired or discriminated against in any way simply because they report violations of the Act. Along the same line, this section authorizes EPA to investigate any business that threatens to close its facility or reduce its workforce on the rationale that it cannot meet permit requirements without doing so.

A private business's ability to supply the federal government with goods and services is limited by Section 508. Anyone convicted of an offense under Section 309 cannot contract for new government work at facilities where the violations leading to the offense occurred. In extreme cases of national importance this procurement ban can be lifted, but the President must notify Congress whenever he makes an exception.

Administrative and judicial review procedures appear in Section 509, while authorities reserved to the states are treated in Section 510. Other responsibilities outside those covered in the Clean Water Act that relate to programs created under this statute are safeguarded in Section 511. Section 512 maintains the validity of the Act in all instances except where a provision is held invalid in a particular case. Section 513 applies the requirements of the Davis-Bacon Act to construction and labor supported by the construction grants program in Title II.

Section 514 requires the agency issuing NPDES permits under Section 402 to help a permit applicant coordinate the permit's requirements with those of the appropriate public health agencies. Section 515 sets us the Effluent Standards and Water Quality Information Advisory Board. Section 516 directs EPA to produce several types of routine reports; among them are the Needs Survey of municipal wastewater contruction addressed in Title II and the state revolving funds created in Title VI.

General authorizations to pay for programs elsewhere in the Act fall into Section 517. Larger programs in other titles often have separate authorizations and thus are excluded from the scope of this section.

Section 518 is a 1987 amendment to the Act. It treats American Indian tribes as states for the purposes of the statute. Under this mandate, tribes may apply for municipal construction grants, establish their own water quality standards for water bodies under their control, receive grants for nonpoint source control, and forge cooperative agreements with any state in which the tribe's lands are situated to carry out Clean Water Act programs.

Title V concludes with Section 519, which allows the statute to be cited as the "Federal Water Pollution Control Act" and which acknowledges that it is commonly referred to as the "Clean Water Act."

Title VI - State Water Pollution Control Revolving Funds

Section 601 empowers EPA to make capitalization grants to States so that they can establish water pollution control revolving funds to: (1) construct municipal treatment works; (2) implement the management program called for in Section 319; and (3) prepare and carry out the conservation and management plan described in Section 320. Capitalization grants must be made in quarterly installments. Each payment must be completed no later than two years after funds are obligated by the state or four years after the fund are allotted to state, whichever is earlier.

Section 602 outlines a 10-point agreement with EPA. For example, they must match any federal contribution with a sum that equals 20% of that contribution. States also have to commit the monies in their fund within a year of receiving each sum. Each year, the state must report how the monies in the fund are actually used, demonstrating it is maintaining progress towards the enforceable requirements of the Act.

How a state can actually use the money in its revolving fund is controlled by Section 603. In certain cases, money from the fund can be used to pay for the nonfederal share of POTW construction also receiving grant funds under Section 201. This special condition aside, only seven uses are allowed.

First, loans for wastewater treatment can be made at market rates, below market rates, or at no interest rate at all. Second, states can buy or refinance a POTW's own debt obligations, thus reducing the carrying cost to the original issuer. Third, states can guarantee or insure a local obligation to increase its attractiveness. Fourth, the fund can be used as a form of collateral on the state's own bond sales, provided the proceeds of the sales are deposted in the fund. Fifth, fund monies can be used to guarantee smaller revolving funds set up by local governments. Sixth, a state's fund can earn interest for itself. And seventh, a maximum of 4% of the federal deposits made to the fund can be used to pay for operating the fund.

Section 604 requires EPA to use the grant allotment formula in Title II to also set capitalization grants for revolving funds. The section permits states to reserve 1% or $100,000--whichever is greater--to carry out the planning they must do under Sections 205 and 303. Like grant allotments, revolving fund allotments are available to a state for two fiscal year. Any uncommitted monies return to EPA and are re-allotted to all other states.

Section 605 allows EPA to withhold capitalization grants if the agency determines that a state is not meeting its 10-point agreement. Once notified that they are not meeting the purposes of the revolving loan fund program, states have 60 days to correct their noncompliance. Any state that cannot correct its problems within a year of EPA's notice loses its remaining grants to the re-allotment process.

Section 606 stipulates the fiscal controls and accounting procedures that a state must use for its fund. Federal audits must be done at least once a year. States must prepare an Intended Use Plan annually, describing exactly how they will commit the monies in the fund. At the beginning of each fiscal year, states must also tell EPA how well it did in meeting its goals and objectives the previous year. Finally, EPA must conduct an annual oversight review of each state's complete operation and can require revolving loan fund beneficiaries to provide reasonable amounts of information to complete that review.

Section 607 authorizes Congress to appropriate money for capitalization grants as follows:

1989: $1.2 billion	1992: $1.8 billion
1990: $1.2 billion	1993: $1.2 billion
1991: $2.4 billion	1994: $0.6 billion

Appendix A - Short-Term Precursors to the 1972 Act

Before PL 92-500 was enacted on October 18, 1972, Congress passed several short term extensions to the Federal Water Pollution Control Act of 1956. Known as PL 84-660, that statute had already been amended several times before. For historical accuracy, certain sections of the extensions enacted in 1972 deserve to be listed with the 1972 law. They are short and relatively easy to understand. For this reason, no summaries of the provisions appear in this publication. Full text entries, however, appear on pages 291-299.

Appendix B - Stand-Alone Sections of PL 95-217, the 1977 Act

Several provisions in the 1977 amendments to PL 92-500 do not amend that statute. They stand as separate mandates and requirements and are cited as provisions of PL 95-217 only. Nevertheless, they bear directly on the programs created by the 1972 law and reflect accommodations and adjustments that were important at the time.

Appendix C - Section 26 of PL 97-117, the 1981 Act

Section 26 of the Municipal Wastewater Treatment Construction Grant Amendments of 1981 did not amend PL 92-500. However, it makes recommendations regarding consent decrees reached between EPA and certain plaintiffs before the 1981 law was enacted. Section 26 is short and need not be summarized here. Please see page 303 for the full text.

Appendix D - List of Priority Pollutants Referred to in Section 307

This appendix contains the list of toxic substances called "priority pollutants." Substances on this list have received special attention in EPA's standard-setting process since the list was incorporated into the statute by reference in the 1977 amendments to the Act.

Appendix E - Stand-Alone Sections of PL 100-4, the 1987 Act

Below is a list of 18 provisions in PL 100-4 that do not amend the 1972 law. They bear directly on some of the programs created by the latter and reflect several important additions or changes to it. The full text of these stand-alone provisions starts on page 306.

Sec. 317 - National Estuary Program
Sec. 318 - Unconsolidated Quaternary Aquifer
Sec. 407 - Log Transfer Facilities
Sec. 508 - Special Provisions Regarding Certain Dumping Sites
Sec. 509 - Ocean Discharge Research Projects
Sec. 510 - San Diego, California
Sec. 511 - Limitation on Discharge of Raw Sewage by New York City
Sec. 512 - Oakwood Beach and Red Hook Projects, New York
Sec. 513 - Boston Harbor and Adjacent Waters
Sec. 514 - Wastewater Reclamation Demonstration

* * * * * * * *

FEDERAL WATER POLLUTION CONTROL ACT, AS AMENDED
BY THE CLEAN WATER ACT OF 1977

[Commonly Referred to as Clean Water Act] [Enacted by Public Law
92-500, October 18, 1972, 86 Stat. 816; 33 U.S.C. 1251 et seq.;
Amended by PL 93-207, December 28, 1973, and PL 93-243, January 2,
1974; PL 93-592, January 2, 1975; PL 94-238, March 23, 1976; PL
94-273, April 21, 1976; PL 94-558, October 19, 1976; PL 95-217,
December 28, 1977; PL 95-576, November 2, 1978; PL 96-148, December
16, 1979; PL 96-478, PL 96-483, October 21, 1980; PL 96-510,
December 11, 1980; PL 96-561, December 22, 1980; PL 97-35, August
13, 1981; PL 97-117, December 29, 1981; PL 97-164, April 2, 1982; PL
97-440, January 8, 1983; Amended by PL 100-4, February 4, 1987]

[The Federal Water Pollution Control Act Amendments of 1972, PL
92-500, replaced the previous language of the Act entirely including
the Water Quality Act of 1965, the Clean Water Restoration Act of
1966, and the Water Quality Improvement Act of 1970, all of which
had been amendments of the Federal Water Pollution Control Act first
passed in 1956. The 1977 amendments, PL 95-217, further amended PL
92-500, as did PL 95-576.]

TITLE I -- RESEARCH AND RELATED PROGRAMS

Sec. 101. Declaration of Goals and Policy.

(a) The objective of this Act is to restore and maintain the
chemical, physical, and biological integrity of the Nation's waters.
In order to achieve this objective it is hereby declared that,
consistent with the provisions of this Act --

(1) it is the national goal that the discharge of pollutants
into the navigable waters be eliminated by 1985;

(2) it is the national goal that wherever attainable, an interim
goal of water quality which provides for the protection and
propagation of fish, shellfish, and wildlife and provides for
recreation in and on the water be achieved by July 1, 1983;

(3) it is the national policy that the discharge of toxic
pollutants in toxic amounts be prohibited;

(4) it is the national policy that Federal financial assistance
be provided to construct publicly owned waste treatment works;

(5) it is the national policy that areawide waste treatment
management planning processes be developed and implemented to
assure adequate control of sources of pollutants in each State;

(6) it is the national policy that a major research and
demonstration effort be made to develop technology necessary to
eliminate the discharge of pollutants into the navigable waters,
waters of the contiguous zone, and the oceans; and

(7) it is the national policy that programs for the control of nonpoint sources of pollution be developed and implemented in an expeditious manner so as to enable the goals of this Act to be met through the control of both point and nonpoint sources of pollution.

[101(a)(7) added by PL 100-4]

(b) It is the policy of the Congress to recognize, preserve, and protect the primary responsibilities and rights of States to prevent, reduce, and eliminate pollution, to plan the development and use (including restoration, preservation, and enhancement) of land and water resources, and to consult with the Administrator in the exercise of his authority under this Act. It is the policy of Congress that the States manage the construction grant program under this Act and implement the permit programs under sections 402 and 404 of this Act. It is further the policy of the Congress to support and aid research relating to the prevention, reduction, and elimination of pollution, and to provide Federal technical services and financial aid to State and interstate agencies and municipalities in connection with the prevention, reduction, and elimination of pollution.

(c) It is further the policy of Congress that the President, acting through the Secretary of State and such national and international organizations as he determines appropriate, shall take such action as may be necessary to insure that to the fullest extent possible all foreign countries shall take meaningful action for the prevention, reduction, and elimination of pollution in their waters and in international waters and for the achievement of goals regarding the elimination of discharge of pollutants and the improvement of water quality to at least the same extent as the United States does under its laws.

(d) Except as otherwise expressly provided in this Act, the Administrator of the Environmental Protection Agency (hereinafter in this Act called "Administrator") shall administer this Act.

(e) Public participation in the development, revision, and enforcement of any regulation, standard, effluent limitation, plan, or program established by the Administrator or any State under this Act shall be provided for, encouraged, and assisted by the Administrator and the States. The Administrator, in cooperation with the States, shall develop and publish regulations specifying minimum guidelines for public participation in such processes.

(f) It is the national policy that to the maximum extent possible the procedures utilized for implementing this Act shall encourage the drastic minimization of paperwork and interagency decision procedures, and the best use of available manpower and funds, so as to prevent needless duplication and unnecessary delays at all levels of government.

(g) It is the policy of Congress that the authority of each State to allocate quantities of water within its jurisdiction shall not be superseded, abrogated or otherwise impaired by this Act. It is the further policy of Congress that nothing in this Act shall be construed to supersede or abrogate rights to quantities of water which have been established by any State. Federal agencies shall cooperate with State and local agencies to develop comprehensive solutions to prevent, reduce and eliminate pollution in concert with programs for managing water resources.

Sec. 102. Comprehensive Programs for Water Pollution Control

(a) The Administrator shall, after careful investigation, and in cooperation with other Federal agencies, State water pollution control agencies, interstate agencies, and the municipalities and industries involved, prepare or develop comprehensive programs for preventing, reducing, or eliminating the pollution of the navigable waters and ground waters and improving the sanitary condition of surface and underground waters. In the development of such comprehensive programs due regard shall be given to the improvements which are necessary to conserve such waters for the protection and propagation of fish and aquatic life and wildlife, recreational purposes, and the withdrawal of such waters for public water supply, agricultural, industrial, and other purposes. For the purpose of this section, the Administrator is authorized to make joint investigations with any such agencies of the condition of any waters in any State or States, and of the discharges of any sewage, industrial wastes, or substance which may adversely affect such waters.

(b) (1) In the survey of planning of any reservoir by the Corps of Engineers, Bureau of Reclamation, or other Federal agency, consideration shall be given to inclusion of storage for regulation of streamflow, except that any such storage and water releases shall not be provided as a substitute for adequate treatment or other methods of controlling waste at the source.

(2) The need for and the value of storage or regulation of streamflow (other than for water quality) including but not limited to navigation, salt water intrusion, recreation, esthetics, and fish and wildlife, shall be determined by the Corps of Engineers, Bureau of Reclamation, or other Federal agencies.

(3) The need for, the value of, and the impact of, storage for water quality control shall be determined by the Administrator, and his views on these matters shall be set forth in any report or presentation to Congress proposing authorization or construction of any reservoir including such storage.

(4) The value of such storage shall be taken into account in determining the economic value of the entire project of which it is a part, and costs shall be allocated to the purpose of regulation of streamflow in a manner which will insure that all project purposes share equitably in the benefits of multiple-purpose construction.

(5) Costs of regulation of streamflow features incorporated in any Federal reservoir or other impoundment under the provisions of this Act shall be determined and the beneficiaries identified

and if the benefits are widespread or national in scope, the costs of such features shall be nonreimbursable.

(6) No license granted by the Federal Power Commission for a hydroelectric power project shall include storage for regulation of streamflow for the purpose of water quality control unless the Administrator shall recommend its inclusion and such reservoir storage capacity shall not exceed such proportion of the total storage required for the water quality control plan as the drainage area of such reservoir bears to the drainage area of the river basin or basins involved in such water quality control plan.

(c) (1) The Administrator shall, at the request of the Governor of a State, or a majority of the Governors when more than one State is involved, make a grant to pay not to exceed 50 per centum of the administrative expenses of a planning agency for a period not to exceed three years, which period shall begin after the date of enactment of the Federal Water Pollution Control Act Amendments of 1972, if such agency provides for adequate representation of appropriate State, interstate, local, or (when appropriate) international interests in the basin or portion thereof involved and is capable of developing an effective, comprehensive water quality control plan for a basin or portion thereof.

(2) Each planning agency receiving a grant under this subsection shall develop a comprehensive pollution control plan for the basin or portion thereof which --

(A) is consistent with any applicable water quality standards, effluent and other limitations, and thermal discharge regulations established pursuant to current law within the basin;

(B) recommends such treatment works as will provide the most effective and economical means of collection, storage, treatment, and elimination of pollutants and recommends means to encourage both municipal and industrial use of such works;

(C) recommends maintenance and improvement of water quality within the basin or portion thereof and recommends methods of adequately financing those facilities as may be necessary to implement the plan; and

(D) as appropriate, is developed in cooperation with, and is consistent with any comprehensive plan prepared by the Water Resources Council, any areawide waste management plans developed pursuant to section 208 of this Act, and any State plan developed pursuant to section 303(e) of this Act.

(3) For the purposes of this subsection the term "basin" includes, but is not limited to, rivers and their tributaries, streams, coastal waters, sounds, estuaries, bays, lakes, and portions thereof, as well as the lands drained thereby.

(d) The Administrator, after consultation with the States, and River Basin Commissions established under the Water Resources Planning Act, shall submit a report to Congress on or before July 1, 1978, which analyzes the relationship between programs under this Act, and the programs by which State and Federal agencies allocate quantities of water. Such report shall include recommendations concerning the policy in section 101(g) of the Act to improve coordination of efforts to reduce and eliminate pollution in concert with programs for managing water resources.

Sec. 103. Interstate Cooperation and Uniform Laws.

(a) The Administrator shall encourage cooperative activities by the States for the prevention, reduction, and elimination of pollution, encourage the enactment of improved and, so far as practicable, uniform State laws relating to the prevention, reduction, and elimination of pollution; and encourage compacts between States for the prevention and control of pollution.

(b) The consent of the Congress is hereby given to two or more States to negotiate and enter into agreements, or compacts, not in conflict with any law or treaty of the United States, for (1) cooperative effort and mutual assistance for the prevention and control of pollution and the enforcement of their respective laws relating thereto, and (2) the establishment of such agencies, joint or otherwise, as they may deem desirable for making effective such agreements and compacts. No such agreement or compact shall be binding or obligatory upon any State a party thereto unless and until it has been approved by the Congress.

[Section 105 of PL 100-4 provides:

"Sec. 105. Research On Effects Of Pollutants.

In carrying out the provisions of section 104(a) of the Federal Water Pollution Control Act, the Administrator shall conduct research on the harmful effects on the health and welfare of persons caused by pollutants in water, in conjunction with the United States Fish and Wildlife Service, the National Oceanic and Atmospheric Administration, and other Federal, State, and interstate agencies carrying on such research. Such research shall include, and shall place special emphasis on, the effect that bioaccumulation of these pollutants in aquatic species has upon reducing the value of aquatic commercial and sport industries. Such research shall further study methods to reduce and remove these pollutants from the relevant affected aquatic species so as to restore and enhance these valuable resources."]

Sec. 104. Research, Investigations, Training and Information.

(a) The Administrator shall establish national programs for the prevention, reduction, and elimination of pollution and as part of such programs shall --

(1) in cooperation with other Federal, State, and local agencies, conduct and promote the coordination and acceleration of, research, investigations, experiments, training,

demonstrations, surveys, and studies relating to the causes, effects, extent, prevention, reduction, and elimination of pollution;

(2) encourage, cooperate with, and render technical services to pollution control agencies and other appropriate public or private agencies, institutions, and organizations, and individuals, including the general public, in the conduct of activities referred to in paragraph (1) of this subsection;

(3) conduct, in cooperation with State water pollution control agencies and other interested agencies, organizations and persons, public investigations concerning the pollution of any navigable waters, and report on the results of such investigations;

(4) establish advisory committees composed of recognized experts in various aspects of pollution and representatives of the public to assist in the examination and evaluation of research progress and proposals and to avoid duplication of research;

(5) in cooperation with the States, and their political subdivisions, and other Federal agencies establish, equip, and maintain a water quality surveillance system for the purpose of monitoring the quality of the navigable waters and ground waters and the contiguous zone and the oceans and the Administrator shall, to the extent practicable, conduct such surveillance by utilizing the resources of the National Aeronautics and Space Administration, the National Oceanic and Atmospheric Administration, the Geological Survey, and the Coast Guard, and shall report on such quality in the report required under subsection (a) of section 516; and

(6) initiate and promote the coordination and acceleration of research designed to develop the most effective practicable tools and techniques for measuring the social and economic costs and benefits of activities which are subject to regulation under this Act; and shall transmit a report on the results of such research to the Congress not later than January 1, 1974.

(b) In carrying out the provisions of subsection (a) of this section the Administrator is authorized to --

(1) collect and make available, through publications and other appropriate means, the results of an other information, including appropriate recommendations by him in connection therewith, pertaining to such research and other activities referred to in paragraph (1) of subsection (a);

(2) cooperate with other Federal departments and agencies, State water pollution control agencies, interstate agencies, other public and private agencies, institutions, organizations, industries involved, and individuals, in the preparation and conduct of such research and other activities referred to in paragraph (1) of subsection (a);

(3) make grants to State water pollution control agencies, interstate agencies, other public or nonprofit private agencies, institutions, organizations, and individuals, for purposes stated in paragraph (1) of subsection (a) of this section;

(4) contract with public or private agencies, institutions, organizations, and individuals, without regard to sections 3648 and 3709 of the Revised Statutes (31 U.S.C. 529; 41 U.S.C. 5), referred to in paragraph (1) of subsection (a);

(5) establish and maintain research fellowships at public or nonprofit private educational institutions or research organizations;

(6) collect and disseminate, in cooperation with other Federal departments and agencies, and with other public or private agencies, institutions, and organizations having related responsibilities, basic data on chemical, physical, and biological effects of varying water quality and other information pertaining to pollution and the prevention, reduction, and elimination thereof; and

(7) develop effective and practical processes, methods, and prototype devices for the prevention, reduction, and elimination of pollution.

(c) In carrying out the provisions of subsection (a) of this section the Administrator shall conduct research on, and survey the results of other scientific studies on, the harmful effects on the health or welfare of persons caused by pollutants. In order to avoid duplication of effort, the Administrator shall, to the extent practicable, conduct such research in cooperation with and through the facilities of the Secretary of Health, Education, and Welfare.

(d) In carrying out the provisions of this section the Administrator shall develop and demonstrate under varied conditions (including conducting such basic and applied research, studies, and experiments as may be necessary:

(1) Practicable means of treating municipal sewage, and other waterborne wastes to implement the requirements of section 201 of this Act;

(2) Improved methods and procedures to identify and measure the effects of pollutants, including those pollutants created by new technological developments; and

(3) Methods and procedures for evaluating the effects on water quality of augmented streamflows to control pollution not susceptible to other means of prevention, reduction, or elimination.

(e) The Administrator shall establish, equip, and maintain field laboratory and research facilities, including, but not limited to, one to be located in the northeastern area of the United States, one in the Middle Atlantic area, one in the southeastern area, one in the midwestern area, one in the southwestern area, one in the

Pacific Northwest, and one in the State of Alaska, for the conduct of research, investigations, experiments, field demonstrations and studies, and training relating to the prevention, reduction and elimination of pollution. Insofar as practicable, each such facility shall be located near institutions of higher learning in which graduate training in such research might be carried out. In conjunction with the development of criteria under section 403 of this Act, the Administrator shall construct the facilities authorized for the National Marine Water Quality Laboratory established under this subsection.

(f) The Administrator shall conduct research and technical development work, and make studies, with respect to the quality of the waters of the Great Lakes, including an analysis of the present and projected future water quality of the Great Lakes under varying conditions of waste treatment and disposal, an evaluation of the water quality needs of those to be served by such waters, an evaluation of municipal, industrial, and vessel waste treatment and disposal practices with respect to such waters, and a study of alternate means of solving pollution problems (including additional waste treatment measures) with respect to such waters.

(g) (1) For the purpose of providing an adequate supply of trained personnel to operate and maintain existing and future treatment works and related activities, and for the purpose of enhancing substantially the proficiency of those engaged in such activities, the Administrator shall finance pilot programs, in cooperation with State and interstate agencies, municipalities, educational institutions, and other organizations and individuals, of manpower development and training and retraining of persons in, on entering into, the field of operation and maintenance of treatment works and related activities. Such program and any funds expended for such a program shall supplement, not supplant, other manpower and training programs and funds available for the purposes of this paragraph. The Administrator is authorized under such terms and conditions as he deems appropriate, to enter into agreements with one or more States, acting jointly or severally, or with other public or private agencies or institutions for the development and implementation of such a program.

(2) The Administrator is authorized to enter into agreements with public and private agencies and institutions, and individuals to develop and maintain an effective system for forecasting the supply of, and demand for, various professional and other occupational categories needed for the prevention, reduction, and elimination of pollution in each region, State, or area of the United States and, from time to time, to publish the results of such forecasts.

(3) In furtherance of the purposes of this Act, the Administrator is authorized to --

(A) make grants to public or private agencies and institutions and to individuals for training projects, and provide for the conduct of training by contract with public or private agencies and institutions and with individuals without regard to sections 3648 and 3709 of the Revised Statutes;

(B) establish and maintain research fellowships in the Environmental Protection Agency with such stipends and allowances, including traveling and subsistence expenses, as he may deem necessary to procure the assistance of the most promising research fellows; and

(C) provide, in addition to the program established under paragraph (1) of this subsection, training in technical matters relating to the causes, prevention, reduction, and elimination of pollution for personnel of public agencies and other persons with suitable qualifications.

(4) The Administrator shall submit, through the President, a report to the Congress not later than December 31, 1973, summarizing the actions taken under this subsection and the effectiveness of such actions, and setting forth the number of persons trained, the occupational categories for which training was provided, the effectiveness of other Federal, State, and local training programs in this field, together with estimates of future needs, recommendations on improving training programs, and such other information and recommendations, including legislative recommendations, as he deems appropriate.

(h) The Administrator is authorized to enter into contracts with, or make grants to, public or private agencies and organizations and individuals for (A) the purpose of developing and demonstrating new or improved methods for the prevention, removal, reduction, and elimination of pollution in lakes, including the undesirable effects of nutrients and vegetation, and (B) the construction of publicly owned research facilities for such purpose.

(i) The Administrator, in cooperation with the Secretary of the department in which the Coast Guard is operating, shall --

(1) engage in such research, studies, experiments, and demonstrations as he deems appropriate, relative to the removal of oil from any waters and to the prevention, control, and elimination of oil and hazardous substances pollution;

(2) publish from time to time the results of such activities; and

(3) from time to time, develop and publish in the Federal Register specifications and other technical information on the various chemical compounds used in the control of oil and hazardous substances spills.

In carrying out this subsection, the Administrator may enter into contracts with, or make grants to, public or private agencies and organizations and individuals.

(j) The Secretary of the department in which the Coast Guard is operating shall engage in such research, studies, experiments, and demonstrations as he deems appropriate relative to equipment which is to be installed on board a vessel and is designed to receive, retain, treat, or discharge human body wastes and the wastes from toilets and other receptacles intended to receive or retain body wastes with particular emphasis on equipment to be installed on small recreational vessels. The Secretary of the department in which the Coast Guard is operating shall report to Congress the results of such research, studies, experiments, and demonstrations prior to the effective date of any regulations established under section 312 of this Act. In carrying out this subsection the Secretary of the department in which the Coast Guard is operating may enter into contracts with, or make grants to, public or private organizations and individuals.

(k) In carrying out the provisions of this section relating to the conduct by the Administrator of demonstration projects and the development of field laboratories and research facilities, the Administrator may acquire land and interests therein by purchase, with appropriated or donated funds, by donation, or by exchange for acquired or public lands under his jurisdiction which he classifies as suitable for disposition. The values of the properties so exchanged either shall be approximately equal, or if they are not approximately equal, the values shall be equalized by the payment of cash to the grantor or to the Administrator as the circumstances require.

(l) (1) The Administrator shall, after consultation with appropriate local, State, and Federal agencies, public and private organizations, and interested individuals, as soon as practicable but not later than January 1, 1973, develop and issue to the States for the purpose of carrying out this Act the latest scientific knowledge available in indicating the kind and extent of effects on health and welfare which may be expected from the presence of pesticides in the water in varying quantities. He shall revise and add to such information whenever necessary to reflect developing scientific knowledge.

(2) The President shall, in consultation with appropriate local, State, and Federal agencies, public and private organizations, and interested individuals, conduct studies and investigations of methods to control the release of pesticides into the environment which study shall include examination of the persistency of pesticides in the water environment and alternatives thereto. The President shall submit reports, from time to time, on such investigations to Congress together with his recommendations for any necessary legislation.

(m) (1) The Administrator shall, in an effort to prevent degradation of the environment from the disposal of waste oil, conduct a study of:

(A) the generation of used engine, machine, cooling, and similar waste oil, including quantities generated, the nature and quality of such oil, present collecting methods and disposal practices, and alternate uses of such oil;

(B) the long-term chronic biological effects of the disposal of such waste oil; and

(C) the potential market for such oils, including the economic and legal factors relating to the sale of products made from such oils, the level of subsidy, if any, needed to encourage the purchase by public and private nonprofit agencies of products from such oil, and the practicability of Federal procurement, on a priority basis, of products made from such oil. In conducting such study, the Administrator shall consult with affected industries and other persons.

(2) The Administrator shall report the preliminary results of such study to Congress within six months after the date of enactment of the Federal Water Pollution Control Act Amendments of 1972, and shall submit a final report to Congress within 18 months after such date of enactment.

(n) (1) The Administrator shall, in cooperation with the Secretary of the Army, the Secretary of Agriculture, the Water Resources Council, and with other appropriate Federal, State, interstate, or local public bodies and private organizations, institutions, and individuals, conduct and promote, encourage contributions to, continuing comprehensive studies of the effects of pollution, including sedimentation, in the estuaries and estuarine zones of the United States on fish and wildlife, on sport and commercial fishing, on recreation, on water supply and water power, and on other beneficial purposes. Such studies shall also consider the effect of demographic trends, the exploitation of mineral resources and fossil fuels, land and industrial development, navigation, flood and erosion control, and other uses of estuaries and estuarine zones upon the pollution of the waters therein.

(2) In conducting such studies, the Administrator shall assemble, coordinate, and organize all existing pertinent information on the Nation's estuaries and estuarine zones; carry out a program of investigations and surveys to supplement existing information in representative estuaries and estuarine zones; and identify the problems and areas where further research and study are required.

(3) The Administrator shall submit to Congress, from time to time, reports of the studies authorized by this subsection but at least one such report during any six-year period. Copies of each such report shall be made available to all interested parties, public and private.

(4) For the purpose of this subsection, the term "estuarine zones" means an environmental system consisting of an estuary and those transitional areas which are consistently influenced or affected by water from an estuary such as, but not limited to, salt marshes, coastal and intertidal areas, bays, harbors, lagoons, inshore waters, and channels, and the term "estuary" means all or part of the mouth of a river or stream or other body of water having unimpaired natural connection with open sea and within which the sea water is measurably diluted with fresh water derived from land drainage.

(o) (1) The Administrator shall conduct research and investigations on devices, systems, incentives, pricing policy, and other methods of reducing the total flow of sewage, including, but not limited to, unnecessary water consumption in order to reduce the requirements for, and the costs of, sewage and waste treatment services. Such research and investigations shall be directed to develop devices, systems, policies, and methods capable of achieving the maximum reduction of unnecessary water consumption.

(2) The Administrator shall report the preliminary results of such studies and investigations to the Congress within one year after the date of enactment of the Federal Water Pollution Control Act Amendments of 1972, and annually thereafter in the report required under subsection (a) of section 516. Such report shall include recommendations for any legislation that may be required to provide for the adoption and use of devices, systems, policies, or other methods of reducing water consumption and reducing the total flow of sewage. Such report shall include an estimate of the benefits to be derived from adoption and use of such devices, systems, policies, or other methods and also shall reflect estimates of any increase in private, public, or other cost that would be occasioned thereby.

(p) In carrying out the provisions of subsection (a) of this section the Administrator shall, in cooperation with the Secretary of Agriculture, other Federal agencies, and the States, carry out a comprehensive study and research program to determine new and improved methods and the better application of existing methods of preventing, reducing, and eliminating pollution from agriculture, including the legal, economic, and other implications of the use of such methods.

(q) (1) The Administrator shall conduct a comprehensive program of research and investigation and pilot project implementation into new and improved methods of preventing, reducing, storing, collecting, treating, or otherwise eliminating pollution from sewage in rural and other areas where collection of sewage in conventional, community-wide sewage collection systems is impractical, uneconomical, or otherwise infeasible, or where soil conditions or other factors preclude the use of septic tank and drainage field systems.

(2) The Administrator shall conduct a comprehensive program of research and investigation and pilot project implementation into new and improved methods for the collection and treatment of sewage and other liquid wastes combined with the treatment and disposal of solid wastes.

(3) The Administrator shall establish, either within the Environmental Protection Agency, or through contract with an appropriate public or private non-profit organization, a national clearinghouse which shall:

(A) receive reports and information resulting from research, demonstrations, and other projects funded under this Act related to paragraph (1) of this subsection and to subsection (e)(2) of section 105;

(B) coordinate and disseminate such reports and information for use by Federal and State agencies, municipalities, institutions, and persons in developing new and improved methods pursuant to this subsection; and

(C) provide for the collection and dissemination of reports and information relevant to this subsection from other Federal and State agencies, institutions, universities, and persons.

(4) Small Flows Clearinghouse. -- Notwithstanding section 205(d) of this Act, from amounts that are set aside for a fiscal year under section 205(i) of this Act and are not obligated by the end of the 24-month period of availability for such amounts under section 205(d), the Administrator shall make available $1,000,000 or such unobligated amount, whichever is less, to support a national clearinghouse within the Environmental Protection Agency to collect and disseminate information on small flows of sewage and innovative or alternative wastewater treatment processes and techniques, consistent with paragraph (3). This paragraph shall apply with respect to amounts set aside under section 205(i) for which the 24-month period of availability referred to in the preceding sentence ends on or after September 30, 1986.

[Sec. 104(q)(4) added by PL 100-4]

(r) The Administrator is authorized to make grants to colleges and universities to conduct basic research into the structure and function of fresh water aquatic ecosystems, and to improve understanding of the ecological characteristics necessary to the maintenance of the chemical, physical, and biological integrity of freshwater aquatic ecosystems.

(s) The Administrator is authorized to make grants to one or more institutions of higher education (regionally located and to be designated as "River Study Centers") for the purpose of conducting and reporting on interdisciplinary studies on the nature of river systems, including, hydrology, biology, ecology, economics, the relationship between river uses and land uses, and the effects of development within river basins on river systems and on the value of water resources and water related activities. No such grant in any fiscal year shall exceed $1,000,000.

(t) The Administrator shall, in cooperation with State and Federal agencies and public and private organizations, conduct continuing comprehensive studies of the effects and methods of control of thermal discharges. In evaluating alternative methods of control the studies shall consider (1) such data as are available on the latest available technology, economic feasibility including cost-effectiveness analysis, and (2) the total impact on the environment, considering not only water quality but also air quality, land use, and effective utilization and conservation of fresh water and other natural resources. Such studies shall consider methods of minimizing adverse effects and maximizing beneficial effects of thermal discharges. The results of these studies shall be reported by the Administrator as soon as practicable, but not later than 270 days after enactment of this subsection, and shall be made available to the public and the States, and considered as they become available by the Administrator in carrying out section 316 of this Act and by the States in proposing thermal water quality standards.

(u) There is authorized to be appropriated:

(1) not to exceed $100,000,000 per fiscal year ending June 30, 1973, the fiscal year ending June 30, 1974, and the fiscal year ending June 30, 1975, not to exceed $14,039,000 for the fiscal year ending September 30, 1980, not to exceed $20,697,000 for the fiscal year ending September 30, 1981, not to exceed $22,770,000 for the fiscal year ending September 30, 1982, such sums as may be necessary for fiscal years 1983 through 1985, and not to exceed $22,770,000 per fiscal year for each of the fiscal years 1986 through 1990, for carrying out the provisions of this section, other than subsections (g)(1) and (2), (p), (r), and (t), except that such authorizations are not for any research, development, or demonstration activity pursuant to such provisions;

(2) not to exceed $7,500,000 for fiscal years 1973, 1974, and 1975, $2,000,000 for fiscal year 1977, $3,000,000 for fiscal year 1978, $3,000,000 for fiscal year 1979, $3,000,000 for fiscal year 1980, $3,000,000 for fiscal year 1981, $3,000,000 for fiscal year 1982, such sums as may be necessary for fiscal years 1983 through 1985, and $3,000,000 per fiscal year for each of the fiscal years 1986 through 1990, for carrying out the provisions of subsection (g)(1);

(3) not to exceed $2,500,000 for fiscal year 1973, 1974, and 1975. $1,000,000 for fiscal year 1977, $1,500,000 for fiscal year 1978, $1,500,000 for fiscal year 1979, $1,500,000 for fiscal year 1980, $1,500,000 for fiscal year 1981, $1,500,000 for fiscal year 1982, such sums as may be necessary for fiscal years 1983 through 1985, and $1,500,000 per fiscal year for each of the fiscal years 1986 through 1990, for carrying out the provisions of subsection (g)(2);

(4) not to exceed $10,000,000 for each of the fiscal years ending June 30, 1973, June 30, 1974, and June 30, 1975, for carrying out the provisions of subsection (p);

(5) not to exceed $15,000,000 per fiscal year for the fiscal years ending June 30, 1973, June 30, 1974, and June 30, 1975, for carrying out the provisions of subsection (r); and

(6) not to exceed $10,000,000 per fiscal year for the fiscal years ending June 30, 1973, June 30, 1974, and June 30, 1975, for carrying out the provisions of subsection (t).

[Sec. 104(u) amendment by PL 95-576; PL 96-483; PL 100-4]

Sec. 105. Grants for Research and Development.

(a) The Administrator is authorized to conduct in the Environmental Protection Agency, and to make grants to any State, municipality, or intermunicipal or interstate agency for the purpose of assisting in the development of --

(1) any project which will demonstrate a new or improved method of preventing, reducing, and eliminating the discharge into any waters of pollutants from sewers which carry storm water or both storm water and pollutants; or

(2) any project which will demonstrate advanced waste treatment and water purification methods (including the temporary use of new or improved chemical additives which provide substantial immediate improvement to existing treatment processes), or new or improved methods of joint treatment systems for municipal and industrial wastes; and to include in such grants such amounts as are necessary for the purpose of reports, plans, and specifications in connection therewith.

(b) The Administrator is authorized to make grants to any State or States or interstate agency to demonstrate, in river basins or portions thereof, advanced treatment and environmental enhancement techniques to control pollution from all sources, within such basins or portions thereof, including nonpoint sources, together with in stream water quality improvement techniques.

(c) In order to carry out the purposes of section 301 of this Act, the Adminstrator is authorized to (1) conduct in the Environmental Protection Agency, (2) make grants to persons, and (3) enter into contracts with persons, for research and demonstration projects for prevention of pollution of any waters by industry including, but not limited to, the prevention, reduction, and elimination of the discharge of pollutants. No grant shall be made for any project under this subsection unless the Administrator determines that such project will develop or demonstrate a new or improved method of treating industrial wastes or otherwise prevent pollution by industry, which method shall have industrywide application.

(d) In carrying out the provisions of this section, the Administrator shall conduct, on a priority basis, and accelerated effort to develop, refine, and achieve practical application of:

(1) waste management methods applicable to point and nonpoint sources of pollutants to eliminate the discharge of pollutants, including, but not limited to, elimination of runoff of pollutants and the effects of pollutants from in place or accumulated sources;

(2) advanced waste treatment methods applicable to point and nonpoint sources, including in place or accumulated sources of pollutants, and methods for reclaiming and recycling water and confining pollutants so they will not migrate to cause water or other environmental pollution; and

(3) improved methods and procedures to identify and measure the effects of pollutants on the chemical, physical, and biological integrity of water, including those pollutants created by new technological developments.

(e) (1) The Administrator is authorized to (A) make, in consultation with the Secretary of Agriculture, grants to persons for research and demonstration projects with respect to new and improved methods of preventing, reducing, and eliminating pollution from agriculture, and (B) disseminate, in cooperation with the Secretary of Agriculture, such information obtained under this subsection, section 104(p), and section 304 as will encourage and enable the adoption of such methods in the agricultural industry.

(2) The Administrator is authorized, (A) in consultation with other interested Federal agencies, to make grants for demonstration projects with respect to new improved methods of preventing, reducing, storing, collecting, treating, or otherwise eliminating pollution from sewage in rural and other areas where collection of sewage in conventional, community-wide sewage collection systems is impractical, uneconomical, or otherwise infeasible, or where soil conditions or other factors preclude the use of septic tank and drainage field systems, and (B) in cooperation with other interested Federal and State agencies, to disseminate such information obtained under this subsection as will encourage and enable the adoption of new and improved methods developed pursuant to this subsection.

(f) Federal grants under subsection (a) of this section shall be subject to the following limitations:

(1) No grant shall be made for any project unless such project shall have been approved by the appropriate State water pollution control agency or agencies and by the Administrator;

(2) No grant shall be made for any project in an amount exceeding 75 per centum of cost thereof as determined by the Administrator; and

(3) No grant shall be made for any project unless the Administrator determines that such project will serve as a useful demonstration for the purpose set forth in clause (1) or (2) of subsection (a).

(g) Federal grants under subsections (c) and (d) of this section shall not exceed 75 per centum of the cost of the project.

(h) For the purpose of this section there is authorized to be appropriated $75,000,000 per fiscal year for the fiscal year ending June 30, 1973, the fiscal year ending June 30, 1974, and the fiscal year ending June 30, 1975, and from such appropriations at least 10 per centum of the funds actually appropriated in each fiscal year shall be available only for the purposes of subsection (e).

(i) The Administrator is authorized to make grants to a municipality to assist in the costs of operating and maintaining a project which received a grant under this section, section 104, or section 113 of this Act prior to the date of enactment of this subsection so as to reduce the operation and maintenance costs borne by the recipients of services from such project to costs comparable to those for projects assisted under title II of this Act.

(j) The Administrator is authorized to make a grant to any grantee who received an increased grant pursuant to section 202(a)(2) of this Act. Such grant may pay up to 100 per centum of the costs of technical evaluation of the operation of the treatment works, costs of training of persons (other than employees of the grantee), and costs of disseminating technical information on the operation of the treatment works.

Sec. 106. Grants for Pollution Control Programs.

(a) There are hereby authorized to be appropriated the following sums, to remain available until expended, to carry out the purposes of this section --

(1) $60,000,000 for the fiscal year ending June 30, 1973; and

(2) $75,000,000 for the fiscal year ending June 30, 1974, and the fiscal year ending June 30, 1975, $100,000,000 per fiscal year for the fiscal years 1977, 1978, 1979, 1980, $75,000,000 per fiscal year for the fiscal years 1981 and 1982, such sums as may be necessary for fiscal years 1983 through 1985, and $75,000,000 per fiscal year for each of the fiscal years 1986 through 1990; for grants to States and to interstate agencies to assist them in administering programs for the prevention, reduction, and elimination of pollution, including enforcement directly or through appropriate State law enforcement officers or agencies.

[Sec. 106(a)(2) amended by PL 96-483; PL 100-4]

(b) From the sums appropriated in any fiscal year, the Administrator shall make allotments to the several States and interstate agencies in accordance with regulations promulgated by him on the basis of the extent of the pollution problem in the respective States.

(c) The Administrator is authorized to pay each State and interstate agency each fiscal year either --

(1) the allotment of such State or agency for such fiscal year under subsection (b), or

(2) the reasonable costs as determined by the Administrator of developing and carrying out a pollution program by such State or agency during such fiscal year, whichever amount is the lesser.

(d) No grant shall be made under this section to any State or interstate agency for any fiscal year when the expenditure of non-Federal funds by such State or interstate agency during such fiscal year for the recurrent expenses of carrying out its pollution control program are less than the expenditure by such State or interstate agency of non-Federal funds for such recurrent program expenses during the fiscal year ending June 30, 1971.

(e) Beginning in fiscal year 1974 the Administrator shall not make any grant under this section to any State which has not provided or is not carrying out as a part of its program --

(1) the establishment and operation of appropriate devices, methods, systems, and procedures necessary to monitor, and to compile and analyze data on (including classification according to eutrophic condition), the quality of navigable waters and to the extent practicable, ground waters including biological monitoring; and provision for annually updating such data and including it in the report required under section 305 of this Act;

(2) authority comparable to that in section 504 of this Act and adequate contingency plans to implement such authority.

(f) Grants shall be made under this section on condition that --

(1) Such State (or interstate agency) filed with the Administrator within one hundred and twenty days after the date of enactment of this section:

(A) a summary report of the current status of the State pollution control program, including the criteria used by the State in determining priority of treatment works; and

(B) such additional information, data, and reports as the Administrator may require.

(2) No federally assumed enforcement as defined in section 309 (a)(2) is in effect with respect to such State or interstate agency.

(3) Such State (or interstate agency) submits within one hundred and twenty days after the date of enactment of this section and before October 1 of each year thereafter for the Administrator's approval of its program for the prevention, reduction, and elimination of pollution in accordance with purposes and provisions of this Act in such form and content as the Administrator may prescribe.

[Sec. 106 (f)(3) amended by PL 94-273]

(g) Any sums allotted under subsection (b) in any fiscal year which are not paid shall be reallotted by the Administrator in accordance with regulations promulgated by him.

Sec. 107. Mine Water Pollution Control Demonstrations.

(a) The Administrator in cooperation with the Appalachian Regional Commission and other Federal agencies is authorized to conduct, to make grants for, or to contract for, projects to demonstrate comprehensive approaches to the elimination or control of acid or other mine water pollution resulting from active or abandoned mining operations and other environmental pollution affecting water quality within all or part of a watershed or river basin, including siltation from surface mining. Such projects shall demonstrate the engineering and economic feasibility and practicality of various abatement techniques which will contribute substantially to effective and practical methods of acid or other mine water pollution elimination or control, and other pollution affecting water quality, including techniques that demonstrate the engineering and economic feasibility and practicality of using sewage sludge materials and other municipal wastes to diminish or prevent pollution affecting water quality from acid, sedimentation, or other pollutants and in such projects to restore affected lands to usefulness for forestry, agriculture, recreation, or other beneficial purposes.

(b) Prior to undertaking any demonstration project under this section in the Appalachian region (as defined in section 403 of the Appalachian Regional Development Act of 1965, as amended), the Appalachian Regional Commission shall determine that such demonstration project is consistent with the objectives of the Appalachian Regional Development Act of 1965, as amended.

(c) The Administrator, in selecting watersheds for the purposes of this section, shall be satisfied that the project area will not be affected adversely by the influx of acid or other mine water pollution from nearby sources.

(d) Federal participation in such projects shall be subject to the conditions --

(1) that the State shall acquire any land or interests therein necessary for such project; and

(2) that the State shall provide legal and practical protection to the project area to insure against any activities which will cause future acid or other mine water pollution.

(e) There is authorized to be appropriated $30,000,000 to carry out the provisions of this section, which sum shall be available until expended.

Sec. 108. Pollution Control in Great Lakes.

(a) The Administrator, in cooperation with other Federal departments, agencies, and instrumentalities is authorized to enter, into agreements with any State, political subdivision, interstate agency, or other public agency, or combination thereof, to carry out one or more projects to demonstrate new methods and techniques and to develop preliminary plans for the elimination or control of pollution, within all or any part of the watersheds of the Great Lakes. Such projects shall demonstrate the engineering and economic feasibility and practicality of removal of pollutants and prevention of any polluting matter from entering into the Great Lakes in the future and other reduction and remedial techniques which will contribute substantially to effective and practical methods of pollution prevention, reduction, or elimination.

(b) Federal participation in such projects shall be subject to the condition that the State, political subdivision, interstate agency, or other public agency, or combination thereof, shall pay not less than 25 per centum of the actual project costs, which payment may be in any form, including, but not limited to, land or interests therein that is needed for the project, and personal property or services the value of which shall be determined by the Administrator.

(c) There is authorized to be appropriated $20,000,000 to carry out the provisions of subsections (a) and (b) of this section, which sum shall be available until expended.

(d) (1) In recognition of the serious conditions which exist in Lake Erie, the Secretary of the Army, acting through the Chief of Engineers, is directed to design and develop a demonstration waste water management program for the rehabilitation and environmental repair of Lake Erie. Prior to the initiation of detailed engineering and design, the program, along with the specific recommendations shall be submitted to the Congress for statutory approval. This authority is in addition to, and not in lieu of, other waste water studies aimed at eliminating pollution emanating from select sources around Lake Erie.

(2) This program is to be developed in cooperation with the Environmental Protection Agency, other interested departments, agencies, and instrumentalities of the Federal Government, and the States and their political subdivisions. This program shall set forth alternative systems for managing waste water on a regional basis and shall provide local and State governments with a range of choice as to the type of system to be used for the treatment of waste water. These alternative systems shall include both advanced waste treatment technology and land disposal systems including aerated treatment-spray irrigation technology and will also include provisions for the disposal of solid wastes, including sludge. Such program should include measures to control point sources of pollution, area sources of pollution, including acid-mine drainage, urban runoff and rural runoff, and in place sources of pollution, including bottom loads, sludge banks, and polluted harbor dredgings.

(e) There is authorized to be appropriated $5,000,000 to carry out the provisions of subsection (d) of this section, which sum shall be available until expended.

Sec. 109. Training Grants and Contracts.

(a) The Administrator is authorized to make grants to or contracts with institutions of higher education, or combinations of such institutions, to assist them in planning, developing, strengthening, improving, or carrying out programs or projects for the preparation of undergraduate students to enter an occupation which involves the design, operation, and maintenance of treatment works, and other facilities whose purpose is water quality control. Such grants or contracts may include payment of all or part of the cost of programs or projects such as --

(A) planning for the development or expansion of programs or projects for training persons in the operation and maintenance of treatment works;

(B) training and retraining of faculty members;

(C) conduct of short-term or regular session institutes for study by persons engaged in, or preparing to engage in, the preparation of students preparing to enter an occupation involving the operation and maintenance of treatment works;

(D) carrying out innovative and experimental programs of cooperative education involving alternate periods of full-time or part-time academic study at the institution and periods of full-time or part-time employment involving the operation and maintenance of treatment works; and

(E) research into, and development of, methods of training students or faculty, including the preparation of teaching materials and the planning of curriculum.

(b) (1) The Administrator may pay 100 per centum of any additional cost of construction of treatment works required for a facility to train and upgrade waste treatment works operation and maintenance personnel and for the costs of other State treatment works operator training programs, including mobile training units, classroom rental, specialized instructors, and instructional material.

(2) The Administrator shall make no more than one grant for such additional construction in any State (to serve a group of States, where, in his judgment, efficient training programs require multi-State programs), and shall make such grant after consultation with and approval by the State or States on the basis of (A) the suitability of such facility for training operation and maintenance personnel for treatment works throughout such State or States; and (B) a commitment by the State agency or agencies to carry out at such facility a program of training approved by the Administrator. In any case where a grant is made to serve two or more States, the Administrator is authorized to make an additional grant for a supplemental facility in each such State.

(3) The Administrator may make such grant out of the sums allocated to a State under section 205 of this Act, except that in no event shall the Federal cost of any such training facilities exceed $500,000.

(4) The Administrator may exempt a grant under this section from any requirement under section 204(a)(3) of this Act. Any grantee who received a grant under this section prior to enactment of the Clean Water Act of 1977 shall be eligible to have its grant increased by funds made available under such Act.

Sec. 110.   Application for Training Grant or Contract; Allocation of Grants or Contracts.

(1) A grant or contract authorized by section 109 may be made only upon application to the Administrator at such time or times and containing such information as he may prescribe, except that no such application shall be approved unless it --

(A) sets forth programs, activities, research, or development for which a grant is authorized under section 109 and describes the relation to any program set forth by the applicant in an application, if any, submitted pursuant to section 111;

(B) provides such fiscal control and fund accounting procedures as may be necessary to assure proper disbursement of and accounting for Federal funds paid to the applicant under this section; and

(C) provides for making such reports, in such form and containing such information, as the Administrator may require to carry out his functions under this section, and for keeping such records and for affording such access thereto as the Administrator may find necessary to assure the correctness and verification of such reports.

(2) The Administrator shall allocate grants or contracts under section 109 in such manner as will most nearly provide an equitable distribution of the grants or contracts throughout the United States among institutions of higher education which show promise of being able to use funds effectively for the purpose of this section.

(3) (A) Payments under this section may be used in accordance with regulations of the Administrator, and subject to the terms and conditions set forth in an application approved under paragraph (1), to pay part of the compensation of students employed in connection with the operation and maintenance of treatment works, other than as an employee in connection with the operation and maintenance of treatment works or as an employee in any branch of the Government of the United States, as part of a program for which a grant has been approved pursuant to this section.

(B) Departments and agencies of the United States are encouraged, to the extent consistent with efficient administration, to enter into arrangements with institutions of higher education for the full-time, part-time, or temporary employment, whether in the competitive or excepted service, of students enrolled in programs set forth in applications approved under paragraph (1).

Sec. 111.   Award of Scholarships

(1) The Administrator is authorized to award scholarships in accordance with the provisions of this section for undergraduate study by persons who plan to enter an occupation involving the operation and maintenance of treatment works. Such scholarships

shall be awarded for such periods as the Administrator may determine but not to exceed four academic years.

(2) The Administrator shall allocate scholarships under this section among institutions of higher education with programs approved under the provisions of this section for the use of individuals accepted into such programs, in such manner and accordance to such plan as will insofar as practicable --

(A) provide an equitable distribution of such scholarships throughout the United States; and

(B) attract recent graduates of secondary schools to enter an occupation involving the operation and maintenance of treatment works.

(3) The Administrator shall approve a program of any institution of higher education for the purposes of this section only upon application by the institution and only upon his finding --

(A) that such program has a principal objective the education and training of persons in the operation and maintenance of treatment works;

(B) that such program is in effect and of high quality, or can be readily put into effect and may reasonably be expected to be of high quality;

(C) that the application describes the relation of such program to any program, activity, research, or development set forth by the applicant in an application, if any, submitted pursuant to section 110 of this Act; and

(D) that the application contains satisfactory assurances that (i) the institution will recommend to the Administrator for the award of scholarships under this section, for study in such program, only persons who have demonstrated to the satisfaction of the institution a serious intent, upon completing the program, to enter an occupation involving the operation and maintenance of treatment works, and (ii) the institution will make reasonable continuing efforts to encourage recipients of scholarships under this section, enrolled in such program, to enter occupations involving the operation and maintenance of treatment works upon completing the program.

(4) (A) The Administrator shall pay to persons awarded scholarships under this section such stipends (including such allowances for subsistence and other expenses for such persons and their dependents) as he may determine to be consistent with prevailing practices under comparable federally supported programs.

(B) The Administrator shall (in addition to the stipends paid to persons under paragraph (1)) pay to the institution of higher education at which such person in pursuing his course of study such amount as he may determine to be consistent with prevailing practices under comparable federally supported programs.

(5) A person awarded a scholarship under the provisions of this section shall continue to receive the payments provided in this section only during such periods as the Administrator finds that he is maintaining satisfactory proficiency and devoting full time to study or research in the field in which such scholarship was awarded in an institution of higher education, and is not engaging in gainful employment other than employment approved by the Administrator by or pursuant to regulation.

(6) The Administrator shall by regulation provide that any person awarded a scholarship under this section shall agree in writing to enter and remain in an occupation involving the design, operation, or maintenance of treatment works for such period after completion of this course of studies as the Administrator determines appropriate.

Sec. 112. **Definitions and Authorizations.**

(a) As used in sections 109 through 112 of this Act --

(1) The term "institution of higher education" means an educational institution described in the first sentence of section 1201 of the Higher Education Act of 1965 (other than an institution of any agency of the United States) which is accredited by a nationally recognized accrediting agency of association approved by the Administrator for this purpose. For purposes of this subsection, the Administrator shall publish a list of nationally recognized accrediting agencies or associations which he determines to be reliable authority as to the quality of training offered.

(2) The term "academic year" means an academic year or its equivalent, as determined by the Administrator.

(b) The Administrator shall annually report his activities under section 109 through 112 of this Act, including recommendations for needed revisions in the provisions thereof.

(c) There are authorized to be appropriated $25,000,000 per fiscal year for the fiscal years ending June 30, 1973, June 30, 1974, and June 30, 1975, $6,000,000 for the fiscal year ending September 30, 1977, $7,000,000 for the fiscal year ending September 30, 1978, $7,000,000 for the fiscal year ending September 30, 1979, $7,000,000 for the fiscal year ending September 30, 1980, $7,000,000 for the fiscal year ending September 30, 1981, $7,000,000 for the fiscal year ending September 30, 1982, such sums as may be necessary for fiscal years 1983 through 1985, and $7,000,000 per fiscal year for each of the fiscal years 1986 through 1990, to carry out sections 109 through 112 of this Act.

[NB: Sec. 112(c) amended by PL 96-483; PL 100-4]

Sec. 113. **Alaska Village Demonstration Projects.**

(a) The Administrator is authorized to enter into agreements with the State of Alaska to carry out one or more projects to demonstrate methods to provide for central community facilities for safewater and elimination or control of pollution in those native villages of Alaska without such facilities. Such project shall include provisions for community safe water supply systems, toilets, bathing and laundry facilities, sewage disposal facilities, and other similar facilities, and educational and informational facilities and programs relating to health and hygiene. Such demonstration projects shall be for the further purpose of developing preliminary plans for providing such safe water and such elimination or control of pollution for all native villages in such State.

(b) In carrying out this section the Administrator shall cooperate with the Secretary of Health, Education, and Welfare for the purpose of utilizing such of the personnel and facilities of that Department as may be appropriate.

(c) The Administrator shall report to Congress not later than July 1, 1973, the results of the demonstration projects authorized by this section together with his recommendations, including any necessary legislation, relating to the establishment of a statewide program.

(d) There is authorized to be appropriated not to exceed $2,000,000 to carry out this section. In addition, there is authorized to be appropriated to carry out this section not to exceed $200,000 for the fiscal year ending September 30, 1978 and $220,000 for the fiscal year ending September 30, 1979.

(e) The Administrator is authorized to coordinate with the Secretary of the Department of Health, Education, and Welfare, the Secretary of the Department of Housing and Urban Development, the Secretary of the Department of the Interior, the Secretary of the Department of Agriculture, and the heads of any other departments or agencies he may deem appropriate to conduct a joint study with representatives of the State of Alaska and the appropriate Native organizations (as defined in Public Law 92-203) to develop a comprehensive program for achieving adequate sanitation services in Alaska villages. This study shall be coordinated with the programs and projects authorized by sections 104(q) and 105(e)(2) of this Act. The Administrator shall submit a report of the results of the study, together with appropriate supporting data and such recommendations as he deems desirable, to the Committee on Environment and Public Works of the Senate and to the Committee on Public Works and Transportation of the House of Representatives not later than December 31, 1979. The Administrator shall also submit recommended administrative actions, procedures, and any proposed legislation necessary to the recommendations of the study no later than June 30, 1980.

(f) The Administrator is authorized to provide technical, financial and management assistance for operation and maintenance of the demonstration projects constructed under this section, until such time as the recommendations of subsection (e) are implemented.

(g) For the purpose of this section, the term "village" shall mean an incorporated or unincorporated community with a population of ten to six hundred people living within a two-mile radius. The term "sanitation services" shall mean water supply, sewage disposal, solid waste disposal and other services necessary to maintain generally accepted standards of personal hygiene and public health.

Sec. 114. Lake Tahoe Study.

(a) The Administrator, in consultation with the Tahoe Regional Planning Agency, the Secretary of Agriculture, other Federal agencies, representatives of State and local governments, and members of the public, shall conduct a thorough and complete study on the adequacy of and need for extending Federal oversight and control in order to preserve the fragile ecology of Lake Tahoe.

(b) Such study shall include an examination of the interrelationships and responsibilities of the various agencies of the Federal Government and State and local governments with a view to establishing the necessity for redefinition of legal and other arrangements between these various governments, and making specific legislative recommendations to Congress. Such study shall consider the effect of various actions in terms of their environmental impact on the Tahoe Basin, treated as an ecosystem.

(c) The Administrator shall report on such study to Congress not later than one year after the date of enactment of this subsection.

(d) There is authorized to be appropriated to carry out this section not to exceed $500,000.

Sec. 115. In-Place Toxic Pollutants.

The Administrator is directed to identify the location of in-place pollutants with emphasis on toxic pollutants in harbors and navigable waterways and is authorized, acting through the Secretary of the Army, to make contracts for the removal and appropriate disposal of such materials from critical port and harbor areas. There is authorized to be appropriated $15,000,000 to carry out the provisions of this section, which sum shall be available until expended.

Sec. 116. Hudson River PCB Reclamation Demonstration Project.

(a) The Administrator is authorized to enter into contracts and other agreements with the State of New York to carry out a project to demonstrate methods for the selective removal of polychlorinated biphenyls contaminating bottom sediments of the Hudson River, treating such sediments as required, burying such sediments in secure landfills, and installing monitoring systems for such landfills. Such demonstration project shall be for the purpose of determining the feasibility of indefinite storage in secure landfills of toxic substances and of ascertaining the improvement of the rate of recovery of a toxic contaminated national waterway. No pollutants removed pursuant to this paragraph shall be placed in any landfill unless the Administrator first determines that disposal of the pollutants in such landfill would provide a higher standard of protection of the public health, safety, and welfare than disposal of such pollutants by any other method including, but not limited to, incineration or a chemical destruction process.

(b) The Administrator is authorized to make grants to the State of New York to carry out this section from funds allotted to such State under section 205(a) of this Act, except that the amount of any such grant shall be equal to 75 per centum of the cost of the project and such grant shall be made on condition that non-Federal sources provide the remainder of the cost of such project. The authority of this section shall be available until September 30, 1983. Funds allotted to the State of New York under section 205(a) shall be available under this subsection only to the extent that funds are not available, as determined by the Administrator, to the State of New York for the work authorized by this section under section 115 or 311 of this Act or a comprehensive hazardous substance response and clean up fund. Any funds used under the authority of this subsection shall be deducted from any estimate of the needs of the State of New York prepared under section 616(b) of this Act. The Administrator may not obligate or expend more than $20,000,000 to carry out this section.

[Sec. 116 added by PL 96-483]

[Section 12 of PL 96-483 provides:

"Sec. 12. The Administrator of the Environmental Protection Agency is authorized to make grants to States to undertake a demonstration program for the cleanup of State-owned abandoned mines which can be used as hazardous waste disposal sites. The State shall pay 10 percentum of project costs. At a minimum, the Administrator shall undertake projects under such program in the States of Ohio, Illinois, and West Virginia. There are authorized to be appropriated $10,000,000 per fiscal year for each of the fiscal years ending September 30, 1982, September 30, 1983, and September 30, 1984, to carry out this section. Such projects shall be undertaken in accordance with all applicable laws and regulations."]

Sec. 117. Chesapeake Bay.

[Sec. 117 added by PL 100-4]

(a) Office. -- The Administrator shall continue the Chesapeake Bay Program and shall establish and maintain in the Environmental Protection Agency an office, division, or branch of Chesapeake Bay Programs to --

(1) collect and make available, through publications and other appropriate means, information pertaining to the environmental quality of the Chesapeake Bay (hereinafter in this subsection referred to as the 'Bay');

(2) coordinate Federal and State efforts to improve the water quality of the Bay;

(3) determine the impact of sediment deposition in the Bay and identify the sources, rates, routes, and distribution patterns of such sediment deposition; and

(4) determine the impact of natural and man-induced environmental changes on the living resources of the Bay and the

relationships among such changes, with particular emphasis
placed on the impact of pollutant loadings of nutrients,
chlorine, acid precipitation, dissolved oxygen, and toxic
pollutants, including organic chemicals and heavy metals, and
with special attention given to the impact of such changes on
striped bass.

(b) Interstate Development Plan Grants. --

(1) Authority. -- The Administrator shall, at the request of
the Governor of a State affected by the interstate management
plan developed pursuant to the Chesapeake Bay Program
(hereinafter in this section referred to as the 'plan'), make a
grant for the purpose of implementing the management mechanisms
contained in the plan if such State has, within 1 year after the
date of the enactment of this section, approved and committed to
implement all or substantially all aspects of the plan. Such
grants shall be made subject to such terms and conditions as the
Administrator considers appropriate.

(2) Submission of Proposal. -- A State or combination of States
may elect to avail itself of the benefits of this subsection by
submitting to the Administrator a comprehensive proposal to
implement management mechanisms contained in the plan which
shall include (A) a description of proposed abatement actions
which the State or combination of States commit to take within a
specified time period to reduce pollution in the Bay and to meet
applicable water quality standards, and (B) the estimated cost
of the abatement actions proposed to be taken during the next
fiscal year. If the Administrator finds that such proposal is
consistent with the national policies set forth in section
101(a) of this Act and will contribute to the achievement of the
national goals set forth in such section, the Administrator
shall approve such proposal and shall finance the costs of
implementing segments of such proposal.

(3) Federal share. -- Grants under this subsection shall not
exceed 50 percent of the costs of implementing the management
mechanisms contained in the plan in any fiscal year and shall be
made on condition that non-Federal sources provide the remainder
of the cost of implementing the management mechanisms contained
in the plan during such fiscal year.

(b) Administrative costs. -- Administrative costs in the form of
salaries, overhead, or indirect costs for services provided and
charged against programs or projects supported by funds made
available under this subsection shall not exceed in any one fiscal
year 10 percent of the annual Federal grant made to a State under
this subsection.

(c) Reports. -- Any State or combination of States that receives a
grant under subsection (b) shall, within 18 months after the date of
receipt of such grant and biennially thereafter, report to the
Administrator on the progress made in implementing the interstate
management plan developed pursuant to the Chesapeake Bay Program.
The Administrator shall transmit each such report along with the
comments of the administrator on such report to Congress.

(d) Authorization of Appropriations. -- There are hereby authorized to be appropriated the following sums, to remain available until expended, to carry out the purposes of this section:

(1) $3,000,000 per fiscal year for each of the fiscal years 1987, 1988, 1989, and 1990, to carry out subsection (a); and

(2) $10,000,000 per fiscal year for each of the fiscal years 1987, 1988, 1989, and 1990, for grants to States under subsection (b).

Sec. 118. Great Lakes.

[Sec. 118 added by PL 100-4]

(a) Findings, Purpose, and Definitions.

(1) Findings. -- The Congress finds that --

(A) the Great Lakes are a valuable national resource, continuously serving the people of the United States and other nations as an important source of food, fresh water, recreation, beauty, and enjoyment;

(B) the United States should seek to attain the goals embodied in the Great Lakes Water Quality Agreement of 1978 with particular emphasis on goals related to toxic pollutants; and

(C) the Environmental Protection Agency should take the lead in the effort to meet those goals, working with other Federal agencies and State and local authorities.

(2) Purpose. -- It is the purpose of this section to achieve the goals embodied in the Great Lakes Water Quality Agreement of 1978 through improved organization and definition of mission on the part of the Agency, funding of State grants for pollution control in the Great Lakes area, and improved accountability for implementation of such agreement.

(3) Definitions. -- For purposes of this section, the term --

(A) "Agency" means the Environmental Protection Agency;

(B) "Great Lakes" means Lake Ontario, Lake Erie, Lake Huron (including Lake St. Clair), Lake Michigan, and Lake Superior, and the connecting channels (Saint Mary's River, Saint Clair River, Detroit River, Niagara River, and Saint Lawrence River to the Canadian Border);

(C) "Great Lakes System" means all the streams, rivers, lakes and other bodies of water within the drainage basin of the Great Lakes:

(D) "Program Office" means the Great Lakes National Program Office established by this section; and

(E) "Research Office" means the Great Lakes Research Office established by subsection (d).

(b) Great Lakes National Program Office. -- The Great Lakes National Program Office (previously established by the Administrator) is hereby established within the Agency. The Program Office shall be headed by a Director who, by reason of management experience and technical expertise relating to the Great Lakes, is highly qualified to direct the development of programs and plans on a variety of Great Lakes issues. The Great Lakes National Program Office shall be located in a Great Lakes State.

(c) Great Lakes Management. --

(1) Functions. -- The Program Office shall --

(A) in cooperation with appropriate Federal, State, tribal, and international agencies, and in accordance with section 101(e) of this Act, develop and implement specific action plans to carry out the responsibilities of the United States under the Great Lakes Water Quality Agreement of 1978;

(B) establish a Great Lakes system-wide surveillance network to monitor the water quality of the Great Lakes, with specific emphasis on the monitoring of toxic pollutants;

(C) serve as the liaison with, and provide information to, the Canadian members of the International Joint Commission and the Canadian counterpart to the Agency;

(D) coordinate actions of the Agency (including actions by headquarters and regional offices thereof) aimed at improving Great Lakes water quality; and

(E) coordinate actions of the Agency with the actions of other Federal agencies and State and local authorities, so as to ensure the input of those agencies and authorities in developing water quality strategies and obtain the support of those agencies and authorities in achieving the objectives of such agreement.

(2) 5-Year Plan and Program. -- The Program Office shall develop, in consultation with the States, a five-year plan and program for reducing the amount of nutrients introduced into the Great Lakes. Such program shall incorporate any management program for reducing nutrient runoff from nonpoint sources established under section 319 of this Act and shall include a program for monitoring nutrient runoff into, and ambient levels in, the Great Lakes.

(3) 5-Year Study and Demonstration Projects. -- The Program Office shall carry out a five-year study and demonstration projects relating to the control and removal of toxic pollutants in the Great Lakes, with emphasis on the removal of toxic pollutants from bottom sediments. In selecting locations for conducting demonstration projects under this paragraph, priority consideration shall be given to projects at the following

locations: Saginaw Bay, Michigan; Sheboygan Harbor, Wisconsin, Grand Calument River, Indiana; Ashtabula River, Ohio; and Buffalo River, New York.

(4) Administrator's Responsibility. -- The Administrator shall ensure that the Program Office enters into agreements with the various organizational elements of the Agency involved in Great Lakes activities and the appropriate State agencies specifically delineating --

(A) the duties and responsibilities of each such element in the Agency with respect to the Great Lakes;

(B) the time periods for carrying out such duties and responsibilities; and

(C) the resources to be committed to such duties and responsibilities.

(5) Budget Item. -- The Administrator shall, in the Agency's annual budget submission to Congress, include a funding request for the Program Office as a separate budget line item.

(6) Comprehensive Report. -- Within 90 days after the end of each fiscal year, the Administrator shall submit to Congress a comprehensive report which --

(A) describes the achievements in the preceding fiscal year in implementing the Great Lakes Water Quality Agreement of 1978 and shows by categories (including judicial enforcement, research, State cooperative efforts, and general administration) the amounts expended on Great Lakes water quality initiatives in such preceding fiscal year;

(B) describes the progress made in such preceding fiscal year in implementing the system of surveillance of the water quality in the Great Lakes System, including the monitoring of groundwater and sediment, with particular reference to toxic pollutants;

(C) describes the long-term prospects for improving the condition of the Great Lakes; and

(D) provides a comprehensive assessment of the planned efforts to be pursued in the succeeding fiscal year for implementing the Great Lakes Water Quality Agreement of 1978, which assessment shall --

(i) show by categories (including judicial enforcement, research, State cooperative efforts, and general administration) the amount anticipated to be expended on Great Lakes water quality initiatives in the fiscal year to which the assessment relates; and
(ii) include a report of current programs administered by other Federal agencies which make available resources to the Great Lakes water quality management efforts.

(d) Great Lakes Research. --

(1) Establishment of Research Office. -- There is established within the National Oceanic and Atmospheric Administration the Great Lakes Research Office.

(2) Identification of Issues. -- The Research Office shall identify issues relating to the Great Lakes resources on which research is needed. The Research Office shall submit a report to Congress on such issues before the end of each fiscal year which shall identify any changes in the Great Lakes system with respect to such issues.

(3) Inventory. -- The Research Office shall identify and inventory Federal, State, university, and tribal environmental research programs (and, to the extent feasible, those of private organizations and other nations) relating to the Great Lakes system, and shall update that inventory every four years.

(4) Research Exchange. -- The Research Office shall establish a Great Lakes research exchange for the purpose of facilitating the rapid identification, acquisition, retrieval, dissemination, and use of information concerning research projects which are ongoing or completed and which affect the Great Lakes System.

(5) Research Program. -- The Research Office shall develop, in cooperation with the Coordination Office, a comprehensive environmental research program and data base for the Great Lakes system. The data base shall include, but not be limited to, data relating to water quality, fisheries, and biota.

(6) Monitoring. -- The Research Office shall conduct, through the Great Lakes Environmental Research Laboratory, the National Sea Grant College program, other Federal laboratories, and the private sector, appropriate research and monitoring activities which address priority issues and current needs relating to the Great Lakes.

(7) Location. -- The Research Office shall be located in a Great Lakes State.

(e) Research and Management Coordination. --

(1) Joint Plan. Before October 1 of each year, the Program Office and the Research Office shall prepare a joint research plan for the fiscal year which begins in the following calendar year.

(2) Contents of Plan. -- Each plan prepared under paragraph (1) shall --

(A) identify all proposed research dedicated to activities conducted under the Great Lakes Water Quality Agreement of 1978;

(B) include the Agency's assessment of priorities for research needed to fulfill the terms of such Agreement; and

(C) identify all proposed research that may be used to develop a comprehensive environmental data base for the Great Lakes System and establish priorities for development of such data base.

(f) Interagency Cooperation. -- The head of each department, agency, or other instrumentality of the Federal Government which is engaged in, is concerned with, or has authority over programs relating to research, monitoring, and planning to maintain, enhance, preserve, or rehabilitate the environmental quality and natural resources of the Great Lakes, including the Chief of Engineers of the Army, the Chief of the Soil Conservation Service, the Commandant of the Coast Guard, the Director of the Fish and Wildlife Service, and the Administrator of the National Oceanic and Atmospheric Administration, shall submit an annual report to the Administrator with respect to the activities of that agency or office affecting compliance with the Great Lakes Water Quality Agreement of 1978.

(g) Relationship to Existing Federal and State Laws and International Treaties. -- Nothing in this section shall be construed to affect the jurisdiction, powers, or prerogatives of any department, agency, or officer of the Federal Government or of any State government, or of any tribe, nor any powers, jurisdiction, or prerogatives of any international body created by treaty with authority relating to the Great Lakes.

(h) Authorizations of Great Lakes Appropriations. -- There are authorized to be appropriated to the Administrator to carry out this section not to exceed $11,000,000 per fiscal year for the fiscal years 1987, 1988, 1989, 1990, and 1991. Of the amounts appropriated each fiscal year --

(1) 40 percent shall be used by the Great Lakes National Program Office on demonstration projects on the feasibility of controlling and removing toxic pollutants;

(2) 7 percent shall be used by the Great Lakes National Program Office for the program of nutrient monitoring; and

(3) 30 percent shall be transferred to the National Oceanic and Atmospheric Administration for use by the Great Lakes Research Office.

TITLE II -- GRANTS FOR CONSTRUCTION OF TREATMENT WORKS

[Section 202(f) of PL 100-4 states:

"(f) Availability of Certain Funds for Non-Federal Share. -- Notwithstanding any other provision of law, Federal assistance made available by the Farmers Home Administration to any political subdivision of a State may be used to provide the non-Federal share of the cost of any construction project carried out under section 201 of the Federal Water Pollution Control Act."]

Sec. 201. Purpose.

(a) It is the purpose of this title to require and to assist the development and implementation of waste treatment management plans and practices which will achieve the goals of this Act.

(b) Waste treatment management plans and practices shall provide for the application of the best practicable waste treatment technology before any discharge into receiving waters, including reclaiming and recycling of water, and confined disposal of pollutants so they will not migrate to cause water or other environmental pollution and shall provide for consideration of advanced waste treatment techniques.

(c) To the extent practicable, waste treatment management shall be on an areawide basis and provide control or treatment of all point and nonpoint sources of pollution, including in place or accumulated pollution sources.

(d) The Administrator shall encourage waste treatment management which results in the construction of revenue producing facilities providing for --

    (1) the recycling of potential sewage pollutants through the production of agriculture, silviculture, or aquaculture products, or any combination thereof;

    (2) the confined and contained disposal of pollutants not recycled;

    (3) the reclamation of wastewater; and

    (4) the ultimate disposal of sludge in a manner that will not result in environmental hazards.

(e) The Administrator shall encourage waste treatment management which results in integrating facilities for sewage treatment and recycling with facilities to treat, dispose of, or utilize other industrial and municipal wastes, including but not limited to solid waste and waste heat and thermal discharges. Such integrated facilities shall be designed and operated to produce revenues in excess of capital and operation and maintenance costs and such revenues shall be used by the designated regional management agency to aid in financing other environmental improvement programs.

(f) The Administrator shall encourage waste treatment management which combines "open space" and recreational considerations with such management.

(g) (1) The Administrator is authorized to make grants to any State, municipality, or intermunicipal or interstate agency for the construction of publicly owned treatment works. On and after October 1, 1984, grants under this title shall be made only for projects for secondary treatment or more stringent treatment, or any cost effective alternative thereto, new interceptors and appurtenances, and infiltration-in-flow correction. Notwithstanding the preceding sentences, the Administrator may make grants on and after October 1, 1984, for (A) any project within the definition set forth in section 212(2) of this Act, other than for a project referred to in the preceding sentence, and (B) any purpose for which a grant may be made under sections 319(h) and (i) of this Act (including any innovative and alternative approaches for the control of nonpoint sources of pollution), except that not more than 20 per centum (as determined by the Governor of the State) of the amount allotted to a State under section 205 of this Act for any fiscal year shall be obligated in such State under authority of this sentence.

[Sec. 201(g)(1) revised by PL 97-117; amended by PL 100-4]

[Section 213(b)-(d) and Section 214 of PL 100-4, stipulate:

"**(b)** Walker and Smithfield Townships, Pennsylvania. Under the third sentence of section 201(g)(1) of the Federal Water Pollution Control Act in fiscal year 1987, the Administrator shall make grants --

(1) to Walker Township, Pennsylvania, for developing a collector system and connecting its wastewater treatment system into the Huntingdon Borough, Pennsylvania, sewage treatment plant, and

(2) to Smithfield Township, Pennsylvania, for rehabilitating and extending its collector system.

(c) Taylor Mill, Kentucky. -- Notwithstanding section 201(g)(1) of the Federal Water Pollution Control Act or any other provision of law, the Administrator shall make a grant of $250,000 from funds allotted under section 205 of such Act to the State of Kentucky for fiscal year 1986 to the city of Taylor Mill, Kentucky, for the repair and reconstruction, as necessary, of the publicly owned treatment works of such city.

(d) Nevada County, California. -- Out of funds available for grants in the State of California under the third sentence of section 201(g)(1) of the Federal Water Pollution Control Act in fiscal year 1987, the Administrator shall make a grant for the construction of a collection system serving the Glenshire/Devonshire area of Nevada County, California, to deliver waste to the Tahoe-Truckee Sanitary District's regional wastewater treatment facility."]

"Sec. 214.   Chicago Tunnel and Reservoir Project.

The Chicago tunnel and reservoir project may receive grants under
the last sentence of section 201(g)(1) of the Federal Water
Pollution Control Act without regard to the limitation contained in
such sentence if the Administrator determines that such project
meets the cost-effectiveness requirements of sections 217 and 218 of
such Act without any redesign or reconstruction and if the Governor
of the affected State demonstrates to the satisfaction of the
Administrator the water quality benefits of such project."]

(2) The Administrator shall not make grants from funds
authorized for any fiscal year beginning after June 30, 1974, to
any State, municipality, or intermunicipal or interstate agency
for the erection, building, acquisition, alteration, remodeling,
improvement, or extension of treatment works unless the grant
applicant has satisfactorily demonstrated to the Administrator
that --

(A) alternative waste management techniques have been
studied and evaluated and the works proposed for grant
assistance will provide for the application of the best
practicable waste treatment technology over the life of the
works consistent with the purposes of this title; and

(B) as appropriate, the works proposed for grant assistance
will take into account and allow to the extent practicable
the application of technology at a later date which will
provide for the reclaiming or recycling of water or
otherwise eliminate the discharge of pollutants.

(3) The Administrator shall not approve any grant after July 1,
1973, for treatment works under this section unless the
applicant shows to the satisfaction of the Administrator that
each sewer collection system discharging into such treatment
works is not subject to excessive infiltration.

(4) The Administrator is authorized to make grants to applicants
for treatment works grants under this section for such sewer
system evaluation studies as may be necessary to carry out the
requirements of paragraph (3) of this subsection. Such grants
shall be made in accordance with rules and regulations
promulgated by the Administrator. Initial rules and regulations
shall be promulgated under this paragraph not later than 120
days after the date of enactment of the Federal Water Pollution
Control Act Amendments of 1972.

(5) The Administrator shall not make grants from funds
authorized for any fiscal year beginning after September 30,
1978, to any State, municipality, or intermunicipal or
interstate agency for the erection, building, acquisition,
alteration, remodeling, improvement, or extension of treatment
works unless the grant applicant has satisfactorily demonstrated
to the Administrator that innovative and alternative wastewater
treatment processes and techniques which provide for the
reclaiming and reuse of water, otherwise eliminate the discharge

of pollutants, and utilize recycling techniques, land treatment, new or improved methods of waste treatment management for municipal and industrial waste (discharged into municipal systems) and the confined disposal of pollutants, so that pollutants will not migrate to cause water or other environmental pollution, have been fully studied and evaluated by the applicant taking into account section 201(d) of this Act and taking into account and allowing to the extent practicable the more efficient use of energy and resources.

[Section 517 of PL 100-4 provides:

"Sec. 517. Study of Effectiveness of Innovative and Alternative Processes and Techniques.

(a) Effectiveness Study. -- The Administrator shall study the effectiveness on waste treatment of innovative and alternative wastewater treatment processes and techniques referred to in section 201(g)(5) of the Federal Water Pollution Control Act which have been utilized in treatment works constructed under such Act. In conducting such study, the Administrator shall compile information, by State, on the types of such processes and techniques utilized, on the number of facilities constructed with such processes and techniques which have not performed to design standards. The Administrator shall also determine which States have not obligated the full amount set aside under section 205(i) of such Act for such processes and techniques and the reasons for each such State's failure to make such obligations.

(b) Report. -- Not later than one year after the date of the enactment of this Act, the Administrator shall submit to the Committee on Public Works and Transportation of the House of Representatives and the Committee on Environment and Public Works of the Senate a report on the results of such study, along with recommendations for providing more effective incentives for innovative and alternative wastewater treatment processes and techniques."]

(6) The Administrator shall not make grants from funds authorized for any fiscal year beginning after September 30, 1978, to any State, municipality, or intermunicipal or interstate agency for the erection, building, acquisition, alteration, remodeling, improvement, or extension of treatment works unless the grant applicant has satisfactorily demonstrated to the Administrator that the applicant has analyzed the potential recreation and open space opportunities in the planning of the proposed treatment works.

(h) A grant may be made under this section to construct a privately owned treatment works serving one or more principal residences or small commercial establishments constructed prior to, and inhabited on the date of enactment of this subsection where the Administrator finds that --

(1) a public body otherwise eligible for a grant under subsection (g) of this section has applied on behalf of a number

of such units and certified that public ownership of such works is not feasible;

(2) such public body has entered into an agreement with the Administrator which guarantees that such treatment works will be properly operated and maintained and will comply with all other requirements of section 204 of this Act and includes a system of charges to assure that each recipient of waste treatment services under such a grant will pay its proportionate share of the cost of operation and maintenance (including replacement); and

(3) the total cost and environmental impact of providing waste treatment services to such residences or commercial establishments will be less than the cost of providing a system of collection and central treatment of such wastes.

(i) The Administrator shall encourage waste treatment management methods, processes, and techniques which will reduce total energy requirements.

(j) The Administrator is authorized to make a grant for any treatment works utilizing processes and techniques meeting the guidelines promulgated under section 304(d)(3) of this Act, if the Administrator determines it is in the public interest and if in the cost effectiveness study made of the construction grant application for the purpose of evaluating alternative treatment works, the life cycle cost of the treatment works for which the grant is to be made does not exceed the life cycle cost of the most effective alternative by more than 15 per centum.

(k) No grant made after November 15, 1981, for a publicly owned treatment works, other than for facility planning and the preparation of construction plans and specifications, shall be used to treat, store, or convey the flow of any industrial user into such treatment works in excess of a flow per day equivalent to fifty thousand gallons per day of sanitary waste. This subsection shall not apply to any project proposed by a grantee which is carrying out an approved project to prepare construction plans and specifications for a facility to treat wastewater, which received its grant approval before May 15, 1980. This subsection shall not be in effect after November 15, 1981.

[Sec. 201(k) added by PL 96-483; amended by PL 97-117]

[Section 4 of PL 96-483 provides:

"Sec. 4.

The Administrator of the Environmental Protection Agency shall study and report to the Congress not later than March 15, 1981, on the effect of the amendment by section 3 [Section 3 of PL 96-483 amended Section 201 of this Act by adding subsection (k)] on the construction of publicly owned treatment works, industrial participation in publicly owned treatment works, treatment of industrial discharges, and the appropriate degree of Federal and non-Federal participation in the funding of publicly owned treatment works."]

(1) (1) After the date of enactment of this subsection, Federal grants shall not be made for the purpose of providing assistance solely for facility plans, or plans specifications, and estimates for any proposed project for the construction of treatment works. In the event that the proposed project receives a grant under this section for construction, the Administrator shall make an allowance in such grant for non-Federal funds expended during the facility planning and advanced engineering and design phase at the prevailing Federal share under section 202(a) of this Act, based on the percentage of total project costs which the Administrator determines is the general experience for such projects.

(2) (A) Each State shall use a portion of the funds allotted to such State each fiscal year, but not to exceed 10 per centum of such funds, to advance to potential grant applicants under this title the costs of facility planning or the preparation of plans, specifications, and estimates.

(B) Such an advance shall be limited to the allowance for such costs which the Administrator establishes under paragraph (1) of this subsection, and shall be provided only to a potential grant applicant which is a small community and which in the judgment of the State would otherwise be unable to prepare a request for a grant for construction costs under this section.

(C) In the event a grant for construction costs is made under this section for a project for which an advance has been made under · this paragraph, the Administrator shall reduce the amount of such grant by the allowance established under paragraph (1) of this subsection. In the event no such grant is made, the State is authorized to seek repayment of such advance on such terms and conditions as it may determine.

[Sec. 201(1) added by PL 97-117]

(m) Mitigation and Special Processes.

(1) Notwithstanding any other provisions of this title, the Administrator is authorized to make a grant from any funds otherwise allotted to the State of California under section 205 of this Act to the project (and in the amount) specified in Order WQG 81-1 of the California State Water Resources Control Board.

(2) Notwithstanding any other provisions of this Act, the Administrator shall make a grant from any funds otherwise allotted to the State of California to the city of Eureka, California, in connection with project numbered C-06-2772, for the purchase of one hundred and thirty-nine acres of property as environmental mitigation for siting of the proposed treatment plant.

(3) Notwithstanding any other provision of this Act, the Administrator shall make a grant from any funds otherwise allotted to the State of California to the city of San Diego, California, in connection with that city's aquaculture sewage process (total resources recovery system) as an innovative and alternative waste treatment process.

[Sec. 201(m) added by PL 97-117]

(n) Combined Sewer Overflow

(1) On and after October 1, 1984, upon the request of the Governor of an affected State, the Administrator is authorized to use funds available to such State under section 205 to address water quality problems due to the impacts of discharges from combined storm water and sanitary sewer overflows, which are not otherwise eligible under this subsection, were correction of such discharges is a major priority for such State.

(2) Beginning fiscal year 1983, the Administrator shall have available $200,000,000 per fiscal year in addition to those funds authorized in section 207 of this Act to be utilized to address water quality problems of marine bays and estuaries subject to lower levels of water quality due to the impacts of discharges from combined storm water and sanitary sewer overflows from adjacent urban complexes, not otherwise eligible under this subsection. Such sums may be used as deemed appropriate by the Administrator as provided in paragraphs (1) and (2) of this subsection, upon the request of and demonstration of water quality benefits by the Governor of an affected State.

[Sec. 201(n) added by PL 97-117]

(o) The Administrator shall encourage and assist applicants for grant assistance under this title to develop and file with the Administrator a capital financing plan which, at a minimum --

(1) projects the future requirements for waste treatment services within the applicant's jurisdiction for a period of no less than ten years;

(2) projects the nature, extent, timing, and costs of future expansion and reconstruction of treatment works which will be necessary to satisfy the applicant's projected future requirements for waste treatment services; and

(3) sets forth with specificity the manner in which the applicant intends to finance such future expansion and reconstruction.

[Sec. 201(o) added by PL 97-117]

(p) Time Limit on Resolving Certain Disputes. -- In any case in which a dispute arises with respect to the awarding of a contract for construction of treatment works by a grantee of funds under this title and a party to such dispute files an appeal with the Administrator under this title for resolution of such dispute, the Administrator shall make a final decision on such appeal within 90 days of the filing of such appeal.

[Sec. 201(p) added by PL 100-4]

Sec. 202. Federal Share.

(a) (1) The amount of any grant for treatment works made under this Act from funds authorized for any fiscal year beginning after June 30, 1971, and ending before October 1, 1984, shall be 75 per centum at the cost of construction thereof (as approved by the Administrator), and for any fiscal year beginning on or after October 1, 1984, shall be 55 per centum of the cost of construction thereof (as approved by the Administrator), unless modified to a lower percentage rate uniform throughout a State by the Governor of that State with the concurrence of the Administrator. Within ninety days after the enactment of this sentence the Adminstrator shall issue guidelines for concurrence in any such modification, which shall provide for the consideration of the unobligated balance of sums allocated to the State under section 205 of this Act, the need for assistance under this title in such State, and the availability of State grant assistance to replace the Federal share reduced by such modification. The payment of any such reduced Federal share shall not constitute an obligation on the part of the United States or a claim on the part of any State or grantee to reimbursement for the portion of the Federal share reduced in any such State. Any grant (other than for reimbursement) made prior to the date of enactment of the Federal Water Pollution Control Act Amendments of 1972 from any funds authorized for any fiscal year beginning after June 30, 1971, shall, upon the request of the applicant, be increased to the applicable percentage under this section. Notwithstanding the first sentence of this paragraph, in any case where a primary, secondary, or advanced waste treatment facility or its related interceptors or a project for infiltration-in-flow correction has received a grant for erection, building, acquisition, alteration, remodeling, improvement, extension, or correction before October 1, 1984, all segments and phases of such facility, interceptors, and project for infiltration-in-flow correction shall be eligible for grants at 75 per centum of the cost of construction thereof for any grant made pursuant to a State obligation which obligation occurred before October 1, 1990. Notwithstanding the first sentence of this paragraph, in the case of a project for which an application for a grant under this title has been made to the Administrator before October 1, 1984, and which project is under judicial injunction on such date prohibiting its construction, such project shall be eligible for grants at 75 percent of the cost of construction thereof. Notwithstanding the first sentence of this paragraph, in the case of the Wyoming Valley Sanitary Authority project mandated by judicial order under a proceeding begun prior to October 1, 1984, and a project for wastewater treatment for Altoona, Pennsylvania, such projects shall be eligible for grants at 75 percent of the cost of construction thereof.

[Sec. 202(a)(1) amended by PL 96-483; PL 97-117; PL 100-4]

(2) The amount of any grant made after September 30, 1978, and before October 1, 1981, for any eligible treatment works or significant portion thereof utilizing innovative or alternative wastewater treatment processes and techniques referred to in section 201(g) (5) shall be 85 per centum of the cost of construction thereof unless modified by the Governor of the State with the concurrence of the Administrator to a percentage rate no less than 15 percentum greater than the modified uniform percentage rate in which the Administrator has concurred pursuant to paragraph (1) of this subsection. The amount of any grant made after September 30, 1981, for any eligible treatment works or unit processes and techniques thereof utilizing innovative or alternative wastewater treatment processes and techniques referred to in section 201(g)(5) shall be a percentage of the cost of construction thereof equal to 20 per centum greater than the percentage in effect under paragraph (1) of this subsection for such works or unit processes and techniques, but in no event greater than 85 per centum of the cost of construction thereof. No grant shall be made under this paragraph for construction of a treatment works in any State unless the proportion of the State contribution to the non-Federal share of construction costs for all treatment works in such State receiving a grant under this paragraph is the same as or greater than the proportion of the State contribution (if any) to the non-Federal share of construction costs for all treatment works receiving grants in such State under paragraph (1) of this subsection.

[Sec. 202(a)(2) amended by PL 96-483; PL 97-117]

[Section 202(e) of PL 100-4 stipulates:

"(e) Innovative Process. -- The activated bio-filter feature of the project for treatment works of the city of Little Falls, Minnesota, shall be deemed to be an innovative wastewater process and technique for purposes of section 202(a)(2) of the Federal Water Pollution Control Act and the amount of any grant under such Act for such feature shall be 85 percent of the cost thereof."]

(3) In addition to any grant made pursuant to paragraph (2) of this subsection, the Administrator is authorized to make a grant to fund all of the costs of the modification or replacement of any facilities constructed with a grant made pursuant to paragraph (2) if the Administrator finds that such facilities have not met design performance specifications unless such failure is attributable to negligence on the part of any person and if such failure has significantly increased capital or operating and maintenance expenditures. In addition, the Administrator is authorized to make a grant to fund all of the costs of the modification or replacement of biodisc equipment (rotating biological contractors) in any publicly owned treatment works if the Administrator finds that such equipment has failed to meet design performance specifications, unless such failure is attributable to negligence on the part of any

person, and if such failure has significantly increased capital or operating and maintenance expenditures.

[Sec. 202(a)(3) amended by PL 100-4]

(4) For the purposes of this section, the term "eligible treatment works" means those treatment works in each State which meet the requirements of section 201(g) (5) of this Act and which can be fully funded from funds available for such purpose in such State.

[Sec. 202(a)(4) amended by PL 97-117]

(b) The amount of the grant for any project approved by the Administrator after January 1, 1971, and before July 1, 1971, for the construction of treatment works, the actual erection, building or acquisition of which was not commenced prior to July 1, 1971, shall, upon the request of the applicant, be increased to the applicable percentage under subsection (a) of this section for grants for treatment works from funds for fiscal years beginning after June 30, 1971, with respect to the cost of such actual erection, building, or acquisition. Such increased amount shall be paid from any funds allocated to the State in which the treatment works is located without regard to the fiscal year for which such funds were authorized. Such increased amount shall be paid for such project only if --

(1) a sewage collection system that is a part of the same total waste treatment system as the treatment works for which such grant was approved is under construction or is to be constructed for use in conjunction with such treatment works, and if the cost of such sewage collection system exceeds the cost of such treatment works, and

(2) the State water pollution control agency or other appropriate State authority certifies that the quantity of available ground water will be insufficient, inadequate, or unsuitable for public use, including the ecological preservation and recreational use of surface water bodies, unless effluents from publicly owned treatment works after adequate treatment are returned to the ground water consistent with acceptable technological standards.

[Section 27 of PL 97-117 provides:

"Sec. 27. Bath Township.

For purposes of the Federal Water Pollution Control Act, the project for publicly owned treatment works for Bath Township, Michigan, shall be eligible for payments from sums allocated to the State of Michigan under such Act in an amount equal to the amount such works would be eligible for under section 202 of such Act if such works were to be constructed after the date of enactment of this Act, at the original construction costs."]

Sec. 203. Plans, Specifications, Estimates, and Payments.

(a) (1) Each applicant for a grant shall submit to the Administrator for his approval, plans, specifications, and estimates for each proposed project for the construction of treatment works for which a grant is applied for under section 201(g)(1) from funds allotted to the State under section 205 and which otherwise meets the requirements of this Act. The Administrator shall act upon such plans, specifications, and estimates as soon as practicable after the same have been submitted, and his approval of any such plans, specifications, and estimates shall be deemed a contractual obligation of the United States for the payment of its proportional contribution to such project.

[Sec. 203(a) amended by PL 96-483; (a)(1) designated by PL 100-4]

(2) Agreement on Eligible Costs. --

(A) Limitation on Modifications. -- Before taking final action on any plans, specifications, and estimates submitted under this subsection after the 60th day following the date of the enactment of the Water Quality Act of 1987, the Administrator shall enter into a written agreement with the applicant which establishes and specifies which items of the proposed project are eligible for Federal payments under this section. The Administrator may not later modify such eligibility determinations unless they are found to have been made in violation of applicable Federal statutes and regulations.

(B) Limitation on Effect. -- Eligibility determinations under this paragraph shall not preclude the Administrator from auditing a project pursuant to section 501 of this Act, or other authority, or from withholding of recovering Federal funds for costs which are found to be unreasonable, unsupported by adequate documentation, or otherwise unallowable under applicable Federal costs to meet the design specifications or effluent limitations contained in the grant agreement and permit pursuant to section 402 of this Act for such project.

[Sec. 203(a)(2) added by PL 100-4]

(3) In the case of a treatment works that has an estimated total cost of $8,000,000 or less (as determined by the Administrator), and the population of the applicant municipality is twenty-five thousand or less (according to the most recent United States census), upon completion of an approved facility plan, a single grant may be awarded for the combined Federal share of the cost of preparing construction plans and specifications, and the building and erection of the treatment works.

[Sec. 203(a)(3) designated by PL 100-4]

(b) The Administrator shall, from time to time as the work progresses, make payments to the recipient of a grant for costs of construction incurred on a project. These payments shall at no time exceed the Federal share of the cost of construction incurred to the date of the voucher covering such payment plus the Federal share of the value of the materials which have been stockpiled in the vicinity of such construction in conformity to plans and specifications for the project.

(c) After completion of a project and approval of the final voucher by the Administrator, he shall pay out of the appropriate sums the unpaid balance of the Federal share payable on account of such project.

(d) Nothing in this Act shall be construed to require, or to authorize the Administrator to require, that grants under this Act for construction of treatment works be made only for projects which are operable units usable for sewage collection, transportation, storage, waste treatment, or for similar purposes without additional construction.

(e) At the request of a grantee under this title, the Administrator is authorized to provide technical and legal assistance in the administration and enforcement of any contract in connection with treatment works assisted under this title, and to intervene in any civil action involving the enforcement of such a contract.

(f) Design/Build Projects.   --

[Sec. 203(f) added by PL 100-4]

    (1) Agreement.   -- Consistent with State law, an applicant who proposes to construct waste water treatment works may enter into an agreement with the Administrator under this subsection providing for the preparation of construction plans and specifications and the erection of such treatment works, in lieu of proceeding under the other provisions of this section.

    (2) Limitation on Projects.   -- Agreements under this subsection shall be limited to projects under an approved facility plan which projects are --

        (A) treatment works that have an estimated total cost of $8,000,000 or less; and

        (B) any of the following types of waste water treatment systems: aerated lagoons, trickling filters, stabilization ponds, land application systems, sand filters, and subsurface disposal systems.

    (3) Required Terms.   -- An agreement entered into under this subsection shall --

        (A) set forth an amount agreed to as the maximum Federal contribution to the project, based upon a competitively bid document of basic design data and applicable standard construction specifications and a determination of the federally eligible costs of the project at the applicable Federal share under section 202 of this Act;

(B) set forth dates for the start and completion of construction of the treatment works by the applicant and a schedule of payments of the Federal contribution to the project;

(C) contain assurances by the applicant that (i) engineering and management assistance will be provided to manage the project; (ii) the proposed treatment works will be an operable unit and will meet all the requirements of this title; and (iii) not later than 1 year after the date specified as the date of completion of construction of the treatment works, the treatment works will be operating so as to meet the requirements of any applicable permit for such treatment works under section 402 of this Act;

(D) require the applicant to obtain a bond from the contractor in an amount determined necessary by the Administrator to protect the Federal interest in the project; and

(E) contain such other terms and conditions as are necessary to assure compliance with this title (except as provided in paragraph (4) of this subsection).

(4) Limitation on Application. -- Subsections (a), (b), and (c) of this section shall not apply to grants made pursuant to this subsection.

(5) Reservation to Assure Compliance. -- The Administrator shall reserve a portion of the grant to assure contract compliance until final project approval as defined by the Administrator. If the amount agreed to under paragraph (3)(A) exceeds the cost of designing and constructing the treatment works, the Administrator shall reallot the amount of the excess to the State in which such treatment works are located for the fiscal year in which such audit is completed.

(6) Limitation on Obligations. -- The Administrator shall not obligate more than 20 percent of the amount allotted to a State for a fiscal year under section 205 of this Act for grants pursuant to this subsection.

(7) Allowance. -- The Administrator shall determine an allowance for facilities planning for projects constructed under this subsection in accordance with section 201(l).

(8) Limitation on Federal Contributions. -- In no event shall the Federal contribution for the cost of preparing construction plans and specifications and the building and erection of treatment works pursuant to this subsection exceed the amount agreed upon under paragraph (3).

(9) Recovery Action. -- In any case in which the recipient of a grant made pursuant to this subsection does not comply with the

terms of the agreement entered into under paragraph (3), the Administrator is authorized to take such action as may be necessary to recover the amount of the Federal contribution to the project.

(10) Prevention of Double Benefits. -- A recipient of a grant made pursuant to this subsection shall not be eligible for any other grants under this title for the same project.

Sec. 204. Limitations and Conditions.

(a) Before approving grants for any project for any treatment works under section 201(g)(1) the Administrator shall determine --

(1) that any required areawide waste treatment management plan under section 208 of this Act (A) is being implemented for such area and the proposed treatment works are included in such plan, or (B) is being developed for such area and reasonable progress is being made toward its implementation and the proposed treatment works will be included in such plan;

(204(a)(1) and (2) revised by PL 100-4)

(2) that (A) the State in which the project is to be located (i) is implementing any required plan under section 303(e) of this Act and the proposed treatment works are in conformity with such plan, or (ii) is developing such a plan and the proposed treatment works will be in conformity with such plan, and (B) such State is in compliance with section 305(b) of this Act;

[Sec. 205(f) of PL 100-4 states the revisions to 204(a)(1) and (2) "shall take effect on the last day of the two-year period" beginning on the date of enactment that law (February 4, 1987.)]

(3) that such works have been certified by the appropriate State water pollution control agency as entitled to priority over such other works in the State in accordance with any applicable State plan under section 303(e) of this Act, except that any priority list developed pursuant to section 303(e)(3)(H) may be modified by such State in accordance with regulations promulgated by the Administrator to give higher priority for grants for the Federal share of the cost of preparing construction drawings and specifications for any treatment works utilizing processes and techniques meeting the guidelines promulgated under section 304(d)(3) of this Act and for grants for the combined Federal share of the cost of preparing construction drawings and specifications and the building and erection of any treatment works meeting the requirements of the next to the last sentence of section 203(a) of this Act which utilizes processes and techniques meeting the guidelines promulgated under section 304(d)(3) of this Act;

(4) that the applicant proposing to construct such works agrees to pay the non-Federal costs of such works and has made adequate provisions satisfactory to the Administrator for assuring proper and efficient operation, including the employment of trained management and operations personnel, and the maintenance of such

works in accordance with a plan of operation approved by the State water pollution control agency or, as appropriate, the interstate agency, after construction thereof;

(5) that the size and capacity of such works relate directly to the needs to be served by such works, including sufficient reserve capacity. The amount of reserve capacity provided shall be approved by the Administrator on the basis of a comparison of the cost of constructing such reserves as a part of the works to be funded and the anticipated cost of providing expanded capacity at a date when such capacity will be required after taking into account, in accordance with regulations promulgated by the Administrator, efforts to reduce total flow of sewage and unnecessary water consumption. The amount of reserve capacity eligible for a grant under this title shall be determined by the Administrator taking into account the projected population and associated commercial and industrial establishments within the jurisdiction of the applicant to be served by such treatment works as identified in an approved facilities plan, an areawide plan under section 208; or an applicable municipal master plan of development. For the purpose of this paragraph, section 208, and any such plan, projected population shall be determined on the basis of the latest information available from the United States Department of Commerce or from the States as the Administrator, by regulation, determines appropriate. Beginning October 1, 1984, no grant shall be made under this title to construct that portion of any treatment works providing reserve capacity in excess of existing needs (including existing needs of residential, commercial, industrial, and other users) on the date of approval of a grant for the erection, building, acquisition, alteration, remodeling, improvement, or extension of a project for secondary treatment or more stringent treatment or new interceptors and appurtenances, except that in no event shall reserve capacity of a facility and its related interceptors to which this subsection applies be in excess of existing needs on October 1, 1990. In any case in which an applicant proposes to provide reserve capacity greater than that eligible for Federal financial assistance under this title, the incremental costs of the additional reserve capacity shall be paid by the applicant;

[Sec. 204(a)(5) amended by PL 97-117]

(6) that no specification for bids in connection with such works shall be written in such a manner as to contain proprietary, exclusionary, or discriminatory requirements other than those based upon performance, unless such requirements are necessary to test or demonstrate a specific thing or to provide for necessary interchangeability of parts and equipment. When in the judgment of the grantee, it is impractical or uneconomical to make a clear and accurate description of the technical requirements, a "brand name or equal" description may be used as a means to define the performance or other salient requirements of a procurement, and in doing so the grantee need not establish the existence of any source other than the brand or source so named.

[Sec. 204(a)(6) amended by PL 97-117]

(b) (1) Notwithstanding any other provision of this title, the Administrator shall not approve any grant for any treatment works under section 201(g)(1) after March 1, 1973, unless he shall first have determined that the applicant (A) has adopted or will adopt a system of charges to assure that each recipient of waste treatment services within the applicant's jurisdiction, as determined by the Administrator, will pay its proportionate share (except as otherwise provided in this paragraph) of the costs of operation and maintenance (including replacement) of any waste treatment services provided by the applicant; and (B) has legal, institutional managerial, and financial capability to insure adequate construction, operation, and maintenance of treatment works throughout the applicant's jurisdiction, as determined by the Administrator. In any case where an applicant which, as of the date of enactment of this sentence, uses a system of dedicated ad valorem taxes and the Administrator determines that the applicant has a system of charges which results in the distribution of operation and maintenance costs for treatment works within the applicant's jurisdiction, to each user class, in proportion to the contribution to the total costs of operation and maintenance of such works by each user class (taking into account total waste water loading of such works, the constituent elements of the waste, and other appropriate factors) and such applicant is otherwise in compliance with clause (A) of this paragraph with respect to each industrial user, then such dedicated ad valorem tax system shall be deemed to be the user charge system meeting the requirements of clause (A) of this paragraph for the residential user class and such small non-residential user classes as defined by the Administrator. In defining small non-residential users, the Administrator shall consider the volume of wastes discharged into the treatment works by such users and the constituent elements of such wastes as well as such other factors as he deems appropriate. A system of user charges which imposes a lower charge for low-income residential users (as defined by the Administrator) shall be deemed to be a user charge system meeting the requirements of clause (A) of this paragraph if the Administrator determines that such system was adopted after public notice and hearing.

[Sec. 204(b)(1) amended by PL 96-483; PL 100-4]

[Section 215 of PL 100-4 provides:

"Sec. 215. **Ad Valorem Tax Dedication.**

For the purposes of complying with section 204(b)(1) of the Federal Water Pollution Control Act, the ad valorem tax user charge systems of the town of Hampton and the city of Nashua, New Hampshire, shall be deemed to have been dedicated as of December 27, 1977. The Administrator shall review such ad valorem tax user charge systems for compliance with the remaining requirements of such section and related regulations of the Environmental Protection Agency."]

(2) The Administrator shall, within one hundred and eighty days after the date of enactment of the Federal Water Pollution Control Act Amendments of 1972, and after consultation with appropriate State, interstate, municipal, and intermunicipal agencies, issue guidelines applicable to payment of waste treatment costs by industrial and nonindustrial recipients of waste treatment services which shall establish (A) classes of users of such services, including categories of industrial users; (B) criteria against which to determine the adequacy of charges imposed on classes and categories of users reflecting all factors that influence the cost of waste treatment, including strength, volume, and delivery flow rate characteristics of waste; and (C) model systems and rates of user charges typical of various treatment works serving municipal-industrial communities.

(3) Approval by the Administrator of a grant to an interstate agency established by interstate compact for any treatment works shall satisfy any other requirement that such works be authorized by Act of Congress.

[Sec. 204(b)(3) repealed and (4) redesignated as (3) by PL 96-483]

(4) A system of charges which meets the requirement of clause (A) of paragraph (1) of this subsection may be based on something other than metering the sewage or water supply flow of residential recipients of waste treatment services, including ad valorem taxes. If the system of charges is based on something other than metering the Administrator shall require (A) the applicant to establish a system by which maintenance of the treatment works; and (B) the applicant to establish a procedure under which the residential user will be notified as to that portion of his total payment which will be allocated to the costs of the waste treatment services.

[Sec. 204(b)(5) redesignated as (4) by PL 96-483]

(6) [Sec. 204(b)(6) repealed by PL 96-483]

[Section 2(c) of PL 96-483 provides:

(c) "The Administrator of the Environmental Protection Agency shall take such action as may be necessary to remove from any grant made under section 201(g)(1) of the Federal Water Pollution Control Act after March 1, 1973, and prior to the date of enactment of this Act any condition or requirement no longer applicable as a result of the repeals made by subsections (a) and (b)

[Section 2(a) and (b) of PL 96-483 amended or repealed portions of Section 204 (b) of the Federal Water Pollution Control Act.] of this section or release any grant recipient of the obligations established by such conditions of other requirement."]

[Section 2(g) of PL 96-483 provides:

"(g) The amendments made by this section [Sec. 2 of PL 96-483] shall take effect on December 27, 1977."]

(c) The next to the last sentence of paragraph (5) of subsection (a) of this section shall not apply in any case where a primary, secondary, or advanced waste treatment facility or its related interceptors has received a grant for erection, building, acquisition, alteration, remodeling, improvement, or extension before October 1, 1984, and all segments and phases of such facility and interceptors shall be funded based on a 20-year reserve capacity in the case of such facility and a 20-year reserve capacity in the case of such interceptors, except that, if a grant for such interceptors has been approved prior to the date of enactment of the Municipal Wastewater Treatment Construction Grant Amendments of 1981, such interceptors shall be funded based on the approved reserve capacity not to exceed 40 years.

[Sec. 204(c) added by PL 97-117]

(d) (1) A grant for the construction of treatment works under this title shall provide that the engineer or engineering firm supervising construction or providing architect engineering services during construction shall continue its relationship to the grant applicant for a period of one year after the completion of construction and intitial operation of such treatment works. During such period such engineer or engineering firm shall supervise operation of the treatment works, train operating personnel, and prepare curricula and training material for operating personnel. Costs associated with the implementation of this paragraph shall be eligible for Federal assistance in accordance with this title.

(2) On the date one year after the completion of construction and initial operation of such treatment works, the owner and operator of such treatment works shall certify to the Administrator whether or not such treatment works meet the design specifications and effluent limitations contained in the grant agreement and permit pursuant to section 402 of the Act for such works. If the owner and operator of such treatment works cannot certify that such treatment works meet such design specifications and effluent limitations, any failure to meet such design specifications and effluent limitations shall be corrected in a timely manner, to allow such affirmative certification, at other than Federal expense.

(3) Nothing in this section shall be construed to prohibit a grantee under this title from requiring more assurances, guarantees, or indemnit or other contractual requirements from any party to a contract pertaining to a project assisted under this title, than those provided under this subsection. (Sec. 204(d) added by PL 97-117)

Sec. 205. Allotment.

(a) Sums authorized to be appropriated pursuant to section 207 for each fiscal year beginning after June 30, 1972, and before September 30, 1977, shall be allotted by the Administrator not later than the January 1st immediately preceding the beginning of the fiscal year for which authorized, except that the allotment for fiscal year 1973 shall be made not later than 30 days after the date of enactment of the Federal Water Pollution Control Act Amendments of 1972. Such sums shall be allotted among the States by the Administrator in accordance with regulations promulgated by him, in the ratio that the estimated costs of constructing all needed publicly owned treatment works in each State bears to the estimated cost of construction of all needed publicly owned treatment works in all of the States. For the fiscal years ending June 30, 1973, and June 30, 1974, such ratio shall be determined on the basis of the table III of House Public Works Committee Print No. 92-50.

For the fiscal year ending June 30, 1975, such ratio shall be determined one-half on the basis of table I of House Public Works Committee Print Numbered 93-28 and one-half on the basis of table II of such print, except that no State shall receive an allotment less than that which it received for the fiscal year ending June 30, 1972, as set forth in table III of such print. Allotments for fiscal years which begin after the fiscal year ending June 30, 1975 shall be made only in accordance with a revised cost estimate made and submitted to Congress in accordance with section 516(b) of this Act and only after such revised cost estimate shall have been approved by law specifically enacted hereafter.

(b) (1) Any sums allotted to a State under subsection (a) shall be available for obligation under section 203 on and after the date of such allotment. Such sums shall continue available for obligation in such State for a period of one year after the close of the fiscal year for which such sums are authorized. Any amount so allotted which are not obligated by the end of such one-year period shall be immediately reallotted by the Administrator, in accordance with regulations promulgated by him, generally on the basis of the ratio used in making the last allotment of sums under this section. Such reallotted sums shall be added to the last allotments made to the States. Any sum made available to a State by reallotment under this subsection shall be in addition to any funds otherwise allotted to such State for grants under this title during any fiscal year.

(2) Any sums which have been obligated under section 203 and which are released by the payment of the final voucher for the project shall be immediately credited to the State to which such sums were last allotted. Such released sums shall be added to the amounts last allotted to such State and shall be immediately available for obligation in the same manner and to the same extent as such last allotment.

(c) (1) Sums authorized to be appropriated pursuant to section 207 for the fiscal years during the period beginning October 1, 1977, and ending September 30, 1981, shall be allotted for each such year by the Adminstrator not later than the tenth day which begins after the date of enactment of the Clean Water Act of 1977. Notwithstanding any other provision of law, sums authorized for the fiscal years ending September 30, 1978, September 30, 1979, September 30, 1980, and September 30, 1981, shall be allotted in accordance with table 3 of Committee Print Numbered 95-30 of the Committee on Public Works and Transportation of the House of Representatives.

(2) Sums authorized to be appropriated pursuant to section 207 for the fiscal years 1982, 1983, 1984, and 1985 shall be allotted for each such year by the Administrator not later than the tenth day which begins after the date of enactment of the Municipal Wastewater Treatment Construction Grant Amendments of 1981. Notwithstanding any other provision of law, sums authorized for the fiscal year ending September 30, 1982, shall be allotted in accordance with table 3 of Committee Print Numbered 95-30 of the Committee on Public Works and Transportation of the House of Representatives. Sums authorized for the fiscal years ending September 30, 1983, September 30, 1984, September 30, 1985, and September 30, 1986, shall be allotted in accordance with the following table:

States	Fiscal Years 1983 Through 1985
Alabama	.011398
Alaska	.006101
Arizona	.006885
Arkansas	.006668
California	.072901
Colorado	.008154
Connecticut	.012487
Delaware	.004965
District of Columbia	.004965
Florida	.034407
Georgia	.017234
Hawaii	.007895
Idaho	.004965
Illinois	.046101
Indiana	.024566
Iowa	.013796
Kansas	.009201
Kentucky	.012973
Louisiana	.011205
Maine	.007788
Maryland	.024653
Massachusetts	.034603
Michigan	.043829
Minnesota	.018735
Mississippi	.009184
Missouri	.028257
Montana	.004965
Nebraska	.005214
Nevada	.004965
New Hampshire	.010186
New Jersey	.041654
New Mexico	.004965
New York	.113097
North Carolina	.018396
North Dakota	.004965
Ohio	.057383
Oklahoma	.008235
Oregon	.011515
Pennsylvania	.040377
Rhode Island	.006750

South Carolina	.010442
South Dakota	.004965
Tennessee	.014807
Texas	.038726
Utah	.005371
Vermont	.004965
Virginia	.020861
Washington	.017726
West Virginia	.015890
Wisconsin	.027557
Wyoming	.004965
Samoa	.000915
Guam	.000662
Northern Marianas	.000425
Puerto Rico	.013295
Pacific Trust Territories	.001305
Virgin Islands	.000531

United States Totals   .999996

[Sec. 205(c)(2) added by PL 97-117; amended by PL 100-4]

(3) Fiscal years 1987-1990. -- Sums authorized to be
appropriated pursuant to section 207 for the fiscal years 1987,
1988, 1989, and 1990 shall be allotted for each such year by the
Administrator not later than the 10th day which begins after the
date of the enactment of this paragraph.   Sums authorized for
such fiscal years shall be allotted in accordance with the
following table:

States	Fiscal Years 1987-1990
Alabama	.011309
Alaska	.006053
Arizona	.006831
Arkansas	.006616
California	.072333
Colorado	.008090
Connecticut	.012390
Delaware	.004965
District of Columbia	.004965
Florida	.034139
Georgia	.017100
Hawaii	.007833
Idaho	.004965
Illinois	.045741
Indiana	.024374
Iowa	.013688
Kansas	.009129
Kentucky	.012872
Louisiana	.011118
Maine	.007829
Maryland	.024461
Massachusetts	.034338
Michigan	.043487
Minnesota	.018589

Mississippi	.009112
Missouri	.028037
Montana	.004965
Nebraska	.005173
Nevada	.004965
New Hampshire	.010107
New Jersey	.041329
New Mexico	.004965
New York	.111632
North Carolina	.018253
North Dakota	.004965
Ohio	.056936
Oklahoma	.008171
Oregon	.011425
Pennsylvania	.040062
Rhode Island	.006791
South Carolina	.010361
South Dakota	.004965
Tennessee	.014692
Texas	.046226
Utah	.005329
Vermont	.004965
Virginia	.020698
Washington	.017588
West Virginia	.015766
Wisconsin	.027342
Wyoming	.004965
American Samoa	.000908
Guam	.000657
Northern Marianas	.000422
Puerto Rico	.023191
Pacific Trust Territories	.001295
Virgin Islands	.000527

[205(c)(3) added by PL 100-4]

[Section 213(a) and (e)-(g) of PL 100-4 state:

"Sec. 213. Improvement Projects.

(a) Avalon, California. -- The Administrator shall make a grant of $3,000,000 from funds allotted under section 205 of the Federal Water Pollution Control Act to the State of California for fiscal year 1987 to the city of Avalon, California, for improvements to the publicly owned treatment works of such city.

(e) Treatment Works for Wanaque, New Jersey. -- In fiscal year 1987 and succeeding fiscal years, the Administrator shall make grants to the Wanaque Valley Regional Sewerage Authority, New Jersey from funds allotted under section 205 of the Federal Water Pollution Control Act to the State of New Jersey for such fiscal year, for the construction of treatment works with a total treatment capacity of 1,050,000 gallons per day (including a treatment module with a treatment capacity of 350,000 gallons per day). Notwithstanding section 202 of such Act, the Federal share of the cost of construction of such treatment works shall be 75 percent.

(f) Treatment Works for Lena, Illinois. -- The Administrator shall make grants to the village of Lena, Illinois, from funds allotted under section 205 of the Federal Water Pollution Control Act to the State of Illinois for fiscal years beginning after September 30, 1986, for the construction of a replacement moving bed filter press of the treatment works of such village. Notwithstanding section 202 of the Federal Water Pollution Control Act, the Federal share of the cost of construction of such project shall be 75 percent.

(g) Priority for Court-Ordered and Other Projects. -- The State of Pennsylvania, from funds allotted to it under section 205 of the Federal Water Pollution Control Act, shall give priority for construction of --

(1) the Wyoming Valley Sanitary Authority Secondary Treatment project mandated under Federal court order, regardless of the date of start of construction made pursuant to the court order; and

(2) a project for wastewater treatment for Altoona, Pennsylvania."]

(d) Sums allotted to the States for a fiscal year shall remain available for obligation for the fiscal year for which authorized and for the period of the next succeeding twelve months. The amount of any allotment not obligated by the end of such twenty-four-month period shall be immediately reallotted by the Administrator on the basis of the same ratio as applicable to sums allotted for the then current fiscal year, except that none of the funds reallotted by the Administrator for fiscal year 1978 and for fiscal years thereafter shall be allotted to any State which failed to obligate any of the funds being reallotted. Any sum made available to a State by reallotment under this subsection shall be in addition to any funds otherwise allotted to such State for grants under this title during any fiscal year.

[Section 7 of PL 96-483 provides:

"Sec. 7.

Notwithstanding section 205(d) of the Federal Water Pollution Control Act (33 U.S.C. 1285), sums allotted to the States for the fiscal year 1979 shall remain available for obligation for the fiscal year for which authorized and for the period of the next succeeding twenty-four months. The amount of any allotment not obligated by the end of such thirty-six month period shall be immediately reallotted by the Administrator on the basis of the same ratio as applicable to sums allotted for the then current fiscal year, except that none of the funds reallotted by the Administrator for fiscal year 1979 shall be allotted to any State which failed to obligate any of the funds being reallotted. Any sum made available to a State by reallotment under this section shall be in addition to any funds otherwise allotted to such State for grants under title II of the Federal Water Pollution Control Act during any fiscal year. This section shall take effect on September 30, 1980."]

(e) For the fiscal years, 1978, 1979, 1980, 1981, 1982, 1983, 1984, 1985, 1986, 1987, 1988, 1989, and 1990, no State shall receive less than one-half of 1 per centum of the total allotment under subsection (c) of this section, except that in the case of Guam, Virgin Islands, American Samoa, and the Trust Territories not more than thirty-three one-hundredths of 1 per centum on the aggregate shall be allotted to all four of these jurisdictions. For the purpose of carrying out this subsection there are authorized to be appropriated, subject to such amounts as are provided in appropriation Acts, not to exceed $75,000,000 for each of fiscal years 1978, 1979, 1980, 1981, 1982, 1983, 1984, 1985, 1986, 1987, 1988, 1989, and 1990. If for any fiscal year the amount appropriated under authority of this subsection is less than the amount necessary to carry out this subsection, the amount each State receives under this subsection for such year shall bear the same ratio to the amount such State would have received under this subsection in such year if the amount necessary to carry it out had been appropriated as the amount appropriated for such year bears to the amount necessary to carry out this subsection for such year.

[Sec. 205(e) amended by PL 97-117; PL 100-4]

(f) Notwithstanding any other provision of this section, sums made available between January 1, 1975, and March 1, 1975, by the Administrator for obligation shall be available for obligation until September 30, 1978.

(g) (1) The Administrator is authorized to reserve each fiscal year not to exceed 2 percentum of the amount authorized under section 207 of this title for purposes of the allotment made to each State under this section on or after October 1, 1977, except in the case of any fiscal year beginning on or after October 1, 1981, and ending before October 1, 1994, in which case the percentage authorized to be reserved shall not exceed 4 per centum, or $400,000 whichever amount is the greater. Sums so reserved shall be available for making grants to such State under paragraph (2) of this subsection for the same period as sums are available from such allotment under subsection (d) of this section, and any such grant shall be available for obligation only during such period. Any grant made from sums reserved under this subsection which has not been obligated by the end of the period for which available shall be added to the amount last allotted to such State under this section and shall be immediately available for obligation in the same manner and to the same extent as such last allotment. Sums authorized to be reserved by this paragraph shall be in addition to and not in lieu of any other funds which may be authorized to carry out this subsection.

[Sec. 205(g)(1) amended by PL 96-483; PL 97-117; PL 100-4]

(2) The Administrator is authorized to grant to any State from amounts reserved to such State under this subsection, the reasonable costs of administering any aspects of section 201, 203, 204, and 212 of this Act the responsibility for administration of which the Administrator has delegated to such State. The Administrator may increase such grant to take into

account the reasonable costs of administering an approved program under section 402 or 404, administering a statewide waste treatment management planning program under section 208(b)(4), and managing waste treatment construction grants for small communities.

(h) The Administrator shall set aside from funds authorized for each fiscal year beginning on or after October 1, 1978, a total (as determined by the Governor of the State) of not less than 4 percent nor more than 7 1/2 percent of the sums allotted to any State with a rural population of 25 per centum or more of the total population of such State, as determined by the Bureau of the Census. The Administrator may set aside no more than 7 1/2 percent of the sums allotted to any other State for which the Governor requests such action. Such sums shall be available only for alternatives to conventional sewage treatment works for municipalities having a population of three thousand five hundred or less, or for the highly dispersed sections of larger municipalities, as defined by the Administrator.

[Sec. 205(h) amended by PL 100-4]

(i) Set-Aside for Innovative and Alternative Projects. -- Not less than 1/2 of 1 percent of funds allotted to a State for each of the fiscal years ending September 30, 1979, through September 30, 1990, under subsection (c) of this section shall be expended only for increasing the Federal share of grants for construction of treatment works utilizing innovative processes and techniques pursuant to section 202(a)(2) of this Act. Including the expenditures authorized by the preceding sentence, a total of 2 percent of the funds allotted to a State for each of the fiscal years ending September 30, 1979, and September 30, 1980, and 3 percent of the funds allotted to a State for the fiscal year ending September 30, 1981, under subsection (c) of this section shall be expended only for increasing grants for construction of treatment works pursuant to section 202(a)(2) of this Act. Including the expenditures authorized by the first sentence of this subsection, a total (as determined by the Governor of the State) of not less than 4 percent nor more than 7 1/2 percent of the funds allotted to such State under subsection (c) of this section for each of the fiscal years ending September 30, 1982, through September 30, 1990, shall be expended only for increasing the Federal share of grants for construction of treatment works pursuant to section 202(a)(2) of this Act.

[Sec. 205(i) amended by PL 97-117; PL 100-4]

(j) (1) The Administrator shall reserve each fiscal year not to exceed 1 per centum of the sums allotted and available for obligation to each State under this section for each fiscal year beginning on or after October 1, 1981, or $100,000, whichever amount is the greater.

[Sec. 205(j) added by PL 97-117]

(2) Such sums shall be used by the Administrator to make grants to the States to carry out water quality management planning, including, but not limited to --

(A) identifying most cost effective and locally acceptable facility and non-point measures to meet and maintain water quality standards;

(B) developing an implementation plan to obtain State and local financial and regulatory commitments to implement measures developed under subparagraph (A);

(C) determining the nature, extent, and causes of water quality problems in various areas of the State and interstate region, and reporting on these annually; and

(D) determining those publicly owned treatment works which should be constructed with assistance under this title, in which areas and in what sequence, taking into account the relative degree of effluent reduction attained, the relative contributions to water quality of other point or nonpoint sources, and the consideration of alternatives to such construction, and implementing section 303(e) of this Act.

(3) In carrying out planning with grants made under paragraph (2) of this subsection, a State shall develop jointly with local, regional, and interstate entities, a plan for carrying out the program and give funding priority to such entities and designated or undesignated public comprehensive planning organizations to carry out the purposes of this subsection. In giving such priority, the State shall allocate at least 40 percent of the amount granted to such State for a fiscal year under paragraph (2) of this subsection to regional public comprehensive planning organizations in such State and appropriate interstate organizations for the development and implementation of the plan described in this paragraph. In any fiscal year for which the Governor, in consultation with such organizations and with the approval of the Administrator, determines that allocation of at least 40 percent of such amount to such organizations will not result in significant participation by such organizations in water quality management planning and not significantly assist in development and implementation of the plan described in this paragraph and achieving the goals of this Act, the allocation to such organization may be less than 40 percent of such amount.

[Sec. 205(j)(3) amended by PL 100-4]

(4) All activities undertaken under this subsection shall be in coordination with other related provisions of this Act.

(5) Nonpoint Source Reservation. -- In addition to the sums reserved under paragraph (1), the Administrator shall reserve each fiscal year for each State 1 percent of the sums allotted and available for obligation to such State under this section for each fiscal year beginning on or after October 1, 1986, or $100,000, whichever is greater, for the purpose of carrying out

section 319 of this Act. Sums so reserved in a State in any fiscal year for which such State does not request the use of such sums, to the extent such sums exceed $100,000, may be used by such State for other purposes under this title.

[Sec. 205(j)(5) added by PL 100-4]

(k) Convention Center. The Administrator shall allot to the State of New York from sums authorized to be appropriated for the fiscal year ending September 30, 1982, an amount necessary to pay the entire cost of conveying sewage from the Convention Center of the city of New York to the Newtown sewage treatment plant, Brooklyn-Queens area, New York. The amount allotted under this subsection shall be in addition to and not in lieu of any other amounts authorized to be allotted to such State under this Act.

[Sec. 205(k) added by PL 97-117]

(l) Marine Estuary Reservation. --

    (1) Reservation of Funds. --

        (A) General Rule. -- Prior to making allotments among the States under subsection (c) of this section, the Administrator shall reserve funds from sums appropriated pursuant to section 207 for each fiscal year beginning after September 30, 1986.

        (B) Fiscal Years 1987 and 1988. -- For each of fiscal years 1987 and 1988 the reservation shall be 1 percent of the sums appropriated pursuant to section 207 for each fiscal year.

        (C) Fiscal Years 1989 and 1990. -- For each of fiscal years 1989 and 1990 the reservation shall be 1 1/2 percent of the funds appropriated pursuant to section 207 for such fiscal year.

    (2) Use of Funds. -- Of the sums reserved under this subsection, two-thirds shall be available to address water quality problems of marine bays and estuaries subject to lower levels of water quality due to the impacts of discharges from combined storm water and sanitary sewer overflows from adjacent urban complexes, and one-third shall be available for the implementation of section 320 of this Act, relating to the national estuary program.

    (3) Period of availability. -- Sums reserved under this subsection shall be subject to the period of availability for obligation established by subsection (d) of this section.

    (4) Treatment of Certain Body of Water. -- For purposes of this section and section 201(n), Newark Bay, New Jersey, and the portion of the Passaic River up to Little Falls, in the vicinity of Beatties Dam, shall be treated as a marine bay and estuary.

[Sec. 205(l) added by PL 100-4]

(m) Discretionary Deposits Into State Water Pollution Control
Revolving Funds. --

(1) From Construction Grant Allotments. -- In addition to any
amounts deposited in a water pollution control revolving fund
established by a State under title VI, upon request of the
Governor of such State, the Administrator shall make available
to the State for deposit, as capitalization grants, in such fund
in any fiscal year beginning after September 30, 1986, such
portion of the amounts allotted to such State under this section
for such fiscal year as the Governor considers appropriate;
except that (A) in fiscal year 1987, such deposit may not exceed
50 percent of the amounts allotted to such State under this
section for such fiscal year, and (B) in fiscal year 1988, such
deposit may not exceed 75 percent of the amounts allotted to
such State under this section for this fiscal year.

(2) Notice Requirement. -- The Governor of a State may make a
request under paragraph (1) for a deposit into the water
pollution control revolving fund of such State -- (A) in fiscal
year 1987 only if no later than 90 days after the date of the
enactment of this subsection, and (B) in each fiscal year
thereafter only if 90 days before the first day of such fiscal
year, the State provides notice of its intent to make such
deposit.

(3) Exception. -- Sums reserved under section 205(j) of this
Act shall not be available for obligation under this subsection.

[Sec. 205(m) added by PL 100-4]

Sec. 206. **Reimbursement and Advanced Construction.**

(a) Any publicly owned treatment works in a State on which
construction was initiated after June 30, 1966, but before July 1,
1973, which was approved by the appropriate State water pollution
control agency and which the Administrator finds meets the
requirements of section 8 of this Act in effect at the time of the
initiation of construction shall be reimbursed a total amount equal
to the difference between the amount of Federal financial
assistance, if any, received under such section 8 for such project
and 50 per centum of the cost of such project, or 55 per centum of
the project cost where the Administrator also determines that such
treatment works was constructed in conformity with a comprehensive
metropolitan treatment plan as described in section 8(f) of the
Federal Water Pollution Control Act as in effect immediately prior
to the date of enactment of the Federal Water Pollution Control Act
Amendments of 1972. Nothing in this subsection shall result in any
such works receiving Federal grants from all sources in excess of 80
per centum of the cost of such project.

(b) Any publicly owned treatment works constructed with or eligible
for Federal financial assistance under this Act in a State between
June 30, 1956, and June 30, 1966, which was approved by the State
water pollution control agency and which the Administrator finds
meets the requirements of section 8 of this Act prior to the date of
enactment of the Federal Water Pollution Control Act Amendments of

1972 but which was constructed without assistance under such section 8 or which received such assistance in an amount less than 30 per centum of the cost of such project shall qualify for payments and reimbursement of State or local funds used for such project from sums allocated to such State under this section in an amount which shall not exceed the difference between the amount of such assistance, if any, received for such project and 30 per centum of the cost of such project.

(c) No publicly owned treatment works shall receive any payment or reimbursement under subsection (a) or (b) of this section unless an application for such assistance is filed with the Administrator within the one year period which begins on the date of enactment of the Federal Water Pollution Control Act Amendments of 1972. Any application filed within such one year period may be revised from time to time, as may be necessary.

[Section 29 of Public Law 93-207 states:

"Sec. 29.   Notwithstanding section 206(c) of the Federal Water Pollution Control Act and section 2 of Public Law 93-207, in the case of publicly owned treatment works for which a grant was made under the Federal Water Pollution Control Act, as amended by the Water Pollution Control Act Amendments of 1956 (Public Law 660, 84th Congress) before July 1, 1972, and on which construction was initiated before July 1, 1973, applications for assistance under such section 206 shall be filed not later than the ninetieth day after the date of enactment of the Clean Water Act of 1977."]

(d) The Administrator shall allocate to each qualified project under subsection (a) of this section each fiscal year for which funds are appropriated under subsection (e) of this section an amount which bears the same ratio to the unpaid balance of the reimbursement due such project as the total of such funds for such year bears to the total unpaid balance of reimbursement due all such approved projects on the date of enactment of such appropriations. The Administrator shall allocate to each qualified project under subsection (b) of this section each fiscal year for which funds are appropriated under subsection (e) of this section an amount which bears the same ratio to the unpaid balance of the reimbursement due such project as the total of such funds for such years bears to the total unpaid balance of reimbursement due all such approved projects on the date of enactment of such appropriation.

[Section 3 of Public Law 93-207 provides:

"Sec. 3.   Funds available for reimbursement under Public Law 92-399 shall be allocated in accordance with subsection (d) of section 206 of the Federal Water Pollution Control Act (86 Stat. 838), pro rata among all projects eligible under subsection (a) of such section 206 for which applications have been submitted and approved by the Administrator pursuant to such Act. Notwithstanding the provisions of subsection (d) of such section 206, (1) the Administrator is authorized to make interim payments to each such project for which an application has been approved on the basis of estimates of maximum pro rata entitlement of all applicants under section 206(a) and (2) for the purpose of determining allocation of sums available under Public Law 92-399, the unpaid balance of reimbursement due such projects shall be computed as of January 31, 1974. Upon completion by the Administrator of his audit and approval of all projects for which an application has been filed under subsection (a) of such section 206, the Administrator shall, within the limits of appropriated funds, allocate to each such qualified project the amount remaining, if any, of its total entitlement. Amounts allocated to projects which are later determined to be in excess of entitlement shall be available for reallocation, until expended, to other qualified projects under subsection (a) of such section 206. In no event, however, shall any payments exceed the Federal share of the cost of construction incurred to the date of the voucher covering such payments plus the Federal Share of the value of the materials which have been stockpiled in the vicinity of such construction in conformity to plans and specifications for the project."]

(e) There is authorized to be appropriated to carry out subsection (a) of this section not to exceed $2,600,000,000 and to carry out subsection (b) of this section, not to exceed $750,000,000. The authorizations contained in this subsection shall be the sole source of funds for reimbursements authorized by this section.

(f) (1) In any case where a substantial portion of the funds allotted to a State for the current fiscal year under this title have been obligated under section 201(g), or will be so obligated in a timely manner (as determined by the Administrator), and there is construction of any treatment work project without the aid of Federal funds and in accordance with all procedures and all requirements applicable to treatment works projects, except those procedures and requirements which limit construction of projects to those constructed with the aid of previously allotted Federal funds, the Administrator, upon his approval of an application made under this subsection therefore, is authorized to pay the Federal share of the cost of construction of such project when additional funds are allotted to the State under this title if prior to the construction of the project the Administrator approves plans, specifications, and estimates therefore in the same manner as other treatment works projects. The Administrator may not approve an application under this subsection unless an authorization is in effect for the first fiscal year in the period for which the application requests payment and such requested payment for that fiscal year does not exceed the State's expected allotment from such authorization. The Administrator shall not be required to make such requested payment for any fiscal year --

   (A) to the extent that such payment would exceed such State's allotment of the amount appropriated for such fiscal year; and

   (B) unless such payment is for a project which, on the basis of an approved funding priority list of such State, is eligible to receive such payment based on the allotment and appropriation for such fiscal year. To the extent that sufficient funds are not appropriated to pay the full Federal share with respect to a project for which

obligations under the provisions of this subsection have
been made, the Administrator shall reduce the Federal share
to such amount less than 75 percentum as such appropriations
do provide. (Sec. 206(f)(1) amended by PL 96-483) (2) In
determining the allotment for any fiscal year under this
title, any treatment works project constructed in accordance
with this section and without the aid of Federal funds shall
not be considered completed until an application under the
provisions of this subsection with respect to such project
has been approved by the Administrator, or the availability
of funds from which this project is eligible for
reimbursement has expired, whichever first occurs.

Sec. 207. Authorization.

There is authorized to be appropriated to carry out this title,
other than sections 206(e), 208 and 209, for the fiscal year ending
June 30, 1973, not to exceed $5,000,000,000, for the fiscal year
ending June 30, 1974, not to exceed $6,000,000,000, and for the
fiscal year ending June 30, 1975, not to exceed $7,000,000,000, and,
subject to such amounts as are provided in appropriation Acts, for
the fiscal year ending September 30, 1977, $1,000,000,000 for the
fiscal year ending September 30, 1978, $4,500,000,000 and for the
fiscal years ending September 30, 1979, September 30, 1980, not to
exceed $5,000,000,000; for the fiscal year ending September 30,
1981, not to exceed $2,548,837,000; and for the fiscal years ending
September 30, 1982, September 30 1983, September 30, 1984, and
September 30, 1985, not to exceed $2,400,000,000 per fiscal year;
and for each of the fiscal years ending September 30, 1986,
September 30, 1987, and September 30, 1988, not to exceed
$2,400,000,000; and for each of the fiscal years ending September
30, 1989, and September 30, 1990, not to exceed $1,200,000,000.

[Sec. 207 amended by PL 97-35; 97-117; PL 100-4]

Sec. 208. Areawide Waste Treatment Management.

(a) For the purpose of encouraging and facilitating the development
and implementation of areawide waste treatment management plans --

(1) The Administrator, within ninety days after the the date of
enactment of this Act and after consultation with appropriate
Federal, State, and local authorities, shall be regulation
publish guidelines for the identification of those areas which,
as a result of urban-industrial concentrations or other factors,
have substantial water quality control problems.

(2) The Governor of each State, within sixty days after
publication of the guidelines issued pursuant to paragraph (1)
of this subsection, shall identify each area within the State
which, as a result of urban-industrial concentrations or other
factors, has substantial water quality control problems. Not
later than one hundred and twenty days following such
identification and after consultation with appropriate elected
and other officials of local governments having jurisdiction in
such areas, the Governor shall designate (A) the boundaries of
each such area, and (B) a single representative organization,

including elected officials from local governments or their designees, capable of developing effective areawide waste treatment management plans for such area. The Governor may in the same manner at any later time identify any additional area (or modify an existing area) for which he determines areawide waste treatment management to be appropriate, designate the boundaries of such area, and designate an organization capable of developing effective areawide waste treatment management plans for such area.

(3) With respect to any area which, pursuant to the guidelines published under paragraph (1) of this subsection, is located in two or more States, the Governors of the respective States shall consult and cooperate in carrying out the provisions of paragraph (2), with a view toward designating the boundaries of the interstate area having common water quality control problems and for which areawide waste treatment management plans would be most effective, and toward designating, within one hundred and eighty days after publication of guidelines issued pursuant to paragraph (1) of this subsection, of a single representative organization capable of developing effective areawide waste treatment management plans for such area.

(4) If a Governor does not act, either by designating or determining not to make a designation under paragraph (2) of this subsection, within the time required by such paragraph, or if, in the case of an interstate area, the Governors of the States involved do not designate a planning organization within the time required by paragraph (3) of this subsection, the chief elected officials of local governments within an area may be agreement designate (A) the boundaries for such an area, and (B) a single representative organization including elected officials from such local governments, or their designees, capable of developing an areawide waste treatment management plan for such area.

(5) Existing regional agencies may be designated under paragraphs (2), (3), and (4) of this subsection.

(6) The State shall act as a planning agency for all portions of such State which are not designated under paragraphs (2), (3), or (4) of this subsection.

(7) Designations under this subsection shall be subject to the approval of the Administrator.

(b) (1) (A) Not later than one year after the date of designation of any organization under subsection (a) of this section such organization shall have in operation a continuing areawide waste treatment management planning process consistent with section 201 of this Act. Plans prepared in accordance with this process shall contain alternatives for waste treatment management, and be applicable to all wastes generated within the area involved. The initial plan prepared in accordance with such process shall be certified by the Governor and submitted to the Administrator not later than two years after the planning process is in operation.

(B) For any agency designated after 1975 under subsection (a) of this section and for all portions of a State for which the State is required to act as the planning agency in accordance with subsection (a)(6), the initial plan prepared in accordance with such process shall be certified by the Governor and submitted to the Administrator not later than three years after the receipt of the initial grant award authorized under subsection (f) of the section.

(2) Any plan prepared under such process shall include, but not be limited to --

(A) the identification of treatment works necessary to meet the anticipated municipal and industrial waste treatment needs of the area over a twenty-year period, annually updated (including an analysis of alternative waste treatment systems), including any requirements for the acquisition of land for treatment purposes; the necessary waste water collection and urban storm water runoff systems; and a program to provide the necessary financial arrangements for the development of such treatment works, and an identification of open space and recreation opportunities that can be expected to result from improved water quality, including consideration of potential use of lands associated with treatment works and increased access to water-based recreation;

(B) the establishment of construction priorities for such treatment works and time schedules for the initiation and completion of all treatment works;

(C) the establishment of a regulatory program to --

(i) implement the waste treatment management requirements of section 201(c),
(ii) regulate the location, modification, and construction of any facilities within such area which may result in any discharge in such area, and
(iii) assure that any industrial or commercial waste discharged into any treatment works in such area meet applicable pretreatment requirements;

(D) the identification of those agencies necessary to construct, operate, and maintain all facilities required by the plan and otherwise to carry out the plan;

(E) the identification of the measures necessary to carry out the plan (including financing), the period of time necessary to carry out the plan, the costs of carrying out the plan within such time, and the economic, social, and environmental impact of carrying out the plan within such time;

(F) a process to
(i) identify, if appropriate, agriculturally and silviculturally related nonpoint sources of pollution, including return flows from irrigated agriculture, and

their cumulative effects, runoff from manure disposal areas, and from land used for livestock and crop production, and

(ii) set forth procedures and methods (including land use requirements) to control to the extent feasible such sources;

(G) a process to

(i) identify, if appropriate, mine-related sources of pollution including new, current, and abandoned surface and underground mine runoff, and

(ii) set forth procedures and methods (including land use requirements) to control to the extent feasible such sources;

(H) a process to

(i) identify construction activity related sources of pollution, and

(ii) set forth procedures and methods (including land use requirements) to control to the extent feasible such sources;

(I) a process to

(i) identify, if appropriate, salt water intrusion into rivers, lakes, and estuaries resulting from reduction of fresh water flow from any cause, including irrigation, obstruction, ground water extraction, and diversion, and

(ii) set forth procedures and methods to control such intrusion to the extent feasible where such procedures and methods are otherwise a part of the waste treatment management plan;

(J) a process to control the disposition of all residual waste generated in such area which could affect water quality; and

(K) a process to control the disposal of pollutants on land or in subsurface excavations within such area to protect ground and surface water quality.

(3) Areawide waste treatment management plans shall be certified annually by the Governor or his designee (or Governors or their designees, where more than one State is involved) as being consistent with applicable basin plans and such areawide waste treatment management plans shall be submitted to the Administrator for his approval.

(4) (A) Whenever the Governor of any State determines (and notifies the Administrator) that consistency with a statewide regulatory program under section 303 so requires, the requirements of clauses (F) through (K) of paragraph (2) of this subsection shall be developed and submitted by the Governor to the Administrator for approval for application to a class or category of activity throughout each State.

(B) Any program submitted under subparagraph (A) of this paragraph which, in whole or in part, is to control the discharge or other placement of dredged or fill material into the navigable waters shall include the following:

(i) A consultation process which includes the State agency with primary jurisdiction over fish and wildlife resources.

(ii) A process to identify and manage the discharge or other placement of dredged or fill material which adversely affects navigable waters, which shall complement and be coordinated with a State program under section 404 conducted pursuant to this Act.

(iii) A process to assure that any activity conducted pursuant to a best management practice will comply with the guidelines established under section 404(b)(1), and sections 307 and 403 of this Act.

(iv) A process to assure that any activity conducted pursuant to a best management practice can be terminated or modified for cause including, but not limited to the following:

(I) violation of any condition of the best management practice;

(II) change in any activity that requires either a temporary or permanent reduction or elimination of the discharge pursuant to the best management practice.

(v) A process to assure continued coordination with Federal and Federal-State water-related planning and reviewing processes, including the National Wetlands Inventory.

(C) If the Governor of a State obtains approval from the Administrator of a statewide regulatory program which meets the requirements of subparagraph (B) of this paragraph and if such State is administering a permit program under section 404 of this Act, no person shall be required to obtain an individual permit pursuant to such section, or to comply with a general permit issued pursuant to such section, with respect to any appropriate activity within such State for which a best management practice has been approved by the Administrator under the program approved by the Administrator pursuant to this paragraph.

(D) (i) Whenever the Administrator determines after public hearing that a State is not administering a program approved under this section in accordance with the requirements of this section, the Administrator shall so notify the State, and if appropriate corrective action is not taken within a reasonable time, not to exceed ninety days, the Administrator shall withdraw approval of such program. The Administrator shall not withdraw approval of any such program unless he shall first have notified the State, and made public, in writing, the reasons for such withdrawal.

(ii) In the case of a State with a program submitted and approved under this paragraph, the Administrator shall withdraw approval of such program under this subparagraph only for a substantial failure of the State to administer its program under this subparagraph only for a substantial failure of the State to administer its program in accordance with the requirements of this paragraph.

(c) (1) The Governor of each State, in consultation with the planning agency designated under subsection (a) of this section, at the time a plan is submitted to the Administrator, shall designate one or more waste treatment management agencies (which may be an existing or newly created local, regional or State agency or potential subdivision) for each area designated under subsection (a) of this section and submit such designations to the Administrator.

(2) The Administrator shall accept any such designation, unless, within 120 days of such designation, he finds that the designated management agency (or agencies) does not have adequate authority --
> (A) to carry out appropriate portions of an areawide waste treatment management plan developed under subsection (b) of this section;
> (B) to manage effectively waste treatment works and related facilities servicing such area in conformance with any plan required by subsection (b) of this section;
> (C) directly or by contract, to design and construct new works, and to operate and maintain new and existing works as required by any plan developed pursuant to subsection (b) of this section;
> (D) to accept and utilize grants, or other funds from any source, for waste treatment management purposes;
> (E) to raise revenues, including the assessment of waste treatment charges;
> (F) to incur short- and long-term indebtedness;
> (G) to assure in implementation of an areawide waste treatment management plan that each participating community pays its proportionate share of treatment costs;
> (H) to refuse to receive any wastes from any municipality or subdivision thereof, which does not comply with any provisions of an approved plan under this section applicable to such area; and
> (I) to accept for treatment industrial wastes.

(d) After a waste treatment management agency having the authority required by subsection (c) has been designated under such subsection for an area and a plan for such area has been approved under subsection (b) of this section, the Administrator shall not make any grant for construction of a publicly owned treatment works under section 201(g)(1) within such area except to such designated agency and for works in conformity with such plan.

(e) No permit under section 402 of this Act shall be issued for any point source which is in conflict with a plan approved pursuant to subsection (b) of this section.

(f) (1) The Administrator shall make grants to any agency designated under subsection (a) of this section for payment of the reasonable costs of developing and operating a continuing

areawide waste treatment management planning process under
subsection (b) of this section.

(2) For the two-year period beginning on the date the first
grant is made under paragraph (1) of this subsection to an
agency, if such first grant is made before October 1, 1977, the
amount of each such grant to such agency shall be 100 per centum
of the costs of developing and operating a continuing areawide
waste treatment management planning process under subsection (b)
of this section, and thereafter the amount granted to such
agency shall not exceed 75 per centum of such costs in each
succeeding one-year period. In the case of any other grant made
to an agency under such paragraph (1) of this subsection, the
amount of such grant shall not exceed 75 per centum of the costs
of developing and operating a continuing areawide waste
treatment management planning process in any year.

(3) Each applicant for a grant under this subsection shall
submit to the Administrator for his approval each proposal for
which a grant is applied for under this subsection. The
Administrator shall act upon such proposal as soon as
practicable after it has been submitted, and his approval of
that proposal shall be deemed a contractual obligation of the
United States for the payment of its contribution to such
proposal, subject to such amounts as are provided in
appropriation Acts. There is authorized to be appropriated to
carry out this subsection not to exceed $50,000,000 for the
fiscal year ending June 30, 1973, not to exceed $100,000,000 for
the fiscal year ending June 30, 1974, not to exceed $150,000,000
per fiscal year for the fiscal years ending June 30, 1975,
September 30, 1977, September 30, 1978, September 30, 1979, and
September 30, 1980, not to exceed $100,000,000 per fiscal year
for the fiscal years ending September 30, 1981, and September
30, 1982, and such sums as may be necessary for fiscal years
1983 through 1990.

[Sec. 208(f)(3) amended by PL 96-483; PL 100-4]

(g) The Administrator is authorized, upon request of the Governor or
the designated planning agency, and without reimbursement, to
consult with, and provide technical assistance to, any agency
designated under subsection (a) of this section in the development
of areawide waste treatment management plans under subsection (b) of
this section.

(h) (1) The Secretary of the Army, acting through the Chief of
Engineers, in cooperation with the Administrator is authorized
and directed, upon request of the Governor or the designated
planning organization, to consult with, and provide technical
assistance to, any agency designed under subsection (a) of this
section in developing and operating a continuing areawide waste
treatment management planning process under subsection (b) of
this section.

(2) There is authorized to be appropriated to the Secretary of
the Army, to carry out this subsection, not to exceed

$50,000,000 per fiscal year for the fiscal years ending June 30, 1973, and June 30, 1974.

(i) (1) The Secretary of the Interior, acting through the Director of the United States Fish and Wildlife Service, shall, upon request of the Governor of a State, and without reimbursement, provide technical assistance to such State in developing a statewide program for submission to the Administrator under subsection (b)(4)(B) of this section and in implementing such program after its approval.

(2) There is authorized to be appropriated to the Secretary of the Interior $6,000,000 to complete the National Wetlands Inventory of the United States, by December 31, 1981, and to provide information from such Inventory to States as it becomes available to assist such States in the development and operation of programs under this Act.

(j) (1) The Secretary of Agriculture, with the concurrence of the Administrator, and acting through the Soil Conservation Service and such other agencies of the Department of Agriculture as the Secretary may designate, is authorized and directed to establish and administer a program to enter into contracts of not less than five years nor more than ten years with owners and operators having control of rural land for the purpose of installing and maintaining measures incorporating best management practices to control nonpoint source pollution for improved water quality in those States or areas for which the Administrator has approved a plan under subsection (b) of this section where the practices to which the contracts apply are certified by the management agency designated under subsection (c)(1) of this section to be consistent with such plans and will result in improved water quality. Such contracts may be entered into during the period ending not later than September 31, 1988. Under such contracts the land owner or operator shall agree --

(i) to effectuate a plan approved by a soil conservation district, where one exists, under this section for his farm, ranch, or other land substantially in accordance with the schedule outlined therein unless any requirement thereof is waived or modified by the Secretary;
(ii) to forfeit all rights to further payments or grants under the contract and refund to the United States all payments and grants received thereunder, with interest, upon his violation of the contract at any stage during the time he has control of the land if the Secretary, after considering the recommendations of the soil conservation district where one exists, and the Administrator, determines that such violation is of such a nature as to warrant termination of the contract, or to make refunds or accept such payment adjustments as the Secretary may deem appropriate if he determines that the violation by the owner or operator does not warrant termination of the contract;
(iii) upon transfer of his right and interest in the farm, ranch, or other land during the contract period to forfeit all rights to further payments or grants under the contract and refund to the United States all payments or grants

received thereunder, with interest, unless the transferee of
any such land agrees with the Secretary to assume all
obligations of the contract;
(iv) not to adopt any practice specified by the Secretary on
the advice of the Administrator in the contract as a
practice which would tend to defeat the purposes of the
contract;
(v) to such additional provisions as the Secretary
determines are desirable and includes in the contract to
effectuate the purposes of the program or to facilitate the
practical administration of the program.

(2) In return for such agreement by the landowner or operator
the Secretary shall agree to provide technical assistance and
share the cost of carrying out those conservation practices and
measures set forth in the contract for which he determines that
cost sharing is appropriate and in the public interest and which
are approved for cost sharing by the agency designated to
implement the plan developed under subsection (b) of this
section. The portion of such cost (including labor) to be
shared shall be that part which the Secretary determines is
necessary and appropriate to effectuate the installation of the
water quality management practices and measures under the
contract, but not to exceed 50 per centum of the total cost of
the measures set forth in the contract; except the Secretary may
increase the matching cost share where he determines that (1)
the main benefits to be derived from the measures are related to
improving offsite water quality, and (2) the matching share
requirement would place a burden on the landowner which would
probably prevent him from participating in the program.

(3) The Secretary may terminate any contract with a landowner or
operator by mutual agreement with the owner or operator if the
Secretary determines that such termination would be in the
public interest, and may agree to such modification of contracts
previously entered into as he may determine to be desirable to
carry out the purposes of the program or facilitate the
practical administration thereof or to accomplish equitable
treatment with respect to other conservation, land use, or water
quality programs.

(4) In providing assistance under this subsection the Secretary
will give priority to those areas and sources that have the most
significant effect upon water quality. Additional
investigations or plans may be made, where necessary, to
supplement approved water quality management plans, in order to
determine priorities.

(5) The Secretary shall, where practicable, enter into
agreements with soil conservation districts, State soil and
water conservation agencies, or State water quality agencies to
administer all or part of the program established in this
subsection under regulations developed by the Secretary. Such
agreements shall provide for the submission of such reports as
the Secretary deems necessary, and for payment by the United
States of such portion of the costs incurred in the

administration of the program as the Secretary may deem appropriate.

(6) The contracts under this subsection shall be entered into only in areas where the management agency designated under subsection (c)(1) of this section assures an adequate level of participation by owners and operators having control of rural land in such areas. Within such areas the local soil conservation district, where one exists, together with the Secretary of Agriculture, will determine the priority of assistance among individual landowners and operators to assure that the most critical water quality problems are addressed.

(7) The Secretary, in consultation with the Administrator and subject to section 304(k) of this Act, shall, not later than September 30, 1978, promulgate regulations for carrying out this subsection and for support and cooperation with other Federal and non-Federal agencies for implementation of this subsection.

(8) This program shall not be used to authorize or finance projects that would otherwise be eligible as assistance under the terms of Public Law 83-566.

(9) There are hereby authorized to be appropriated to the Secretary of Agriculture $200,000,000 for fiscal year 1979, $400,000,000 for fiscal year 1980, $100,000,000 for fiscal year 1981, $100,000,000 for fiscal year 1982, and such sums as may be necessary for fiscal years 1983 through 1990, to carry out this subsection. The program authorized under this subsection shall be in addition to, and not in substitution of, other programs in such area authorized by this or any other public law.

[Sec. 208(j)(9) amended by PL 96-483; PL 100-4]

Sec. 209. Basin Planning.

(a) The President, acting through the Water Resources Council, shall, as soon as practicable, prepare a Level B plan under the Water Resources Planning Act for all basins in the United States. All such plans shall be completed not later than January 1, 1980, except that priority in the preparation of such plans shall be given to those basins and portions thereof which are within those areas designated under paragraphs (2), (3), and (4) of subsection (a) of section 208 of this Act.

(b) The President, acting through the Water Resources Council, shall report annually to Congress on progress being made in carrying out this section. The first such report shall be submitted not later than January 31, 1973.

(c) There is authorized to be appropriated to carry out this section not to exceed $200,000,000.

Sec. 210. Annual Survey.

The Administrator shall annually make a survey to determine the efficiency of the operation and maintenance of treatment works

constructed with grants made under this Act, as compared to the
efficiency planned at the time the grant was made. The results of
such annual survey shall be included in the report required under
section 516(a) of this Act.

Sec. 211. Sewage Collection Systems.

(a) No grant shall be made for a sewage collection system under this
title unless such grant (1) is for replacement or major
rehabilitation of an existing collection system and is necessary to
the total integrity and performance of the waste treatment works
servicing such community, or (2) is for a new collection system in
an existing community with sufficient existing or planned capacity
adequately to treat such collected sewage and is consistent with
section 201 of this Act.

(b) If the Administrator uses population density as a test for
determining the eligibility of a collector sewer for assistance it
shall be only for the purpose of evaluating alternatives and
determining the needs for such system in relation to ground or
surface water quality impact.

(c) No grant shall be made under this title from funds authorized
for any fiscal year during the period beginning October 1, 1977, and
ending September 30, 1990, for treatment works for control of
pollutant discharges from separate storm sewer systems.

[Sec. 211(c) amended by PL 97-117; PL 100-4]

Sec. 212. Definitions.

As used in this title --

(1) The term "construction" means any one or more of the following:
preliminary planning to determine the feasibility of treatment
works, engineering, architectural, legal, fiscal, or economic
investigations or studies, surveys, designs, plans, working
drawings, specifications, procedures, field testing of innovative or
alternative waste water treatment processes and techniques meeting
guidelines promulgated under section 304 (d)(3) of this Act, or
other necessary actions, erection, building, acquisition,
alteration, remodeling, improvement, or extension of treatment
works, or the inspection or supervision of any of the foregoing
items.

[Sec. 212(1) amended by PL 97-117]

(2) (A) The term "treatment works" means any devices and systems
    used in the storage, treatment, recycling, and reclamation of
    municipal sewage or industrial wastes of a liquid nature to
    implement section 201 of this act, or necessary to recycle or
    reuse water at the most economical cost over the estimated life
    of the works, including intercepting sewers, outfall sewers,
    sewage collection systems, pumping, power, and other equipment,
    and their appurtenances; extensions, improvements, remodeling,
    additions, and alterations thereof; elements essential to
    provide a reliable recycled supply such as standby treatment

units and clear well facilities; and any works, including site acquisition of the land that will be an integral part of the treatment process (including land use for the storage of treated wastewater in land treatment systems prior to land application) or is used for ultimate disposal of residues resulting from such treatment.

(B) In addition to the definition contained in subparagraph (A) of this paragraph, "treatment works" means any other method or system for preventing, abating, reducing, storing, treating, separating, or disposing of municipal waste, including storm water runoff, or industrial waste, including waste in combined storm water and sanitary sewer systems. Any application for construction grants which includes wholly or in part such methods or systems shall, in accordance with guidelines published by the Administrator pursuant to subparagraph (C) of this paragraph, contain adequate data and analysis demonstrating such proposal to be, over the life of such works, the most cost efficient alternative to comply with sections 301 or 302 of this act, or the requirements of section 201 of this act.

(C) For the purposes of subparagraph (B) of this paragraph, the Administrator shall, within one hundred and eighty days after the date of enactment of this title, publish and thereafter revised no less often than annually, guidelines for the evaluation of methods, including cost effective analysis, described in subparagraph (B) of this paragraph.

(3) The term "replacement" as used in this title means those expenditures for obtaining and installing equipment, accessories, or appurtenances during the useful life of the treatment works necessary to maintain the capacity and performance for which such works are designed and constructed.

Sec. 213. Loan Guarantees for Construction of Treatment Works.

(a) Subject to the conditions of this section and to such terms and conditions as the Administrator determines to be necessary to carry out the purposes of this title, the Administrator is authorized to guarantee, and to make commitments to guarantee, the principal and interest (including interest accruing between the date of default and the date of the payment in full of the guarantee) of any loan, obligation, or participation therein of any State, municipality, or intermunicipal or interstate agency issued directly and exclusively to the Federal Financing Bank to finance that part of the cost of any grant-eligible project for the construction of publicly owned treatment works not paid for with Federal financial assistance under this title (other than in section), which project the Administrator has determined to be eligible for such financial assistance under this title, including, but not limited to, projects eligible for reimbursement under section 206 of this title.

(b) No guarantee, or commitment to make a guarantee, may be made pursuant to this section --

(1) unless the Administrator certifies that the issuing body is unable to obtain on reasonable terms sufficient credit to finance its actual needs without such guarantee; and

(2) unless the Administrator determines that there is a reasonable assurance of repayment of the loan, obligation, or participation therein. A determination of whether financing is available at reasonable rates shall be made by the Secretary of the Treasury with relationship to the current average yield on outstanding marketable obligations of municipalities of comparable maturity.

(c) The Administrator is authorized to charge reasonable fees for the investigation of an application for a guarantee and for the issuance of a commitment to make a guarantee.

(d) The Administrator, in determining whether there is a reasonable assurance of repayment, may require a commitment which would apply to such repayment. Such commitment may include, but not be limited to, any funds received by such grantee from the amounts appropriated under section 206 of this act.
[Sec. 213(d) amended by PL 96-483]

Sec. 214. Public Information.

The Administrator shall develop and operate within one year of the date of enactment of this section, a continuing program of public information and education on recycling and reuse of wastewater (including sludge), the use of land treatment, and methods for the reduction of wastewater volume.

Sec. 215. Requirements for American Materials.

Notwithstanding any other provision of law, no grant for which application is made after February 1, 1978, shall be made under this title for any treatment works unless only such unmanufactured articles, materials, and supplies as have been mined or produced in the United States, and only such manufactured articles, materials, and supplies as have been manufactured in the United States, substantially all from articles, materials, or supplies mined, produced, or manufactured, as the case may be, in the United States will be used in such treatment works. This section shall not apply in any case where the Administrator determines, based upon those factor the Administrator deems relevant, including the available resources of the agency, it to be inconsistent with the public interest (including multilateral government procurement agreements) or the cost to be unreasonable, or if articles, materials, or supplies of the class or kind to be used or the articles, material, or supplies from which they are manufactured are not mined, produced, or manufactured, as the case may be, in the United States in sufficient and reasonably available commercial quantities and of a satisfactory quality.

Sec. 216. Determination of Priority.

Notwithstanding any other provision of this Act, the determination of the priority to be given each category of projects for

construction of publicly owned treatment works within each State
shall be made solely by that State, except that if the
Administrator, after a public hearing, determines that a specific
project will not result in compliance with the enforceable
requirements of this Act, such project shall be removed from the
State's priority list and such State shall submit a revised priority
list. These categories shall include, but not be limited to (A)
secondary treatment, (B) more stringent treatment, (C)
infiltration-in-flow correction, (D) major sewer system
rehabilitation, (E) new collector sewers and appurtenances, (F) new
interceptors and appurtenances, and (G) correction of combined sewer
overflows. Not less than 25 per centum of funds allocated to a
State in any fiscal year under this title for construction of
publicly owned treatment works in such State shall be obligated for
those types of projects referred to in clauses (D), (E), (F), and
(G) of this section, if such projects are on such State's priority
list for that year and are otherwise eligible for funding in that
fiscal year. It is the policy of Congress that projects for
wastewater treatment and management undertaken with Federal
financial assistance under this Act by any State, municipality, or
intermunicipal or interstate agency shall be projects which, in the
estimation of the State, are designed to achieve optimum water
quality management, consistent with the public health and water
quality goals and requirements of the Act.

[Sec. 216 amended by PL 97-117]

Sec. 217. Cost-Effectiveness Guidelines.

Any guidelines for cost-effectiveness analysis published by the
Administrator under this title shall provide for the identification
and selection of cost effective alternatives to comply with the
objective and goals of this Act and sections 201(b), 201(d),
201(g)(2)(A), and 301(b)(2)(B) of this Act.

Sec. 218. Cost Effectiveness.

(a) It is the policy of Congress that a project for waste treatment
and management undertaken with Federal financial assistance under
this Act by any State, municipality, or intermunicipal or interstate
agency shall be considered as an overall waste treatment system for
waste treatment and management, and shall be that system which
constitutes the most economical and cost-effective combination of
devices and systems used in the storage, treatment, recycling, and
reclamation of municipal sewage or industrial wastes of a liquid
nature to implement section 201 of this Act, or necessary to recycle
or reuse water at the most economical cost over the estimated life
of the works, including intercepting sewers, outfall sewers, sewage
collection systems, pumping power, and other equipment, and their
appurtenances; extension, improvements, remodeling, additions, and
alterations thereof; elements essential to provide a reliable
recycled supply such as standby treatment units and clear well
facilities; and any works, including site acquisition of the land
that will be an integral part of the treatment process (including
land use for the storage of treated wastewater in land treatment
systems prior to land application) or which is used for ultimate
disposal of residues resulting from such treatment; water efficiency

measures and devices; and any other method or system for preventing, abating, reducing, storing, treating, separating, or disposing of municipal waste, including storm water runoff, or industrial waste, including waste in combined storm water and sanitary sewer systems; to meet the requirements of this Act.

(b) In accordance with the policy set forth in subsection (a) of this section, before the Administrator approves any grant to any State, municipality, or intermunicipal or interstate agency for the erection, building, acquisition, alteration, remodeling, improvement, or extension of any treatment works the Administrator shall determine that the facilities plan of which such treatment works are a part constitutes the most economical and cost-effective combination of treatment works over the life of the project to meet the requirements of this Act, including, but not limited to, consideration of construction costs, operation, maintenance, and replacement costs.

(c) In furtherance of the policy set forth in subsection (a) of this section, the Administrator shall require value engineering review in connection with any treatment works, prior to approval of any grant for the erection, building, acquisition, alteration, remodeling, improvement, or extension of such treatment works, in any case in which the cost of such erection, building, acquisition, alteration, remodeling, improvement, or extension is projected to be in excess of $10,000,000. For purposes of this subsection, the term "value engineering review" means a specialized cost control technique which uses a systematic and creative approach to identify and to focus on unnecessarily high cost in a project in order to arrive at a cost saving without sacrificing the reliability or efficiency of the project.

(d) This section applies to projects for waste treatment and management for which no treatment works including a facilities plan for such project have received Federal financial assistance for the preparation of construction plans and specifications under this Act before the date of enactment of this section.

[Sec. 218 added by PL 97-117]

Sec. 219. **State Certification of Projects**.

Whenever the Governor of a State which has been delegated sufficient authority to administer the construction grant program under this title in that State certifies to the Administrator that a grant application meets applicable requirements of Federal and State law for assistance under this title, the Administrator shall approve or disapprove such application within 45 days of the date of receipt of such application. If the Administrator does not approve or disapprove such application within 45 days of receipt, the application shall be deemed approved. If the Administrator disapproves such application the Administrator shall state in writing the reasons for such disapproval. Any grant approved or deemed approved under this section shall be subject to amounts provided in appropriation Acts.

[Sec. 219 added by PL 97-117]

TITLE III -- STANDARDS AND ENFORCEMENT EFFLUENT LIMITATIONS

Sec. 301. Effluent Limitations.

(a) Except as in compliance with this section and sections 302, 306, 307, 318, 402, and 404 of this Act, the discharge of any pollutant by any person shall be unlawful.

(b) In order to carry out the objective of this Act there shall be achieved --

(1) (A) not later than July 1, 1977, effluent limitations for point sources, other than publicly owned treatment works, (i) which shall require the application of the best practicable control technology currently available as defined by the Administrator pursuant to section 304(b) of this Act, or (ii) in the case of a discharge into a publicly owned treatment works which meets the requirements of subparagraph (B) of this paragraph, which shall require compliance with any applicable pretreatment requirements and any requirements under section 307 of this Act; and

(B) for publicly owned treatment works in existence on July 1, 1977, or approved pursuant to section 203 of this Act prior to June 30, 1974 (for which construction must be completed within four years of approval), effluent limitations based upon secondary treatment as defined by the Administrator pursuant to section 304(d)(1) of this Act; or

(C) not later than July 1, 1977, any more stringent limitation, including those necessary to meet water quality standards, treatment standards, or schedule of compliance, established pursuant to any State law or regulations, (under authority preserved by section 510) or any other Federal law or regulation, or required to implement any applicable water quality standard established pursuant to this Act.

(2) (A) for pollutants identified in subparagraphs (C), (D), and (F) of this paragraph, effluent limitations for categories and classes of point sources, other than publicly owned treatment works, which (i) shall require application of the best available technology economically achievable for such category or class, which will result in reasonable further progress toward the national goal of eliminating the discharge of all pollutants, as determined in accordance with regulations issued by the Administrator pursuant to section 304(b)(2) of this Act, which such effluent limitations shall require the elimination of discharges of all pollutants if the Administrator finds, on the basis of information available to him (including information developed pursuant to section 315), that such elimination is technologically and economically achievable for category or class of point sources as determined in accordance with regulations issued by the Administrator pursuant to section 304(b)(2) of this Act or (ii) in the case of the introduction of a pollutant into a publicly owned treatment

works which meets the requirements of subparagraph (b) of this paragraph, shall require compliance with any applicable pretreatment requirements and any other requirement under section 307 of this Act;

(B) [Sec. 301(b)(2)(B) repealed by PL 97-117]

(C) with respect to all toxic pollutants referred to in table 1 of Committee Print Number 95-30 of the Committee on Public Works and Transportation of the House of Representatives compliance with effluent limitations in accordance with subparagraph (A) of this paragraph as expeditiously as practicable but in no case later than three years after the date such limitations are promulgated under section 304(b), and in no case later than March 31, 1989.

[Sec. 301(b)(2)(C) amended by PL 100-4]

[Section 301(f) of PL 100-4 provides:

"(f) Deadlines for Regulations for Certain Toxic Pollutants. -- The Administrator shall promulgate final regulations establishing effluent limitations in accordance with sections 301(b)(2)(A) and 307(b)(1) of the Federal Water Pollution Control Act for all toxic pollutants referred to in table 1 of Committee Print Numbered 95-30 of the Committee on Public Works and Transportation of the House of Representatives which are discharged from the categories of point sources in accordance with the following table:

Category	Date by which the final regulation shall be promulgated
Organic chemicals and plastics and synthetic fibers	December 31, 1986.
Pesticides	December 31, 1986."]

(D) for all toxic pollutants listed under paragraph (1) of subsection (a) of section 307 of this Act which are not referred to in subparagraph (C) of this paragraph compliance with effluent limitation in accordance with subparagraph (A) of this paragraph as expeditiously as practicable, but in no case later than three years after date such limitations are promulgated under section 304(b), and in no case later than March 31, 1989;

[Sec. 301(b)(2)(D) amended by PL 100-4]

(E) as expeditiously as practicable but in no case later than three years after the date such limitations are promulgated under section 304(b), and in no case later than March 31, 1989, compliance with effluent limitations for categories and classes of point sources, other than publicly owned treatment works, which in the case of pollutants identified pursuant to section 304(a)(4) of this Act shall require application of the best conventional pollutant

control technology as determined in accordance with
regulations issued by the Administrator pursuant to section
304(b)(4) of this Act; and

[301(b)(2)(E) amended by PL 100-4]

(F) for all pollutants (other than those subject to
subparagraphs (C), (D), or (E) of this paragraph) compliance
with effluent limitations in accordance with subparagraph
(A) of this paragraph as expeditiously as practicable but in
no case later than 3 years after the date such limitations
are established, and in no case later than March 31, 1989.

[Sec. 301(b)(2)(F) amended by PL 100-4]

(3) (A) for effluent limitations under paragraph (1)(A)(i) of
this subsection promulgated after January 1, 1982, and
requiring a level of control substantially greater or based
on fundamentally different control technology than under
permits for an industrial category issued before such date,
compliance as expeditiously as practicable but in no case
later than three years after the date such limitations are
promulgated under section 304(b), and in no case later than
March 31, 1989; and

(B) for any effluent limitation in accordance with paragraph
(1)(A)(i), (2)(A)(i), or (2)(E) of this subsection
established only on the basis of section 402(a)(1) in a
permit issued after enactment of the Water Quality Act of
1987, compliance as expeditiously as practicable but in no
case later than three years after the date such limitations
are established, and in no case later than March 31, 1989.

[Sec. 301(b)(3) added by PL 100-4]

(c) The Administrator may modify the requirements of subsection
(b)(2)(A) of this section with respect to any point source for which
a permit application is filed after July 1, 1977, upon a showing by
the owner or operator of such point source satisfactory to the
Administrator that such modified requirements (1) will represent the
maximum use of technology within the economic capability of the
owner or operator; and (2) will result in reasonable further
progress toward the elimination of the discharge of pollutants.

(d) Any effluent limitation required by paragraph (2) of subsection
(b) of this section shall be reviewed at least every five years and,
if appropriate, revised pursuant to the procedure established under
such paragraph.

(e) Effluent limitations established pursuant to this section or
section 302 of this Act shall be applied to all point sources of
discharge of pollutants in accordance with the provisions of this
Act.

(f) Notwithstanding any other provisions of this Act it shall be
unlawful to discharge any radiological, chemical, or biological

warfare agent or high-level radioactive waste into the navigable waters.

(g) Modifications for Certain Nonconventional Pollutants. --

(1) General Authority. -- The Administrator, with the concurrence of the State, may modify the requirements of subsection (b)(2)(A) of this section with respect to the discharge from any point source of ammonia, chlorine, color, iron, and total phenols (4AAP) (when determined by the Administrator to be a pollutant covered by subsection (b)(2)(F)) and any other pollutant which the Administrator lists under paragraph (4) of this subsection.

[Former Sec. 301(g)(1) deleted and new (1) and (2) added by PL 100-4]

(2) Requirements for Granting Modifications. -- A modification under this subsection shall be granted only upon a showing by the owner or operator of a point source satisfactory to the Administrator that --

(A) such modified requirements will result at a minimum in compliance with the requirements of subsection (b)(1)(A) or (C) of this section, whichever is applicable;

(B) such modified requirements will not result in any additional requirements on any other point or nonpoint source; and

(C) such modification will not interfere with the attainment of maintenance of that water quality which shall assure protection of public water supplies, and the protection and propagation of a balanced population of shellfish, fish, and wildlife, and allow recreational activities, in and on the water and such modification will not result in the discharge of pollutants in quantities which may reasonably be anticipated to pose an unacceptable risk to human health or the environment because of bioaccumulation, persistency in the environment, acute toxicity, chronic toxicity (including carcinogenicity, mutagenicity or teratogenicity), or synergistic propensities.

(3) Limitation on Authority to Apply for Subsection (c) Modification -- If an owner or operator of a point source applies for a modification under this subsection with respect to the discharge of any pollutant, such owner or operator shall be eligible to apply for modification under subsection (c) of this section with respect to such pollutant only during the same time-period as he is eligible to apply for a modification under this subsection.

[Former Sec. 301(g)(2) amended and redesignated as (3) by PL 100-4]

(4) Procedures for Listing Additional Pollutants. --

(A) General Authority. -- Upon petition of any person, the Administrator may add any pollutant to the list of pollutants for which modification under this section is authorized (except for pollutants identified pursuant to section 304(a)(4) of this Act, toxic pollutants subject to section 307(a) of this Act, and the thermal component of discharges) in accordance with the provisions of this paragraph.

(B) Requirements for Listing. --
    (i) Sufficient Information. -- The person petitioning for listing of an additional pollutant under this subsection shall submit to the Administrator sufficient information to make the determinations required by this subparagraph.
    (ii) Toxic Criteria Determination. -- The Administrator shall determine whether or not the pollutant meets the criteria for listing as a toxic pollutant under section 307(a) of this Act.
    (iii) Listing as Toxic Pollutant. -- If the Administrator determines that the pollutant meets the criteria for listing as a toxic pollutant under section 307(a), the Administrator shall list the pollutant as a toxic pollutant under section 307(a).
    (iv) Nonconventional Criteria Determination. -- If the Administrator determines that the pollutant does not meet the criteria for listing as a toxic pollutant under such section and determines that adequate test methods and sufficient data are available to make the determinations required by paragraph (2) of this subsection with respect to the pollutant, the Administrator shall add the pollutant to the list of pollutants specified in paragraph (1) of this subsection for which modifications are authorized under this subsection.

(C) Requirements for Filing of Petitions. -- A petition for listing of a pollutant under this paragraph --
    (i) must be filed not later than 270 days after the date of promulgation of an applicable effluent guideline under section 304;
    (ii) may be filed before promulgation of such guideline; and
    (iii) may be filed with an application for a modification under paragraph (1) with respect to the discharge of such pollutant.

(D) Deadline for Approval of Petition. -- A decision to add a pollutant to the list of pollutants for which modifications under this subsection are authorized must be made within 270 days after the date of promulgation of an applicable effluent guideline under section 304.

(E) Burden of Proof. -- The burden of proof for making the determinations under subparagraph (B) shall be on the petitioner.

[Sec. 301(g)(4) added by PL 100-4]

(5) Removal of Pollutants. -- The Administrator may remove any pollutant from the list of pollutants for which modifications are authorized under this subsection if the Administrator determines that adequate test methods and sufficient data are no longer available for determining whether or not modifications may be granted with respect to such pollutant under paragraph (2) of this subsection.

[Sec. 301(g)(5) added by PL 100-4]

[Section 302(e) of PL 100-4 states:

"(e) Application. --

(1) General Rule. -- Except as provided in paragraph (2), the amendments made by this section shall apply to all requests for modifications under section 301(g) of the Federal Water Pollution Control Act pending on the date of the enactment of this Act and shall not have the effect of extending the deadline established in section 301(j)(1)(B) of such Act.

(2) Exception. -- The amendments made by this section shall not affect any application for a modification with respect to the discharge of ammonia, chlorine, color, iron, or total phenols (4AAP) under section 301(g) of the Federal Water Pollution Control Act pending on the date of the enactment of this Act; except that the Administrator must approve or disapprove such application not later than 365 days after the date of such enactment."]

(h) The Administrator, with the concurrence of the State, may issue a permit under section 402 which modifies the requirements of subsection (b)(1)(B) of this section with respect to the discharge of any pollutant from a publicly owned treatment works into marine waters, if the applicant demonstrates to the satisfaction of the Administrator that --

(1) there is an applicable water quality standard specific to the pollutant for which the modification is requested, which has been identified under section 304(a)(6) of this Act;

(2) the discharge of pollutants in accordance with such modified requirements will not interfere, alone or in combination with pollutants from other sources, with the attainment or maintenance of that water quality which assures protection of public water supplies and protection and propagation of a balanced, indigenous population of shellfish, fish and wildlife, and allows recreational activities, in and on the water;

(3) the applicant has established a system for monitoring the impact of such discharge on a representative sample of aquatic biota, to the extent practicable, and the scope of such monitoring is limited to include only those scientific investigations which are necessary to study the effects of the proposed discharge;

[Sec. 301(h)(3) amended by PL 100-4]

[Section 303(b)(2) of PL 100-4 states the amendment to 301(h)(3), "shall only apply to modifications and renewals of modifications which are tentatively or finally approved after the date of the enactment of this Act."]

(4) such modified requirements will not result in any additional requirements on any other point or nonpoint source;

(5) all applicable pretreatment requirements for sources introducing waste into such treatment works will be enforced;

(6) in the case of any treatment works serving a population of 50,000 or more, with respect to any toxic pollutant introduced into such works by an industrial discharger for which pollutant there is no applicable pretreatment requirement in effect, sources introducing waste into such works are in compliance with all applicable pretreatment requirements, the applicant will enforce such requirements, and the applicant has in effect a pretreatment program which, in combination with the treatment of discharges from such works, removes the same amount of such pollutant as would be removed if such works were to apply secondary treatment to discharges and if such works had no pretreatment program with respect to such pollutant;

[New Sec. 301(h)(6) added by PL 100-4]

(7) to the extent practicable, the applicant has established a schedule of activities designed to eliminate the entrance of toxic pollutants from nonindustrial sources into such treatment works;

[Former Sec. 301(h)(8) deleted by PL 97-117; former (6) and (7) redesignated as (7) and (8) by PL 100-4]

(8) there will be no new or substantially increased discharges from the point source of the pollutant to which the modification applies above that volume of discharge specified in the permit;

(9) the applicant at the time such modification becomes effective will be discharging effluent which has received at least primary or equivalent treatment and which meets the criteria established under section 304(a)(1) of this Act after initial mixing in the waters surrounding or adjacent to the point at which such effluent is discharged.

[Sec. 301(h)(9) added by PL 100-4]

For the purposes of this subsection the phrase "the discharge of any pollutant into marine waters" refers to a discharge into deep waters of the territorial sea or the waters of the contiguous zone, or into saline estuarine waters where there is strong tidal movement and other hydrological and geological characteristics which the Administrator determines necessary to allow compliance with paragraph (2) of this subsection, and section 101(a)(2) of this Act. For the purposes of paragraph

(9), "primary or equivalent treatment" means treatment by screening, sedimentation, and skimming adequate to remove at least 30 percent of the biological oxygen demanding material and of the suspending solids in the treatment works influent, and disinfection, where appropriate. A municipality which applies secondary treatment shall be eligible to receive a permit pursuant to this subsection which modifies the requirements of subsection (b)(1)(B) of this section with respect to the discharge of any pollutant from any treatment works owned by such municipality into marine waters. No permit issued under this subsection shall authorize the discharge of sewage sludge into marine waters. In order for a permit to be issued under this subsection for the discharge of a pollutant into marine waters, such marine waters must exhibit characteristics assuring that water providing dilution does not contain significant amounts of previously discharged effluent from such treatment works. No permit issued under this subsection shall authorize the discharge of any pollutant into saline estuarine waters which at the time of application do not support a balanced indigenous population of shellfish, fish and wildlife, or allow recreation in and on the waters or which exhibit ambient water quality below applicable water quality standards adopted for the protection of public water supplies, shellfish, fish and wildlife or recreational activities or such other standards necessary to assure support and protection of such uses. The prohibition contained in the preceding sentence shall apply without regard to the presence or absence of a causal relationship between such characteristics and the applicant's current or proposed discharge. Notwithstanding any other provisions of this subsection, no permit may be issued under this subsection for discharge of a pollutant into the New York Bight Apex consisting of the ocean waters of the Atlantic Ocean westward of 73 degrees 30 minutes west longitude and northward of 40 degrees 10 minutes north latitude.

[Sec. 301(h) amended by PL 97-117; PL 100-4]

[Section 303(g) of PL 100-4 states the amendments to 301(h) and (h)(2), as well as the provisions of (h)(6) and (h)(9), "shall not apply to an application for a permit under section 301(h) of the Federal Water Pollution Control Act which has been tentatively or finally approved by the Administrator before the date of the enactment of this Act; except that such amendments shall apply to renewals of such permits after such date of enactment."]

(i) (1) Where construction is required in order for a planned or existing publicly owned treatment works to achieve limitations under subsection (b)(1)(B) or (b)(1)(C) of this section, but (A) construction cannot be completed within the time required in such subsection, or (B) the United States has failed to make financial assistance under this Act available in time to achieve such limitations by the time specified in such subsection, the owner or operator of such treatment works may request the Administrator (or if appropriate the State) to issue a permit pursuant to section 402 of this Act or to modify a permit issued pursuant to that section to extend such time for compliance. Any such request shall be filed with the Administrator (or if appropriate the State) within 180 days after the date of enactment of the Water Quality Act of 1987. The Administrator (or if appropriate the State) may grant such request and issue or modify such a permit, which shall contain a schedule of compliance for the publicly owned treatment works based on the earliest date by which such financial assistance will be available from the United States and construction can be completed, but in no event later than July 1, 1988, and shall contain such other terms and conditions, including those necessary to carry out subsections (b) through (g) of section 201 of this Act, section 307 of this Act, and such interim effluent limitations applicable to that treatment works as the Administrator determines are necessary to carry out the provisions of this Act.

[Sec. 301(i)(1) amended by PL 100-4]

[Section 304(b) of PL 100-4 states the amendment to 301(i)(1), "shall not apply to those treatment works which are subject to a compliance schedule established before the date of the enactment of this Act by a court order or a final administrative order."]

    (2) (A) Where a point source (other than a publicly owned treatment works) will not achieve the requirements of subsections (b)(1)(A) and (b)(1)(C) of this section and --
        (i) if a permit issued prior to July 1, 1977, to such point source is based upon a discharge into a publicly owned treatment works; or
        (ii) if such point source (other than a publicly owned treatment works) had before July 1, 1977, a contract (enforceable against such point source) to discharge into a publicly owned treatment works; or
        (iii) if either an application made before July 1, 1977, for a construction grant under this Act for a publicly owned treatment works, or engineering or architectural plans or working drawings made before July 1, 1977, for a publicly owned treatment works, show that such point source was to discharge into such publicly owned treatment works, and such publicly owned treatment works is presently unable to accept such discharge without construction, and in the case of a discharge to an existing publicly owned treatment works, such treatment works has an extension pursuant to paragraph (1) of this subsection, the owner or operator of such point source may request the Administrator (or if appropriate the State) to issue or modify such a permit pursuant to such section 402 to extend such time for compliance. Any such request shall be filed with the Administrator (or if appropriate the State) within 180 days after the date of enactment of this subsection or the filing of a request by the appropriate publicly owned treatment works under paragraph (1) of this subsection, whichever is later. If the Administrator (or if appropriate the State) finds that the owner or operator of such point source has acted in good faith, he may grant such request and issue or modify such a permit, which shall contain a schedule of compliance for the point source to

achieve the requirements of subsections (b)(1)(A) and (C) of this section and shall contain such other terms and conditions, including pretreatment and interim effluent limitations and water conservation requirements applicable to that point source, as the Administrator determines are necessary to carry out the provisions of this Act.

(B) No time modification granted by the Administrator (or if appropriate the State) pursuant to paragraph (2)(A) of this subsection shall extend beyond the earliest date practicable for compliance or beyond the date of any extension granted to the appropriate publicly owned treatment works pursuant to paragraph (1) of this subsection, but in no event shall it extend beyond July 1, 1988; and no such time modification shall be granted unless (i) the publicly owned treatment works will be in operation and available to the point source before July 1, 1988, and will meet the requirements to subsections (b)(1)(B) and (C) of this section after receiving the discharge from that point source; and (ii) the point source and the publicly owned treatment works have entered into an enforceable contract requiring the point source to discharge into the publicly owned treatment works, the owner or operator of such point source to pay the costs required under section 204 of this Act, and the publicly owned treatment works to accept the discharge from the point source; and (iii) the permit for such point source requires point source to meet all requirements under section 307 (a) and (b) during the period of such time modification.

[Sec. 301(i) amended by PL 97-117]

[Section 21 of PL 97-117 in addition to extending the compliance date from July 1, 1983 to July 1, 1988, also provides: "The amendment made by this subsection shall not be interpreted or applied to extend the date for compliance with section 301(b)(1)(B) or (C) of the Federal Water Pollution Control Act beyond schedules for compliance in effect as of the date of enactment of this Act, except in cases where reductions in the amount of financial assistance under this Act or changed conditions affecting the rate of construction beyond the control of the owner or operator will make it impossible to complete construction by July 1, 1983."]

(j) (1) Any application filed under this section for a modification of the provisions of --

(A) subsection (b)(1)(B) under subsection (h) of this section shall be filed not later that(n) the 365th day which begins after the date of enactment of the Municipal Wastewater Treatment Construction Grant Amendments of 1981, except that a publicly owned treatment works which prior to December 31, 1982, had a contractual arrangement to use a portion of the capacity of an ocean outfall operated by another publicly owned treatment works which has applied for or received modification under subsection (h), may apply for a modification of subsection (h) in its own right not later than 30 days after the date of the enactment of the Water Quality Act of 1987;

[Sec. 301(j)(1)(A) amended by PL 100-4]

[Sec. 301(j)(1)(A) revised by PL 97-117]

[Section 22(e) of PL 97-117 provides:

"(e) The amendments made by this section shall take effect on the date of enactment of this Act, except that no applicant, other than the city of Avalon, California, who applies after the date of enactment of this Act for a permit pursuant to subsection (h) of section 301 of the Federal Water Pollution Control Act which modifies the requirements of subsection (b)(1)(B) of section 301 of such Act shall receive such permit during the one-year period which begins on the date of enactment of this Act."]

> (B) subsection (b)(2)(A) as it applies to pollutants identified in subsection (b)(2)(F) shall be filed not later than 270 days after the date of promulgation of an applicable effluent guideline under section 304 or not later than 270 days after the date of enactment of the Clean Water Act of 1977, whichever is later.
>
> (2) Subject to paragraph (3) of this section, any application for a modification filed under subsection (g) of this section shall not operate to stay any requirement under this Act, unless in the judgment of the Administrator such a stay or the modification sought will not result in the discharge of pollutants in quantities which may reasonably be anticipated to pose an unacceptable risk to human health or the environment because of bioaccumulation, persistency in the environment, acute toxicity, chronic toxicity (including carcinogenicity, mutagenicity or teratogenicity), or synergistic propensities, and that there is a substantial likelihood that the applicant will succeed on the merits of such application. In the case of an applicant filed under subsection (g) of this section, the Administrator may condition any stay granted under this paragraph on requiring the filing of a bond or other appropriate security to assure timely compliance with the requirements from which a modification is sought.
>
> (3) Compliance Requirements Under Subsection (g). --
>
> > (A) Effect of Filing. -- An application for a modification under subsection (g) and a petition for listing of a pollutant as a pollutant for which modifications are authorized under such subsection shall not stay the requirement that the person seeking such modification or listing comply with effluent limitations under this Act for all pollutants not the subject of such application or petition.
> >
> > (B) Effect of Disapproval. -- Disapproval of an application for a modification under subsection (g) shall not stay the requirement that the person seeking such modification comply with all applicable effluent limitations under this Act. •

[Sec. 301(j)(3) and (4) added by PL 100-4]

(4) Deadline for Subsection (g) Decision. -- An application for a modification with respect to a pollutant filed under subsection (g) must be approved or disapproved not later than 365 days after the date of such filing; except that in any case in which a petition for listing such pollutant as a pollutant for which modifications are authorized under such subsection is approved, such application must be approved or disapproved not later than 365 days after the date of approval of such petition.

(k) In the case of any facility subject to a permit under section 402 which proposes to comply with the requirements of subsection (b)(2)(A) or (b)(2)(E) of this section by replacing existing production capacity with an innovative production process which will result in an effluent reduction significantly greater than that required by the limitation otherwise applicable to such facility and moves toward the national goal of eliminating the discharge of all pollutants, or with the installation of an innovative control technique that has a substantial likelihood for enabling the facility to comply with the applicable effluent limitation by achieving a significantly greater effluent reduction than that required by the applicable effluent limitation and moves toward the national goal of eliminating the discharge of all pollutants, or by achieving the required reduction with an innovative system that has the potential for significantly lower costs than the systems which have been determined by the Administrator to be economically achievable, the Administrator (or the State with an approved program under section 402, in consultation with the Administrator) may establish a date for compliance under subsection (b)(2)(A) or (b)(2)(E) of this section no later than two years after the date for compliance with such effluent limitation which would otherwise be applicable under such subsection, if it is also determined that such innovative system has the potential for industrywide application.

[Sec. 301(k) amended by PL 100-4]

(1) Other than as provided in subsection (n) of this section, the Administrator may not modify any requirement of this section as it applies to any specific pollutant which is on the toxic pollutant list under section 307(a)(1) of this Act.

[Sec. 301(1) amended by PL 100-4]

(m) (1) The Administrator, with the concurrence of the State, may issue a permit under section 402 which modifies the requirements of subsections (b)(1)(A) and (b)(2)(E) of this section, and of section 403, with respect to effluent limitations to the extent such limitations relate to biochemical oxygen demand and pH from discharges by an industrial discharger in such State into deep waters of the territorial seas, if the applicant demonstrates and the Administrator finds that --

[Sec. 301(m) added by PL 97-440]

(A) the facility for which modification is sought is covered at the time of the enactment of this subsection by National Pollutant Discharge Elimination System permit number CA0005894 or CA0005282;

(B) the energy and environmental costs of meeting such requirements of subsections (b)(1)(A) and (b)(2)(E) and section 403 exceed by an unreasonable amount the benefits to be obtained, including the objectives of this Act;

(C) the applicant has established a system for monitoring the impact of such discharges on a representative sample of aquatic biota;

(D) such modified requirements will not result in any additional requirements on any other point or nonpoint source;

(E) there will be no new or substantially increased discharges from the point source of the pollutant to which the modification applies above that volume of discharge specified in the permit;

(F) the discharge is into waters where there is strong tidal movement and other hydrological and geological characteristics which are necessary to allow compliance with this subsection and section 101(a)(2) of this Act;

(G) the applicant accepts as a condition to the permit a contractural obligation to use funds in the amount required (but not less than $250,000 per year for ten years) for research and development of water pollution control technology, including but not limited to closed cycle technology;

(H) the facts and circumstances present a unique situation which, if relief is granted, will not establish a precedent or the relaxation of the requirements of this Act applicable to similarly situated discharges; and

(I) no owner or operator of a facility comparable to that of the applicant situated in the United States has demonstrated that it would be put at a competitive disadvantage to the applicant (or the parent company or any subsidiary thereof) as a result of the issuance of a permit under this subsection.

(2) The effluent limitations established under a permit issued under paragraph (1) shall be sufficient to implement the applicable State water quality standards, to assure the protection of public water supplies and protection and propagation of a balanced, indigenous population of shellfish, fish, fauna, wildlife, and other aquatic organisms, and to allow recreational activities in and on the water. In setting such limitations, the Administrator shall take into account any seasonal variations and the need for an adequate margin of safety, considering the lack of essential knowledge of the effects of discharges on beneficial uses of the receiving waters.

(3) A permit under this subsection may be issued for a period not to exceed five years, and such a permit may be renewed for

one additional period not to exceed five years upon a
demonstration by the applicant and a finding by the
Administrator at the time of application for any such renewal
that the provisions of this subsection are met.

(4) The Administrator may terminate a permit issued under this
subsection if the Administrator determines that there has been a
decline in ambient water quality of the receiving waters during
the period of the permit even if a direct cause and effect
relationship cannot be shown: Provided, that if the effluent
from a source with a permit issued under this subsection is
contributing to a decline in ambient water quality of the
receiving waters, the Administrator shall terminate such permit.

(n) Fundamentally Different Factors. --

[Sec. 301(n) added by PL 100-4]

(1) General Rule. -- The Administrator, with the concurrence of
the State, may establish an alternative requirement under
subsection (b)(2) or section 307(b) for a facility that modifies
the requirements of national effluent limitation guidelines or
categorical pretreatment standards that would otherwise be
applicable to such facility, if the owner or operator of such
facility demonstrates to the satisfaction of the Administrator
that --

   (A) the facility is fundamentally different with respect to
   the factors (other than cost) specified in section 304(b) or
   304(g) and considered by the Administrator in establishing
   such national effluent limitation guidelines or categorical
   pretreatment standards;

   (B) the application --
      (i) is based solely on information and supporting data
      submitted to the Administrator during the rulemaking for
      establishment of the applicable national effluent
      limitation guidelines or categorical pretreatment
      standard specifically raising the factors that are
      fundamentally different for such facility; or
      (ii) is based on information and supporting data
      referred to in clause (i) and information and supporting
      data the applicant did not have a reasonable opportunity
      to submit during such rulemaking;

   (C) the alternative requirement is no less stringent than
   justified by the fundamental difference; and

   (D) the alternative requirement will not result in a
   non-water quality environmental impact which is markedly
   more adverse than the impact considered by the Administrator
   in establishing such national effluent limitation guideline
   or categorical pretreatment standard.

(2) Time Limit for Applications. -- An application for an
alternative requirement which modifies the requirements of an
effluent limitation or pretreatment standard under this

subsection must be submitted to the Administrator within 180 days after the date on which such limitation or standard is established or revised, as the case may be.

(3) Time Limit for Decision. -- The Administrator shall approve or deny by final agency action an application submitted under this subsection within 180 days after the date such application is filed with the Administrator.

(4) Submission of Information. -- The Administrator may allow an applicant under this subsection to submit information and supporting data until the earlier of the date the application is approved or denied or the last day that the Administration has to approve or deny such application.

(5) Treatment of Pending Applications. -- For the purposes of this subsection, an application for an alternative requirement based on fundamentally different factors which is pending on the date of the enactment of this subsection shall be treated as having been submitted to the Administrator on the 180th day following such date of enactment. The applicant may amend the application to take into account the provisions of this subsection.

(6) Effect of Submission of Application. -- An application for an alternative requirement under this subsection shall not stay the applicant's obligation to comply with the effluent limitation guideline or categorical pretreatment standard which is the subject of the application.

(7) Effect of Denial. -- If an application for an alternative requirement which modifies the requirements of an effluent limitation or pretreatment standard under this subsection is denied by the Administrator, the applicant must comply with such limitation or standard as established or revised, as the case may be.

(8) Reports. -- Every 6 months after the date of the enactment of this subsection, the Administrator shall submit to the Committee on Environment and Public Works of the Senate and the Committee on Public Works and Transportation of the House of Representatives a report on the status of applications for alternative requirements which modify the requirements of effluent limitations under section 301 or 304 of this Act or any national categorical pretreatment standard under section 307(b) of this Act filed before, on, or after such date of enactment.

(o) Application Fees. -- The Administrator shall prescribe and collect from each applicant fees reflecting the reasonable administrative costs incurred in reviewing and processing applications for modifications submitted to the Administrator pursuant to subsections (c), (g), (i), (k), (m), and (n) of section 301, section 304(d)(4), and section 316(a) of this Act. All amounts collected by the Administrator under this subsection shall be deposited into a special fund of the Treasury entitled "Water Permits and Related Services" which shall thereafter be available for appropriation to carry out activities of the Environmental Protection Agency for which such fees were collected.

[Sec. 301(o) added by PL 100-4]

(p) Modified Permit for Coal Remining Operations. --

[Sec. 301(p) added by PL 100-4]

(1) In General. -- Subject to paragraphs (2) through (4) of this subsection, the Administrator, or the State in any case which the State has an approved permit program under section 402(b), may issue a permit under section 402 which modifies the requirements of subsection (b)(2)(A) of this section with respect to the pH level of any pre-existing discharge, and with respect to pre-existing discharges of iron and manganese from the remined area of any coal remining operation or with respect to the pH level or level of iron or manganese in any pre-existing discharge affected by the remining operation. Such modified requirements shall apply the best available technology economically achievable on a case-by-case basis, using best professional judgment, to set specific numerical effluent limitations in each permit.

(2) Limitations. -- The Administrator or the State may only issue a permit pursuant to paragraph (1) if the applicant demonstrates to the satisfaction of the Administrator or the State, as the case may be, that the coal remining operation will result in the potential for improved water quality from the remining operation but in no event shall such a permit allow the pH level of any discharge, and in no event shall such a permit allow the discharges of iron and manganese, to exceed the levels being discharged from the remined area before the coal remining operation begins. No discharge from, or affected by, the remining operation shall exceed State water quality standards established under section 303 of this Act.

(3) Definitions. -- For purposes of this subsection --

(A) Coal Remining Operation. -- The term "coal remining operation" means a coal mining operation which begins after the date of the enactment of this subsection at a site on which coal mining was conducted before the effective date of the Surface Mining Control and Reclamation Act of 1977.

(B) Remined Area. -- The term "remined area" means only that area of any coal remining operation on which coal mining was conducted before the effective date of the Surface Mining Control and Reclamation Act of 1977.

(C) Pre-existing Discharge. -- The term "pre-existing discharge" means any discharge at the time of permit application under this subsection.

(4) Applicability of Strip Mining Laws. -- Nothing in this subsection shall affect the application of the Surface Mining Control and Reclamation Act of 1977 to any coal remining

operation, including the application of such Act to suspended solids.

Sec. 302. Water Quality Related Effluent Limitations.

(a) Whenever, in the judgment of the Administrator or as identified under section 304(1) discharges of pollutants from a point source or group of point sources, with the application of effluent limitations required under section 301(b)(2) of this Act, would interfere with the attainment or maintenance of that water quality in a specific portion of the navigable waters which shall assure protection of public health, public water supplies, agricultural and industrial uses, and the protection and propagation of a balanced population of shellfish, fish and wildlife, and allow recreational activities in and on the water, effluent limitations (including alternative effluent control strategies) for such point source or sources shall be established which can reasonably be expected to contribute to the attainment or maintenance of such water quality.

[Sec. 302(a) amended by PL 100-4]

(b) Modifications of Effluent Limitations. --

(1) Notice and Hearing. -- Prior to establishment of any effluent limitation pursuant to subsection (a) of this section, the Administrator shall publish such proposed limitation and within 90 days of such publication hold a public hearing.

(2) Permits. --

(A) No Reasonable Relationship. -- The Administrator, with the concurrence of the State, may issue a permit which modifies the effluent limitations required by subsection (a) of this section for pollutants other than toxic pollutants if the applicant demonstrates at such hearing that (whether or not technology or other alternative control strategies are available) there is no reasonable relationship between the economic and social costs and the benefits to be obtained (including attainment of the objective of this Act) from achieving such limitation.

(B) Reasonable Progress. -- The Administrator, with the concurrence of the State, may issue a permit which modifies the effluent limitations required by subsection (a) of this section for toxic pollutants for a single period not to exceed 5 years if the applicant demonstrates to the satisfaction of the Administrator that such modified requirements (i) will represent the maximum degree of control within the economic capability of the owner and operator of the source, and (ii) will result in reasonable further progress beyond the requirements of section 301(b)(2) toward the requirements of subsection (a) of this section.

[Sec. 302(b) revised by PL 100-4]

(c) The establishment of effluent limitations under this section shall not operate to delay the application of any effluent limitation established under section 301 of this Act.

Sec. 303. **Water Quality Standards and Implementation Plans.**

(a) (1) In order to carry out the purpose of this Act, any water quality standard applicable to interstate waters which was adopted by any State and submitted to, and approved by, or is awaiting approval by, the Administrator pursuant to this Act as in effect immediately prior to the date of enactment of the Federal Water Pollution Control Act Amendments of 1972, shall remain in effect unless the Administrator determined that such standard is not consistent with the applicable requirements of this Act as in effect immediately prior to the date of enactment of the Federal Water Pollution Control Act Amendments of 1972. If the Administrator makes such a determination he shall, within three months after the date of enactment of the Federal Water Pollution Control Act Amendments of 1972, notify the State and specify the changes needed to meet such requirements. If such changes are not adopted by the State within ninety days after the date of such notification, the Administrator shall promulgate such changes in accordance with subsection (b) of this section.

(2) Any State which, before the date of enactment of the Federal Water Pollution Control Act Amendments of 1972, has adopted pursuant to its own law, water quality standards applicable to intrastate waters shall submit such standards to the Administrator within thirty days after the date of enactment of the Federal Water Pollution Control Act Amendments of 1972. Each such standard shall remain in effect, in the same manner and to the same extent as any other water quality standard established under this Act unless the Administrator determines that such standard is inconsistent with the applicable requirements of this Act as in effect immediately prior to the date of enactment of the Federal Water Pollution Control Act Amendments of 1972. If the Administrator makes such a determination he shall not later than the one hundred and twentieth day after the date of submission of such standards, notify the State and specify the changes needed to meet such requirements. If such changes are not adopted by the State within ninety days after such notification, the Administrator shall promulgate such changes in accordance with subsection (b) of this section.

(3) (A) Any State which prior to the date of enactment of the Federal Water Pollution Control Act Amendments of 1972 has not adopted pursuant to its own laws water quality standards applicable to intrastate waters shall, not later than one hundred and eighty days after the date of enactment of the Federal Water Pollution Control Act Amendments of 1972, adopt and submit such standards to the Administrator.

(B) If the Administrator determines that any such standards are consistent with the applicable requirements of this Act as in effect immediately prior to the date of enactment of the Federal Water Pollution Control Act Amendments of 1972, he shall approve such standards.

(C) If the Administrator determines that any such standards are not consistent with the applicable requirements of this Act as in effect immediately prior to the date of enactment of the Federal Water Pollution Control Act Amendments of 1972, he shall, not later than the ninetieth day after the date of submission of such standards, notify the State and specify the changes to meet such requirements. If such changes are not adopted by the State within ninety days after the date of notification, the Administrator shall promulgate such standards pursuant to subsection (b) of this section.

(b) (1) The Administrator shall promptly prepare and publish proposed regulations setting forth water quality standards for a State in accordance with the applicable requirements of this Act as in effect immediately prior to the date of enactment of the Federal Water Pollution Control Act Amendments of 1972, if --

(A) the State fails to submit water quality standards within the times prescribed in subsection (a) of this section,

(B) a water quality standard submitted by such State under subsection (a) of this section is determined by the Administrator not to be consistent with the applicable requirements of subsection (a) of this section.

(2) The Administrator shall promulgate any water quality standard published in a proposed regulation not later than one hundred and ninety days after the date he publishes any such proposed standard, unless prior to such promulgation, such State has adopted a water quality standard which the Administrator determines to be in accordance with subsection (a) of this section.

(c) (1) The Governor of a State or the State water pollution control agency of such State shall from time to time (but at least once each three year period beginning with the date of enactment of the Federal Water Pollution Control Act Amendments of 1972) hold public hearings for the purpose of reviewing applicable water quality standards and, as appropriate, modifying and adopting standards. Results of such review shall be made available to the Administrator.

(2) (A) Whenever the State revises or adopts a new standard, such revised or new standard shall be submitted to the Administrator. Such revised or new water quality standard shall consist of the designated uses of the navigable waters involved and the water quality criteria for such waters based upon such uses. Such standards shall be such as to protect the public health or welfare, enhance the quality of water and serve the purposes of this Act. Such standards shall be established taking into consideration their use and value for public water supplies, propagation of fish and

wildlife, recreational purposes, and also taking into consideration their use and value for navigation.

[Sec. 303(c)(2)(A) designated by PL 100-4]

(B) Whenever a State reviews water quality standards pursuant to paragraph (1) of this subsection, or revises or adopts new standards pursuant to this paragraph, such State shall adopt criteria for all toxic pollutants listed pursuant to section 307(a)(1) of this Act for which criteria have been published under section 304(a), the discharge or presence of which in the affected waters could reasonable be expected to interfere with those designated uses adopted by the State, as necessary to support such designated uses. Such criteria shall be specific numerical criteria for such toxic pollutants. Where such numerical criteria are not available, whenever a State reviews water quality standards pursuant to paragraph (1), or revises or adopts new standards pursuant to this paragraph, such State shall adopt criteria based on biological monitoring or assessment methods consistent with information published pursuant to section 304(a)(8). Nothing in this section shall be construed to limit or delay the use of effluent limitations or other permit conditions based on or involving biological monitoring or assessment methods or previously adopted numerical criteria.

[Sec. 303(c)(2)(B) added by PL 100-4]

(3) If the Administrator, within sixty days after the date of submission of the revised or new standard, determines that such standard meets the requirements of this Act, such standard shall thereafter be the water quality standard for the applicable waters of that State. If the Administrator determines that any such revised or new standard is not consistent with the applicable requirements of this Act, he shall not later than the ninetieth day after the date of submission of such standard notify the State and specify the changes to meet such requirements. If such changes are not adopted by the State within ninety days after the date of notification, the Administrator shall promulgate such standard pursuant to paragraph (4) of this subsection.

(4) The Administrator shall promptly prepare and publish proposed regulations setting forth a revised or new water quality standard for the navigable waters involved --

(A) if a revised or new water quality standard submitted by such State under paragraph (3) of this subsection for such waters is determined by the Administrator not to be consistent with the applicable requirements of this Act, or

(B) in any case where the Administrator determines that a revised or new standard is necessary to meet the requirements of this Act. The Administrator shall promulgate any revised or new standard under this paragraph not later than ninety days after he publishes such proposed standards, unless prior to such promulgation, such State has adopted a revised or new water quality standards which the Administrator determines to be in accordance with this Act.

[Section 24 of PL 97-117 provides:

"**Sec. 24. Revised Water Quality Standards**

The review, revision, and adoption or promulgation of revised or new water quality standards pursuant to section 303(c) of the Federal Water Pollution Control Act shall be completed by the date three years after the enactment of the Municipal Wastewater Treatment Construction Grant Amendments of 1981. No grant shall be made under title II of the Federal Water Pollution Control Act after such date until water quality standards are reviewed and revised pursuant to section 303(c), except where the State has in good faith submitted such revised water quality standards and the Administrator has not acted to approve or disapprove such submission within one hundred and twenty days of receipt."]

[Section 404(c) of PL 100-4 provides:

"(c) Study. -- The Administrator shall study --

(1) the extent to which States have reviewed, revised, and adopted water quality standards in accordance with section 24 of the Municipal Wastewater Treatment Construction Grant Amendments of 1981; and

(2) the extent to which modifications of permits issued under section 402(a)(1)(B) of the Federal Water Pollution Control Act for the purpose of reflecting any revisions to water quality standards should be encouraged or discouraged. The Administrator shall submit a report on such study, together with recommendations, to Congress not later than 2 years after the date of the enactment of this Act."]

(d) (1) (A) Each State shall identify those waters within its boundaries for which the effluent limitations required by section 301(b)(1)(A) and section 301(b)(1)(B) are not stringent enough to implement any water quality standard applicable to such waters. The State shall establish a priority ranking for such waters. The State shall establish a priority ranking for such waters, taking into account the severity of the pollution and the uses to be made of such waters.

(B) Each State shall identify those waters or parts thereof within its boundaries for which controls on thermal discharges under section 301 are not stringent enough to assure protection and propagation of a balanced indigenous population of shellfish, fish, and wildlife.

(C) Each State shall establish for the waters identified in paragraph (1)(A) of this subsection, and in accordance with the priority ranking, the total maximum daily load, for those pollutants which the Administrator identifies under

section 304(a)(2) as suitable for such calculation. Such
load shall be established at a level necessary to implement
the applicable water quality standards with seasonal
variations and a margin of safety which takes into account
any lack of knowledge concerning the relationship between
effluent limitations and water quality.

(D) Each State shall estimate for the waters identified in
paragraph (1)(D) of this subsection the total maximum daily
thermal load required to assure protection and propagation
of a balanced, indigenous population of shellfish, fish and
wildlife. Such estimates shall take into account the normal
water temperatures, flow rates, seasonal variations,
existing sources of heat input, and the dissipative capacity
of the identified waters or parts thereof. Such estimates
shall include a calculation of the maximum heat input that
can be made into each such part and shall include a margin
of safety which takes into account any lack of knowledge
concerning the development of thermal water quality criteria
for such protection and propagation in the identified waters
or parts thereof.

(2) Each State shall submit to the Administrator from time to
time, with the first such submission not later than one hundred
and eighty days after the date of publication of the first
identification of pollutants under section 304(a)(2)(D), for his
approval the waters identified and the loads established under
paragraphs (1)(A), (1)(B), (1)(C), and (1)(D) of this
subsection. The Administrator shall either approve or
disapprove such identification and load not later than thirty
days after the date of submission. If the Administrator
approves such identification and load, such State shall
incorporate them into its current plan under subsection (e) of
this section. If the Administrator disapproves such
identification and load, he shall not later than thirty days
after the date of such disapproval identify such waters in such
State and establish such loads for such waters as he determines
necessary to implement the water quality standards applicable to
such waters and upon such identification and establishment the
State shall incorporate them into its current plan under
subsection (e) of this section.

(3) For the specific purpose of developing information, each
State shall identify all waters within its boundaries which it
has not identified under paragraph (1)(A) and (1)(B) of this
subsection and estimate for such waters the total maximum daily
load with seasonal variations and margins of safety, for those
pollutants which the Administrator identifies under section
304(a)(2) as suitable for such calculation and for thermal
discharges, at a level that would assure protection and
propagation of a balanced indigenous population of fish,
shellfish and wildlife.

(4) Limitations on Revision of Certain Effluent Limitations. --

[Sec. 303(d)(4) added by PL 100-4]

(A) Standard Not Attained. -- For waters identified under paragraph (1)(A) where the applicable water quality standard has not yet been attained, any effluent limitation based on a total maximum daily load or other waste load allocation established under this section may be revised only if (i) the cumulative effect of all such revised effluent limitations based on such total maximum daily load or waste load allocation will assure the attainment of such water quality standard, or (ii) the designated use which is not being attained is removed in accordance with regulations established under this section.

(B) Standard Attained. -- For waters identified under paragraph (1)(A) where the quality of such waters equals or exceeds levels necessary to protect the designated use for such waters or otherwise required by applicable water quality standards, any effluent limitation based on a total maximum daily load or other waste load allocation established under this section, or any water quality standard established under this section, or any other permitting standard may be revised only if such revision is subject to and consistent with the antidegradation policy established under this section.

(e) (1) Each State shall have a continuing planning process approved under paragraph (2) of this subsection which is consistent with this Act.

(2) Each State shall submit not later than 120 days after the date of the enactment of the Water Pollution Control Amendments of 1972 to the Administrator for his approval a proposed continuing planning process which is consistent with this Act. Not later than thirty days after the date of submission of such a process the Administrator shall either approve or disapprove such process. The Administrator shall from time to time review each State's approved planning process for the purpose of insuring that such planning process is at all times consistent with this Act. The Administrator shall not approve any State permit program under title IV of this Act for any State which does not have an approved continuing process under this section.

(3) The Administrator shall approve any continuing planning process submitted to him under this section which will result in plans for all navigable waters within such State, which include, but are not limited to, the following:

(A) effluent limitations and schedules of compliance at least as stringent as those required by section 301(b)(1), section 301(b)(2), section 306, and section 307, and at least as stringent as any requirements contained in any applicable water quality standard in effect under authority of this section;

(B) the incorporation of all elements of any applicable areawide waste management plans under section 208, and applicable basin plans under section 209 of this Act;

(C) total maximum daily load for pollutants in accordance with subsection (d) of this section;

(D) procedures for revision;

(E) adequate authority for intergovernmental cooperation;

(F) adequate implementation, including schedules of compliance, for revised or new water quality standards, under subsection (c) of this section;

(G) controls over the disposition of all residual waste from any water treatment processing; (H) an inventory and ranking, in order of priority, of needs for construction of waste treatment works required to meet the applicable requirements of sections 301 and 302.

(f) Nothing in this section shall be construed to affect any effluent limitation, or schedule of compliance required by any State to be implemented prior to the dates set forth in sections 301(b)(1) and 301(b)(2) nor to preclude any State from requiring compliance with any effluent limitation of schedule of compliance at dates earlier than such dates.

(g) Water quality standards relating to heat shall be consistent with the requirements of section 316 of this Act.

(h) For the purposes of this Act the term "water quality standards" includes thermal water quality standards.

Sec. 304. Information and Guidelines.

(a) (1) The Administrator, after consultation with appropriate Federal and State agencies and other interested persons, shall develop and publish, within one year after the date of enactment of this title (and from time to time thereafter revise) criteria for water quality accurately reflecting the latest scientific knowledge (A) on the kind and extent of all identifiable effects on health and welfare including, but not limited to, plankton, fish, shellfish, wildlife, plant life, shorelines, beaches, esthetics, and recreation which may be expected from the presence of pollutants in any body of water, including ground water; (B) on the concentration and dispersal of pollutants, or their byproducts, through biological, physical, and chemical processes; and (C) on the effects of pollutants on biological community diversity, productivity, and stability, including information on the factors affecting rates of eutrophication and rates of organic and inorganic sedimentation for varying types of receiving waters.

(2) The Administrator, after consultation with appropriate Federal and State agencies and other interested persons, shall develop and publish, within one year after the date of enactment of this title (and from time to time thereafter revise information (A) on the factors necessary to restore and maintain the chemical, physical, and biological integrity of all navigable waters, ground waters, waters of the contiguous zone,

and the oceans; (B) on the factors necessary for the protection and propagation of shellfish, fish, and wildlife for classes and categories of receiving waters and to allow recreational activities in and on the water; and (C) on the measurement and classification of water quality; and (D) for the purpose of section 303, on and the identification of pollutants suitable for maximum daily load measurement correlated with the achievement of water quality objectives.

(3) Such criteria and information and revisions thereof shall be issued to the States and shall be published in the Federal Register and otherwise made available to the public.

(4) The Administrator shall, within 90 days after the date of enactment of the Clean Water Act of 1977 and from time to time thereafter, publish and revise as appropriate information identifying conventional pollutants, including but not limited to, pollutants classified as biological oxygen demanding, suspended solids, fecal coliform, and pH. The thermal component of any discharge shall not be identified as a conventional pollutant under this paragraph.

(5) (A) The Administrator, to the extent practicable before consideration of any request under section 301(g) of this Act and within six months after the date of enactment of the Clean Water Act of 1977, shall develop and publish information on the factors necessary for the protection of public water supplies, and the protection and propagation of a balanced population of shellfish, fish and wildlife, and to allow recreational activities, in and on the water.

(B) The Administrator, to the extent practicable before consideration of any application under section 301(h) of this Act and within six months after the date of enactment of the Clean Water Act of 1977, shall develop and publish information on the factors necessary for the protection of public water supplies, and the protection and propagation of a balanced indigenous population of shellfish, fish and wildlife, and to allow recreational activities, in and on the water.

(6) The Administrator shall, within three months after enactment of the Clean Water Act of 1977 and annually thereafter, for purposes of section 301(h) of this Act publish and revise as appropriate information identifying each water quality standard in effect under this Act of State law, the specific pollutants associated with such water quality standard, and the particular waters to which such water quality standard applies.

(7) Guidance to States. -- The Administrator, after consultation with appropriate State agencies and on the basis of criteria and information published under paragraphs (1) and (2) of this subsection, shall develop and publish, within 9 months after the date of the enactment of the Water Quality Act of 1987, guidance to the States on performing the identification required by section 304(1)(1) of this Act.

[Sec. 304(a)(7) added by PL 100-4]

(8) Information on Water Quality Criteria. -- The Administrator, after consultation with appropriate State agencies and within 2 years after the date of the enactment of the Water Quality Act of 1987, shall develop and publish information on methods for establishing and measuring water quality criteria for toxic pollutants on other bases than pollutant-by-pollutant criteria, including biological monitoring and assessment methods.

[Sec. 304(a)(8) added by PL 100-4]

(b) For the purpose of adopting or revising effluent limitations under this Act the Administrator shall, after consultation with appropriate Federal and State agencies and other appropriate Federal and State agencies and other interested persons, publish within one year of enactment of this title, regulations, providing guidelines for effluent limitations, and, at least annually thereafter, revise, if appropriate, such regulations. Such regulations shall --

(1) (A) identify, in terms of amounts of constituents and chemical, physical, and biological characteristics of pollutants, the degree of effluent reduction attainable through the application of the best practicable control technology currently available for classes and categories of point sources (other than publicly owned treatment works); and

(B) specify factors to be taken into account in determining the control measures and practices to be applicable to point sources (other than publicly owned treatment works) within such categories or classes. Factors relating to the assessment of best practicable control technology currently available to comply with subsection (b)(1) of section 301 of this Act shall include consideration of the total cost of application of technology in relation to the effluent reduction benefits to be achieved from such application, and shall also take into account the age of equipment and facilities involved, the process employed, the engineering aspects of the application of various types of control techniques, process changes, non-water quality environmental impact (including energy requirements), and such other factors as the Administrator deems appropriate;

(2) (A) identify, in terms of amounts of constituents and chemical, physical, and biological characteristics of pollutants, the degree of effluent reduction attainable through the application of the best control measures and practices achievable including treatment techniques, process and procedure innovations, operating methods, and other alternatives for classes and categories of point sources (other than publicly owned treatment works); and

(B) specify factors to be taken into account in determining the best measures and practices available to comply with subsection (b)(2) of section 301 of this Act to be applicable to any point source (other than publicly owned treatment works) within such categories of classes. Factors relating to the assessment of best available technology shall take into account the age of equipment and facilities involved, the process employed, the engineering aspects of the application of various types of control techniques, process changes, the cost of achieving such effluent reduction, non-water quality environmental impact (including energy requirements), and such other factors as the Administrator deems appropriate;

(3) identify control measures and practices available to eliminate the discharge of pollutants from categories and classes of point sources, taking into account the cost of achieving such elimination of the discharge of pollutants; and

(4) (A) identify, in terms of amounts of constituents and chemical, physical, and biological characteristics of pollutants, the degree of effluent reduction attainable through the application of the best conventional pollutant control technology (including measures and practices) for classes and categories of point sources (other than publicly owned treatment works); and

(B) specify factors to be taken into account in determining the best conventional pollutant control technology measures and practices to comply with section 301(b)(2)(E) of this Act to be applicable to any point source (other than publicly owned treatment works) within such categories or classes. Factors relating to the assessment of best conventional pollutant control technology (including measures and practices) shall include consideration of the reasonableness of the relationship between the costs of attaining a reduction in effluents and the effluent reduction benefits derived, and the comparison of the cost and level of reduction of such pollutants from the discharge from publicly owned treatment works to the cost and level of reduction of such pollutants from a class or category of industrial sources, and shall take into account the age of equipment and facilities involved, the process employed, the engineering aspects of the application of various types of control techniques, process changes, non-water quality environmental impact (including energy requirements), and such other factors as the Administrator deems appropriate.

(c) The Administrator, after consultation, with appropriate Federal and State agencies and other interested persons, shall issue to the States and appropriate water pollution control agencies within 270 days after enactment of this title (and from time to time thereafter) information on the processes, procedures, or operating methods which result in the elimination or reduction of the discharge of pollutants to implement standards of performance under section 306 of this Act. Such information shall include technical and other data, including costs, as are available on alternative methods of elimination or reduction of the discharge of pollutants. Such information, and revisions thereof, shall be published in the

Federal Register and otherwise shall be made available to the public.

(d) (1) The Administrator, after consultation with appropriate Federal and State agencies and other interested persons, shall publish within sixty days after enactment of this title (and from time to time thereafter) information, in terms of amounts of constituents and chemical, physical, and biological characteristics of pollutants, on the degree of effluent reduction attainable through the application of secondary treatment.

(2) The Administrator, after consultation with appropriate Federal and State agencies and other interested persons, shall publish within nine months after the date of enactment of this title (and from time to time thereafter) information on alternative waste treatment management techniques and systems available to implement section 201 of this Act.

(3) The Administrator, after consultation with appropriate Federal and State agencies and other interested persons, shall promulgate within one hundred and eighty days after the date of enactment of this subsection guidelines for identifying and evaluating innovative and alternative wastewater treatment processes and techniques referred to in section 201(g)(5) of this Act.

(4) For the purposes of this subsection, such biological treatment facilities as oxidation ponds, lagoons, and ditches and trickling filters shall be deemed the equivalent of secondary treatment. The Administrator shall provide guidance under paragraph (1) of this subsection on design criteria for such facilities, taking into account pollutant removal efficiencies and, consistent with the objective of the Act, assuring that water quality will not be adversely affected by deeming such facilities as the equivalent of secondary treatment.

[Sec. 304(d)(4) added by PL 97-117]

(e) The Administrator, after consultation with appropriate Federal and State agencies and other interested persons, may publish regulations, supplemental to any effluent limitations specified under subsections (b) and (c) of this section for a class or category of point sources, for any specific pollutant which the Administrator is charged with a duty to regulate as a toxic or hazardous pollutant under section 307(a)(1) or 311 of this Act, to control plant site runoff, spillage or leaks, sludge or waste disposal, and drainage from raw material storage which the Administrator determines are associated with or ancillary to the industrial manufacturing or treatment process within such class or category of point sources and may contribute significant amounts of such pollutants to navigable waters. Any applicable controls established under this subsection shall be included as a requirement for the purposes of section 301, 302, 306, 307, or 403, as the case may be, in any permit issued to a point source pursuant to section 402 of this Act.

(f) The Administrator, after consultation with appropriate Federal and State agencies and other interest persons, shall issue to appropriate Federal agencies, the States, water pollution control agencies, and agencies designated under section 208 of this Act, within one year after the effective date of this subsection (and from time to time thereafter) information including

(1) guidelines for identifying and evaluating the nature and extent of nonpoint sources of pollutants, and

(2) processes, procedures, and methods to control pollution resulting from --

(A) agricultural and silvicultural activities, including runoff from fields and crop and forest lands;

(B) mining activities, including runoff and siltation from new, currently operating, and abandoned surface and underground mines;

(C) all construction activity, including runoff from the facilities resulting from such construction;

(D) the disposal of pollutants in wells or in subsurface excavations;

(E) salt water intrusion resulting from reductions of fresh water flow from any cause, including extraction of ground water, irrigation, obstruction, and diversion; and

(F) changes in the movement, flow, or circulation of any navigable waters or ground waters, including changes caused by the construction of dams, levees, channels, causeways, or flow diversion facilities.

Such information and revisions thereof shall be published in the Federal Register and otherwise made available to the public.

(g) (1) For the purpose of assisting States in carrying out programs under section 402 of this Act, the Administrator shall publish, within one hundred and twenty days after the date of enactment of this title, and review at least annually thereafter and, if appropriate, revise guidelines for pretreatment of pollutants which he determines are not susceptible to treatment by publicly owned treatment works. Guidelines under this subsection shall be established to control and prevent the discharge into the navigable waters, the contiguous zone, or the ocean (either directly or through publicly owned treatment works) of any pollutant which interferes with, passes through, or otherwise is incompatible with such works.

(2) When publishing guidelines under this subsection, the Administrator shall designate the category or categories of treatment works to which the guidelines shall apply.

(h) The Administrator shall, within one hundred and eighty days from the date of enactment of this title, promulgate guidelines establishing test procedures for the analysis of pollutants that shall include the factors which must be provided in any certification pursuant to section 401 of this Act or permit application pursuant to section 402 of this Act.

[Section 518 of PL 100-4 provides:

"Sec. 518. **Study of Testing Procedures**.

(a) Study. -- The Administrator shall study the testing procedures for analysis of pollutants established under section 304(h) of the Federal Water Pollution Control Act. Such study shall include, but not be limited to, an analysis of the adequacy and standardization of such procedures. In conducting the analysis of the standardization of such procedures, the Administrator shall consider the extent to which such procedures are consistent with comparable procedures established under other Federal laws.

(b) Report. -- Not later than 1 year after the date of the enactment of this Act, the Administrator shall submit a report on the results of the study conducted under this subsection, together with recommendations for modifying the test procedures referred to in subsection (a) to improve their effectiveness, to the Committee on Public Works and Transportation of the House of Representatives and the Committee on Environment and Public Works of the Senate."]

[See also the provisions of Section 519 of PL 100-4 published at the end of this Act.]

(i) The Administrator shall

(1) within sixty days after the enactment of this title promulgate guidelines for the purpose of establishing uniform application forms and other minimum requirements for the acquisition of information from owners and operators of point-sources of discharge subject to any State program under section 402 of this Act, and

(2) within sixty days from the date of enactment of this title promulgate guidelines establishing the minimum procedural and other elements of any State program under section 402 of this Act which shall include:

(A) monitoring requirements;

(B) reporting requirements (including procedures to make information available to the public);

(C) enforcement provisions; and

(D) funding, personnel qualifications, and manpower requirements (including a requirement that no board or body which approves permit applications or portions thereof shall include, as a member, any person who receives, or has during the previous two years received, a significant portion of his income directly or indirectly from permit holders or applicants for a permit).

(j) Lake Restoration Guidance Manual -- The Administrator shall, within 1 year after the date of the enactment of the Water Quality Act of 1987 and biennially thereafter, publish and disseminate a lake restoration guidance manual describing methods, procedures, and processes to guide State and local efforts to improve, restore, and enhance water quality in the Nation's publicly owned lakes.

[304(j) revised by PL 100-4]

(k) (1) The Administrator shall enter into agreements with the Secretary of Agriculture, the Secretary of the Army, and the Secretary of the Interior, and the heads of such other departments, agencies, and instrumentalities of the United States as the Administrator determines, to provide for the maximum utilization of other Federal laws and programs for the purpose of achieving and maintaining water quality through appropriate implementation of plans approved under section 208 of this Act and nonpoint source pollution management programs approved under section 319 of this Act.

[Sec. 304(k)(1) amended by PL 100-4]

(2) The Administrator is authorized to transfer to the Secretary of Agriculture, the Secretary of the Army, and the Secretary of the Interior and the heads of such other departments, agencies, and instrumentalities of the United States as the Administrator determines, any funds appropriated under paragraph (3) of this subsection to supplement funds otherwise appropriated to programs authorized pursuant to any agreement under paragraph (1).

(3) There is authorized to be appropriated to carry out the provisions of this subsection, $100,000,000 per fiscal year for the fiscal years 1979 through 1983 and such sums as may be necessary for fiscal years 1984 through 1990.

[Sec. 304(k)(3) amended by PL 100-4]

(l) Individual Control Strategies for Toxic Pollutants. --

[Sec. 304(l) added by PL 100-4]

(1) State List of Navigable Waters and Development of Strategies. -- Not later than 2 years after the date of the enactment of this subsection, each State shall submit to the Administrator for review, approval, and implementation under this subsection --

(A) a list of those waters within the State which after the application of effluent limitations required under section 301(b)(2) of this Act cannot reasonably be anticipated to attain or maintain (i) water quality standards for such waters reviewed, revised, or adopted in accordance with section 303(c)(2)(B) of this Act, due to toxic pollutants, or (ii) that water quality which shall assure protection of public health, public water supplies, agricultural and industrial uses, and the protection and propagation of a balanced population of shellfish, fish and wildlife, and allow recreational activities in and on the water;

(B) a list of all navigable waters in such State for which the State does not expect the applicable standard under section 303 of this Act will be achieved after the requirements of sections 301(b), 306, and 307(b) are met, due entirely or substantially to discharges from point sources of any toxic pollutants listed pursuant to section 307(a);

(C) for each segment of the navigable waters included on such lists, a determination of the specific point sources discharging any such toxic pollutant which is believed to be preventing or impairing such water quality and the amount of each such toxic pollutant discharged by each such source; and

(D) for each such segment, an individual control strategy which the State determines will produce a reduction in the discharge of toxic pollutants from point sources identified by the State under this paragraph through the establishment of effluent limitations under section 402 of this Act and water quality standards under section 303(c)(2)(B) of this Act, which reduction is sufficient, in combination with existing controls on point and nonpoint sources of pollution, to achieve the applicable water quality standard as soon as possible, but not later than 3 years after the date of the establishment of such strategy.

(2) Approval or Disapproval. -- Not later than 120 days after the last day of the 2-year period referred to in paragraph (1), the Administrator shall approve or disapprove the control strategies submitted under paragraph (1) by any State.

(3) Administrator's Action. -- If a State fails to submit control strategies in accordance with paragraph (1) or the Administrator does not approve the control strategies submitted by such State in accordance with paragraph (1), then, not later than 1 year after the last day of the period referred to in paragraph (2), the Administrator, in cooperation with such State and after notice and opportunity for public comment, shall implement the requirements of paragraph (1) in such State. In the implementation of such requirements, the Administrator shall, at a minimum, consider for listing under this subsection any navigable waters for which any person submits a petition to the Administrator for listing not later than 120 days after such last day.

[Section 308(g) of PL 100-4 requires:

"(g) Water Quality Improvement Study. --

(1) Study. -- The Administrator shall study the water quality improvements which have been achieved by application of best available technology economically achievable pursuant to section 301(b)(2) of the Federal Water Pollution Control Act. Such

study shall include, but not be limited to, an analysis of the effectiveness of the application of best available technology economically achievable pursuant to such section in attaining applicable water quality standards (including the standard specified in section 302(a) of such Act) and an analysis of the effectiveness of the water quality program under such Act and methods of improving such program, including site specific levels of treatment which will achieve the water quality goals of such Act.

(2) Report. -- Not later than 2 years after the date of the enactment of this Act, the Administrator shall submit a report on the results of the study conduct under subsection (a) together with recommendations for improving the water quality program and its effectiveness to the Committee on Public Works and Transportation of the House of Representatives and the Committee on Environment and Public Works of the Senate."]

(m) Schedule for Review of Guidelines. --

[Sec. 304(m) added by PL 100-4]

(1) Publication. -- Within 12 months after the date of the enactment of the Water Quality Act of 1987, and biennially thereafter, the Administrator shall publish in the Federal Register a plan which shall --

(A) establish a schedule for the annual review and revision of promulgated effluent guidelines, in accordance with subsection (b) of this section;

(B) identify categories of sources discharging toxic or nonconventional pollutants for which guidelines under subsection (b)(2) of this section and section 306 have not previously been published; and

(C) establish a schedule for promulgation of effluent guidelines for categories identified in subparagraph (B), under which promulgation of such guidelines shall be no later than 4 years after such date of enactment for categories identified in the first published plan or 3 years after the publication of the plan for categories identified in later published plans.

(2) Public Review. -- The Administrator shall provide for public review and comment on the plan prior to final publication.

Sec. 305. Water Quality Inventory

(a) The Administrator, in cooperation with the States and with the assistance of appropriate Federal agencies shall prepare a report to be submitted to the Congress on or before January 1, 1974, which shall --

(1) describe the specific quality, during 1973, with appropriate supplemental descriptions as shall be required to take into

account seasonal, tidal, and other variations, of all navigable waters and the waters of the contiguous zone;

(2) include an inventory of all point sources of discharge (based on a qualitative and quantitative analysis of discharges) of pollutants, into all navigable waters and the waters of the contiguous zone; and

(3) identify specifically those navigable waters, the quality of which --

(A) is adequate to provide for the protection and propagation of a balanced population of shellfish, fish, and wildlife and allow recreational activities in and on the water;

(B) can reasonably be expected to attain such level by 1977 or 1983; and

(C) can reasonably be expected to attain such level by any later date.

(b) (1) Each State shall prepare and submit to the Administrator by April 1, 1975, and shall bring up to date by April 1, 1976, and biennially thereafter, a report which shall include --

(A) a description of the water quality of all navigable waters in such State during the preceding year, with appropriate supplemental descriptions as shall be required to take into account seasonal, tidal, and other variations, correlated with the quality of water required by the objective of this Act (as identified by the Administrator pursuant to criteria published under section 304(a) of this Act) and the water quality described in subparagraph (B) of this paragraph;

(B) an analysis of the extent to which all navigable waters of such State provide for the protection and propagation of a balanced population of shellfish, fish, and wildlife, and allow recreational activities in and on the water;

(C) an analysis of the extent to which the elimination of the discharge of pollutants and a level of water quality which provides for the protection and propagation of a balanced population of shellfish, fish, and wildlife and allows recreational activities in and on the water, have been or will be achieved by the requirements of this Act, together with recommendations as to additional action necessary to achieve such objectives and for what waters such additional action is necessary;

(D) an estimate of (i) the environmental impact, (ii) the economic and social costs necessary to achieve the objective of this Act in such State, (iii) the economic and social benefits of such achievement, and (iv) an estimate of the date of such achievement; and

(E) a description of the nature and extent of nonpoint sources of pollutants, and recommendations as to the programs which must be undertaken to control each category of such sources, including an estimate of the costs of implementing such programs.

(2) The Administrator shall transmit such State reports, together with an analysis thereof, to Congress on or before October 1, 1975, and October 1, 1976, and biennially thereafter.

Sec. 306. National Standards of Performance

(a) For purposes of this section:

(1) The term "standard of performance" means a standard for the control of the discharge of pollutants which reflects the greatest degree of effluent reduction which the Administrator determines to be achievable through application of the best available demonstrated control technology, processes, operating methods, or other alternatives, including, where practicable, a standard permitting no discharge of pollutants.

(2) The term "new source" means any source, the construction of which is commenced after the publication of proposed regulations prescribing a standard of performance under this section which will be applicable to such source, if such standard is thereafter promulgated in accordance with this section.

(3) The term "source" means any building, structure, facility, or installation from which there is or may be the discharge of pollutants.

(4) The term "owner or operator" means any person who owns, leases, operates, controls, or supervises a source.

(5) The term "construction" means any placement, assembly, or installation of facilities or equipment) at the premises where such equipment will be used, including preparation work at such premises.

(b) (1) (A) The Administrator shall, within ninety days after the date of enactment of this title publish (and from time to time thereafter shall revise) a list of categories of sources, which shall, at the minimum, include:

> pulp and paper mills;
> paper board, builders paper and board mills;
> meat product and rendering processing;
> dairy product processing;
> grain mills;
> canned and preserved fruits and vegetable
>   processing;
> canned and preserved seafood processing;
> sugar processing;
> textile mills;
> cement manufacturing;
> feedlots;

electroplating;
organic chemicals manufacturing;
inorganic chemicals manufacturing;
plastic and synthetic materials manufacturing;
soap and detergent manufacturing;
fertilizer manufacturing;
petroleum refining;
iron and steel manufacturing;
nonferrous metals manufacturing;
phosphate manufacturing;
steam electric powerplants;
ferroalloy manufacturing;
leather tanning and finishing;
glass and asbestos manufacturing;
rubber processing; and
timber products processing.

(B) As soon as practicable, but in no case more than one year, after a category of sources is included in a list under subparagraph (A) of this paragraph, the Administrator shall propose and publish regulations establishing Federal standards of performance for new sources within such category. The Administrator shall afford interested persons an opportunity for written comment on such proposed regulations. (After considering such comments, he shall promulgate, within one hundred and twenty days after publication of such proposed regulations, such standards with such adjustments as he deems appropriate. The Administrator shall, from time to time, as technology and alternatives change, revise such standards following the procedure required by this subsection for promulgation of such standards. Standards of performance, or revisions thereof, shall become effective upon promulgation. In establishing or revising Federal standards of performance for new sources under this section, the Adminstrator shall take into consideration the cost of achieving such effluent reduction, and any non-water quality environmental impact and energy requirements.

(2) The Administrator may distinguish among classes, types, and sizes within categories of new sources for the purpose of establishing such standards and shall consider the type of process employed (including whether batch or continuous).

(3) The provisions of this section shall apply to any new source owned or operated by the United States.

(c) Each State may develop and submit to the Administrator a procedure under State law for applying and enforcing standards of performance for new sources located in such State. If the Administrator finds that the procedure and the law of any State require the application and enforcement of standards of performance to at least the same extent as required by this section, such State is authorized to apply and enforce such standards of performance (except with respect to new sources owned or operated by the United States).

(d) Notwithstanding any other provision of this Act, any point source the construction of which is commenced after the date of enactment of the Federal Water Pollution Control Act Amendments of 1972 and which is so constructed as to meet all applicable standards of performance shall not be subject to any more stringent standard of performance during a ten-year period beginning on the date of completion of such construction or during the period of depreciation or amortization of such facility for the purposes of section 167 or 169 (or both) of the Internal Revenue Code of 1954, whichever period ends first.

(e) After the effective date of standards of performance promulgated under this section, it shall be unlawful for any owner or operator of any new source to operate such source in violation of any standard of performance applicable to such source.

Sec. 307.   **Toxic and Pretreatment Effluent Standards.**

(a) (1) On and after the date of enactment of the Clean Water Act of 1977, the list of toxic pollutants or combination of pollutants subject to this Act shall consist of those toxic pollutants listed in table 1 of Committee Print Numbered 95-30 of the Committee on Public Works and Transporation of the House of Representatives, and the Administrator shall publish, not later than the thirtieth day after date of enactment of the Clean Water Act of 1977, that list. From time to time thereafter, the Administrator may revise such list and the Administrator is authorized to add to or remove from such list any pollutant. The Administrator in publishing any revised list, including the addition or removal of any pollutant from such list, shall take into account the toxicity of the pollutant, its persistence, degradability, the usual or potential presence of the affected organisms in any waters, the importance of the affected organisms, and the nature and extent of the effect of the organisms, and the nature and extent of the effect of the toxic pollutant on such organisms. A determination of the Administrator under this paragraph shall be final except that if, on judicial review, such determination was based on arbitrary and capricious action of the Administrator, the Administrator shall make a redetermination.

[Table 1 is published at the end of the Act. See also Section 301(b)(2)(C) editor's note and the provisions of Section 519 of PL 100-4 published at the end of this Act.]

(2) Each toxic pollutant listed in accordance with paragraph (1) of this subsection shall be subject to effluent limitations resulting from the application of the best available technology economically achievable for the applicable category or class of point sources established in accordance with section 301(b)(2)(A) and 304(b)(2) of this Act. The Administrator, in his discretion, may publish in the Federal Register a proposed effluent standard (which may include a prohibition) establishing requirements for a toxic pollutant which, if an effluent limitation is applicabble to a class or category of point sources, shall be applicable to such category or class only if such standard imposes more stringent requirements. Such

published effluent standard (or prohibition) shall take into account the toxicity of the pollutant, its persistence, degradability, the usual or potential presence of the affected organisms in any waters, the importance of the affected organisms and the nature and extent of the effect of the toxic pollutant on such organisms, and the extent to which effective control is being or may be achieved under other regulatory authority. The Administrator shall allow a period of not less than sixty days following publication of any such proposed effluent standard (or prohibition) for written comment by interested persons on such proposed standard. In addition, if within thirty days of publication of any such proposed effluent standard (or prohibition) any interested person so requests, the Administrator shall hold a public hearing in connection therewith. Such a public hearing shall provide an opportunity for oral and written presentations, such cross-examination as the Administrator determines is appropriate on disputed issues of material fact, and the transcription of a verbatim record which shall be available to the public. After consideration of such comments and any information and material presented at any public hearing held on such proposed standard or prohibition, the Administrator shall promulgate such standards (or prohibition). Such standard (or prohibition) shall be final except that if, on judicial review, such standard was not based on substantial evidence, the Administrator shall promulgate a revised standard. Effluent limitations shall be established in accordance with sections 301(b)(2)(A) and 304(b)(2) for every toxic pollutant referred to in Table 1 of Committee on Public Works and Transportation of the House of Representatives as soon as practicable after the date of enactment of the Clean Water Act of 1977, but no later than July 1, 1980. Such effluent limitations or effluent standards (or prohibitions) shall be established for every other toxic pollutant listed under paragraph (1) of this subsection as soon as practicable after it is so listed.

(3) Each such effluent standard (or prohibition) shall be reviewed and, if appropriate, revised at least every three years.

(4) Any effluent standard promulgated under this seciton shall be at that level which the Administrator determines provides an ample margin of safety.

(5) When proposing or promulgating any effluent standard (or prohibition) under this section, the Administrator shall designate the category or categories of sources to which the effluent standard (or prohibition) shall apply. Any disposal of dredged material may be included in such a category of sources after consultation with the Secretary of the Army.

(6) Any effluent standard (or prohibition) established pursuant to this section shall take effect on such date or dates as specified in the order promulgating such standard, but in no case, more than one year from the date of such promulgation. If the Administrator determines that compliance within one year from the date of promulgation is technologically infeasible for

a category of sources, the Administrator may establish the effective date of the effluent standard (or prohibition) for such category at the earliest date upon which compliance can be feasibly attained by sources within such category, but in no event more than three years after the date of such promulgation.

(7) Prior to publishing any regulations pursuant to this section the Administrator shall, to the maximum extent practicable within the time provided, consult with appropriate advisory committees, States, independent experts, and Federal departments and agencies.

(b) (1) The Administrator shall, within one hundred and eighty days after the date of enactment of this title and from time to time thereafter, publish proposed regulations establishing pretreatment standards for introduction of pollutants into treatment works (as defined in section 212 of this Act) which are publicly owned for those pollutants which are determined not to be susceptible to treatment by such treatment works or which would interfere with the operation of such treatment works. Not later than ninety days after such publication, and after opportunity for public hearing, the Administrator shall promulgate such pretreatment standards. Pretreatment standards under this subsection shall specify a time for compliance not to exceed three years from the date of promulgation and shall be established to prevent the discharge of any pollutant through treatment works (as defined in section 212 of this Act) which are publicly owned, which pollutant interferes with, passes through, or otherwise is incompatible with such works. If, in the case of any toxic pollutant under subsection (a) of this section introduced by a source into a publicly owned treatment works, the treatment by such works removes all or any part of such toxic pollutant and the discharge from such works does not violate that effluent limitation or standard which would be applicable to such toxic pollutant if it were discharged by such source other than through a publicly owned treatment works, and does not prevent sludge use or disposal by such works in accordance with section 405 of this Act, then the pretreatment requirements for the sources actually discharging such toxic pollutant into such publicly owned treatment works may be revised by the owner or operator of such works to reflect the removal of such toxic pollutant by such works.

(2) The Administrator shall, from time to time, as control technology, processes, operating methods, or other alternative change, revise such standards following the procedure established by this subsection for promulgation of such standards.

(3) When proposing or promulgating any pretreatment standard under this section, the Administrator shall designate the category or categories of sources to which such standard shall apply.

(4) Nothing in this subsection shall affect any pretreatment requirement established by any State or local law not in

conflict with any pretreatment standard established under this subsection.

(c) In order to insure that any source introducing pollutants into a publicly owned treatment works, which source would be a new source subject to section 306 if it were to discharge pollutants, will not cause a violation of the effluent limitations established for any such treatment works, the Administrator shall promulgate pretreatment standards for the category of such sources simultaneously with the promulgation of standards of performance under section 306 for the equivalent category of new sources. Such pretreatment standards shall prevent the discharge of any pollutant into such treatment works, which pollutant may interfere with, pass through, or otherwise be incompatible with such works.

(d) After the effective date of any effluent standard or prohibition or pretreatment standard promulgated under this section, it shall be unlawful for any owner or operator of any source to operate any source in violation of any such effluent standard or prohibition or pretreatment standard.

(e) Compliance Date Extension for Innovative Pretreatment Systems. -- In the case of any existing facility that proposes to comply with the pretreatment standards of subsection (b) of this section by applying an innovative system that meets the requirements of section 301(k) of this Act, the owner or operator of the publicly owned treatment works receiving the treated effluent from such facility may extend the date for compliance with the applicable pretreatment standard established under this section for a period not to exceed 2 years --

(1) if the Administrator determines that the innovative system has the potential for industrywide application, and

(2) if the Administrator (or the State in consultation with the Administrator, in any case in which the State has a pretreatment program approved by the Administrator) --

(A) determines that the proposed extension will not cause the publicly owned treatment works to be in violation of its permit under section 402 or of section 405 or to contribute to such a violation, and (B) concurs with the proposed extension.

[307(e) added by PL 100-4]

[Section 309(b) of PL 100-4 provides:

"(b) Increase in EPA Employees. -- The Administrator shall take such actions as may be necessary to increase the number of employees of the Environmental Protection Agency in order to effectively implement pretreatment requirements under section 307 of the Federal Water Pollution Control Act."]

Sec. 308. Inspections, Monitoring and Entry.

(a) Whenever required to carry out the objective of this Act, including but not limited to

(1) developing or assisting in the development of any effluent limitation, or other limitation, prohibition, or effluent standard, pretreatment standard, or standard of performance under this Act;

(2) determining whether any person is in violation of any such effluent limitation, or other limitation, prohibition, or effluent standard, pretreatment standard, or standard of performance;

(3) any requirement established under this section; or (4) carrying out sections 305, 311, 402, 404 (relating to State permit programs), 405, and 504 of this Act -- (Sec. 308(a)(4) amended by PL 100-4)

(A) the Administrator shall require the owner or operator of any point source to (i) establish and maintain such records, (ii) make such reports, (iii) install, use, and maintain such monitoring equipment or methods (including where appropriate, biological monitoring methods), (iv) sample such effluents (in accordance with such methods, at such locations, at such intervals, and in such manner as the Administrator shall prescribe), and (v) provide such other information as he may reasonably require; and

(B) the Administrator or his authorized representative (including an authorized contractor acting as a representative of the Administrator), upon presentation of his credentials -- (i) shall have a right of entry to, upon, or through any premises in which an effluent source is located or in which any records required to be maintained under clause (A) of this subsection are located, and (ii) may at reasonable times have access to and copy any records, inspect any monitoring equipment or method required under clause (A), and sample any effluents which the owner or operator of such source is required to sample under such clause.

[Sec. 308(a)(B) amended by PL 100-4]

(b) Any records, reports, or information obtained under this section (1) shall, in the case of effluent data be related to any applicable effluent limitations, toxic, pretreatment, or new source performance standards, and (2) shall be available to the public, except that upon a showing satisfactory to the Administrator by any person that records, reports, or information, or particular part thereof (other than effluent data), to which the Administrator has access under this section, if made public would divulge methods or processes entitled to protection as trade secrets of such person, the Administrator shall consider such record, report, or information, or particular portion thereof confidential in accordance with the purposes of section 1905 of title 18 of the United States Code. Any authorized representative of the Administrator (including an authorized contractor acting as a representative of the Administrator) who knowingly or willfully publishes, divulges, discloses, or makes known in any manner or to any extent not authorized by law any information which is required to be considered confidential under this subsection shall be fined not more than $1,000 or imprisoned not more than 1 year, or both. Nothing in this subsection shall prohibit the Administrator or an authorized representative of the Administrator (including any authorized contractor acting as a representative of the Administratory) from disclosing records, reports, or information to other officers, employees, or authorized representatives of the United States concerned with carrying out this Act or when relevant in any proceeding under this Act.

[308(b) amended by PL 100-4]

(c) Each State may develop and submit to the Administrator procedures under State law for inspection, monitoring, and entry with respect to point sources located in such State. If the Administrator finds that the procedures and the law of any State relating to inspection, monitoring, and entry are applicable to at least the same extent as those required by this section, such State is authorized to apply and enforce its procedures for inspection, monitoring, and entry with respect to point sources located in such State (except with respect to point sources owned or operated by the United States).

(d) Access by Congress. -- Notwithstanding any limitation contained in this section or any other provision of law, all information reported to or otherwise obtained by the Administrator (or any representative of the Administrator) under this Act shall be made available, upon written request of any duly authorized committee of Congress, to such committee.

[308(d) added by PL 100-4]

Sec. 309. Federal Enforcement.

[See also Section 318 of PL 100-4, published at the end of this Act, for applicability of this Section to the Unconsolidated Quarternary Aquifer-Rockaway River Basin, New Jersey.]

(a) (1) Whenever, on the basis of any information available to him, the Administrator finds that any person is in violation of any condition or limitation which implements section 301, 302, 306, 307, 308, 318, or 405 of this Act in a permit issued by a State under an approved permit program under section 402 or 404 of this Act, he shall proceed under his authority in paragraph (3) of this subsection or he shall notify the person in alleged violation and such State of such finding. If beyond the thirtieth day after the Administrator's notification the State has not commenced appropriate enforcement action, the Administrator shall issue an order requiring such person to comply with such condition or limitation or shall bring a civil action in accordance with subsection (b) of this section.

(2) Whenever, on the basis of information available to him, the Administrator finds that violations of permit conditions or limitations as set forth in paragraph (1) of this subsection are so widespread that such violations appear to result from a failure of the State to enforce such permit conditions or limitations effectively, he shall so notify the State. If the Administrator finds such failure extends beyond the thirtieth day after such notice, he shall give public notice of such finding. During the period beginning with such public notice and ending when such State satisfies the Administrator that it will enforce such conditions and limitations (hereafter referred to in this section as the period of "federally assumed enforcement"), except where an extension has been granted under paragraph (5)(B) of this subsection, the Administrator shall enforce any permit condition or limitation with respect to any person --

(A) by issuing an order to comply with such condition or limitation, or

(B) by bringing a civil action under subsection (b) of this section.

(3) Whenever on the basis of any information available to him the Administrator finds that any person is in violation of section 301, 302, 306, 307, 308, 318, or 405 of this Act, or is in violation of any permit condition or limitation implementing any of such sections in a permit issued under section 404 of this Act by a State, he shall issue an order requiring such person to comply with such section or requirement, or he shall bring a civil action in accordance with subsection (b) of this section.

(4) A copy of any order issued under this subsection shall be sent immediately by the Administrator to the State in which the violation occurs and other affected States. In any case in which an order under this subsection (or notice to a violator under paragraph (1) of this subsection) is issued to a corporation, a copy of such order (or notice) shall be served on any appropriate corporate officers. An order issued under this subsection relating to a violation of section 308 of this Act shall not take effect until the person to whom it is issued has had an opportunity to confer with the Administrator concerning the alleged violation.

(5) (A) Any order issued under this subsection shall be by personal service, shall state with reasonable specifity the nature of the violation, and shall specify a time for compliance not to exceed thirty days in the case of a violation of an interim compliance schedule or operation and maintenance requirement and not to exceed a time the Administrator determines to be reasonable in the case of a violation of a final deadline, taking into account the seriousness of the violation and any good faith efforts to comply with applicable requirements.

(B) The Administrator may, if he determines (i) that any
person who is a violator of, or any person who is otherwise
not in compliance with, the time requirements under this Act
or in any permit issued under this Act, has acted in good
faith, and has made a commitment (in the form of contracts
or other securities) of necessary resources to achieve
compliance by the earliest possible date after July 1, 1977,
but not later than April 1, 1979; (ii) that any extension
under this provision will not result in the imposition of
any additional controls on any other point or nonpoint
source; (iii) that an application for a permit under section
402 of this Act was filed for such person prior to December
31, 1974; and (iv) that the facilities necessary for
compliance with such requirements are under construction,
grant an extension of the date referred to in section
301(b)(1)(A) to a date which will achieve compliance at the
earliest time possible but not later than April 1, 1979.

(6) Whenever, on the basis of information available to him, the
Administrator finds (A) that any person is in violation of
section 301(b)(1)(A) or (C) of this Act, (B) that such person
cannot meet the requirements for a time extension under section
301(i)(2) of this Act, and (C) that the most expeditious and
appropriate means of compliance with this Act by such person is
to discharge into a publicly owned treatment works, then, upon
request of such person, the Administrator may issue an order
requiring such person to comply with this Act at the earliest
date practicable, but not later than July 1, 1983, by
discharging into a publicly owned treatment works if such works
concur with such order. Such order shall include a schedule of
compliance.

(b) The Administrator is authorized to commence a civil action for
appropriate relief, including a permanent or temporary injunction,
for any violation for which he is authorized to issue a compliance
order under subsection (a) of this section. Any action under this
subsection may be brought in the district court of the United States
for the district in which the defendant is located or resides or is
doing business, and such court shall have jurisdiction to restrain
such violation and to require compliance. Notice of the
commencement of such action shall be given immediately to the
appropriate State.

(c) Criminal Penalties. --

[309(c) revised by PL 100-4]

(1) Negligent Violations. -- Any person who --

(A) negligently violates section 301, 302, 306, 307, 308,
318, or 405 of this Act, or any permit condition or
limitation implementing any of such sections in a permit
issued under section 402 of this Act by the Administrator or
by a State, or any requirement imposed in a pretreatment
program approved under section 402(a)(3) or 402(b)(8) of
this Act or in a permit issued under section 404 of this Act
by the Secretary of the Army or by a State; or

(B) negligently introduces into a sewer system or into a publicly owned treatment works any pollutant or hazardous substance which such person knew or reasonably should have known could cause personal injury or property damage or, other than in compliance with all applicable Federal, State, or local requirements or permits, which causes such treatment works to violate any effluent limitation or condition in any permit issued to the treatment works under section 402 of this Act by the Administrator or a State; shall be punished by a fine of not less than $2,500 nor more than $25,000 per day of violation, or by imprisonment for not more than 1 year, or by both. If a conviction of a person is for a violation committed after a first conviction of such person under this paragraph, punishment shall be by a fine of not more than $50,000 per day of violation, or by imprisonment of not more than 2 years, or by both.

(2) Knowing Violations. -- Any person who --

(A) knowingly violates section 301, 302, 306, 307, 308, or 405 of this Act, or any permit condition or limitation implementing any of such sections in a permit issued under section 402 of this Act by the Administrator or by a State, or any requirement imposed in a pretreatment program approved under section 402(a)(3) or 402(b)(8) of this Act or in a permit issued under section 404 of this Act by the Secretary of the Army or by a State; or

(B) knowingly introduces into a sewer system or into a publicly owned treatment works any pollutant or hazardous substance which such person knew or reasonably should have known could cause personal injury or property damage or, other than in compliance with all applicable Federal, State, or local requirements or permits, which causes such treatment work to violate any effluent limitation or condition in a permit issued to the treatment works under section 402 of this Act by the Administrator of a State;

shall be punished by a fine of not less than $5,000 nor more than $50,000 per day of violation, or by imprisonment for not more than 3 years, or by both. If a conviction of a person is for a violation committed after a first conviction of such person under this paragraph, punishment shall be a fine of not more than $100,000 per day of violation, or by imprisonment of not more than 6 years, or by both.

(3) Knowing Endangerment. --

(A) General Rule. -- Any person who knowingly violates section 301, 302, 303, 306, 307, 308, 318, or 405 of this Act, or any permit condition or limitation implementing any of such sections in a permit issued under section 402 of this Act by the Administrator or by a State, or in a permit issued under section 404 of this Act by the Secretary of the Army or by a State, and who knows at that time that he thereby places another person in imminent danger of death or serious bodily injury, shall, upon conviction, be subject to

a fine of not more than $250,000 or imprisonment of not more
than 15 years, or both. A person which is an organization
shall, upon conviction of violating this subparagraph, be
subject to a fine of not more than $1,000,000. If a
conviction of a person is for a violation committed after a
first conviction of such person under this paragraph, the
maximum punishment shall be doubled with respect to both
fine and imprisonment.

(B) Additional Provisions. -- For the purpose of
subparagraph (A) of this paragraph --
    (i) in determining whether a defendant who is an
individual knew that his conduct placed another person
in imminent danger of death or serious bodily injury --
        (I) the person is responsible only for actual
awareness or actual belief that he possessed; and
        (II) knowledge possessed by a person other than the
defendant but not by the defendant himself may not
be attributed to the defendant; except that in
proving the defendant's possession of actual
knowledge, circumstantial evidence may be used,
including evidence that the defendant took
affirmative steps to shield himself from relevant
information;
    (ii) it is an affirmative defense to prosecution that
the conduct charged was consented to by the person
endangered and that the danger and conduct charged were
reasonably foreseeable hazards of --
        (I) an occupation, a business, or a profession; or
        (II) medical treatment or medical or scientific
experimentation conducted by professionally approved
methods and such other person had been made aware of
the risks involved prior to giving consent; and such
defense may be established under this subparagraph
by a preponderance of the evidence;
    (iii) the term "organization" means a legal entity,
other than a government, established or organized for
any purpose, and such term includes a corporation,
company, association, firm, partnership, joint stock
company, foundation, institution, trust, society, union,
or any other association of persons; and
    (iv) the term "serious bodily injury" means bodily
injury which involves a substantial risk of death,
unconsciousness, extreme physical pain, protracted and
obvious disfigurement, or protracted loss or impairment
of the function of a bodily member, organ, or mental
faculty.

(4) False Statements. -- Any person who knowingly makes any
false material statement, representation, or certification in
any application, record, report, plan, or other document filed
or required to be maintained under this Act or who knowingly
falsifies, tampers with, or renders inaccurate any monitoring
device or method required to be maintained under this Act, shall
upon conviction, be punished by a fine of not more than $10,000,
or by imprisonment for not more than 2 years, or by both. If a
conviction of such person is for a violation committed after a

first conviction of such person under this paragraph, punishment shall be by a fine of not more than $20,000 per day of violation, or by imprisonment of not more than 4 years, or by both.

(5) Treatment of Single Operational Upset. -- For purposes of this subsection, a single operational upset which leads to simultaneous violations of more than one pollutant parameter shall be treated as a single violation.

(6) Responsible Corporate Officer as "Person". -- For the purpose of this subsection, the term "person" means, in addition to the definition contained in section 502(5) of this Act, any responsible corporate officer.

(7) Hazardous Substance Defined. -- For the purpose of this subsection, the term "hazardous substance" means (A) any substance designated pursuant to section 311(b)(2)(A) of this Act, (B) any element, compound, mixture, solution, or substance designated pursuant to section 102 of the Comprehensive Environmental Response, Compensation, and Liability Act of 1980, (C) any hazardous waste having the characteristics identified under or listed pursuant to section 3001 of the Solid Waste Disposal Act (but not including any waste the regulation of which under the Solid Waste Disposal Act has been suspended by Act of Congress), (D) any toxic pollutant listed under section 307(a) of this Act, and (E) any imminently hazardous chemical substance or mixture with respect to which the Administrator has taken action pursuant to section 7 of the Toxic Substances Control Act.

(d) Any person who violates section 301, 302, 306, 307, 308, 318, or 405 of this Act, or any permit condition or limitation implementing any of such sections in a permit issued under section 402 of this Act by the Administrator, or by a State, or in a permit issued under section 404 of this Act by a State, or any requirement imposed in a pretreatment program approved under section 402(a)(3) or 402(b)(8) of this Act, and any person who violates any order issued by the Administrator under subsection (a) of this section, shall be subject to a civil penalty not to exceed $25,000 per day for each violation. In determining the amount of a civil penalty the court shall consider the seriousness of the violation or violations, the economic benefit (if any) resulting from the violation, any history of such violations, any good-faith efforts to comply with the applicable requirements, the economic impact of the penalty on the violator, and such other matters as justice may require. For purposes of this subsection, a single operational upset which leads to simultaneous violations of more than one pollutant parameter shall be treated as a single violation.

[Sec. 309(d) amended by PL 100-4]

[Section 313(a)(2) and (b)(2) of PL 100-4 state the following concerning the amendments to 309(d):

"(a)(2) Savings Provision. -- No State shall be required before July 1,1988, to modify a permit program approved or submitted under section 402 of the Federal Water Pollution Control Act as a result of the amendment made by paragraph (a)(1)." [Note: Section 313(a)(1) amended 309(d).]

"(b)(2) Increased Penalties Not Required Under State Programs. -- The Federal Water Pollution Control Act shall not be construed as requiring a State to have a civil penalty for violations described in section 309(d) of such Act which has the same monetary amount as the civil penalty established by such section, as amended by paragraph (b)(1). Nothing in this paragraph shall affect the Administrator's authority to establish or adjust by regulation a minimum acceptable State civil penalty."]

(e) Whenever a municipality is a party to a civil action brought by the United States under this section, the State in which such municipality is located shall be joined as a party. Such State shall be liable for payment of any judgment, or any expenses incurred as a result of complying with any judgment, entered against the municipality in such action to the extent that the laws of that State prevent the municipality from raising revenues needed to comply with such judgment.

(f) Whenever, on the basis of an information available to him, the Administrator finds that an owner or operator of any source is introducing a pollutant into a treatment works in violation of subsection (d) of section 307, the Administrator may notify the owner or operator of such treatment works and the State of such violation. If the owner or operator of the treatment works does not commence appropriate enforcment action within 30 days of the date of such notification, the Administrator may commence a civil action for appropriate relief, including but not limited to, a permanent or temporary injunction, against the owner or operator of such treatment works. In any such civil action the Administrator shall join the owner or operator of such source as a party to the action. Such action shall be brought in the district court of the United States in the district in which the treatment works is located. Such court shall have jurisdiction to restrain such violation and to require the owner or operator of the treatment works and the owner or operator of the source to take such action as may be necessary to come into compliance with this Act. Notice of commencement of any such action shall be given to the State. Nothing in this subsection shall be construed to limit or prohibit any other authority the Administrator may have under this Act.

(g) Administrative Penalties. --

[Sec. 309(g) added by PL 100-4]

(1) Violations. -- Whenever on the basis of any information available --

(A) the Administrator finds that any person has violated section 301, 302, 306, 307, 308, 318, or 405 of this Act, or has violated any permit condition or limitation implementing any of such sections in a permit issued under section 402 of this Act by the Administrator or by a State, or in a permit issued under section 404 by a State, or

(B) the Secretary of the Army (hereinafter in this subsection referred to as the "Secretary") finds that any person has violated any permit condition or limitation in a permit issued under section 404 of this Act by the Secretary.

the Administrator or Secretary, as the case may be, may, after consultation with the State in which the violation occurs, assess a class I civil penalty or a class II civil penalty under this subsection.

(2) Classes of Penalties. --

(A) Class I. -- The amount of a class I civil penalty under paragraph (1) may not exceed $10,000 per violation, except that the maximum amount of any class I civil penalty under this subparagraph shall not exceed $25,000. Before issuing an order assessing a civil penalty under this subparagraph, the Administrator or the Secretary, as the case may be, shall give to the person to be assessed such penalty written notice of the Administrator's or Secretary's proposal to issue such order and the opportunity to request, within 30 days of the date the notice is received by such person, a hearing on the proposed order. Such hearing shall not be subject to section 554 or 556 of title 5, United States Code, but shall provide a reasonable opportunity to be heard and to present evidence.

(B) Class II. -- The amount of a class II civil penalty under paragraph (1) may not exceed $10,000 per day for each day during which the violation continues; except that the maximum amount of any class II civil penalty under this subparagraph shall not exceed $125,000. Except as otherwise provided in this subsection, a class II civil penalty shall be assessed and collected in the same manner, and subject to the same provisions, as in the case of civil penalties assessed and collected after notice and opportunity for a hearing on the record in accordance with section 554 of title 5, United States Code. The Administrator and the Secretary may issue rules for discovery procedures for hearings under this subparagraph.

(3) Determining Amount. -- In determining the amount of any penalty assessed under this subsection, the Administrator or the Secretary, as the case may be, shall take into account the nature, circumstances, extent and gravity of the violation, or violations, and, with respect to the violator, ability to pay, any prior history of such violations, the degree of culpability, economic benefit or savings (if any) resulting from the violation, and such other matters as justice may require. For purposes of this subsection, a single operational upset which leads to simultaneous violations of more than one pollutant parameter shall be treated as a single violation.

(4) Rights of Interested Persons. --

(A) Public Notice. -- Before issuing an order assessing a civil penalty under this subsection the Administrator or Secretary, as the case may be, shall provide public notice of and reasonable opportunity to comment on the proposed issuance of such order.

(B) Presentation of Evidence. -- Any person who comments on a proposed assessment of a penalty under this subsection shall be given notice of any hearing held under this subsection and of the order assessing such penalty. In any hearing held under this subsection, such person shall have a reasonable opportunity to be heard and to present evidence.

(C) Rights of Interested Persons to a Hearing. -- If no hearing is held under paragraph (2) before issuance of an order assessing a penalty under this subsection, any person who commented on the proposed assessment may petition, within 30 days after the issuance of such order, the Administrator or Secretary, as the case may be, to set aside such order and to provide a hearing on the penalty. If the evidence presented by the petitioner in support of the petition is material and was not considered in the issuance of the order, the Administrator or Secretary shall immediately set aside such order and provide a hearing in accordance with paragraph (2)(A) in the case of a class I civil penalty and paragraph (2)(B) in the case of a class II civil penalty. If the Administrator or Secretary denies a hearing under this subparagraph, the Administrator or Secretary shall provide to the petitioner, and publish in the Federal Register, notice of and the reasons for such denial.

(5) Finality of Order. -- An order issued under this subsection shall become final 30 days after its issuance unless a petition for judicial review is filed under paragraph (8) or a hearing is requested under paragraph (4)(C). If such a hearing is denied, such order shall become final 30 days after such denial.

(6) Effect of Order. --

(A) Limitation on Actions Under Other Sections. -- Action taken by the Administrator or the Secretary, as the case may be, under this subsection shall not affect or limit the Administrator's or Secretary's authority to enforce any provision of this Act; except that any violation --
(i) with respect to which the Administrator or the Secretary has commenced and is diligently prosecuting an action under this subsection,
(ii) with respect to which a State has commenced and is diligently prosecuting an action under a State law comparable to this subsection, or
(iii) for which the Administrator, the Secretary, or the State has issued a final order not subject to further judicial review and the violator has paid a penalty assessed under this subsection, or such comparable State

law, as the case may be, shall not be the subject of a civil penalty action under subsection (d) of this section or section 311(b) or section 505 of this Act.

(B) Applicability of Limitation With Respect to Citizen Suits. -- The limitations contained in subparagraph (A) on civil penalty actions under section 505 of this Act shall not apply with respect to any violation for which --
    (i) a civil action under section 505(a)(1) of this Act has been filed prior to commencement of an action under this subsection, or
    (ii) notice of an alleged violation of section 505(a)(1) of this Act has been given in accordance with section 505(b)(1)(A) prior to commencement of an action under this subsection and an action under section 505(a)(1) with respect to such alleged violation is filed before the 120th day after the date on which such notice is given.

(7) Effect of Action on Compliance. -- No action by the Administrator or the Secretary under this subsection shall affect any person's obligation to comply with any section of this Act or with the terms and conditions of any permit issued pursuant to section 402 or 404 of this Act.

(8) Judicial Review. -- Any person against whom a civil penalty is assessed under this subsection or who commented on the proposed assessment of such penalty in accordance with paragraph (4) may obtain review of such assessment --

(A) in the case of assessment of a class I civil penalty, in the United States District Court for the District of Columbia or in the district in which the violation is alleged to have occurred, or

(B) in the case of assessment of a class II civil penalty, in United States Court of Appeals for the District of Columbia Circuit or for any other circuit in which such person resides or transacts business, by filing a notice of appeal in such court within the 30-day period beginning on the date the civil penalty order is issued and by simultaneously sending a copy of such notice by certified mail to the Administrator or the Secretary, as the case may be, and the Attorney General. The Administrator or the Secretary shall promptly file in such court a certified copy of the record on which the order was issued. Such court shall not set aside or remand such order unless there is not substantial evidence in the record, taken as a whole, to support the finding of a violation or unless the Administrator's or Secretary's assessment of the penalty constitutes an abuse of discretion and shall not impose additional civil penalties for the same violation unless the Administrator's or Secretary's assessment of the penalty constitutes an abuse of discretion.

(9) Collection. -- If any person fails to pay an assessment of a civil penalty --

(A) after the order making the assessment has become final, or

(B) After a court in an action brought under paragraph (8) has entered a final judgment in favor of the Administrator or the Secretary, as the case may be, the Administrator or the Secretary shall request the Attorney General to bring a civil action in an appropriate district court to recover the amount assessed (plus interest at currently prevailing rates from the date of the final order or the date of the final judgment, as the case may be). In such an action, the validity, amount, and appropriateness of such penalty shall not be subject to review. Any person who fails to pay on a timely basis the amount of an assessment of a civil penalty as described in the first sentence of this paragraph shall be required to pay, in addition to such amount and interest, attorneys fees and costs for collection proceedings and a quarterly nonpayment penalty for each quarter during which such failure to pay persits. Such nonpayment penalty shall be in an amount equal to 20 percent of the aggregate amount of such person's penalties and nonpayment penalties which are unpaid as of the beginning of such quarter.

(10) Subpoenas. -- The Administrator or Secretary, as the case may be, may issue subpoenas for the attendance and testimony of witnesses and the production of relevant papers, books, or documents in connection with hearings under this subsection. In case of contumacy or refusal to obey a subpoena issued pursuant to this paragraph and served upon any person, the district court of the United States for any district in which such person is found, resides, or transacts business, upon application by the United States and after notice to such person, shall have jurisdiction to issue an other requiring such person to appear and give testimony before the administrative law judge or both, and any failure to obey such order of the court may be punished by such court as a contempt thereof.

(11) Protection of Existing Procedures. -- Nothing in this subsection shall change the procedures existing on the day before the date of the enactment of the Water Quality Act of 1987 under other subsections of this section for issuance and enforcement of orders by the Administrator.

[Section 314(b) of PL 100-4 provides:

"(b) Reports on Enforcement Mechanisms. -- The Secretary of the Army and the Administrator shall each prepare and submit a report to the Congress, not later than December 1, 1988, which shall examine and analyze various enforcement mechanisms for use by the Secretary or Administrator, as the case may be, including an administrative civil penalty mechanism. Each of such reports shall also include an examination, prepared in consultation with the Comptroller General, of the efficacy of the Secretary's or the Administrator's existing enforcement authorities and shall include recommendations for improvements in their operation."]

Sec. 310. International Pollution Abatement.

(a) Whenever the Administrator, upon receipts of reports, surveys, or studies from any duly constituted international agency, has reason to believe that pollution is occurring which endangers the health or welfare of persons in a foreign country, and the Secretary of State requests him to abate such pollution, he shall give formal notification thereof to the State water pollution control agency of the State or States in which such discharge of discharges originate and to the appropriate interstate agency, if any. He shall also promptly call such a hearing, if he believes that such pollution is occurring in sufficient quantity to warrant such action, and if such foreign country has given the United States essentially the same rights with respect to the prevention and control of pollution occurring in that country as is given that country by this subsection. The Administrator, through the Secretary of State, shall invite the foreign country which may be adversely affected by the pollution to attend and participate in the hearing, and the representative of such country shall, for the purpose of the hearing and any further proceeding resulting from such hearing, have all the rights of a State water pollution control agency. Nothing in this subsection shall be construed to modify, amend, repeal, or otherwise affect the provisions of the 1909 Boundary Waters Treaty between Canada and the United States or the Water Utilization Treaty of 1944 between Mexico and the United States (59 Stat. 1219), relative to the control and abatement of pollution in waters covered by those treaties.

(b) The calling of a hearing under this section shall not be construed by the courts, the Administrator, or any person as limiting, modifying, or otherwise affecting the functions and responsibilities of the Administrator under this section to establish and enforce water quality requirements under this Act.

(c) The Administrator shall publish in the Federal Register a notice of a public hearing before a hearing board of five or more persons appointed by the Administrator. A majority of the members of the board and the chairman who shall be designated by the Administrator shall not be officers or employees of Federal, State, or local governments. On the basis of the evidence presented at such hearing, the board shall within sixty days after completion of the hearing make findings of fact as to whether or not such pollution is occurring and shall thereupon by decision, incorporating its findings therein, make such recommendations to abate the pollution as may be appropriate and shall transmit such decision and the record of the hearings to the Administrator. All such decisions shall be public. Upon receipt of such decision, the Administrator shall promptly implement the board's decision in accordance with the provisions of this Act.

(d) In connection with any hearing called under this subsection, the board is authorized to require any person whose alleged activities result in discharges causing or contributing to pollution to file with it in such forms as it may prescribe, a report based on existing data, furnishing such information as may reasonably be required as to the character, kind, and quantity of such discharges and the use of facilities or other means to prevent or reduce such discharges by the person filing such a report. Such report shall be made under oath or otherwise, as the board may prescribe, and shall be filed with the board within such reasonable period as it may prescribe, unless additional time is granted by it. Upon a showing satisfactory to the board by the person filing such report that such report or portion thereof (other than effluent data), to which the Administrator has access under this section, if made public would divulge trade secrets or secret processes of such person, the board shall consider such report or portion thereof confidential for the purposes of section 1905 of title 18 of the United States Code. If any person required to file any report under this paragraph shall fail to do so within the time fixed by the board for filing the same, and such failure shall continue for thirty days after notice of such default, such person shall forfeit to the United States the sum of $1,000 for each and every day of the continuance of such failure, which forfeiture shall be payable into the Treasury of the United States, and shall be recoverable in a civil suit in the name of the United States in the district court of the United States where such person has his principal office or in any district in which he does business. The Administrator may upon application therefor remit or mitigate any forfeiture provided for under this subsection.

(e) Board members, other than officers or employees of Federal, State, or local governments, shall be for each day (including travel-time) during which they are performing board business, entitled to receive compensation at a rate fixed by the Administrator but not in excess of the maximum rate of pay for grade GS-18, as provided in the General Schedule under section 5332 of title 5 of the United States Code, and shall, notwithstanding the limitations of sections 5703 and 5704 of of title 5 of the United States Code, be fully reimbursed for travel, subsistence, and related expenses.

(f) When any such recommendation adopted by the Administrator involves the institution of enforcement proceedings against any person to obtain the abatement of pollution subject to such recommendation, the Administrator shall institute such proceedings if he believes that the evidence warrants such proceedings. The district court of the United States shall consider and determine de novo all relevant issues, but shall receive in evidence the record of the proceedings before the conference or hearing board. The court shall have jurisdiction to enter such judgment and orders enforcing such judgment as it deems appropriate or to remand such proceedings to the Administrator for such further action as it may direct.

Sec. 311. Oil and Hazardous Substance Liability.

(a) For the purpose of this section, the term --

(1) "oil" means oil of any kind or in any form, including, but not limited to, petroleum, fuel oil, sludge, oil refuse, and oil mixed with wastes other than dredged spoil;

(2) "discharge" includes, but is not limited to, any spilling, leaking, pumping, pouring, emitting, emptying or dumping, but excludes (A) discharges in compliance with a permit under section 402 of this Act, (B) discharges resulting from circumstances identified and reviewed and made a part of the public record with respect to a permit issued or modified under section 402 of this Act, and subject to a condition in such permit, and (C) continuous or anticipated intermittent discharges from a point source, identified in a permit or permit application under section 402 of this Act, which are caused by events occurring within the scope of relevant operating or treatment systems.

(311(a)(2) amended by PL 95-576) (3) "vessel" means every description of watercraft or other artificial contrivance used, or capable of being used, as a means of transportation on water other than a public vessel;

(4) "public vessel" means a vessel owned or bareboat-chartered and operated by the United States, or by a State or political subdivision thereof, or by a foreign nation, except when such vessel is engaged in commerce;

(5) "United States" means the States, the District of Columbia, the Commonwealth of Puerto Rico, the Commonwealth of the Northern Mariana Islands, Guam, American Samoa, the Virgin Islands and the Trust Territory of the Pacific Islands;

[Sec. 311(a)(5) amended by PL 100-4]

(6) "owner or operator" means (A) in the case of a vessel, any person owning, operating, or chartering by demise, such vessel, and (B) in the case of an onshore facility, an offshore facility, any person owning or operating such onshore facility or offshore facility, and (C) in the case of any abandoned offshore facility, the person who owned or operated such facility immediately prior to such abandonment;

(7) "person" includes an individual, firm, corporation, association, and a partnership;

(8) "remove" or "removal" refers to removal of the oil or hazardous substances from the water and shorelines or the taking of such other actions as may be necessary to minimize or mitigate damage to the public health or welfare, including, but not limited to, fish, shellfish, wildlife, and public and private property, shorelines, and beaches;

(9) "contiguous zone" means the entire zone established or to be established by the United States under article 24 of the Convention on the Territorial Sea and the Contiguous Zone;

(10) "onshore facility" means any facility (including, but not limited to, motor vehicles and rolling stock) of any kind located in, on, or under, any land within the United States other than submerged land;

(11) "offshore facility" means any facility of any kind located in, on, or under, any of the navigable waters of the United States, and any facility of any kind which is subject to the jurisdiction of the United States and is located in, on, or under any other waters, other than a vessel or a public vessel;

(12) "act of God" means an act occasioned by an unanticipated grave natural disaster;

(13) "barrel" means 42 United States gallons at 60 degrees Fahrenheit;

(14) "hazardous substance" means any substance designated pursuant to subsection (b)(2) of this section;

(15) "inland oil barge" means a non-self-propelled vessel carrying oil in bulk as cargo and certificated to operate only in the inland waters of the United States, while operating in such waters;

(16) "inland waters of the United States" means those waters of the United States lying inside the baseline from which the territorial sea is measured and those waters outside such baseline which are a part of the Gulf Intracoastal Waterway.

(17) "Otherwise subject to the jurisdiction of the United States" means subject to the jurisdiction of the Unite States by virtue of United States citizenship, United States vessel documentation or numbering, or as provided for by international agreement to which the United States is a party.

[311(a)(17) added by PL 95-576]

(b) (1) The Congress hereby declares that it is the policy of the United States that there should be no discharges of oil or hazardous substances into or upon the navigable waters of the United States, adjoining shorelines, or into or upon the waters of the contiguous zone, or in connection with activities under the Outer Continental Shelf Lands Act or the Deepwater Port Act of 1977, or which may affect natural resources belonging to, appertaining to, or under the exclusive management authority of the United States (including resources under the Magnuson Fishery Conservation and Management Act of 1976).

[311(b)(1) amended by PL 96-561]

(2) (A) The Administrator shall develop, promulgate, and revise as may be appropriate, regulations designating as hazardous substances, other than oil as defined in this section, such elements and compounds which, when discharged in any quantity into or upon the navigable waters of the United States or adjoining shorelines or the waters of the contiguous zone or in connection with activities under the Outer Continental Shelf Lands Act or the Deepwater Port Act of 1974, or which may affect natural resources belonging to, appertaining to, or under the exclusive management authority

of the United States (including resources under the Magnuson
Fishery Conservation and Management Act of 1976), present an
imminent and substantial danger to the public health or
welfare, including, but not limited to, fish, shellfish,
wildlife, shorelines, and beaches.

[311(b)(2)(A) amended by PL 96-561]

(B) The Administrator shall within 18 months after the date
of enactment of this paragraph, conduct a study and report
to the Congress on methods, mechanisms, and procedures to
create incentives to achieve a higher standard of care in
all aspects of the management and movement of hazardous
substances on the part of owners, operators, or persons in
charge of onshore facilities, offshore facilities or
vessels. The Administrator shall include in such study (1)
limits of liability, (2) liability for third party damages,
(3) penalties and fees, (4) spill prevention plans, (5)
current practices in the insurance and banking industries,
and (6) whether the penalty enacted in subclause (bb) of
clause (iii) of subparagraph (B) of subsection (b)(2) of
section 311 of Public Law 92-500 should be enacted.

[Sec. 311(b)(2)(B) was revised by PL 95-576. As embodied in PL
92-500, subclause (bb) of 311(b)(2)(B) reads as follows:

"(bb) a penalty determined by the number of units
discharged multiplied by the amount established for such
unit under clause (iv) of this subparagraph, but such
penalty shall not be more than $5,000,000 in the case of
a discharge from a vessel and $500,000 in the case of a
discharge from an onshore or offshore facility."]

(3) The discharge of oil or hazardous substances (i) into or
upon the navigable waters of the United States, adjoining
shorelines, or into or upon the waters of the contiguous zone,
or (ii) in connection with activities under the Outer
Continental Shelf Lands Act or the Deepwater Port Act of 1974,
or which may affect natural resources belonging to, appertaining
to, or under the exclusive management authority of the United
States (including resources under the Magnuson Fishery
Conservation and Management Act of 1976), in such quantities as
may be harmful as determined by the President under paragraph
(4) of this subsection, is prohibited, except (A) in the case of
such discharges into the waters of the contiguous zone or which
may affect natural resources belonging to, appertaining to, or
under the exclusive management authority of the United States
(including resources under the Magnuson Fishery Conservation and
Management Act of 1976), where permitted under the Protocol of
1978 Relating to the International Convention for the Prevention
of Pollution from Ships, 1973 and (B) where permitted in
quantities and at times and locations or under such
circumstances or conditions as the President may, by regulation,
determine not to be harmful. Any regulations issued under this
subsection shall be consistent with maritime safety and with
marine and navigation laws and regulations and applicable water
quality standards.

[311(b)(3) revised by PL 95-576; amended by PL 96-478; PL 96-561]

(4) The President shall by regulation determine for the purposes of this section those quantities of oil and any hazardous substances the discharge of which may be harmful to the public health or welfare of the United States, including but not limited to fish, shellfish, wildlife, and public and private property, shorelines, and beaches.

[311(b)(4) amended by PL 95-576]

(5) Any person in charge of a vessel or of an onshore facility or an offshore facility shall, as soon as he has knowledge of any discharge of oil or a hazardous substance from such vessel or facility in violation of paragraph (3) of this subsection, immediately notify the appropriate agency of the United States Government of such discharge. Any such person (A) in charge of a vessel from which oil or a hazardous substance is discharged in violation of paragraph (3)(i) of this subsection, or (B) in charge of a vessel from which oil or a hazardous substance is discharged in violation of paragraph (3)(ii) of this subsection and who is otherwise subject to the jurisdiction of the United States at the time of the discharge, or (C) in charge of an onshore facility or an offshore facility, who fails to notify immediately such agency of such discharge shall, upon conviction, be fined not more than one year or both. Notification received pursuant to this paragraph or information obtained by the exploitation of such notification shall not be used against any such person in any criminal case, except a prosecution for perjury or for giving a false statement.

[311(b)(4) amended by PL 95-576]

(6) (A) Any owner, operator, or person in charge of any onshore facility or offshore facility from which oil or a hazardous substance is discharged in violation of paragraph (3) of this subsection shall be assessed a civil penalty by the Secretary of the department in which the Coast Guard is operating of not more than $5,000 for each offense. Any owner, operator, or person in charge of any vessel from which oil or a hazardous substance is discharged in violation of paragraph (3)(i) of this subsection, and any owner, operator, or person in charge of a vessel from which oil or a hazardous substance is discharged in violation of paragraph (3)(ii) who is otherwise subject to the jurisdiction of the United States at the time of the discharge, shall be assessed a civil penalty by the Secretary of the department in which the Coast Guard is operating of not more than $5,000 for each offense. No penalty shall be assessed unless the owner or operator charged shall have been given notice and opportunity for a hearing on such charge. Each violation is a separate offense. Any such civil penalty may be compromised by such Secretary. In determining the amount of the penalty, or the amount agreed upon in compromise, the appropriateness of such penalty to the size of the business of the owner or operator charged, the effect on the owner or operator's

ability to continue in business, and the gravity of the
violation, shall be considered by such Secretary. The
Secretary of the Treasury shall withhold at the request of
such Secretary the clearance required by section 4197 of the
Revised Statutes of the United States, as amended (46 U.S.C.
91), of any vessel the owner or operator of which is subject
to the foregoing penalty. Clearance may be granted in such
cases upon the filing of a bond or other surety satisfactory
to such Secretary.

(B) The Administrator, taking into account the gravity of
the offense, and the standard of care manifest by the owner,
operator or person in charge, may commence a civil action
against any such person subject to the penalty under
subparagraph (A) of this paragraph to impose a penalty based
on consideration of the size of the business of the owner or
operator, the effect on the ability of the owner or operator
to continue in business, the gravity of the violation, and
the nature, extent, and degree of success of any efforts
made by the owner, operator, or person in charge to minimize
or mitigate the effects of such discharge. The amount of
such penalty shall not exceed $50,000, except that where the
United States can show that such discharge was the result of
willful negligence or willful misconduct within the privity
and knowledge of the owner, operator, or person in charge,
such penalty shall not exceed $250,000. Each violation is a
separate offense.

Any action under this subparagraph may be brought in the
district court of the United States for the district in
which the defendant is located or resides or is doing
business, and such court shall have jurisdiction to assess
such penalty. No action may be commenced under this clause
where a penalty has been assessed under clause (A) of this
paragraph.

(C) In addition to establishing a penalty for the discharge
of a hazardous substance, the Administrator may act to
mitigate the damage to the public health or welfare caused
by such discharge. The cost of such mitigation shall be
deemed a cost incurred under subsection (c) of this section
for the removal of such substance by the United States
Government.

(D) Any cost of removal incurred in connection with a
discharge excluded by subsection (a)(2)(C) of this section
shall be recoverable from the owner or operator of the
source of the discharge in an action brought under section
309(b) of this Act.

(E) Civil penalties shall not be assessed under both this
section and section 309 for the same discharge.

[B)-(E) added by PL 95-576]

(c) (1) Whenever any oil or a hazardous substance is discharged, or
there is a substantial threat of such discharge, into or upon

the navigable waters of the United States, adjoining shorelines, or into or upon the waters of the contiguous zone, or in connection with activities under the Outer Continental Shelf Lands Act or the Deepwater Port Act of 1974, or which may affect natural resources belonging to, appertaining to, or under the exclusive management authority of the United States (including resources under the Magnuson Fishery Conservation and Management Act of 1976) the President is authorized to act to remove or arrange for the removal of such oil or substance at any time, unless he determines such removal will be done properly by the owner or operator of the vessel, onshore facility, or offshore facility from which the discharge occurs.

[311(c)(1) amended by PL 96-561]

(2) Within sixty days after the effective date of this section, the President shall prepare and publish a National Contingency Plan for removal of oil and hazardous substances, pursuant to this subsection. Such National Contingency Plan shall provide for efficient, coordinated, and effective action to minimize damage from oil and hazardous substance discharges, including containment, dispersal, and removal of oil and hazardous substances, and shall include, but not be limited to --

(A) assignment of duties and responsibilities among Federal departments and agencies in coordination with State and local agencies, including, but not limited to, water pollution control, conservation, and port authorities;

(B) identification, procurement, maintenance, and storage of equipment and supplies;

(C) establishment or designation of a strike force consisting of personnel who shall be trained, prepared, and available to provide necessary services to carry out the Plan, including the establishment at major ports, to be determined by the President, of emergency task forces of trained personnel, adequate oil and hazardous substance pollution control equipment and material, and a detailed oil and hazardous substance pollution prevention and removal plan;

(D) a system of surveillance and notice designed to insure earliest possible notice of discharges of oil and hazardous substances and imminent threats of such discharges to the appropriate State and Federal agencies;

(E) establishment of a national center to provide coordination and direction for operations in carrying out the Plan;

(F) procedures and techniques to be employed in identifying, containing, dispersing, and removing oil and hazardous substances;

(G) a schedule, prepared in cooperation with the States, identifying (i) dispersants and other chemicals, if any, that may be used in carrying out the Plan, (ii) the waters in which such dispersants and chemicals may be used, and (iii) the quantities of such dispersant or chemical which can be used safely in such waters, which schedule shall provide in the case of any dispersant, chemical, or waters not specifically identified in such schedule that the President, or his delegate, may, on a case-by-case basis, identify the dispersants and other chemicals which may be used, the waters in which they may be used, and the quantities which can be used safely in such waters; and

(H) a system whereby the State or States affected by a discharge of oil or hazardous substance may act where necessary to remove such discharge and such State or States may be reimbursed from the fund established under subsection (k) of this section for the reasonable costs incurred in such removal. The President may, from time to time, as he deems advisable revise or otherwise amend the National Contingency Plan. After publication of the National Contingency Plan, the removal of oil and hazardous substances and actions to minimize damage from oil and hazardous substance discharges shall, to the greatest extent possible, be in accordance with the National Contingency Plan.

(d) Whenever a marine disaster in or upon the navigable waters of the United States has created a substantial threat of a pollution hazard to the public health or welfare of the United States, including, but not limited to, fish, shellfish, and wildlife and the public and private shorelines and beaches of the United States, because of a discharge, or an imminent discharge, of large quantities of oil, or a hazardous substance from a vessel the United States may (A) coordinate and direct all public and private efforts directed at the removal or elimination of such threat; and (B) summarily remove, and, if necessary, destroy such vessel by whatever means are available without regard to any provisions of law governing the employment of personnel or the expenditure of appropriated funds. Any expense incurred under this subsection or under the Intervention on the High Seas Act (or the convention defined in section 2(3) thereof) shall be a cost incurred by the United States Government for the purposes of subsection (f) in the removal of oil or hazardous substance.

(e) In addition to any other action taken by a State or local government, when the President determines there is an imminent and substantial threat to the public health or welfare of the United States, including, but not limited to, fish, shellfish, and wildlife and public and private property, shorelines, and beaches within the United States, because of an actual or threatened discharge of oil or hazardous substance into or upon the navigable waters of the United States from an onshore or offshore facility, the President may require the United States attorney of the district in which the threat occurs to secure such relief as may be necessary to abate such threat, and the district courts of the United States shall have jurisdiction to grant such relief as the public interest and the equities of the case may require.

(f) (1) Except where an owner or operator can prove that a discharge was caused solely by (A) an act of God, (B) an act of war, (C)

negligence on the part of the United States Government, or (D)
an act or omission of a third party without regard to whether
any such act or omission was or was not negligent, or any
combination of the foregoing clauses, such owner or operator of
any vessel from which oil or a hazardous substance is discharged
in violation of subsection (b)(3) of this section shall,
notwithstanding any other provision of law, be liable to the
United States Government for the actual costs incurred under
subsection (c) for the removal of such oil or substance by the
United States Government in an amount not to exceed, in the case
of an inland oil barge $125 per gross ton of such barge, or
$125,000, whichever is greater, and in the case of any other
vessel, $150 per gross ton of such vessel (or, for a vessel
carrying oil or hazardous substances as cargo, $250,000),
whichever is greater, except that where the United States can
show that such discharge was the result of willful negligence or
willful misconduct within the privity and knowledge of the
owner, such owner or operator shall be liable to the United
States Government for the full amount of such costs. Such costs
shall constitute a maritime lien on such vessel which may be
recovered in an action in rem in the district court of the
United States for any district within which any vessel may be
found. The United States may also bring an action against the
owner or operator of such vessel in any court of competent
jurisdiction to recover such costs.

[Sec. 58(d)(2) of the Clean Water Act of 1977 increased liability
under Subsection 311(f)(1) of the Act. Sec. 58(j) of the 1977 Act
provides:

"(j) No vessel subject to the increased amounts which result from
the amendments made by subsections (d)(2), (d)(3), and (d)(4) of
this section shall be required to establish any evidence of
financial responsibility under section 311(p) of the Federal Water
Pollution Control Act for such increased amounts before October 1,
1978."]

(2) Except where an owner or operator of an onshore facility can
prove that a discharge was caused solely by (A) an act of God,
(B) an act of war, (C) negligence on the part of the United
States Government, or (D) an act or omission of a third part
without regard to whether any such act or omission was or was
not negligent, or any combination of the foregoing clauses, such
owner or operator of any such facility from which oil or a
hazardous substance is discharged in violation of subsection
(b)(3) of this section shall be liable to the United States
Government for the actual costs incurred under subsection (c)
for the removal of such oil or substance by the United States
Government in an amount not to exceed $50,000,000, except that
where the United States can show that such discharge was the
result of willful negligence or willful misconduct within the
privity and knowledge of the owner, such owner or operator shall
be liable to the United States Government for the full amount of
such costs. The United States may bring an action against the
owner or operator of such facility in any court of competent
jurisdiction to recover such costs. The Administrator is
authorized, by regulation, after consultation with the Secretary

of Commerce and the Small Business Administration, to establish reasonable and equitable classifications of those onshore facilities having a total fixed storage capacity of 1,000 barrels or less which he determines because of size, type, and location do not present a substantial risk of the discharge of oil or a hazardous substance in violation of subsection (b)(3) of this section, and apply with respect to such classifications differing limits of liability which may be less than the amount contained in this paragraph.

(3) Except where an owner or operator of an offshore facility can prove that a discharge was caused solely by (A) an act of God, (B) an act of war, (C) negligence on the part of the United States Government, or (D) an act or omission of a third party without regard to whether any such act or omission was or was not negligent, or any combination of the foregoing clauses, such owner or operator of any such facility from which oil or a hazardous substance is discharged in violation of subsection (b)(3) of this section shall, notwithstanding any other provision of law, be liable to the United States Government for the actual costs incurred under subsection (c) for the removal of such oil or substance by the United States Government in an amount not to exceed $50,000,000, except that where the United States can show that such discharge was the result of willful negligence or willful misconduct within the privity and knowledge of the owner, such owner or operator shall be liabile to the United States Government for the full amount of such costs. The United States may bring an action against the owner or operator of such a facility in any court of competent jurisdiction to recover such costs.

[Liability of $50,000 in Section 311(f)(2) and Section 311(f)(3) was established by the Clean Water Act of 1977. Under Sec. 58(h) of the 1977 Act, liability is to be $8,000,000 until June 1978.]

(4) The costs of removal of oil or a hazardous substance for which the owner or operator of a vessel or onshore or offshore facility is liable under subsection (f) of this section shall include any costs or expenses incurred by the Federal Government or any State government in the restoration or replacement of natural resources damaged or destroyed as a result of a discharge of oil or a hazardous substance in violation of subsection (b) of this section.

(5) The President, or the authorized representative of any State, shall act on behalf of the public as trustee of the natural resources to recover for the costs of replacing or restoring such resources. Sums recovered shall be used to restore, rehabilitate, or acquire the equivalent of such natural resources by the appropriate agencies of the Federal Government, or the State government.

(g) Where the owner or operator of a vessel (other than an inland oil barge) carrying oil or hazardous substances as cargo or an onshore or offshore facility which handles or stores oil or hazardous substances in bulk, from which oil or a hazardous substance is discharged in violation of subsection (b) of this section, alleges that such discharge was caused solely by an act or omission of a third party, such owner or operator shall pay to the United States Government the Actual costs incurred under subsection (c) for removal of such oil or substance and shall be entitled by subrogation to all rights of the United States Government to recover such costs from such third party under this subsection. In any case where an owner or operator of a vessel, of an onshore facility, or of an offshore facility, from which oil or a hazardous substance is discharged in violation of subsection (b)(3) of this section, proves that such discharge of oil or hazardous substance was caused solely by an act or omission of a third party, or was caused solely by such an act or omission in combination with an act of God, an act of war, or negligence on the part of the United States Government, such third party shall, not withstanding any other provision of law, be liable to the United States Government for the actual costs incurred under subsection (c) for removal of such oil or substance by the United States Government, except where such third party can prove that such discharge was caused solely by (A) an act of God, (B) an act of war, (C) negligence on the part of the United States Government, or (D) an act or omission of another party without regard to whether such act or omission was or was not negligent, or any combination of the foregoing clauses. If such third party was the owner or operator of a vessel which caused the discharge of oil or a hazardous substance in violation of subsection (b)(3) of this section, the liability of such third party under this subsection shall not exceed, in the case of an inland oil barge, $125 per gross ton of such barge, $125,000, whichever is greater, and in the case of any other vessel, $150 per gross ton of such vessel (or, for a vessel carrying oil or hazardous substances as cargo, $250,000), whichever is greater. In any other case the liability of such third party shall not exceed the limitation which would have been applicable to the owner or operator of the vessel or the onshore or offshore facility from which the discharge actually occurred if such owner or operator were liabile. If the United States can show that the discharge of oil or a hazardous substance in violation of subsection (b)(3) of this section was the result of willful negligence or willful misconduct within the privity and knowledge of such third party, such third party shall be liable to the United States Government for the full amount of such removal costs. The United States may bring an action against the third party in any court of competent jurisdiction to recover such removal costs.

(h) The liabilities established by this section shall in no way affect any rights which (1) the owner or operator of a vessel or of an onshore facility or an offshore facility may have against any third party whose acts may in any way have caused or contributed to such discharge, or (2) The United States Government may have against any third party whose actions may in any way have caused or contributed to the discharge of oil or hazardous substance.

(i) (1) In any case where an owner or operator of a vessel or an onshore facility or an offshore facility from which oil or a hazardous substance is discharged in violation of subsection (b)(3) of this section acts to remove such oil or substance in accordance with regulations promulgated pursuant to this section, such owner or operator shall be entitled to recover the reasonable costs incurred in such removal upon establishing, in a suit which may be brought against the United States Government in the United States Claims Court, that such discharge was caused solely by (A) an act of God, (B) an act of war, (C) negligence on the part of the United States Government or (D) an act or omission of a third party without regard to whether such act or omission was or was not negligent, or of any combination of the foregoing clauses.

(2) The provisions of this subsection shall not apply in any case where liability is established pursuant to the Outer Continental Shelf Lands Act, or the Deepwater Port Act of 1974.

(3) Any amount paid in accordance with a judgment of the United States Claims Court pursuant to this seciton shall be paid from the funds established pursuant to subsection (k).

[Sec. 311(i)(1) and (3) amended by PL 97-164]

(j) (1) Consistent with the National Contingency Plan required by subsection (c)(2) of this section, as soon as practicable after the effective date of this section, and from time to time thereafter, the President shall issue regulations consistent with maritime safety and with marine and navigation laws (A) establishing methods and procedures for removal of discharged oil and hazardous substances, (B) establishing criteria for the development and implementation of local and regional oil and hazardous substance removal contingency plans, (C) establishing procedures, methods, and equipment and other requirements for equipment to prevent discharges of oil and hazardous substances from vessels and from onshore facilities and offshore facilities, and to contain such discharges, and (D) governing the inspection of vessels carrying cargoes of oil and hazardous substances and the inspection of such cargoes in order to reduce the likelihood of discharges of oil from vessels in violation of this section.

(2) Any owner or operator of a vessel or an onshore facility or an offshore facility and any other person subject to any regulation issued under paragraph (1) of this subsection who fails or refuses to comply with the provisions of any such regulations, shall be liable to a civil penalty of not more than $5,000 for each such violation. This paragraph shall not apply to any owner or operator of any vessel from which oil or a hazardous substance is discharged in violation of paragraph (3)(ii) of subsection (b) unless such owner, operator, or person in charge is otherwise subject to the jurisdiction of the United States. Each violation shall be a separate offense. The President may assess and compromise such penalty. No penalty shall be assessed until the owner, operator, or other person charged shall have been given notice and an opportunity for a hearing on such charge. In determining the amount of the penalty, or the amount agreed upon in compromise, the gravity of the violation, and the demonstrated good faith of the owner, operator, or other person charged in attempting to achieve rapid compliance after notification of a violation, shall be considered by the President.

(k) (1) There is hereby authorized to be appropriated to a revolving fund to be established in the Treasury such sums as may be necessary to maintain such fund at a level of $35,000,000 to carry out the provisions of subsections (c), (d), (i), and (1) of this section. Any other funds received by the United States under this section shall also be deposited in said fund for such purposes. All sums appropriated to or deposited in, said fund shall remain available until expended.

[Sec. 311(k)(1) designated by PL 96-483]

(2) The Secretary of Transportation shall notify the Congress whenever the unobligated balance of the fund is less than $12,000,000, and shall include in such notification a recommendation for a supplemental appropriation relating to the sums that are needed to maintain the fund at the level provided in paragraph (1).

[Sec. 311(k)(2) added by PL 96-483]

[Section 304(b) and (c) of the Comprehensive Environmental Response, Compensation and Liability Act of 1980 (PL 96-510) provides:

"(b) One-half of the unobligated balance remaining before the date of the enactment of this Act under subsection (k) of section 311 of the Federal Water Pollution Control Act and all sums appropriated under section 504(b) of the Federal Water Pollution Control Act shall be transferred to the Fund established under title II of this Act.

(c) In any case in which any provision of section 311 of the Federal Water Pollution Control Act is determined to be in conflict with any provisions of this Act, the provisions of this Act shall apply."]

(1) The President is authorized to delegate the administration of this section to the heads of those Federal departments, agencies, and instrumentalities which he determines to be appropriate. Any moneys in the fund established by subsection (k) of this section shall be available to such Federal departments, agencies, and instrumentalities to carry out the provisions of subsections (c) and (i) of this section. Each such department, agency, and instrumentality, in order to avoid duplication of effort, shall, whenever appropriate, utilize the personnel, services, and facilities of other Federal departments, agencies, and instrumentalities.

(m) Anyone authorized by the President to enforce the provisions of this section may, except as to public vessels, (A) board and inspect any vessel upon the navigable waters of the United States or the waters of the contiguous zone, (B) with or without a warrant arrest any person who violates the provisions of this section or any regulation issued thereunder in his presence or view, and (C) execute any warrant or other process issued by an officer or court of competent jurisdiction.

(n) The several district courts of the United States are invested with jurisdiction for any actions, other than actions pursuant to subsection (i)(1), arising under this section. In the case of Guam and the Trust Territory of the Pacific Islands, such actions may be brought in the district court of Guam, and in the case of the Virgin Islands such actions may be brought in the district court of the Virgin Islands. In the case of American Samoa and the Trust Territory of the Pacific Islands, such actions may be brought in the District Court of the United States for the District of Hawaii and such court shall have jurisdiction of such actions. In the case of the Canal Zone, such actions may be brought in the United States District Court for the District of the Canal Zone.

(o) (1) Nothing in this section shall affect or modify in any way the obligations of any owner or operator of any vessel, or of any owner or operator of any onshore facility or offshore facility to any person or agency under any provision of law for damages to any publicly owned or privately owned property resulting from a discharge of any oil or hazardous substance or from the removal of any such oil or hazardous substance.

(2) Nothing in this section shall be construed as preempting any State or political subdivision thereof from imposing any requirement or liability with respect to the discharge of oil or hazardous substance into any waters within such State.

(3) Nothing in this section shall be construed as affecting or modifying any other existing authority of any Federal department, agency, or instrumentality, relative to onshore or offshore facilities under this Act or any other provision of law, or to affect any State or local law not in conflict with this section.

(p) (1) Any vessel over three hundred gross tons, including any barge of equivalent size, but not including any barge that is not self-propelled and that does not carry oil or hazardous substances as cargo or fuel, using any port or place in the United States or the navigable waters of the United States for any purpose shall establish and maintain under regulations to be prescribed from time to time by the President, evidence of financial responsibility of, in the case of an inland oil barge $125 per gross ton of such barge, or $125,000, whichever is greater, and in the case of any other vessel, $150 per gross ton of such vessel (or, for a vessel carrying oil or hazardous substances as cargo, $250,000), whichever is greater, to meet the liability to the United States which such vessel could be subjected under this section. In cases where an owner or operator owns, operates, or charters more than one such vessel, financial responsibility need only be established to meet the maximum liability to which the largest of such vessels could be subjected. Financial responsibility may be established by any one of, or a combination of, the following methods acceptable to the President: (A) evidence of insurance, (B) surety bonds, (C) qualification as a self-insurer, or (D) other evidence of financial responsibility. Any bond filed shall be issued by a bonding company authorized to do business in the United States.

(2) The provisions of paragraph (1) of this subsection shall be effective April 3, 1971, with respect to oil and one year after

the date of enactment of this section with respect to oil and one year after the date of enactment of this section with respect to hazardous substances. The President shall delegate the responsibility to carry out the provisions of this subsection to the appropriate agency within sixty days after the date of enactment of this section. Regulations necessary to implement this subsection shall be issued within six months after the date of enactment of this section.

(3) Any claim for costs incurred by such vessel may be brought directly against the insurer or any other person providing evidence of financial responsibility as required under this subsection. In the case of any action pursuant to this subsection such insurer or other person shall be entitled to invoke all rights and defenses which would have been available to the owner or operator if an action had been brought against him by the claimant, and which would have been available to him if an action had been brought against him by the owner or operator.

(4) Any owner or operator of a vessel subject to this subsection, who fails to comply with the provisions of this subsection or any regulation issued thereunder, shall be subject to a fine of not more than $10,000.

(5) The Secretary of the Treasury may refuse the clearance required by section 4197 of the Revised Statutes of the United States, as amended (4 U.S.C. 91), to any vessel subject to this subsection, which does not have evidence furnished by the President that the financial responsibility provisions of paragraph (1) of this subsection have been complied with.

(6) The Secretary of the Department in which the Coast Guard is operated may (A) deny entry to any port or place in the United States or the navigable waters of the United States, to, and (B) detain at the port or place in the United States from which it is about to depart for any other port or place in the United States, any vessel subject to this subsection, which upon request, does not produce evidence furnished by the President that the financial responsibility provisions of paragraph (1) of this subsection have been complied with.

(q) The President is authorized to establish, with respect to any class or category of onshore or offshore facilities, a maximum limit of liability under subsections (f)(2) and (3) of this section of less than $50,000,000, but not less than $8,000,000.

(r) Nothing in this section shall be construed to impose or authorize the imposition of any limitation on liability under the Outer Continental Shelf Lands Act or the Deepwater Port Act of 1974.

Sec. 312. **Marine Sanitation Devices.**

(a) For the purpose of this section, the term --

(1) "new vessel" includes every description of watercraft or other artificial contrivance used, or capable of being used, as

a means of transportation on the navigable waters, the construction of which is initiated after promulgation of standards and regulation under this section;

(2) "existing vessel" includes every description of watercraft or other artificial contrivance used, or capable of being used, as a means of transportation on the navigable waters, the construction of which is initiated before promulgation of standards and regulations under this section;

(3) "public vessel" means a vessel owned or bare-boat-chartered and operated by the United States, by a State or political subdivision thereof, or by a foreign nation, except when such vessel is engaged in commerce;

(4) "United States" includes the States, the District of Columbia, the Commonwealth of Puerto Rico, the Virgin Islands, Guam, American Samoa, the Canal Zone, and the Trust Territory of the Pacific Islands;

(5) "marine sanitation device" includes any equipment for installation on board a vessel which is designed to receive, retain, treat, or discharge sewage, and any process to treat such sewage;

(6) "sewage" means human body wastes and the wastes from toilets and other receptacles intended to receive or retain body wastes except that, with respect to commercial vessels on the Great Lakes such term shall include graywater;

(7) "manufacture" means any person engaged in the manufacturing, assembling, or importation of marine sanitation devices or of vessels subject to standards and regulations promulgated under this section;

(8) "person" means an individual, partnership, firm, corporation, or association, but does not include an individual on board a public vessel;

(9) "discharge" includes, but is not limited to, any spilling, leaking, pumping, pouring, emitting, emptying or dumping;

(10) "commercial vessels" means those vessels used in the business of transporting property for compensation or hire, or in transporting property in the business of the owner, lessee, or operator of the vessel;

(11) "graywater" means galley, bath, and shower water.

(b) (1) As soon as possible, after the enactment of this section and subject to the provisions of section 101(j) of this Act, the Administrator, after consultation with the Secretary of the department in which the Coast Guard is operating, after giving appropriate consideration to the economic costs involved, and within the limits of available technology, shall promulgate Federal standards of performance for marine sanitation devices (hereafter in this section referred to as "standards") which shall be designed to prevent the discharge of untreated or inadequately treated sewage into or upon the navigable waters from new vessels and existing vessels, except vessels not equipped with installed toilet facilities. Such standards and standards established under subsection (c)(1)(B) of this section shall be consistent with maritime safety and the marine and navigation laws and regulations and shall be coordinated with the regulations issued under this subsection by the Secretary of the department in which the Coast Guard is operating. The Secretary of the department in which the Coast Guard is operating shall promulgate regulations, which are consistent with standards promulgated under this subsection and subsection (c) of this section and with maritime safety and the marine and navigation laws and regulations governing the design, construction, installation, and operation of any marine sanitation device on board such vessels.

(2) Any existing vessel equipped with a marine sanitation device on the date of promulgation of initial standards and regulations under this section, which device is in compliance with such initial standards and regulations, shall be deemed in compliance with this section until such time as the device is replaced or is found not to be in compliance with such initial standards and regulations.

(c) (1) (A) Initial standards and regulations under this section shall become effective for new vessels two years after promulgation; and for existing vessels five years after promulgation. Revisions of standards and regulations shall be effective upon promulgation, unless another effective date is specified, except that no revision shall take effect before the effective date of the standard or regulation being revised.

(B) The Administrator shall, with respect to commercial vessels on the Great Lakes, establish standards which require at a minimum the equivalent of secondary treatment as defined under section 304(d) of this Act. Such standards and regulations shall take effect for existing vessels after such time as the Administrator determines to be reasonable for the upgrading of marine sanitation devices to attain such standard.

(2) The Secretary of the department in which the Coast Guard is operating with regard to his regulatory authority established by this section, after consultation with the Administrator, may distinguish among classes, types, and sizes of vessels as well as between new and existing vessels, and may waive applicability of standards and regulations as necessary or appropriate for such classes, types, and sizes of vessels (including existing vessels equipped with marine sanitation devices on the date of promulgation of the initial standards required by this section), and, upon application, for individual vessels.

(d) The provisions of this section and the standards and regulations promulgated hereunder apply to vessels owned and operated by the United States unless the Secretary of Defense finds that compliance

would not be in the interest of national security. With respect to
vessels owned and operated by the Department of Defense, regulations
under the last sentence of subsection (b)(1) of this section and
certifications under subsection (g)(2) of this section shall be
promulgated and issued by the Secretary of Defense.

(e) Before the standards and regulations under this section are
promulgated, the Administrator and the Secretary of the department
in which the Coast Guard is operating shall consult with the
Secretary of State; the Secretary of Health, Education, and Welfare;
the Secretary of Defense; the Secretary of the Treasury; the
Secretary of Commerce; other interested Federal agencies; and the
States and industries interested; and otherwise comply with the
requirements of section 553 of title 5 of the United States Code.

(f) (1) (A) Except as provided in subparagraph (B), after the
effective date of the initial standards and regulations
promulgated under this section, no State or political
subdivision thereof shall adopt or enforce any statute or
regulation of such State or political subdivision with
respect to the design, manufacture, or installation or use
of any marine sanitation devise on any vessel subject to the
provisions of this section.

[Sec. 312(f)(1)(A) designated and amended by PL 100-4]

(B) A State may adopt and enforce a statute or regulation
with respect to the design, manufacture, or installation or
use of any marine sanitation device on a houseboat, if such
statute or regulation is more stringent than the standards
and regulations promulgated under this section. For
purposes of this paragraph, the term 'houseboat' means a
vessel which, for a period of time determined by the State
in which the vessel is located, is used primarily as a
residence and is not used primarily as a means of
transportation.

[Sec. 312(f)(1)(B) added by PL 100-4]

(2) If after promulgation of the initial standards and
regulations and prior to their effective date, a vessel is
equipped with a marine sanitation device in compliance with such
standards and regulations and the installation and operation of
such device is in accordance with such standards and
regulations, such standards and regulations shall, for the
purposes of paragraph (1) of this subsection, become effective
with respect to such vessel on the date of such compliance.

(3) After the effective date of the initial standards and
regulations promulgated under this section, if any State
determines that the protection and enhancement of the quality of
some or all of the waters within such State require greater
environmental protection, such State may completely prohibit the
discharge from all vessels of any sewage, whether treated or
not, into such waters, except that no such prohibition shall
apply until the Administrator determines that adequate
facilities for the safe and sanitary removal and treatment of

sewage from all vessels are reasonably available for such water to which such prohibition would apply. Upon application of the State, the Administrator shall make such determination within 90 days of the date of such application.

(4) (A) If the Administrator determines upon application by a State that the protection and enhancement of the quality of specified waters within such State requires such a prohibition, he shall by regulation completely prohibit the discharge from a vessel of any sewage (whether treated or not) into such waters.

(B) Upon application by a State, the Administrator shall, by regulation, establish a drinking water intake zone in any waters within such State and prohibit the discharge of sewage from vessels within that zone.

(g) (1) No manufacturer of a marine sanitation device shall sell, offer for sale, or introduce or deliver for introduction in interstate commerce, or import into the United States for sale or resale any marine sanitation device manufactured after the effective date of the standards and regulations promulgated under this section unless such device is in all material respects substantially the same as a test device certified under this subsection.

(2) Upon application of the manufacturer, the Secretary of the department in which the Coast Guard is operating shall so certify a marine sanitation device if he determines, in accordance with the provisions of this paragraph, that it meets the appropriate standards and regulations promulgated under this section. The Secretary of the department in which the Coast Guard is operating shall test or require such testing of the device in accordance with procedures set forth by the Administrator as to standards of performance and for such other purposes as may be appropriate. If the Secretary of the department in which the Coast Guard is operating determines that the device is satisfactory from the standpoint of safety and any other requirements of maritime law or regulation, and after consideration of the design, installation, operation, material, or other appropriate factors, he shall certify the device. Any device manufactured by such manufacturer which is in all material respects substantially the same as the certified test device shall be deemed to be in conformity with the appropriate standards and regulations established under this section.

(3) Every manufacturer shall establish and maintain such records, make such reports, and provide such information as the Administrator or the Secretary of the department in which the Coast Guard is operating may reasonably require to enable him to determine whether such manufacturer has acted or is acting in compliance with this section and regulations issued thereunder and shall, upon request of an officer or employee duly designated by the Administrator or the Secretary of the department in which the Coast Guard is operating, permit such officer or employee at reasonable times to have access to and copy such records. All information reported to or otherwise

obtained by the Administrator or the Secretary of the department in which the Coast Guard is operating or their representatives pursuant to this subsection which contains or relates to a trade secret or other matter referred in section 1905 of title 18 of the United States Code shall be considered confidential for the purpose of that section, except that such information may be disclosed to other officers or employees concerned with carrying out this section. This paragraph shall not apply in the case of the construction of a vessel by an individual for his own use.

(h) After the effective date of standards and regulations promulgated under this section, it shall be unlawful --

(1) for the manufacturer of any vessel subject to such standards and regulations to manufacture for sale, to sell or offer for sale, or to distribute for sale or resale any such vessel unless it is equipped with a marine sanitation device which is in all material respects substantially the same as the appropriate test device certified pursuant to this section;

(2) for any person, prior to the sale or delivery of a vessel subject to such standards and regulations to the ultimate purchaser, wrongfully to remove or render inoperative any certified marine sanitation device or element of design of such device installed in such vessel;

(3) for any person to fail or refuse to permit access to or copying of records or to fail to make reports or provide information required under this section; and

(4) for a vessel subject to such standards and regulations to operate on the navigable waters of the United States, if such vessel is not equipped with an operable marine sanitation device certified pursuant to this section.

(i) The district courts of the United States shall have jurisdictions to restrain violations of subsection (g)(1) of this section and subsections (h)(1) through (3) of this section. Actions to restrain such violations shall be brought by, and in, the name of the United States. In case of contumacy or refusal to obey a subpoena served upon any person under this subsection, the district court of the United States for any district in which such person is found or resides or transacts business, upon application by the United States and after notice to such person, shall have jurisdiction to issue an order requiring such person to appear and give testimony or appear and produce documents, and any failure to obey such order of the court may be punished by such court as a contempt thereof.

(j) Any person who violates subsection (g)(1) of this section or clause (1) or (2) of subsection (h) of this section shall be liable to a civil penalty of not more than $5,000 for each violation. Any person who violates clause (4) of subsection (h) of this section or any regulation issued pursuant to this section shall be liable to a civil penalty of not more than $2,000 for each violation. Each violation shall be a separate offense. The Secretary of the department in which the Coast Guard is operating may assess and compromise any such penalty. No penalty shall be assessed until the person charged shall have been given notice and an opportunity for a hearing on such charge. In determining the amount of the penalty, or the amount agreed upon in compromise, the gravity of the violation, and the demonstrated good faith of the person charged in attempting to achieve rapid compliance, after notification of a violation, shall be considered by said Secretary.

(k) The provisions of this section shall be enforced by the Secretary of the department in which the Coast Guard is operating and he may utilize by agreement, with or without reimbursement, law enforcement officers or other personnel and facilities of the Administrator, other Federal agencies, or the States to carry out the provisions of this section. The provisions of this section may also be enforced by a State.

[Sec. 312(k) amended by PL 100-4]

(l) Anyone authorized by the Secretary of the department in which the Coast Guard is operating to enforce the provisions of this section may, except as to public vessels, (1) board and inspect any vessel upon the navigable waters of the United States and (2) execute any warrant or other process issued by an officer or court of competent jurisdiction.

(m) In the case of Guam and Trust Territory of the Pacific Islands, actions arising under this section may be brought in the district court of Guam, and in the case of the Virgin Islands such actions may be brought in the district court of the Virgin Islands. In the case of American Samoa and the Trust Territory of the Pacific Islands, such actions may be brought in the District Court of the United States for the District of Hawaii and such court shall have jurisdiction of such actions. In the case of the Canal Zone, such action may be brought in the District Court for the District of the Canal Zone.

Sec. 313. Federal Facilities Pollution Control.

(a) Each department, agency, or instrumentality of the executive, legislative, and judicial branches of the Federal Government (1) having jurisdiction over any property or facility, or (2) engaged in any activity resulting, or which may result, in the discharge or runoff of pollutants, and each officer, agent, or employee thereof in the performance of his official duties, shall be subject to, and comply with, all Federal, State, interstate, and local requirements, administrative authority, and process and sanctions respecting the control and abatement of water pollution in the same manner, and to the same extent as any nongovernmental entity including the payment of reasonable service charges. The preceding sentence shall apply (A) to any requirement whether substantive or procedural (including any recordkeeping or reporting requirement, any requirement respecting permits and any other requirement, whatsoever), (B) to the exercise of any Federal, State, or local administrative authority, and (C) to any process and sanction, whether enforced in Federal, State, or local courts or in any other manner. This subsection shall apply notwithstanding any immunity of such agencies, officers, agents, or employees under any law or rule of

law. Nothing in this section shall be construed to prevent any
department, agency, or instrumentality of the Federal Government, or
any officer, agent, or employee thereof in the performance of his
official duties, from reporting to the appropriate Federal district
court any proceeding to which the department, agency, or
instrumentality or officer, agent, or employee thereof is subject
pursuant to this section, and any such proceeding may be removed in
accordance with 28 U.S.C. 1441 et seq. No officer, agent, or
employee of the United States shall be personally liable for any
civil penalty arising from the performance of his official duties,
for which he is not otherwise liable, and the United States shall be
liable only for those civil penalties arising under Federal law or
imposed by a State or local court to enforce an order or the process
of such court. The President may exempt any effluent source of any
department, agency, or instrumentality in the executive branch from
compliance with any such a requirement if he determines it to be in
the paramount interest of the United States to do so; except that no
exemption may be granted from the requirements of section 306 or 307
of this Act. No such exemptions shall be granted due to lack of
appropriation unless the President shall have specifically requested
such appropriation as a part of the budgetary process and the
Congress shall have failed to make available such requested
appropriation. Any exemption shall be for a period not in excess of
one year, but additional exemptions may be granted for periods of
not to exceed one year upon the President'a making a new
determination. The President shall report each January to the
Congress all exemptions from the requirements to this section
granted during the preceding calendar year, together with his reason
for granting such exemption. In addition to any such exemption of a
particular effluent source, the President may, if he determines it
to be in the paramount interest of the United States to do so, issue
regulations exempting from compliance with the requirements of this
section any weaponry, equipment, aircraft, vessels, vehicles, or
other classes or categories of property, and access to such
property, which are owned or operated by the Armed Forces of the
United States (including the Coast Guard) or by the National Guard
of any State and which are uniquely military in nature. The
President shall reconsider the need for such regulations at
three-year intervals.

(b) (1) The Administrator shall coordinate with the head of each
    department, agency, or instrumentality of the Federal Government
    having jurisdiction over any property or facility utilizing
    federally owned wastewater facilities to develop a program of
    cooperation for utilizing wastewater control systems utilizing
    those innovative treatment processes and techniques for which
    guidelines have been promulgated under section 304(d)(3). Such
    program shall include an inventory of property and facilities
    which would utilize such processes and techniques.

    (2) Construction shall not be initiated for facilities for
    treatment of wastewater at any Federal property or facility
    after September 30, 1979, if alternative methods for wastewater
    treatment at such property or facility utilizing innovative
    treatment processes and techniques, including but not limited to
    methods utilizing recycle and reuse techniques and land
    treatment are not utilized, unless the life cycle cost of the

alternative treatment works exceeds the life cycle cost of the
most cost effective alternative by more than 15 per centum. The
Administrator may waive the application of this paragraph in any
case where the Administrator determines it to be in the public
interest, or that compliance with this paragraph would interfere
with the orderly compliance with conditions of a permit issued
pursuant to section 402 of this Act.

Sec. 314. Clean Lakes.

[Sec. 314(a) revised by PL 100-4]

(a) Establishment and Scope of the Program. --

(1) State program requirements. -- Each State on a biennial
basis shall prepare and submit to the Administrator for his
approval --

(A) an identification and classification according to
eutrophic condition of all publicly owned lakes in such
State;

(B) a description of procedures, processes, and methods
(including land use requirements), to control sources of
pollution of such lakes;

(C) a description of methods and procedures, in conjunction
with appropriate Federal agencies, to restore the quality of
such lakes;

(D) methods and procedures to mitigate the harmful effects
of high acidity, including innovative methods of
neutralizing and restoring buffering capacity of lakes and
methods of removing from lakes toxic metals and other toxic
substances mobilized by high acidity;

(E) a list and description of those publicly owned lakes in
such State for which uses are known to be impaired,
including those lakes which are known not to meet applicable
water quality standards or which require implementation of
control programs to maintain compliance with applicable
standards and those lakes in which water quality has
deteriorated as a result of high acidity that may reasonably
be due to acid deposition; and

(F) an assessment of the status and trends of water quality
in lakes in such State, including but not limited to, the
nature and extent of pollution loading from point and
nonpoint sources and the extent to which the use of lakes is
impaired as a result of such pollution, particularly with
respect to toxic pollution.

(2) Submission as Part 305(b)(1) Report. -- The information
required under paragraph (1) shall be included in the report
required under section 305(b)(1) of this Act, beginning with the
report required under such section by April 1, 1988.

(3) Report of Administrator. -- Not later than 180 days after receipt from the States of the biennial information required under paragraph (1), the Administrator shall submit to the Committee on Public Works and Transportation of the House of Representatives and the Committee on Environment and Public Works of the Senate a report on the status of water quality in lakes in the United States, including the effectiveness of the methods and procedures described in paragraph (1)(D).

(4) Eligibility Requirement. -- Beginning after April 1, 1988, a State must have submitted the information required under paragraph (1) in order to receive grant assistance under this section.

(b) The Administrator shall provide financial assistance to States in order to carry out methods and procedures approved by him under subsection (a) of this section. The Administrator shall provide financial assistance to States to prepare the identification and classification surveys required in subsection (a)(1) of this section.

[Sec. 314(b) amended by PL 100-4]

(c) (1) The amount granted to any State for any fiscal year under subsection (b) of this section shall not exceed 70 per centum of the funds expended by such State in such year for carrying out approved methods and procedures under subsection (a) of this Section.

[Sec. 314(c)(1) and (2) amended by PL 100-4]

(2) There is authorized to be appropriated $50,000,000 for the fiscal year ending June 30, 1973; $100,000,000 for the fiscal year 1974; $150,000,000 for the fiscal year 1975, $50,000,000 for fiscal year 1977, $60,000,000 for fiscal year 1978, $60,000,000 for fiscal year 1979, $60,000,000 for fiscal year 1980, $30,000,000 for fiscal year 1981, $30,000,000 for fiscal year 1982, such sums as may be necessary for fiscal years 1983 through 1985, and $30,000,000 per fiscal year for each of the fiscal years 1986 through 1990 for grants to States under subsection (b) of this section which sums shall remain available until expended. The Administrator shall provide for an equitable distribution of such sums to the States with approved methods and procedures under subsection (a) of this section.

(d) Demonstration Program. -- [Sec. 314(d) added by PL 100-4]

(1) General Requirements. -- The Administrator is authorized and directed to establish and conduct at locations throughout the Nation a lake water quality demonstration program. The program shall, at a minimum --

(A) develop cost effective technologies for the control of pollutants to preserve or enhance lake water quality while optimizing multiple lakes uses;

(B) control nonpoint sources of pollution which are contributing to the degradation of water quality in lakes;

(C) evaluate the feasibility of implementing regional consolidated pollution control strategies;

(D) demonstrate environmentally preferred techniques for the removal and disposal of contaminated lake sediments;

(E) develop improved methods for the removal of silt, stumps, aquatic growth, and other obstructions which impair the quality of lakes;

(F) construct and evaluate silt traps and other devices or equipment to prevent or abate the deposit of sediment in lakes; and

(G) demonstrate the costs and benefits of utilizing dredged material from lakes in the reclamation of despoiled land.

(2) Geographical Requirements. -- Demonstration projects authorized by this subsection shall be undertaken to reflect a variety of geographical and environmental conditions. As a priority, the Administrator shall undertake demonstration projects at Lake Houston, Texas, Beaver Lake, Arkansas; Greenwood Lake and Belcher Creek, New Jersey; Deal Lake, New Jersey; Alcyon Lake, New Jersey; Gorton's Pond, Rhode Island; Lake Washington, Rhode Island; Lake Bomoseen, Vermont; Sauk Lake, Minnesota; and Lake Worth, Texas.

(3) Reports. -- The Administrator shall report annually to the Committee on Public Works and Transportation of the House of Representatives and the Committee on Environment and Public Works of the Senate on work undertaken pursuant to this subsection. Upon completion of the program authorized by this subsection, the Administrator shall submit to such committees a final report on the results of such program, along with recommendations for further measures to improve the water quality of the Nation's lakes.

(4) Authorization of Appropriations. --

(A) In General. -- There is authorized to be appropriated to carry out this subsection not to exceed $40,000,000 for fiscal years beginning after September 30, 1986, to remain available until expended.

(B) Special Authorizations. --
(i) Amount. -- There is authorized to be appropriated to carry out subsection (b) with respect to subsection (a)(1)(D) not to exceed $15,000,000 for fiscal years beginning after September 30, 1986, to remain available until expended.
(ii) Distribution of Funds. -- The Administrator shall provide for an equitable distribution of sums appropriated pursuant to this subparagraph among States carrying out approved methods and procedures. Such

distribution shall be based on the relative needs of
each such State for the mitigation of the harmful
effects on lakes and other surface waters of high
acidity that may reasonably be due to acid deposition or
acid mine drainage.
(iii) Grants as Additional Assistance. -- The amount of
any grant to a State under this subparagraph shall be in
addition to, and not in lieu of, any other Federal
financial assistance.

Sec. 315. National Study Commission

(a) There is established a National Study Commission, which shall
make a full and complete investigation and study of all of the
technological aspects of achieving, and all aspects of the total
economic, social, and environmental effects of achieving or not
achieving, the effluent limitations and goals set forth for 1983 in
section 301(b)(2) of this Act.

(b) Such Commission shall be composed of fifteen members, including
five members of the Senate, who are members of the Public Works
committee, appointed by the President of the Senate, five members of
the House, who are members of the Public Works committee, appointed
by the Speaker of the House, and five members of the public
appointed by the President. The Chairman of such Commission shall
be elected from among its members.

(c) In the conduct of such study, the Commission is authorized to
contract with the National Academy of Sciences and the National
Academy of Engineering (acting through the National Research
Council), the National Institute of Ecology, Brookings Institution,
and other nongovernmental entities, for the investigation of matters
within their competence.

(d) The heads of the departments, agencies and instrumentalities of
the executive branch of the Federal Government shall cooperate with
the Commission in carrying out the requirements of this section, and
shall furnish to the Commission such information, as the Commission
deems necessary to carry out this section.

(e) A report shall be submitted to the Congress of the results of
such investigation and study, together with recommendations, not
later than three years after the date of enactment of this title.

(f) The members of the Commission who are not officers or employees
of the United States, while attending conferences or meetings of the
Commission or while otherwise serving at the request of the Chairman
shall be entitled to receive compensation at a rate not in excess of
the maximum rate of pay for grade GS-18, as provided in the General
Schedule under section 5332 of title V of the United States Code,
including traveltime and while away from their homes or regular
places of business they may be allowed travel expenses, including
per diem in lieu of subsistence as authorized by law (5 U.S.C.
73b-2) for persons in the Government service employed
intermittently.

(g) In addition to authority to appoint personnel subject to the provisions of title 5, United States Code, governing appointments in the competitive service, and to pay such personnel in accordance with the provisions of chapter 51 and subchapter III of chapter 53 of such title relating to classification and General Schedule pay rates, the Commission shall have authority to enter into contracts with private or public organizations who shall furnish the Commission with such administrative and technical personnel as may be necessary to carry out the purpose of this section. Personnel furnished by such organizations under this subsection are not, and shall not be considered to be, Federal employees for any purposes, but in the performance of their duties shall be guided by the standards which apply to employees of the legislative branches under rules 41 and 43 of the Senate and House of Representatives, respectively.

(h) There is authorized to be appropriated, for use in carrying out this section, not to exceed $17,250,000.

Sec. 316. Thermal Discharges.

(a) With respect to any point source otherwise subject to the provisions of section 301 or section 306 of this Act, whenever the owner or operator of any such source, after opportunity for public hearing, can demonstrate to the satisfaction of the Administrator (or, if appropriate, the State) that any effluent limitation proposed for the control of the thermal component of any discharge from such source will require effluent limitations more stringent than necessary to assure the projection and propagation of a balanced, indigenous population of shellfish, fish, and wildlife in and on the body of water into which the discharge is to be made, the Administrator (or, if appropriate, the State) may impose an effluent limitation under such sections for such plant, with respect to the thermal component of such discharge (taking into account the interaction of such thermal component with other pollutants), that will assure the protection and propagation of a balanced, indigenous population of shellfish, fish, and wildlife in and on that body of water.

(b) Any standard established pursuant to section 301 or section 306 of this Act and applicable to a point source shall require that the location, design, construction, and capacity of cooling water intake structures reflect the best technology available for minimizing adverse environmental impact.

(c) Notwithstanding any other provision of this Act, any point source of a discharge having a thermal component, the modification of which point source is commenced after the date of enactment of the Federal Water Pollution Control Act Amendments of 1972 and which, as modified, meets effluent limitations established under section 301, or, if more stringent, effluent limitations established under section 303 and which effluent limitations will assure protection and propagation of a balanced, indigenous population of shellfish, fish, and wildlife in or on the water into which the discharge is made, shall not be subject to any more stringent effluent limitation with respect to the thermal component of its discharge during a ten year period beginning on the date of completion of such modification or during the period of depreciation or amortization of such facility for the purpose of section 167 or 169 (or both) of the Internal Revenue Code of 1954, whichever period ends first.

Sec. 317. Financing Study.

(a) The Administrator shall continue to investigate and study the feasibility of alternate methods of financing the cost of preventing, controlling and abating pollution as directed in the Water Quality Improvement Act of 1970 (Public Law 91-224), including, but not limited to, the feasibility of establishing a pollution abatement trust fund. The results of such investigation and study shall be reported to the Congress not later than two years after enactment of this title, together with recommendations of the Administrator for financing the programs for preventing, controlling and abating pollution for the fiscal years beginning after fiscal year 1976, including any necessary legislation.

(b) There is authorized to be appropriated for use in carrying out this section, not to exceed $1,000,000.

Sec. 318. Aquaculture.

(a) The Administrator is authorized, after public hearings, to permit the discharge of a specific pollutant or pollutants under controlled conditions associated with an approved aquaculture project under Federal or State supervision pursuant to section 402 of this Act.

(b) The Administrator shall by regulation establish any procedures and guidelines which the Administrator deems necessary to carry out this section. Such regulations shall require the application to such discharge of each criterion, factor, procedure, and requirement applicable to a permit issued under section 402 of this title, as the Administrator determines necessary to carry out the objective of this Act.

(c) Each State desiring to administer its own permit program within its jurisdiction for discharge of a specific pollutant or pollutants under controlled conditions associated with an approved aquaculture project may do so if upon submission of such program the Administrator determines such program is adequate to carry out the objective of this Act.

Sec. 319. Nonpoint Source Management Programs.

[Sec. 319 added by PL 100-4]

(a) State Assessment Reports. --

(1) Contents. -- The Governor of each State shall, after notice and opportunity for public comment, prepare and submit to the Administrator for approval, a report which --

(A) identifies those navigable waters within the State which, without additional action to control nonpoint sources of pollution, cannot reasonably be expected to attain or maintain applicable water quality standards or the goals and requirements of this Act;

(B) identifies those categories and subcategories of nonpoint sources or, where appropriate, particular nonpoint sources which add significant pollution to each portion of the navigable waters identified under subparagraph (A) in amounts which contribute to such portion not meeting such water quality standards or such goals and requirements;

(C) describes the process, including intergovernmental coordination and public participation, for identifying best management practices and measures to control each category and subcategory of nonpoint sources and, where appropriate, particular nonpoint sources identified under subparagraph (B) and to reduce, to the maximum extent practicable, the level of pollution resulting from such category, subcategory, or source; and

(D) identifies and describes State and local programs for controlling pollution added from nonpoint sources to, and improving the quality of, each such portion of the navigable waters, including but not limited to those programs which are receiving Federal assistance under subsections (h) and (i).

(2) Information Used in Preparation. -- In developing the report required by this section, the State (A) may rely upon information developed pursuant to sections 208, 303(e), 304(f), 305(b), and 314, and other information as appropriate, and (B) may utilize appropriate elements of the waste treatment management plans developed pursuant to sections 208(b) and 303, to the extent such elements are consistent with and fulfill the requirements of this section.

(b) State Management Programs. --

(1) In General. -- The Governor of each State, for that State or in combination with adjacent States, shall, after notice and opportunity for public comment, prepare and submit to the Administrator for approval a management program which such State proposes to implement in the first four fiscal years beginning after the date of submission of such management program for controlling pollution added from nonpoint sources to the navigable waters within the State and improving the quality of such waters.

(2) Specific Contents. -- Each management program proposed for implementation under this subsection shall include each of the following:

(A) An identification of the best management practices and measures which will be undertaken to reduce pollutant loadings resulting from each category, subcategory, or particular nonpoint source designated under paragraph

(1)(B), taking into account the impact of the practice on ground water quality.

(B) An identification of programs (including, as appropriate, nonregulatory or regulatory programs for enforcement, technical assistance, financial assistance, education, training, technology transfer, and demonstration projects) to achieve implementation of the best management practices by the categories, subcategories, and particular nonpoint sources designated under subparagraph (A).

(C) A schedule containing annual milestones for (i) utilization of the program implementation methods identified in subparagraph (B), and (ii) implementation of the best management practices identified in subparagraph (A) by the categories, subcategories, or particular nonpoint sources designated under paragraph (1)(B). Such schedule shall provide for utilization of the best management practices at the earliest practicable date.

(D) A certification of the attorney general of the State or States (or the chief attorney of any State water pollution control agency which has independent legal counsel) that the laws of the State or States, as the case may be, provide adequate authority to implement such management program or, if there is not such adequate authority, a list of such additional authorities as will be necessary to implement such management program. A schedule and commitment by the State or States to seek such additional authorities as expeditiously as practicable.

(E) Sources of Federal and other assistance and funding (other than assistance provided under subsections (h) and (i) which will be available in each of such fiscal years for supporting implementation of such practices and measures and the purposes for which such assistance will be used in each of such fiscal years.

(F) An identification of Federal financial assistance programs and Federal development projects for which the State will review individual assistance applications or development projects for their effect on water quality pursuant to the procedures set forth in Executive Order 12372 as in effect on September 17, 1983, to determine whether such assistance applications or development projects would be consistent with the program prepared under this subsection; for the purposes of this subparagraph, identification shall not be limited to the assistance programs or development projects subject to Executive Order 12372 but may include any programs listed in the most recent Catalog of Federal Domestic Assistance which may have an effect on the purposes and objectives of the State's nonpoint source pollution management program.

(3) Utilization of Local and Private Experts. -- In development and implementing a management program under this subsection, a State shall, to the maximum extent practicable, involve local

public and private agencies and organizations which have expertise in control of nonpoint sources of pollution.

(4) Development on Watershed Basis. -- A State shall, to the maximum extent practicable, develop and implement a management program under this subsection on a watershed-by-watershed basis within such State.

(c) Administrative Provisions. --

(1) Cooperation Requirement. -- Any report required by subsection (a) and any management program and report required by subsection (b) shall be developed in cooperation with local, substate regional, and interstate entities which are actively planning for the implementation of nonpoint source pollution controls and have either been certified by the Administrator in accordance with section 208, have worked jointly with the State on water quality management planning under section 205(j), or have been designated by the State legislative body or Governor as water quality management planning agencies for their geographic areas.

(2) Time Period for Submission of Reports and Management Programs. -- Each report and management program shall be submitted to the Administrator during the 18-month period beginning on the date of the enactment of this section.

(d) Approval or Disapproval of Reports and Management Programs. --

(1) Deadline. -- Subject to paragraph (2), not later than 180 days after the date of submission to the Administrator of any report or management program under this section (other than subsections (h), (i), and (k), the Administrator shall either approve or disapprove such report or management program, as the case may be. The Administrator may approve a portion of a management program under this subsection. If the Administrator does not disapprove a report, management program, or portion of a management program in such 180-day period, such report, management program, or portion shall be deemed approved for purposes of this section.

(2) Procedure for Disapproval. -- If, after notice and opportunity for public comment and consultation with appropriate Federal and State agencies and other interested persons, the Administrator determines that --

(A) the proposed management program or any portion thereof does not meet the requirements of subsection (b)(2) of this section or is not likely to satisfy, in whole or in part, the goals and requirements of this Act;

(B) adequate authority does not exist, or adequate resources are not available, to implement such program or portion;

(C) the schedule for implementing such program or portion is not sufficiently expeditious; or

(D) the practices and measures proposed in such program or portion are not adequate to reduce the level of pollution in navigable waters in the State resulting from nonpoint sources and to improve the quality of navigable waters in the State; the Administrator shall within 6 months of receipt of the proposed program notify the State of any revisions or modifications necessary to obtain approval. The State shall thereupon have an additional 3 months to submit its revised management program and the Administrator shall approve or disapprove such revised program within three months of receipt.

(3) Failure of State to Submit Report. -- If a Governor of State does not submit the report required by subsection (a) within the period specified by subsection (c)(2), the Administrator shall, within 30 months after the date of the enactment of this section, prepare a report for such State which makes the identifications required by paragraphs (1)(A) and (1)(B) of subsection (a). Upon completion of the requirement of the preceding sentence and after notice and opportunity for comment, the Administrator shall report to Congress on his actions pursuant to this section.

(e) Local Management Programs; Technical Assistance. -- If a State fails to submit a management program under subsection (b) or the Administrator does not approve such a management program, a local public agency or organization which has expertise in, and authority to, control water pollution, resulting from nonpoint sources in any area of such State which the Administrator determines is of sufficient geographic size may, with approval of such State, request the Administrator to provide, and the Administrator shall provide, technical assistance to such agency or organization in developing for such area a management program which is described in subsection (b) and can be approved pursuant to subsection (d). After development of such management program, such agency or organization shall submit such management program to the Administrator for approval. If the Administrator approves such management program, such agency or organization shall be eligible to receive financial assistance under subsection (h) for implementation of such management program as if such agency or organization were a State for which a report submitted under subsection (a) and a management program submitted under subsection (b) were approved under this section. Such financial assistance shall be subject to the same terms and conditions as assistance provided to a State under subsection (h).

(f) Technical Assistance for States. -- Upon request of a State, the Administrator may provide technical assistance to such State in developing a management program approved under subsection (b) for those portions of the navigable waters requested by such State.

(g) Interstate Management Conference. --

(1) Convening of Conference; Notification; Purpose. -- If any portion of the navigable waters in any State which is implementing a management program approved under this section is not meeting applicable water quality standards or the goals and

requirements of this Act as a result, in whole or in part, of pollution from nonpoint sources in another State, such State may petition the Administrator to convene, and the Administrator shall convene, a management conference of all States which contribute significant pollution resulting from nonpoint sources to such portion. If, on the basis of information available, the Administrator determines that a State is not meeting applicable water quality standards or the goals and requirements of this Act as a result, in whole or in part, of significant pollution from nonpoint sources in another State, the Administrator shall notify such States. The Administrator may convene a management conference under this paragraph not later than 180 days after giving such notification, whether or not the State which is not meeting such standards requests such conference. The purpose of such conference shall be to develop an agreement among such States to reduce the level of pollution in such portion resulting from nonpoint sources and to improve the water quality of such portion. Nothing in such agreement shall supersede or abrogate rights to quantities of water which have been established by interstate water compacts, Supreme Court decrees, or State water laws. This subsection shall not apply to any pollution which is subject to the Colorado River Basin Salinity Control Act. The requirement that the Administrator convene a management conference shall not be subject to the provisions of section 505 of this Act.

(2) State Management Program Requirement. -- To the extent that the States reach agreement through such conference, the management programs of the States which are parties to such agreements and which contribute significant pollution to the navigable waters or portions thereof not meeting applicable water quality standards or goals and requirements of this Act will be revised to reflect such agreement. Such a management program shall be consistent with Federal and State law.

(h) Grant Program. --

(1) Grants for Implementation of Management Programs. -- Upon application of a State for which a report submitted under subsection (a) and a management program submitted under subsection (b) is approved under this section, the Administrator shall make grants, subject to such terms and conditions as the Administrator considers appropriate, under this subsection to such State for the purpose of assisting the State in implementing such management program. Funds reserved pursuant to section 205(j)(5) of this Act may be used to develop and implement such management program.

(2) Applications. -- An application for a grant under this subsection in any fiscal year shall be in such form and shall contain such other information as the Administrator may require, including an identification and description of the best management practices and measures which the State proposes to assist, encourage, or require in such year with the Federal assistance to be provided under the grant.

(3) Federal Share. -- The Federal share of the cost of each management program implemented with Federal assistance under this subsection in any fiscal year shall not exceed 60 percent of the cost incurred by the State in implementing such management program and shall be made on condition that the non-Federal share is provided from non-Federal sources.

(4) Limitation on Grant Amounts. -- Notwithstanding any other provision of this subsection, not more than 15 percent of the amount appropriated to carry out this subsection may be used to make grants to any one State, including any grants to any local public agency or organization with authority to control pollution from nonpoint sources in any area of such State.

(5) Priority for Effective Mechanisms. -- For each fiscal year beginning after September 30, 1987, the Administrator may give priority in making grants under this subsection, and shall give consideration in determining the Federal share of any such grant, to States which have implemented or are proposing to implement management programs which will --

    (A) control particularly difficult or serious nonpoint source pollution problems, including, but not limited to, problems resulting from mining activities;

    (B) implement innovative methods or practices for controlling nonpoint sources of pollution, including regulatory programs where the Administrator deems appropriate;

    (C) control interstate nonpoint source pollution problems; or

    (D) carry out ground water quality protection activities which the Administrator determines are part of a comprehensive nonpoint source pollution control program, including research, planning, ground water assessments, demonstration programs, enforcement, technical assistance, education, and training to protect ground water quality from nonpoint sources of pollution.

(6) Availability for Obligation. -- The funds granted to each State pursuant to this subsection in a fiscal year shall remain available for obligation by such State for the fiscal year for which appropriated. The amount of any such funds not obligated by the end of such fiscal year shall be available to the Administrator for granting to other States under this subsection in the next fiscal year.

(7) Limitation on Use of Funds. -- States may use funds from grants made pursuant to this section for financial assistance to persons only to the extent that such assistance is related to the costs of demonstration projects.

(8) Satisfactory Progress. -- No grant may be made under this subsection in any fiscal year to a State which in the preceding fiscal year received a grant under this subsection unless the

Administrator determines that such State made satisfactory
progress in such preceding fiscal year in meeting the schedule
specified by such State under subsection (b)(2).

(9) Maintenance of Effort. -- No grant may be made to a State
under this subsection in any fiscal year unless such State
enters into such agreements with the Administrator as the
Administrator may require to ensure that such State will
maintain its aggregate expenditures from all other sources for
programs for controlling pollution added to the navigable waters
in such State from nonpoint sources and improving the quality of
such waters at or above the average level of such expenditures
in its two fiscal years preceding the date of enactment of this
subsection.

(10) Request for Information. -- The Administrator may request
such information, data, and reports as he considers necessary to
make the determination of continuing eligibility for grants
under this section.

(11) Reporting and Other Requirements. -- Each State shall
report to the Administrator on an annual basis concerning (A)
its progress in meeting the schedule of milestones submitted
pursuant to subsection (b)(2)(C) of this section, and (B) to the
extent that appropriate information is available, reductions in
nonpoint source pollutant loading and improvements in water
quality for those navigable waters or watersheds within the
State which were identified pursuant to subsection (a)(1)(A) of
this section resulting from implementation of the management
program.

(12) Limitation on Administrative Costs. -- For purposes of
this subsection, administrative costs in the form of salaries,
overhead, or indirect costs for services provided and charged
against activities and programs carried out with a grant under
this subsection shall not exceed in any fiscal year 10 percent
of the amount of the grant in such year, except that costs of
implementing enforcement and regulatory activities, education,
training, technical assistance, demonstration projects, and
technology transfer programs shall not be subject to this
limitation.

(i) Grants for Protecting Groundwater Quality. --

(1) Eligible Applicants and Activities. -- Upon application of
a State for which a report submitted under subsection (a) and a
plan submitted under subsection (b) is approved under this
section, the Administrator shall make grants under this
subsection to such State for the purpose of assisting such State
in carrying out groundwater quality protection activities which
the Administrator determines will advance the State toward
implementation of a comprehensive nonpoint source pollution
control program. Such activities shall include, but not be
limited to, research planning, groundwater assessments,
demonstration programs, enforcement, technical assistance,
education and training to protect the quality of groundwater and
to prevent contamination of groundwater from nonpoint sources of

pollution.

(2) Applications. -- An application for a grant under this
subsection shall be in such form and shall contain such
information as the Administrator may require.

(3) Federal Share; Maximum Amount. -- The Federal share of the
cost of assisting a State in carrying out groundwater protection
activities in any fiscal year under this subsection shall be 50
percent of the costs incurred by the State in carrying out such
activities, except that the maximum amount of Federal assistance
which any State may receive under this subsection in any fiscal
year shall not exceed $150,000.

(4) Report. -- The Administrator shall include in each report
transmitted under subsection (m) a report on the activities and
programs implemented under this subsection during the preceding
fiscal year.

(j) Authorization of Appropriations. -- There is authorized to be
appropriated to carry out subsections (h) and (i) not to exceed
$70,000,000 for fiscal year 1988, $100,000,000 per fiscal year for
each of fiscal years 1989 and 1990, and $130,000,000 for fiscal year
1991; except that for each of such fiscal years not to exceed
$7,500,000 may be made available to carry out subsection (i). Sums
appropriated pursuant to this subsection shall remain available
until expended.

(k) Consistency of Other Programs and Projects With Management
Programs. -- The Administrator shall transmit to the Office of
Management and Budget and the appropriate Federal departments and
agencies a list of those assistance programs and development
projects identified by each State under subsection (b)(2)(F) for
which individual assistance applications and projects will be
reviewed pursuant to the procedures set forth in Executive Order
12372 as in effect on September 17, 1983. Beginning not later than
sixty days after receiving notification by the Administrator, each
Federal department and agency shall modify existing regulations to
allow States to review individual development projects and
assistance applications under the identified Federal assistance
programs and shall accommodate, according to the requirements and
definitions of Executive Order 12372, as in effect on September 17,
1983, the concerns of the State regarding the consistency of such
applications or projects with the State nonpoint source pollution
management program.

(1) Collection of Information. -- The Administrator shall collect
and make available, through publications and other appropriate
means, information pertaining to management practices and
implementation methods, including, but not limited to, (1)
information concerning the costs and relative efficiencies of best
management practices for reducing nonpoint source pollution; and (2)
available data concerning the relationship between water quality and
implementation of various management practices to control nonpoint
sources of pollution.

(m) Reports of Administrator. --

(1) Annual Reports. -- Not later than January 1, 1988, and each January 1 thereafter, the Administrator shall transmit to the Committee on Public Works and Transportation of the House of Representatives and the Committee on Environment and Public Works of the Senate, a report for the preceding fiscal year on the activities and programs implemented under this section and the progress made in reducing pollution in the navigable waters resulting from nonpoint sources and improving the quality of such waters.

(2) Final Report. -- Not later than January 1, 1990, the Administrator shall transmit to Congress a final report on the activities carried out under this section. Such report, at a minimum, shall --

(A) describe the management programs being implemented by the States by types and amount of affected navigable waters, categories and subcategories of nonpoint sources, and types of best management practices being implemented;

(B) describe the experiences of the States in adhering to schedules and implementing best management practices;

(C) describe the amount and purpose of grants awarded pursuant to subsections (h) and (i) of this section;

(D) identify, to the extent that information is available, the progress made in reducing pollutant loads and improving water quality in the navigable waters;

(E) indicate what further actions need to be taken to attain and maintain in those navigable waters (i) applicable water quality standards; and (ii) the goals and requirements of this Act;

(F) include recommendations of the Administrator concerning future programs (including enforcement programs) for controlling pollution from nonpoint sources; and

(G) identify the activities and programs of departments, agencies, and instrumentalities of the United States which are inconsistent with the management programs submitted by the States and recommend modifications so that such activities and programs are consistent with and assist the States in implementation of such management programs.

(n) Set Aside for Administrative Personnel. -- Not less than 5 percent of the funds appropriated pursuant to subsection (j) for any fiscal year shall be available to the Administrator

to maintain personnel levels at the Environmental Protection Agency at levels which are adequate to carry out this section in such year.

Sec. 320. National Estuary Program

[Sec. 320 added by PL 100-4]

(a) Management Conference. --

(1) Nomination of Estuaries. -- The Governor of any State may nominate to the Administrator an estuary lying in whole or in part within the State as an estuary of national significance and request a management conference to develop a comprehensive management plan for the estuary. The nomination shall document the need for the conference, the likelihood of success, and information relating to the factors in paragraph (2).

(2) Convening of Conference. --

(A) In General. -- In any case where the Administrator determines, on his own initiative or upon nomination of a State under paragraph (1), that the attainment or maintenance of that water quality in an estuary which assures protection of public water supplies and the protection and propagation of a balanced, indigenous population of shellfish, fish, and wildlife, and allows recreational activities, in and on the water, requires the control of point and nonpoint sources of pollution to supplement existing controls of pollution in more than one State, the Administrator shall select such estuary and convene a management conference.

(B) Priority consideration. -- The Administrator shall give priority consideration under this section to Long Island Sound, New York and Connecticut; Narragansett Bay, Rhode Island; Buzzards Bay, Massachusetts; Puget Sound, Washington; New York-New Jersey Harbor, New York and New Jersey; Delaware Bay, Delaware and New Jersey; Delaware Inland Bays, Delaware; Albemarle Sound, North Carolina; Sarasota Bay, Florida; San Francisco Bay, California; and Galveston Bay, Texas.

(3) Boundary Dispute Exception. -- In any case in which a boundary between two States passes through an estuary and such boundary is disputed and is the subject of an action in any court, the Administrator shall not convene a management conference with respect to such estuary before a final adjudication has been made of such dispute.

(b) Purposes of Conference. -- The purposes of any management conference convened with respect to an estuary under this subsection shall be to --

(1) assess trends in water quality, natural resources, and uses of the estuary;

(2) collect, characterize, and assess data on toxics, nutrients, and natural resources within the estuarine zone to identify the causes of environmental problems;

(3) develop the relationship between the inplace loads and point and nonpoint loadings of pollutants to the estuarine zone and the potential uses of the zone, water quality, and natural resources;

(4) develop a comprehensive conservation and management plan that recommends priority corrective actions and compliance schedules addressing point and nonpoint sources of pollution to restore and maintain the chemical, physical, and biological integrity of the estuary, including restoration and maintenance of water quality, a balanced indigenous population of shellfish, fish and wildlife, and recreational activities in the estuary, and assure that the designated uses of the estuary are protected;

(5) develop plans for the coordinated implementation of the plan by the States as well as Federal and local agencies participating in the conference;

(6) monitor the effectiveness of actions taken pursuant to the plan; and

(7) review all Federal financial assistance programs and Federal development projects in accordance with the requirements of Executive Order 12372, as in effect on September 17, 1983, to determine whether such assistance program or project would be consistent with and further the purposes and objectives of the plan prepared under this section. For purposes of paragraph (7), such programs and projects shall not be limited to the assistance programs and development projects subject to Executive Order 12372, but may include any programs listed in the most recent Catalog of Federal Domestic Assistance which may have an effect on the purposes and objectives of the plan developed under this section.

(c) Members of Conference. -- The members of a management conference convened under this section shall include, at a minimum, the Administrator and representatives of --

(1) each State and foreign nation located in whole or in part in the estuarine zone of the estuary for which the conference is convened;

(2) international, interstate, or regional agencies or entities having jurisdiction over all or a significant part of the estuary;

(3) each interested Federal agency, as determined appropriate by the Administrator;

(4) local governments having jurisdiction over any land or water within the estuarine zone, as determined appropriate by the Administrator; and

(5) affected industries, public and private educational institutions, and the general public, as determined appropriate by the Administrator.

(d) Utilization of Existing Data. -- In developing a conservation and management plan under this section, the management conference shall survey and utilize existing reports, data, and studies relating to the estuary that have been developed by or made available to Federal, interstate, State, and local agencies.

(e) Period of Conference. -- A management conference convened under this section shall be convened for a period not to exceed 5 years. Such conference may be extended by the Administrator, and if terminated after the initial period, may be reconvened by the Administrator at any time thereafter, as may be necessary to meet the requirements of this section.

(f) Approval and Implementation of Plans. --

   (1) Approval. -- Not later than 120 days after the completion of a conservation and management plan and after providing for public review and comment, the Administrator shall approve such plan if the plan meets the requirements of this section and the affected Governor or Governors concur.

   (2) Implementation. -- Upon approval of a conservation and management plan under this section, such plan shall be implemented. Funds authorized to be appropriated under titles II and VI and section 319 of this Act may be used in accordance with the applicable requirements of this Act to assist States with the implementation of such plan.

(g) Grants. --

   (1) Recipients. -- The Administrator is authorized to make grants to State, interstate, and regional water pollution control agencies and entities, State coastal zone management agencies, interstate agencies, other public or nonprofit private agencies, institutions, organizations, and individuals.

   (2) Purposes. -- Grants under this subsection shall be made to pay for assisting research, surveys, studies, and modeling and other technical work necessary for the development of a conservation and management plan under this section.

   (3) Federal Share. -- The amount of grants to any person (including a State, interstate, or regional agency or entity) under this subsection for a fiscal year shall not exceed 75 percent of the costs of such research, survey, studies, and work and shall be made on condition that the non-Federal share of such costs are provided from non-Federal sources.

(h) Grant Reporting. -- Any person (including a State, interstate, or regional agency or entity) that receives a grant under subsection (g) shall report to the Administrator not later than 18 months after receipt of such grant and biennially thereafter on the progress being made under this section.

(i) Authorization of Appropriations. -- There are authorized to be appropriated to the Administrator not to exceed $12,000,000 per fiscal year for each of fiscal years 1987, 1988, 1989, 1990, and 1991 for --

(1) expenses related to the administration of management conferences under this section, not to exceed 10 percent of the amount appropriated under this subsection;

(2) making grants under subsection (g); and

(3) monitoring the implementation of a conservation and management plan by the management conference or by the Administrator, in any case in which the conference has been terminated. The Administrator shall provide up to $5,000,000 per fiscal year of the sums authorized to be appropriated under this subsection to the Administrator of the National Oceanic and Atmospheric Administration to carry out subsection (j).

(j) Research. --

(1) Programs. -- In order to determine the need to convene a management conference under this section or at the request of such a management conference, the Administrator shall coordinate and implement through the National Marine Pollution Program Office and the National Marine Fisheries Service of the National Oceanic and Atmospheric Administration, as appropriate, for one or more estuarine zones --

(A) a long-term program of trend assessment monitoring measuring variations in pollutant concentrations, marine ecology, and other physical or biological environmental parameters which may affect estuarine zones, to provide the Administrator the capacity to determine the potential and actual effects of alternative management strategies and measures;

(B) a program of ecosystem assessment assisting in the development of (i) baseline studies which determine the state of estuarine zones and the effects of natural and anthropogenic changes, and (ii) predictive models capable of translating information on specific discharges or general pollutant loadings within estuarine zones into a set of probable effects on such zones;

(C) a comprehensive water quality sampling program for the continuous monitoring of nutrients, chlorine acid precipitation dissolved oxygen, and potentially toxic pollutants (including organic chemicals and metals) in estuarine zones, after consultation with interested States, local, interstate, or international agencies and review and analysis of all environmental sampling data presently collected from estuarine zones; and

(D) a program of research to identify the movements of nutrients, sediments and pollutants through estuarine zones and the impact of nutrients, sediments, and pollutants on water quality, the ecosystem, and designated or potential uses of the estuarine zones.

(2) Reports. -- The Administrator, in cooperation with the Administrator of the National Oceanic and Atmospheric Administration, shall submit to the Congress no less often than biennially a comprehensive report on the activities authorized under this subsection including --

(A) a listing of priority monitoring and research needs;

(B) an assessment of the state and health of the Nation's estuarine zones, to the extent evaluated under this subsection;

(C) a discussion of pollution problems and trends in pollutant concentrations with a direct or indirect effect on water quality, the ecosystem, and designated or potential uses of each estuarine zone, to the extent evaluated under this subsection; and

(D) an evaluation of pollution abatement activities and management measures so far implemented to determine the degree of improvement toward the objectives expressed in subsection (b)(4) of this section,

(k) Definitions. -- For purposes of this section, the terms 'estuary' and 'estuarine zone' have the meanings such terms have in section 104(n)(4) of this Act, except that the term 'estuarine zone' shall also include associated aquatic ecosystems and those portions of tributaries draining into the estuary up to the historic height of migration of anadromous fish or the historic head of tidal influence, whichever is higher.

TITLE IV -- PERMITS AND LICENSES CERTIFICATION

Sec. 401. Certification.

(a) (1) Any applicant for a Federal license or permit to conduct any activity including, but not limited to, the construction or operation of facilities, which may result in any discharge into the navigable waters, shall provide the licensing or permitting agency a certification from the State in which the discharge originates or will originate, or, if appropriate, from the interstate water pollution control agency having jurisdiction over the navigable waters at the point where the discharge originates or will originate, that any such discharge will comply with the applicable provisions of sections 301, 302, 303, 306, and 307 of this Act. In the case of any such activity for which there is not an applicable effluent limitation or other limitation under sections 301(b) and 302, and there is not an applicable standard under sections 306 and 307, the State shall so certify, except that any such certification shall not be deemed to satisfy section 511(c) of this Act. Such State or interstate agency shall establish procedures for public notice in the case of all applications for certification by it and, to the extent it deems appropriate, procedures for public hearings in connection with specific applications. In any case where a State or interstate agency has no authority to give such a certification, such certification shall be from the Administrator. If the State, interstate agency, or Administrator, as the case may be, fails or refuses to act on a request for certification, within a reasonable period of time (which shall not exceed one year) after receipt of such request, the certification requirements of this subsection shall be waived with respect to such Federal application. No license or permit shall be granted until the certification required by this section has been obtained or has been waived as provided in the preceding sentence. No license or permit shall be granted if certification has been denied by the State, interstate agency, or the Administrator, as the case may be.

(2) Upon receipt of such application and certification the licensing or permitting agency shall immediately notify the Administrator of such application and certification. Whenever such a discharge may affect, as determined by the Administrator, the quality of the waters of any other State, the Administrator within thirty days of the date of notice of application for such Federal license or permit shall so notify such other State, the licensing or permitting agency, and the applicant. If, within sixty days after receipt of such notification, such other State determines that such discharge will affect the quality of its waters so as to violate any water quality requirement in such State, and within such sixty-day period notifies the Administrator and the licensing or permitting agency in writing of its objection to the issuance of such license or permit and requests a public hearing on such objection, the licensing or permitting agency shall hold such a hearing. The Administrator shall at such hearing submit his evaluation and recommendations with respect to any such objection to the licensing or

permitting agency. Such agency, based upon the recommendations of such State, the Administrator, and upon any additional evidence, if any, presented to the agency at the hearing, shall condition such license or permit in such manner as may be necessary to insure compliance with applicable water quality requirements. If the imposition of conditions cannot insure such compliance such agency shall not issue such license or permit.

(3) The certification obtained pursuant to paragraph (1) of this subsection with respect to the construction of any facility shall fulfill the requirements of this subsection with respect to ce-tification in connection with any other Federal license or permit required for the operation of such facility unless, after notice to the certifying State, agency, or Administrator, as the case may be, which shall be given by the Federal agency to whom application is made for such operating license or permit, the State, or if appropriate, the interstate agency or the Administrator, notifies such agency within sixty days after receipt of such notice that there is no longer reasonable assurance that there will be compliance with the applicable provisions of sections 301, 302, 303, 306, and 307 of this Act because of changes since the construction license or permit certification was issued in (A) the construction or operation of the facility, (B) the characteristics of the waters into which such discharge is made, (C) the water quality criteria applicable to such waters or (D) applicable effluent limitations or other requirements. This paragraph shall be inapplicable in any case where the applicant for such operating license or permit has failed to provide the certifying State, or, if appropriate, the interstate agency or the Administrator, with notice of any proposed changes in the construction or operation of the facility with respect to which a construction license or permit has been granted, which changes may result in violation of section 301, 302, 303, 306, or 307 of this Act.

(4) Prior to the initial operation of any federally licensed or permitted facility or activity which may result in any discharge into the navigable waters and with respect to which a certification has been obtained pursuant to paragraph (1) of this subsection, which facility or activity is not subject to a Federal operating license or permit, the licensee or permittee shall provide an opportunity for such certifying State, or, if appropriate, the interstate agency or the Administrator to review the manner in which the facility or activity shall be operated or conducted for the purposes of assuring that applicable effluent limitations or other limitations or other applicable water quality requirements will not be violated. Upon notification by the certifying State, or if appropriate, the interstate agency or the Administrator that the operation of any such federally licensed or permitted facility or activity will violate applicable effluent limitations or other limitations or other water quality requirements such Federal agency may, after public hearing, suspend from license or permit. If such license or permit is suspended, it shall remain suspended until notification is received from the certifying State, agency, or Administrator, as the case may be, that there

is reasonable assurance that such facility or activity will not violate the applicable provisions of section 301, 302, 303, 306, or 307 of this Act.

(5) Any Federal license or permit with respect to which a certification has been obtained under paragraph (1) of this subsection may be suspended or revoked by the Federal agency issuing such license or permit upon the entering of a judgment under this Act that such facility or activity has been operated in violation of the applicable provisions of section 301, 302, 303, 306, or 307 of this Act.

(6) Except with respect to a permit issued under section 402 of this Act, in any case where actual construction of a facility has been lawfully commenced prior to April 3, 1970, no certification shall be required under this subsection for a license or permit issued after April 3, 1970, to operate such facility, except that any such license or permit issued without certification shall terminate April 3, 1973, unless prior to such termination date the person having such license or permit submits to the Federal agency which issued such license or permit a certification and otherwise meets the requirements of this section.

(b) Nothing in this section shall be construed to limit the authority of any department or agency pursuant to any other provision of law to require compliance with any applicable water quality requirements. The Administrator shall, upon the request of any Federal department or agency, or State or interstate agency, or applicant, provide, for the purpose of this section, any relevant information on applicable effluent limitations, or other limitations, standards, regulations or requirements, or water quality criteria, and shall, when requested by any such department or agency or State or interstate agency, or applicant, comment on any methods to comply with such limitations, standards, regulations, requirements, or criteria.

(c) In order to implement the provisions of this section, the Secretary of the Army, acting through the Chief of Engineers, is authorized, if he deems it to be in the public interest, to permit the use of spoil disposal areas under his jurisdiction by Federal licensees or permittees, and to make an appropriate charge for such use. Moneys received from such licensees or permittees shall be deposited in the Treasury as miscellaneous receipts.

(d) Any certification provided under this section shall set forth any effluent limitations and other limitations, and monitoring requirements necessary to assure that any applicant for a Federal license or permit will comply with any applicable effluent limitations and other limitations, under section 301 or 302 of this Act, standard of performance under section 306 of this Act, or prohibition, effluent standard, or pretreatment standard under section 307 of this Act, and with any other appropriate requirement of State law set forth in such certification, and shall become a condition on any Federal license or permit subject to the provisions of this section.

Sec. 402. National Pollution Discharge Elimination System.

(a) (1) Except as provided in sections 318 and 404 of this Act, the Administrator may, after opportunity for public hearing, issue a permit for the discharge of any pollutant, or combination of pollutants, notwithstanding section 301 (a), upon condition that such discharge will meet either (A) all applicable requirements under sections 301, 302, 306, 307, 308 and 403 of this Act, or (B) prior to the taking of necessary implementing actions relating to all such requirements, such conditions as the Administrator determines are necessary to carry out the provisions of this Act.

[Sec. 402(a)(1)(A) and (B) designated by PL 100-4]

[Section 306(c) of PL 100-4 provides:

"(c) Phosphate Fertilizer Effluent Limitation. --

(1) Issuance of Permit. -- As soon as possible after the date of the enactment of this Act, but not later than 180 days after such date of enactment, the Administrator shall issue permits under section 402(a)(1)(B) of the Federal Water Pollution Control Act with respect to facilities --

(A) which were under construction on or before April 8, 1974, and

(B) for which the Administrator is proposing to revise the applicability of the effluent limitation established under section 301(b) of such Act for phosphate subcategory of the fertilizer manufacturing point source category to exclude such facilities.

(2) Limitations on Statutory Construction. -- Nothing in this section shall be construed --

(A) to require the Administrator to permit the discharge of gypsum of gypsum waste into the navigable waters,

(B) to affect the procedures and standards applicable to the Administrator in issuing permits under section 402(a)(1)(B) of the Federal Water Pollution Control Act, and

(C) to affect the authority of any State to deny or condition certification under section 401 of such Act with respect to the issuance of permits under section 402(a)(1)(B) of such Act."]

(2) The Administrator shall prescribe conditions for such permits to assure compliance with the requirements of paragraph (1) of this subsection, including conditions on data and information collection, reporting, and such other requirements as he deems appropriate.

(3) The permit program of the Administrator under paragraph (1) of this subsection, and permits issued thereunder, shall be

subject to the same terms, conditions, and requirements as apply
to a State permit program and permits issued thereunder under
subsection (b) of this section.

(4) All permits for discharges into the navigable waters issued
pursuant to section 13 of the Act of March 3, 1899, shall be
deemed to be permits issued under this title, and permits issued
under this title shall be deemed to be permits issued under
section 13 of the Act of March 3, 1899, and shall continue in
force and effect for their term unless revoked, modified, or
suspended in accordance with the provisions of this Act.

(5) No permit for a discharge into the navigable waters shall be
issued under section 13 of the Act of March 3, 1899, after the
date of enactment of this title. Each application for a permit
under section 13 of the Act of March 3, 1899, pending on the
date of enactment of this Act shall be deemed to be an
application for a permit under this section. The Administrator
shall authorize a State, which he determines has the capability
of administering a permit program which will carry out the
objective of this Act, to issue permits for discharges into the
navigable waters within the jurisdiction of such State. The
Administrator may exercise the authority granted him by the
preceding sentence only during the period which begins on the
date of enactment of this Act and ends either on the ninetieth
day after the date of the first promulgation of guidelines
required by section 304 (h)(2) of this Act, or the date of
approval by the Administrator of a permit program for such State
under subsection (b) of this section, whichever date first
occurs, and no such authorization to a State shall extend beyond
the last day of such period. Each such permit shall be subject
to such conditions as the Administrator determines are necessary
to carry out the provisions of this Act. No such permit shall
issue if the Administrator objects to such issuance.

(b) At any time after the promulgation of the guidelines required by
subsection (h)(2) of section 304 of this Act, the Governor of each
State desiring to administer its own permit program for discharges
into navigable waters within its jurisdiction may submit to the
Administrator a full and complete description of the program it
proposes to establish and administer under State law or under an
interstate compact. In addition, such State shall submit a
statement from the attorney general (or the attorney for those State
water pollution control agencies which have independent legal
counsel), or from the chief legal officer in the case of an
interstate agency, that the laws of such State, or the interstate
compact, as the case may be, provide adequate authority to carry out
the described program. The Administrator shall approve each such
submitted program unless he determines that adequate authority does
not exist:

(1) To issue permits which --

(A) apply, and insure compliance with, any applicable
requirements of sections 301, 302, 306, 307, and 403;

(B) are for fixed terms not exceeding five years; and

(C) can be terminated or modified for cause including, but not limited to, the following:

(i) violation of any condition of the permit;

(ii) obtaining a permit by misrepresentation, or failure to disclose fully all relevant facts;

(iii) change in any condition that requires either a temporary or permanent reduction or elimination of the permitted discharge;

(D) control the disposal of pollutants into wells;

(2) (A) To issue permits which apply, and insure compliance with, all applicable requirements of section 308 of this Act, or

(B) To inspect, monitor, enter, and require reports to at least the same extent as required in section 308 of this Act;

(3) To insure that the public, and any other State the waters of which may be affected, receive notice of each application for a permit and to provide an opportunity for public hearing before a ruling on each such application;

(4) To insure that the Administrator receives notice of each application (including a copy thereof) for a permit;

(5) To insure that any State (other than the permitting State), whose waters may be affected by the issuance of a permit may submit written recommendations to the permitting State (and the Administrator) with respect to any permit application and, if any part of such written recommendations are not accepted by the permitting State, that the permitting State will notify such affected State (and the Administrator) in writing of its failure to so accept such recommendations together with its reasons for so doing;

(6) To insure that no permit will be issued if, in the judgment of the Secretary of the Army acting through the Chief of Engineers, after consultation with the Secretary of the department in which the Coast Guard is operating, anchorage and navigation of any of the navigable waters would be substantially impaired thereby;

(7) To abate violations of the permit or the permit program, including civil and criminal penalties and other ways and means of enforcement.

(8) To insure that any permit for a discharge from a publicly owned treatment works includes conditions to require the identification in terms of character and volume of pollutants of any significant source introducing pollutants subject to pretreatment standards under section 307(b) of this Act into such works and a program to assure compliance with such pretreatment standards by each such source, in addition to adequate notice to the permitting agency of (A) new introductions into such works of pollutants from any source

which would be a new source as defined in section 306 if such
source were discharging pollutants, (B) new introductions of
pollutants into such works from a source which would be subject
to section 301 if it were discharging such pollutants, or (C) a
substantial change in volume or character of pollutants being
introduced into such works by a source introducing pollutants
into such works at the time of issuance of the permit. Such
notice shall include information on the quality and quantity of
effluent to be introduced into such treatment works and any
anticipated impact of such change in the quantity or quality of
effluent to be discharged from such publicly owned treatment
works; and

(9) To insure that any industrial user of any publicly owned
treatment works will comply with sections 204(b), 307, and 308.

(c) (1) Not later than ninety days after the date on which a State
has submitted a program (or revision thereof) pursuant to
subsection (b) of this section, the Administrator shall suspend
the issuance of permits under subsection (a) of this section as
to those discharges subject to such program unless he determines
that the State permit program does not meet the requirements of
subsection (b) of this section or does not conform to the
guidelines issued under section 304(i)(2) of this Act. If the
Administrator so determines, he shall notify the State of any
revisions or modifications necessary to conform to such
requirements or guidelines.

[Sec. 402(c)(1) amended by PL 100-4]

(2) Any State permit program under this section shall at all
times be in accordance with this section and guidelines
promulgated pursuant to section 304(h)(2) of this Act.

(3) Whenever the Administrator determines after public hearing
that a State is not administering a program approved under this
section in accordance with requirements of this section, he
shall so notify the State and, if appropriate corrective action
is not taken within a reasonable time, not to exceed ninety
days, the Administrator shall withdraw approval of such program.
The Administrator shall not withdraw approval of any such
program unless he shall first have notified the State, and made
public, in writing, the reasons for such withdrawal.

(4) Limitations on Partial Permit Program Returns and
Withdrawals. -- A State may return to the Administrator
administration, and the Administrator may withdraw under
paragraph (3) of this subsection approval, of --

(A) a State partial permit program approved under subsection
(n)(3) only if the entire permit program being administered
by the State department or agency at the time is returned or
withdrawn; and

(B) a State partial permit program approved under subsection
(n)(4) only if an entire phased component of the permit

program being administered by the State at the time is
returned or withdrawn.

[Sec. 402(c)(4) added by PL 100-4]

(d) (1) Each State shall transmit to the Administrator a copy of
each permit application received by such State and provide
notice to the Administrator of every action related to the
consideration of such permit application, including each permit
proposed to be issued by such State.

(2) No permit shall issue (A) if the Administrator within ninety
days of the date of his notification under subsection (b)(5) of
this section objects in writing to the issuance of such permit,
or (B) if the Administrator within ninety days of the date of
transmittal of the proposed permit by the State objects in
writing to the issuance of such permit as being outside the
guidelines and requirements of this Act. Whenever the
Administrator objects to the issuance of a permit under this
paragraph such written objection shall contain a statement of
the reasons for such objection and the effluent limitations and
conditions which such permit would include if it were issued by
the Administrator.

(3) The Administrator may, as to any permit application, waive
paragraph (2) of this subsection.

(4) In any case where, after the date of enactment of this
paragraph, the Administrator, pursuant to paragraph (2) of this
subsection, objects to the issuance of a permit, or request of
the State, a public hearing shall be held by the Administrator
on such objection. If the State does not resubmit such permit
revised tomeet such objection within 30 days after completion of
the hearing, or, if no hearing is requested within 90 days after
the date of such objection, the Administrator may issue the
permit pursuant to subsection (a) of this section for such
source in accordance with the guidelines and requirements of
this Act.

(e) In accordance with guidelines promulgated pursuant to subsection
(h)(2) of section 304 of this Act, the Administrator is authorized
to waive the requirements of subsection (d) of this section at the
time he approves a program pursuant to subsection (b) of this
section for any category (including any class, type, or size within
such category) of point sources within the State submitting such
program.

(f) The Administrator shall promulgate regulations establishing
categories of point sources which he determines shall not be subject
to the requirements of subsection (d) of this section in any State
with a program approved pursuant to subsection (b) of this section.
The Administrator may distinguish among classes, types, and sizes
within any category of point sources.

(g) Any permit issued under this section for the discharge of
pollutants into the navigable waters from a vessel or other floating
craft shall be subject to any applicable regulations promulgated by

the Secretary of the Department in which the Coast Guard is operating, establishing specifications for safe transportation, handling, carriage, storage, and stowage of pollutants.

(h) In the event any condition of a permit for discharges from a treatment works (as defined in section 212 of this Act) which is publicly owned is violated, a State with a program approved under subsection (b) of this section or the Administrator, where no State program is approved or where the Administrator determines pursuant to section 309(a) of this Act that a State with an approved program has not commenced appropriate enforcement action with respect to such permit, may proceed in a court of competent jurisdiction to restrict or prohibit the introduction of any pollutant into such treatment works by a source not utilizing such treatment works prior to the finding that such condition was violated.

(i) Nothing in this section shall be construed to limit the authority of the Administrator to take action pursuant to section 309 of this Act.

(j) A copy of each permit application and each permit issued under this section shall be available to the public. Such permit application or permit, or portion thereof, shall further be available on request for the purpose of reproduction.

(k) Compliance with a permit issued pursuant to this section, shall be deemed compliance, for purposes of sections 309 and 505, with sections 301, 302, 306, 307, and 403, except any standard imposed under section 307 for a toxic pollutant injurious to human health. Until December 31, 1974, in any case where a permit for discharge has been applied for pursuant to this section, but final administrative disposition of such application has not been made, such discharge shall not be a violation of (1) section 301, 306, and 402, of this Act, or (2) section 13 of the Act of March 3, 1899, unless the Administrator or other plaintiff proves that final administrative disposition of such application has not been made because of the failure of the applicant to furnish information reasonably required or requested in order to process the application. For the 180-day period beginning on the date of enactment of the Federal Water Pollution Control Act Amendments of 1972, in the case of any point source discharging any pollutant or combination of poolutants immediately prior to such date of enactment which source is not subject to section 13 of the Act of March 3, 1899, the discharge by such source shall not be a violation of this Act if such a source applies for a permit for discharge pursuant to this section within such 180-day period.

(1) Limitation on Permit Requirement. --

(1) Agricultural Return Flows. -- The Administrator shall not require a permit under this section, for discharge composed entirely of return flows from irrigated agriculture, nor shall the Administrator directly or indirectly, require any State to require such a permit.

[Sec. 402(1)(1) designated by PL 100-4]

[Sec. 54(c)(2) of the Clean Water Act of 1977 says:

"Any State permit program approved under section 402 of the Federal Water Pollution Control Act before the date of enactment of the Clean Water Act of 1977, which requires modification to conform to the amendment made by paragraph (1) of this subsection, shall not be required to be modified before the end of the one year period which begins on the date of enactment of the Clean Water Act of 1977 unless in order to make the required modification a State must amend or enact a law in which case such modification shall not be required for such State before the end of the two year period which begins on such date of enactment."]

> (2) Stormwater Runoff From Oil, Gas, and Mining Operations. -- The Administrator shall not require a permit under this section, nor shall the Administrator directly or indirectly require any State to require a permit, for discharges of stormwater runoff from mining operations or oil and gas exploration, production, processing, or treatment operations or transmission facilities, composed entirely of flows which are from conveyances or systems of conveyances (including but not limited to pipes, conduits, ditches, and channels) used for collecting and conveying precipitation runoff and which are not contaminated by contact with, or do not come into contact with, any overburden, raw material, intermediate products, finished product, byproduct, or waste products located on the site of such operations.

[Sec. 402(1)(2) added by PL 100-4]

(m) Additional Pretreatment of Conventional Pollutants Not Required. -- To the extent a treatment works (as defined in section 212 of this Act) which is publicly owned is not meeting the requirements of a permit issued under this section for such treatment works as a result of inadequate design or operation of such treatment works, the Administrator, in issuing a permit under this section, shall not require pretreatment by a person introducing conventional pollutants identified pursuant to section 304(a)(4) of this Act into such treatment works other than pretreatment required to assure compliance with pretreatment standards under subsection (b)(8) of this section and section 307(b)(1) of this Act. Nothing in this subsection shall affect the Administrator's authority under sections 307 and 309 of this Act, affect State and local authority under sections 307(b)(4) and 510 of this Act, relieve such treatment works of its obligations to meet requirements established under this Act, or otherwise preclude such works from pursuing whatever feasible options are available to meet its responsibility to comply with its permit under this section.

[Sec. 402(m)-(p) added by PL 100-4]

(n) Partial Permit Program. --

> (1) State Submission. -- The Governor of a State may submit under subsection (b) of this section a permit program for a portion of the discharges into the navigable waters in such State.

(2) Minimum Coverage. -- A partial permit program under this subsection shall cover, at a minimum, administration of a major category of the discharges into the navigable waters of the State or a major component of the permit program required by subsection (b).

(3) Approval of Major Category Partial Permit Programs. -- The Administrator may approve a partial permit program covering administration of a major category of discharges under this subsection if --

(A) such program represents a complete permit program and covers all of the discharges under the jurisdiction of a department or agency of the State; and

(B) the Administrator determines that the partial program represents a significant and identifiable part of the State program required by subsection (b).

(4) Approval of Major Component Partial Permit Programs. -- The Administrator may approve under this subsection a partial and phased permit program covering administration of a major component (including discharge categories) of a State permit program required by subsection (b) if --

(A) the Administrator determines that the partial program represents a significant and identifiable part of the State program required by subsection (b); and

(B) the State submits, and the Administrator approves, a plan for the State to assume administration by phases of the remainder of the State program required by subsection (b) by a specified date not more than 5 years after submission of the partial program under this subsection and agrees to make all reasonable efforts to assume such administration by such date.

(o) Anti-Backsliding. --

(1) General Prohibition. -- In the case of effluent limitations established on the basis of subsection (a)(1)(B) of this section, a permit may not be renewed, reissued, or modified on the basis of effluent guidelines promulgated under section 304(b) subsequent to the original issuance of such permit, to contain effluent limitations which are less stringent than the comparable effluent limitations in the previous permit. In the case of effluent limitations established on the basis of section 301(b)(1)(C) or section 303 (d) or (e), a permit may not be renewed, reissued, or modified to contain effluent limitations which are less stringent than the comparable effluent limitations in the previous permit except in compliance with section 303(d)(4).

(2) Exceptions. -- A permit with respect to which paragraph (1) applies may be renewed, reissued, or modified to contain a less stringent effluent limitation applicable to a pollutant if --

(A) material and substantial alterations or additions to the permitted facility occurred after permit issuance which justify the application of a less stringent effluent limitation;

(B) (i) information is available which was not available at the time of permit issuance (other than revised regulations, guidance, or test methods) and which would have justified the application of a less stringent effluent limitation at the time of permit issuance; or (ii) the Administrator determines that technical mistakes or mistaken interpretations of law were made in issuing the permit under subsection (a)(1)(B);

(C) a less stringent effluent limitation is necessary because of events over which the permittee has no control and for which there is no reasonably available remedy;

(D) the permittee has received a permit modification under section 301(c), 301(g), 301(h), 301(i), 301(k), 301(n), or 316(a); or

(E) the permittee has installed the treatment facilities required to meet the effluent limitations in the previous permit and has properly operated and maintained the facilities but has nevertheless been unable to achieve the previous effluent limitations, in which case the limitations in the reviewed, reissued, or modified permit may reflect the level of pollutant control actually achieved (but shall not be less stringent than required by effluent guidelines in effect at the time of permit renewal, reissuance, or modification). Subparagraph (B) shall not apply to any revised waste load allocations or any alternative grounds for translating water quality standards into effluent limitations, except where the cumulative effect of such revised allocations results in a decrease in the amount of pollutants discharged into the concerned waters, and such revised allocations are not the result of a discharger eliminating or substantially reducing its discharge of pollutants due to complying with the requirements of this Act or for reasons otherwise unrelated to water quality.

(3) Limitations. -- In no event may a permit with respect to which paragraph (1) applies be renewed, reissued, or modified to contain an effluent limitation which is less stringent than required by effluent guidelines in effect at the time the permit is renewed, reissued, or modified. In no event may such a permit to discharge into waters be renewed, reissued, or modified to contain a less stringent effluent limitation if the implementation of such limitation would result in a violation of a water quality standard under section 303 applicable to such waters.

(p) Municipal and Industrial Stormwater Discharges. --

(1) General Rule. -- Prior to October 1, 1992, the Administrator or the State (in the case of a permit program

approved under section 402 of this Act) shall not require a permit under this section for discharges composed entirely of stormwater.

(2) Exceptions. -- Paragraph (1) shall not apply with respect to the following stormwater discharges:

(A) A discharge with respect to which a permit has been issued under this section before the date of the enactment of this subsection.

(B) A discharge associated with industrial activity.

(C) A discharge from a municipal separate storm sewer system serving a population of 250,000 or more.

(D) A discharge from a municipal separate storm sewer system serving a population of 100,000 or more but less than 250,000.

(E) A discharge for which the Administrator or the State, as the case may be, determines that the stormwater discharge contributes to a violation of a water quality standard or is a significant contributor of pollutants to waters of the United States,

(3) Permit Requirements. --

(A) Industrial Discharges. -- Permits for discharges associated with industrial activity shall meet all applicable provisions of this section and section 301.

(B) Municipal Discharge. -- Permits for discharges from municipal storm sewers --

(i) may be issued on a system -- or jurisdiction-wide basis;
(ii) shall include a requirement to effectively prohibit non-stormwater discharges into the storm sewers; and
(iii) shall require controls to reduce the discharge of pollutants to the maximum extent practicable, including management practices, control techniques and system, design and engineering methods, and such other provisions as the Administrator or the State determines appropriate for the control of such pollutants.

(4) Permit Application Requirements. --

(A) Industrial and Large Municipal Discharges. -- Not later than 2 years after the date of the enactment of this subsection, the Administrator shall establish regulations setting forth the permit application requirements for stormwater discharges described in paragraphs (2)(B) and (2)(C). Applications for permits for such discharges shall be filed no later than 3 years after such date of enactment. Not later than 4 years after such date of enactment, the Administrator or the State, as the case may be, shall issue or deny each such permit. Any such permit shall provide for compliance as expeditiously as practicable, but in no event later than 3 years after the date of issuance of such permit.

(B) Other Municipal Discharges. -- Not later than 4 years after the date of the enactment of this subsection, the Administrator shall establish regulations setting forth the permit application requirements for stormwater discharges described in paragraph (2)(D). Applications for permits for such discharges shall be filed no later than 5 years after such date of enactment. Not later than 6 years after such date of enactment, the Administrator or the State, as the case may be, shall issue or deny each such permit. Any such permit shall provide for compliance as expeditiously as practicable, but in no event later than 3 years after the date of issuance of such permit.

(5) Studies. -- The Administrator, in consultation with the States, shall conduct a study for the purposes of --

(A) identifying those stormwater discharges or classes of stormwater discharges for which permits are not required pursuant to paragraphs (1) and (2) of this subsection;

(B) determining, to the maximum extent practicable, the nature and extent of pollutants in such discharges; and

(C) establishing procedures and methods to control stormwater discharges to the extent necessary to mitigate impacts on water quality.

Not later than October 1, 1988, the Administrator shall submit to Congress a report on the results of the study described in subparagraph (A) and (B). Not later than October 1, 1989, the Administrator shall submit to Congress a report on the results of the study described in subparagraph (C).

(6) Regulations. -- Not later than October 1, 1992, the Administrator, in consultation with State and local officials, shall issue regulations (based on the results of the studies conducted under paragraph (5)) which designate stormwater discharges, other than those discharges described in paragraph (2), to be regulated to protect water quality and shall establish a comprehensive program to regulate such designated sources. The program shall, at a minimum, (A) establish priorities, (B) establish requirements for State stormwater management programs, and (C) establish expeditious deadlines. The program may include performance standards, guidelines, guidance, and management practices and treatment requirements, as appropriate.

Sec. 403. Ocean Discharge Criteria.

(a) No permit under section 402 of this Act for a discharge into the territorial sea, the waters of the contiguous zone, or the oceans shall be issued, after promulgation of guidelines established under subsection (c) of this section, except in compliance with such guidelines. Prior to the promulgation of such guidelines, a permit may be issued under such section 402 if the Administrator determines it to be in the public interest.

(b) The requirements of subsection (d) of section 402 of this Act may not be waived in the case of permits for discharges into the territorial sea.

(c) (1) The Administrator shall, within one hundred and eighty days after enactment of this Act (and from time to time thereafter), promulgate guidelines for determining the degradation of the waters of the territorial seas, the contiguous zone, and the oceans, which shall include:

> (A) the effect of disposal of pollutants on human health or welfare, including but not limited to plankton, fish, shellfish, wildlife, shorelines, and beaches;

> (B) the effect of disposal of pollutants on marine life including the transfer, concentration, and dispersal of pollutants or their byproducts through biological, physical, and chemical processes; changes in marine ecosystem diversity, productivity, and stability; and species and community population changes;

> (C) the effect of disposal of pollutants on esthetic, recreation, and economic values;

> (D) the persistence and permanence of the effects of disposal of pollutants;

> (E) the effect of the disposal at varying rates, of particular volumes and concentrations of pollutants;

> (F) other possible locations and methods of disposal or recycling of pollutants including land-based alternatives; and

> (G) the effect on alternate uses of the oceans, such as mineral exploitation and scientific study.

(2) In any event where insufficient information exists on any proposed discharge to make a reasonable judgment on any of the guidelines established pursuant to this subsection no permit shall be issued under section 402 of this Act.

Sec. 404. Permits for Dredged or Fill Material.

(a) The Secretary may issue permits, after notice and opportunity for public hearings for the discharge of dredged or fill material into the navigable waters at specified disposal sites. Not later than the fifteenth day after the date an applicant submits all the information required to complete an application for a permit under this subsection, the Secretary shall publish the notice required by this subsection.

(b) Subject to subsection (c) of this section, each such disposal site shall be specified for each such permit by the Secretary (1) through the application of guidelines developed by the Administrator, in conjunction with the Secretary, which guidelines shall be based upon criteria comparable to the criteria applicable to the territorial seas, the contiguous zones, and the ocean under section 403(c), and (2) in any case where such guidelines under clause (1) alone would prohibit the specification of a site, through the application additionally of the economic impact of the site on navigation and anchorage.

(c) The Administrator is authorized to prohibit the specification (including the withdrawal of specification) of any defined areas as a disposal site, and he is authorized to deny or restrict the use of any defined area for specification (including the withdrawal of specification) as a disposal site, whenever he determines, after notice and opportunity for public hearings, that the discharge of such materials into such area will have an unacceptable adverse effect on municipal water supplies, shellfish beds and fishery areas (including spawning and breeding areas), wildlife, or recreational areas. Before making such determination, the Administrator shall consult with the Secretary. The Administrator shall set forth in writing and make public his findings and his reasons for making any determination under this subsection.

(d) The term "Secretary" as used in this section means the Secretary of the Army, acting through the Chief of Engineers.

(e) (1) In carrying out his functions relating to the discharge of dredged or fill material under this section, the Secretary may, after notice and opportunity for public hearing, issue general permits on a State, regional, or nationwide basis for any category of activities involving discharges of dredged or fill material if the Secretary determines that the activities in such category are similar in nature, will cause only minimal adverse environmental effects when performed separately, and will have only minimal cumulative adverse effect on the environment. Any general permit issued under this subsection shall (A) be based on the guidelines described in subsection (b)(1) of this section, and (B) set forth the requirements and standards which shall apply to any activity authorized by such general permit.

(2) No general permit issued under this subsection shall be for a period of more than five years after the date of its issuance and such general permit may be revoked or modified by the Secretary if, after opportunity for public hearing, the Secretary determines that the activities authorized by such general permit have an adverse impact on the environment or such activities are more appropriately authorized by individual permits.

(f) (1) Except as provided in paragraph (2) of this subsection, the discharge of dredge or fill material --

    (A) from normal farming, silviculture, and ranching activities such as plowing, seeding, cultivating, minor drainage, harvesting for the production of food, fiber, and forest products, or upland soil and water conservation practices;

(B) for the purpose of maintenance, including emergency reconstruction of recently damaged parts, of currently serviceable structures such as dikes, dams, levees, groins, riprap, breakwaters, causeways, and bridge abutments or approaches, and transportation structures;

(C) for the purpose of construction or maintenance of farm or stock ponds or irrigation ditches, or the maintenance of drainage ditches;

(D) for the purpose of construction of temporary sedmentation basins on a construction site which does not include placement of fill material into the navigable waters;

(E) for the purpose of construction or maintenance of farm roads or forest roads, or temporary roads for moving mining equipment, where such roads are constructed and maintained, in accordance with best management practices, to assure that flow and circulation patterns and chemical and biological characteristics of the navigable waters are not impaired, that the reach of the navigable waters is not reduced, and that any adverse effect on the aquatic environment will be otherwise minimized;

(F) resulting from any activity with respect to which a State has an approved program under section 208(b)(4) which meets the requirements of subparagraphs (B) and (C) of such section, is not prohibited by or otherwise subject to regulation under this section or section 301(a) or 402 of this Act (except for effluent standards or prohibitions under section 307).

(2) Any discharge of dredged or fill material into the navigable waters incidental to any activity having as its purpose bringing an area of the navigable waters into a use to which it was not previously subject, where the flow or circulation of navigable waters may be impaired or the reach of such waters be reduced, shall be required to have a permit under this section.

(g) (1) The Governor of any State desiring to administer its own individual and general permit program for the discharge of dredged or fill material into the navigable waters (other than those waters which are presently used, or are susceptible to use in their natural condition or by reasonable improvement as a means to transport interstate or foreign commerce shoreward to their ordinary high water mark, including all waters which are subject to the ebb and flow of the tide shoreward to their mean high water mark, or mean higher high water mark on the west coast, including wetlands adjacent thereto), within its jurisdiction may submit to the Administrator a full and complete description of the program it proposes to establish and administer under State law or under an interstate compact. In addition, such State shall submit a statement from the attorney general (or the attorney for those State agencies which have independent legal counsel), or from the chief legal officer in the case of an interstate agency, that the laws of such State, or the interstate compact, as the case may be, provide adequate authority to carry out the described program.

(2) Not later than the tenth day after the date of the receipt of the program and statement submitted by any State under paragraph (1) of this subsection, the Administrator shall provide copies of such program and statement to the Secretary and the Secretary of the Interior, acting through the Director of the United States Fish and Wildlife Service.

(3) Not later than the ninetieth day after the date of the receipt by the Administrator of the program and statement submitted by any State, under paragraph (1) of this subsection, the Secretary and the Secretary of the Interior, acting through the Director of the United States Fish and Wildlife Service, shall submit any comments with respect to such program and statement to the Administrator in writing.

(h) (1) Not later than the one-hundred-twentieth day after the date of the receipt by the Administrator of a program and statement submitted by any State under paragraph (1) of this subsection, the Administrator shall determine, taking into account any comments submitted by the Secretary and the Secretary of the Interior, acting through the Director of the United States Fish and Wildlife Service, pursuant to subsection (g) of this section, whether such State has the following authority with respect to the issuance of permits pursuant to such program:

    (A) To issue permits which --
        (i) apply and assure compliance with, any applicable requirements of this section, including, but not limited to, the guidelines established under section (b)(1) of this section, and sections 307 and 403 of this Act;
        (ii) are for fixed terms not exceeding five years; and
        (iii) can be terminated or modified for cause including, but not limited to, the following:
            (I) violation of any condition of the permit;
            (II) obtaining a permit by misrepresentation, or failure to disclose fully all relevant facts;
            (III) change in any condition that requires either a temporary or permanent reduction or elimination of the permitted discharge.

    (B) To issue permits which apply, and assure compliance with, all applicable requirements of section 308 of this Act, or to inspect, monitor, enter, and require reports to at least the same extent as required in section 308 of this Act.

    (C) To assure that the public, and any other State the waters of which may be affected, receive notice of each application for a permit and to provide an opportunity for public hearing before a ruling on each such application.

(D) To assure that the Administrator receives notice of each application (including a copy thereof) for a permit.

(E) To assure that any State (other than the permitting State), whose waters may be affected by the issuance of a permit may submit written recommendation to the permitting State (and the Administrator) with respect to any permit application and, if any part of such written recommendations are not accepted by the permitting State, that the permitting State will notify such affected State (and the Administrator) in writing of its failure to so accept such recommendations together with its reasons for so doing.

(F) To assure that no permit will be issued if, in the judgment of the Secretary, after consultation with the Secretary of the department in which the Coast Guard is operating, anchorage and navigation of any of the navigable water would be substantially impaired thereby.

(G) To abate violations of the permit or the permit program, including civil and criminal penalties and other ways and means of enforcement.

(H) To assure continued coordination with Federal and Federal-State water-related planning and review processes.

(2) If, with respect to a State program submitted under subsection (g)(1) of this section, the Administrator determines that such State --

(A) has the authority set forth in paragraph (1) of this subsection, the Administrator shall approve the program and so notify (i) such State, and (ii) the Secretary, who upon subsequent notification from such State that it is administering such program, shall suspend the issuance of permits under subsection (a) and (e) of this section for activities with respect to which a permit may be issued pursuant to such State program; or

(B) does not have the authority set forth in paragraph (1) of this subsection, the Administrator shall so notify such State, which notification shall also describe the revisions or modifications necessary so that such State may resubmit such program for a determination by the Administrator under this subsection.

(3) If the Administrator fails to make a determination with respect to any program submitted by a State under subsection (g)(1) of this section within one-hundred-twenty days after the date of the receipt of such program, such program shall be deemed approved pursuant to paragraph (2)(A) of this subsection and the Administrator shall so notify such State and the Secretary who, upon subsequent notification from such State that it is administering such program, shall suspend the issuance of permits under subsection (a) and (e) of this section for activities with respect to which a permit may be issued by such State.

(4) After the Secretary receives notification from the Administrator under paragraph (2) or (3) of this subsection that a State permit program has been approved, the Secretary shall transfer any applications for permits before the Secretary for activities with respect to which a permit may be issued pursuant to such State program to such State for appropriate action.

(5) Upon notification from a State with a permit program approved under this subsection that such State intends to administer and enforce the terms and conditions of a general permit issued by the Secretary under subsection (e) of this section with respect to activities in such State to which general permit applies, the Secretary shall suspend the administration and enforcement of such general permit with respect to such activities.

(i) Whenever the Administrator determines after public hearing that a State is not administering a program approved under section (h)(2)(A) of this section, in accordance with this section, including, but not limited to, the guidelines established under subsection (b)(1) of this section, the Administrator shall so notify the State, and, if appropriate corrective action is not taken within a reasonable time, not to exceed ninety days after the date of the receipt of such notification, the Administrator shall (1) withdraw approval of such program until the Administrator determines such corrective action has been taken, and (2) notify the Secretary that the Secretary shall resume the program for the issuance of permits under subsections (a) and (e) of this section for activities with respect to which the State was issuing permits and that such authority of the Secretary shall continue in effect until such time as the Administrator makes the determination described in clause (1) of this subsection and such State again has an approved program.

(j) Each State which is administering a permit program pursuant to this section shall transmit to the Administrator (1) a copy of each permit application received by such State and provide notice to the Administrator of every action related to the consideration of such permit application, including each permit proposed to be issued by such State, and (2) a copy of each proposed general permit which such State intends to issue. Not later than the tenth day after the date of the receipt of such permit application or such proposed general permit, the Administrator shall provide copies of such permit application or such proposed general permit to the Secretary and the Secretary of the Interior, acting through the Director of the United States Fish and Wildlife Service. If the Administrator intends to provide written comments to such State with respect to such permit application or such proposed general permit, he shall so notify such State not later than the thirtieth day after the date of the receipt of such application or such proposed general permit and provide such written comments to such State, after consideration of any comments made in writing with respect to such application or such proposed general permit by the Secretary and the Secretary of the Interior, acting through the Director of the United States Fish and Wildlife Service, not later than the ninetieth day after the date of such receipt. If such State is so notified by the Administrator, it shall not issue the proposed permit until after the receipt of such comments from the Administrator, or after such ninetieth day, whichever first occurs. Such State shall not issue such proposed permit after such ninetieth day if it has received such written comments in which the Administrator objects (A) to the issuance of such proposed permit and such proposed permit is one that has been submitted to the Administrator pursuant to subsection (h)(1)(E), or (B) to the issuances of such proposed permit as being outside the requirements of this section, including, but not limited to, the guidelines developed under subsection (b)(1) of this section unless it modifies such proposed permit in accordance with such comments. Whenever the Administrator objects to the issuance of a permit under the preceding sentence such written objection shall contain a statement of the reasons for such objection and the conditions which such permit would include if it were issued by the Administrator. In any case where the Administrator objects to the issuance of a permit, on request of the State, a public hearing shall be held by the Administrator on such objection. If the State does not resubmit such permit revised to meet such objection within 30 days after completion of the hearing or, if no hearing is requested within 90 days after the date of such objection, the Secretary may issue the permit pursuant to subsection (a) or (e) of this section, as the case may be, for such source in accordance with the guidelines and requirements of this Act.

(k) In accordance with guidelines promulgated pursuant to subsection (h)(2) of section 304 of this Act, the Administrator is authorized to waive the requirements of subsection (j) of this section at the time of the approval of a program pursuant to subsection (h)(2)(A) of this section for any category (including any class, type, or size within such category) of discharge within the State submitting such program.

(1) The Administrator shall promulgate regulations establishing categories of discharges which he determines shall not be subject to the requirements of subsection (j) of this section in any State with a program approved pursuant to subsection (h)(2)(A) of this section. The Administrator may distinguish among classes, types, and sizes within any category of discharges.

(m) Not later than the ninetieth day after the date on which the Secretary notifies the Secretary of the Interior, acting through the Director of the United States Fish and Wildlife Service that (1) an application for a permit under subsection (a) of this section has been received by the Secretary, or (2) the Secretary proposes to issue a general permit under subsection (e) of this section, the Secretary of the Interior, acting through the Director of the United States Fish and Wildlife Service, shall submit any comments with respect to such application or such proposed general permit in writing to the Secretary.

(n) Nothing in this section shall be construed to limit the authority of the Administrator to take action pursuant to section 309 of this Act.

(o) A copy of each permit application and each permit issued under this section shall be available to the public. Such permit application or portion thereof, shall further be available on request for the purpose of reproduction.

(p) Compliance with a permit issued pursuant to this section, including any activity carried out pursuant to a general permit issued under this section, shall be deemed compliance, for purposes of sections 309 and 505, with sections 301, 307, and 403.

(q) Not later than the one-hundred-eightieth day after the date of enactment of this subsection, the Secretary shall enter into agreements with the Administrator, the Secretaries of the Departments of Agriculture, Commerce, Interior, and Transportation, and the heads of other appropriate Federal agencies to minimize, to the maximum extent practicable, duplication, needless paperwork, and delays in the issuance of permits under this section. Such agreements shall be developed to assure that, to the maximum extent practicable, a decision with respect to an application for a permit under subsection (a) of this section will be made not later than the ninetieth day after the date the notice of such application is published under subsection (a) of this section.

(r) The discharge of dredged or fill material as part of the construction of a Federal project specifically authorized by Congress, whether prior to or on or after the date of enactment of this subsection, is not prohibited by or otherwise subject to regulation under this section, or a State program approved under this section, or section 301(a) or 402 of the Act (except for effluent standards or prohibitions under section 307), if information on the effects of such discharge, including consideration of the guidelines developed under subsection (b)(1) of this section, is included in an environmental impact statement for such project pursuant to the National Environmental Policy Act of 1969 and such environmental impact statement has been submitted to Congress before the actual discharge of dredged or fill material in connection with the construction of such project and prior to either authorization of such project or an appropriation of funds for each construction.

(s) (1) Whenever on the basis of any information available to him the Secretary finds that any person is in violation of any condition or limitation set forth in a permit issued by the Secretary under this section, the Secretary shall issue an order requiring such persons to comply with such condition or limitation, or the Secretary shall bring a civil action in accordance with paragraph (3) of this subsection.

(2) A copy of any order issued under this subsection shall be sent immediately by the Secretary to the State in which the violation occurs and other affected States. Any order issued under this subsection shall be by personal service and shall state with reasonable specificity the nature of the violation, specify a time for compliance, not to exceed thirty days, which the Secretary determines is reasonable, taking into account the seriousness of the violation and any good faith efforts to comply with applicable requirements. In any case in which an order under this subsection is issued to a corporation, a copy of such order shall be served on any appropriate corporate officers.

(3) The Secretary is authorized to commence a civil action for appropriate relief, including a permanent or temporary injunction for any violation for which he is authorized to issue a compliance order under paragraph (1) of this subsection. Any action under this paragraph may be brought in the district court of the United States for the district in which the defendant is located or resides or is doing business, and such court shall have jurisdiction to restrain such violation and to require compliance. Notice of the commencement of such action shall be given immediately to the appropriate State.

(4) Any person who violates any condition or limitation in a permit issued by the Secretary under this section, and any person who violates any order issued by the Secretary under paragraph (1) of this subsection, shall be subject to a civil penalty not to exceed $25,000 per day for each violation. In determining the amount of a civil penalty the court shall consider the seriousness of the violation or violations, the economic benefit (if any) resulting from the violation, any history of such violations, any good-faith efforts to comply with the applicable requirements, the economic impact of the penalty on the violator, and such other matters as justice may require.

[Sec. 404(s)(4) deleted and (5) amended and redesignated as (4) by PL 100-4]

(t) Nothing in this section shall preclude or deny the right of any State or interstate agency to control the discharge of dredged or fill material in any portion of the navigable waters within the jurisdiction of such State, including any activity of any Federal agency, and each such agency shall comply with such State or interstate requirements both substantive and procedural to control the discharge of dredged or fill material to the same extent that any person is subject to such requirements. This section shall not be construed as affecting or impairing the authority of the Secretary to maintain navigation.

Sec. 405. Disposal of Sewage Sludge.

(a) Notwithstanding any other provision of this Act or any other law, in the case where the disposal of sewage sludge resulting from the operation of a treatment works as defined in section 212 of this Act (including the removal of in-place sewage sludge from one location and its deposit at another location) would result in any pollutant from such sewage sludge entering the navigable waters, such disposal is prohibited except in accordance with a permit issued by the Administrator under section 402 of this Act.

(b) The Administrator shall issue regulations governing the issuance of permits for the disposal of sewage sludge subject to subsection (a) of this section and section 402 of this Act. Such regulations shall require the application to such disposal of each criterion, factor, procedure, and requirement applicable to a permit issued under section 402 of this title.

(c)   Each State desiring to administer its own permit program for
disposal of sewage sludge subject to subsection (a) of this section
within its jurisdiction may do so in accordance with section 402 of
this Act.

(d)   Regulations --

   (1)   Regulations.   -- The Administrator, after consultation with
   appropriate Federal and State agencies and other interested
   persons, shall develop and publish, within one year after the
   date of the enactment of this subsection and from time to time
   thereafter, regulations providing guidelines for the disposal of
   sludge and the utilization of sludge for various purposes.   Such
   regulations shall --

      (A)   identify uses for sludge, including disposal;

      (B)   specify factors to be taken into account in determining
      the measures and practices applicable to each such use or
      disposal (including publication of information on costs);

      (C)   identify concentrations of pollutants which interfere
      with each such use or disposal.

   The Administrator is authorized to revise any regulation issued
   under this subsection.

   (2)   Identification and Regulation of Toxic Pollutants.   --

      (A)   On Basis of Available Information.   --
         (i)   Proposed Regulations.   -- Not later than November
         30, 1986, the Administrator shall identify those toxic
         pollutants which, on the basis of available information
         on their toxicity, persistence, concentration, mobility,
         or potential for exposure, may be present in sewage
         sludge in concentrations which may adversely affect
         public   health   or   the   environment,   and   propose
         regulations specifying acceptable management practices
         for sewage sludge containing each such toxic pollutant
         and establishing numerical limitations for each such
         pollutant for each use identified under paragraph
         (1)(A).
         (ii)   Final Regulations.   -- Not later than August 31,
         1987, and after opportunity for public hearing, the
         Administrator shall promulgate the regulations required
         by subparagraph (A)(i).

      (B)   Others.   --
         (i)   Proposed Regulations.   -- Not later than July 31,
         1987, the Administrator shall identify those toxic
         pollutants not identified under subparagraph (A)(i)
         which may be present in sewage sludge in concentrations
         which   may   adversely   affect   public   health   or   the
         environment,   and   propose   regulations   specifying
         acceptable   management   practices   for   sewage   sludge
         containing each such toxic pollutant and establishing

numerical limitations for each pollutant for each such use identified under paragraph (1)(A).

(ii) Final Regulations. -- Not later than June 15, 1988, the Administrator shall promulgate the regulations required by subparagraph (B)(i).

(C) Review. -- From time to time, but not less often than every 2 years, the Administrator shall review the regulations promulgated under this paragraph for the purpose of identifying additional toxic pollutants and promulgating regulations for such pollutants consistent with the requirements of this paragraph.

(D) Minimum Standards; Compliance Date. -- The management practices and numerical criteria established under subparagraphs (A), (B), and (C) shall be adequate to protect public health and the environment from any reasonably anticipated adverse effects of each pollutant. Such regulations shall require compliance as expeditiously as practicable but in no case later than 12 months after their publication, unless such regulations require the construction of new pollution control facilities, in which case the regulations shall require compliance as expeditiously as practicable but in no case later than two years from the date of their publication.

[Sec. 405(d)(2)-(5) added by PL 100-4]

(3) Alternative Standards. -- For purposes of this subsection, if, in the judgment of the Administrator, it is not feasible to prescribe or enforce a numerical limitation for a pollutant identified under paragraph (2), the Administrator may instead promulgate a design, equipment, management practice, or operational standard, or combination thereof, which in the Administrator's judgment is adequate to protect public health and the environment from any reasonably anticipated adverse effects of such pollutant. In the event the Administrator promulgates a design or equipment standard under this subsection, the Administrator shall include as part of such standard such requirements as will assure the proper operation and maintenance of any such element of design or equipment.

(4) Conditions on Permits. -- Prior to the promulgation of the regulations required by paragraph (2), the Administrator shall impose conditions in permits issued to publicly owned treatment works under section 402 of this Act or take such other measures as the Administrator deems appropriate to protect public health and the environment from any adverse effects which may occur from toxic pollutants in sewage sludge.

(5) Limitation on Statutory Construction. -- Nothing in this section is intended to waive more stringent requirements established by this Act or any other law.

[Section 406(e) of PL 100-4 stipulates:

"(e) Removal Credits. -- The part of the decision of Natural Resources Defense Council, Inc. v. U.S. Environmental Protection Agency, No. 84-3530 (3d Cir. 1986), which addresses section 405(d) of the Federal Water Pollution Control Act is stayed until August 31, 1987, with respect to -- (1) those publicly owned treatment works the owner or operator of which received authority to revise pretreatment requirements under section 307(b)(1) of such Act before the date of the enactment of this section, and (2) those publicly owned treatment works the owner or operator of which has submitted an application for authority to revise pretreatment requirements under such section 307(b)(1) which application is pending on such date of enactment and is approved before August 31, 1987. The Administrator shall not authorize any other removal credits under such Act until the Administrator issues the regulations required by paragraph (2)(A)(ii) of section 406(d) of such Act, as amended by subsection (a) of this section."]

(e) Manner of Sludge Disposal. -- The determination of the manner of disposal or use of sludge is a local determination, except that it shall be unlawful for any person to dispose of sludge from a publicly owned treatment works or any other treatment works treating domestic sewage for any use for which regulations have been established pursuant to subsection (d) of this section, except in accordance with such regulations.

[Sec. 405(e) revised by PL 100-4]

(f) Implementation of Regulations. --

(1) Through Section 402 Permits. -- Any permit issued under section 402 of this Act to a publicly owned treatment works or any other treatment works treating domestic sewage shall include requirements for the use and disposal of sludge that implement the regulations established pursuant to subsection (d) of this section, unless such requirements have been included in a permit issued under the appropriate provisions of subtitle C of the Solid Waste Disposal Act, part C of the Safe Drinking Water Act, the Marine Protection, Research, and Sanctuaries Act of 1972, or the Clean Air Act, or under State permit programs approved by the Administrator, where the Administrator determines that such programs assure compliance with any applicable requirements of this section. Not later than December 15, 1986, the Administrator shall promulgate procedures for approval of State programs pursuant to this paragraph.

(2) Through Other Permits. -- In the case of a treatment works described in paragraph (1) that is not subject to section 402 of this Act and to which none of the other above listed permit programs nor approved State permit authority apply, the Administrator may issue a permit to such treatment works solely to impose requirements for the use and disposal of sludge that implement the regulations established pursuant to subsection (d) of this section. The Administrator shall include in the permit appropriate requirements to assure compliance with the regulations established pursuant to subsection (d) of this

section. The Administrator shall establish procedures for issuing permits pursuant to this paragraph.

[Sec. 405(f) added by PL 100-4]

(g) Studies and Projects. --

(1) Grant Program; Information Gathering. -- The Administrator is authorized to conduct or initiate scientific studies, demonstration projects, and public information and education projects which are designed to promote the safe and beneficial management or use of sewage sludge for such purposes as aiding the restoration of abandoned mine sites, conditioning soil for parks and recreation areas, agricultural and horticultural uses, and other beneficial purposes. For the purposes of carrying out this subsection, the Administrator may make grants to State water pollution control agencies, other public or nonprofit agencies, institutions, organizations, and individuals. In cooperation with other Federal departments and agencies, other public and private agencies, institutions, and organizations, the Administrator is authorized to collect and disseminate information pertaining to the safe and beneficial use of sewage sludge.

(2) Authorization of Appropriations. -- For the purposes of carrying out the scientific studies, demonstration projects, and public information and education projects authorized in this section, there is authorized to be appropriated for fiscal years beginning after September 30, 1986, not to exceed $5,000,000.

[Sec. 405(g) added by PL 100-4]

TITLE V -- GENERAL PROVISIONS ADMINISTRATION

Sec. 501.

(a) The Administrator is authorized to prescribe such regulations as are necessary to carry out his functions under this Act.

(b) The Administrator, with the consent of the head of any other agency of the United States, may utilize such officers and employees of such agency as may be found necessary to assist in carrying out the purposes of this Act.

(c) Each recipient of financial assistance under this Act shall keep such records as the Administrator shall prescribe, including records which fully disclose the amount and disposition by such recipient of the proceeds of such assistance, the total cost of the project or undertaking in connection with which such assistance is given or used, and the amount of that portion of the cost of the project or undertaking supplied by other sources, and such other records as will facilitate an effective audit.

(d) The Administrator and the Comptroller General of the United States, or any of their duly authorized representatives, shall have access, for the purpose of audit and examination, to any books, documents, papers, and records of the recipients that are pertinent to the grants received under this Act. For the purpose of carrying out audits and examinations with respect to recipients of Federal assistance under this Act, the Administrator is authorized to enter into noncompetitive procurement contracts with independent State audit organizations, consistent with chapter 75 of title 31, United States Code. Such contracts may only be entered into to the extent and in such amounts as may be provided in advance in appropriation Acts.

[501(d) amended by PL 100-4]

(e) (1) It is the purpose of this subsection to authorize a program which will provide official recognition by the United States Government to those industrial organizations and political subdivisions of States which during the preceding year demonstrated an outstanding technological achievement or an innovative process, method, or device in their waste treatment and pollution abatement programs. The Administrator shall, in consultation with the appropriate State water pollution control agencies, establish regulations under which such recognition may be applied for and granted, except that no applicant shall be eligible for an award under this subsection if such applicant is not in total compliance with all applicable water quality requirements under this Act, or otherwise does not have a satisfactory record with respect to environmental quality.

(2) The Administrator shall award a certificate or plaque of suitable design to each industrial organization or political subdivision which qualifies for such recognition under regulations established under this subsection.

(3) The President of the United States, the Governor of the appropriate State, the Speaker of the House of Representatives, and the President pro tempore of the Senate shall be notified of the award by the Administrator and the awarding of such recognition shall be published in the Federal Register.

(f) Upon the request of a State water pollution control agency, personnel of the Environmental Protection Agency may be detailed to such agency for the purpose of carrying out the provisions of this Act.

Sec. 502. General Definitions.

Except as otherwise specifically provided, when used in this Act:

(1) The term "State water pollution control agency" means the State agency designated by the Governor having responsibility for enforcing State laws relating to the abatement of pollution.

(2) The term "interstate agency" means an agency of two or more States established by or pursuant to an agreement of compact approved by the Congress, or any other agency of two or more States, having substantial powers or duties pertaining to the control of pollution as determined and approved by the Administrator.

(3) The term "State" means a State, the District of Columbia, the Commonwealth of Puerto Rico, the Virgin Islands, Guam, American Samoa, the Commonwealth of the Northern Mariana Islands, and the Trust Territory of the Pacific Islands.

[Sec. 502(3) amended by PL 100-4]

(4) The term "municipality" means a city, town, borough, county, parish, district, association, or other public body created by or pursuant to State law and having jurisdiction over disposal of sewage, industrial wastes, or other wastes, or an Indian tribe or an authorized Indian tribal organization, or a designated and approved management agency under section 208 of this Act.

(5) The term "person" means an individual, corporation, partnership, association, State, municipality, commission, or political subdivision of a State, or any interstate body.

(6) The term "pollutant" means dredged spoil, solid waste, incinerator residue, sewage, garbage, sewage sludge, munitions, chemical wastes, biological materials, radioactive materials, heat, wrecked or discarded equipment, rock, sand, cellar dirt and industrial, municipal, and agricultural waste discharged into water. This term does not mean (A) "sewage from vessels" within the meaning of section 312 of this Act; or (B) water, gas, or other material which is injected into a well to facilitate production of oil or gas, or water derived in association with oil or gas production and disposed of in a well, if the well used either to facilitate production or for

disposal purposes is approved by authority of the State in which the well is located, and if such State determines that such injection or disposal will not result in the degradation of ground or surface water resources.

(7) The term "navigable waters" means the waters of the United States, including the territorial seas.

(8) The term "territorial seas" means the belt of the seas measured from the line of ordinary low water along that portion of the coast which is in direct contact with the open sea and the line marking the seaward limit of inland waters, and extending seaward a distance of three miles.

(9) The term "contiguous zone" means the entire zone established or to be established by the United States under article 24 of the Convention of the Territorial Sea and the Contiguous Zone.

(10) The term "ocean" means any portion of the high seas beyond the contiguous zone.

(11) The term "effluent limitation" means any restriction established by a State or the Administrator on quantities, rates, and concentrations of chemical, physical, biological, and other concentrations of chemical, physical, biological, and other constituents which are discharged from point sources into navigable waters, the waters of the contiguous zone, or the ocean, including schedules of compliance.

(12) The term "discharge of a pollutant" and the term "discharge of pollutants" each means (A) any addition of any pollutant to navigable waters from any point source, (B) any addition to any pollutant to the waters of the contiguous zone or the ocean from any point source other than a vessel or other floating craft.

(13) The term "toxic pollutant" means those pollutants, or combinations of pollutants, including disease-causing agents, which after discharge and upon exposure, ingestion, inhalation or assimilation into any organism, either directly from the environment or indirectly by ingestion through food chains, will, on the basis of information available to the Administrator, cause death, disease, behavioral abnormalities, cancer, genetic mutations, physiological malfunctions (including malfunctions in reproduction) or physical deformations, in such organisms or their offspring.

(14) The term "point source" means any discernible, confined and discrete conveyance, including but not limited to any pipe, ditch, channel, tunnel, conduit, well, discrete fissure, container, rolling stock, concentrated animal feeding operation, or vessel or other floating craft, from which pollutants are or may be discharged. This term does not include agricultural stormwater discharges and return flows from irrigated agriculture.

[Sec. 502(14) amended by PL 100-4]

[Section 507 of PL 100-4 states:

"Sec. 507. Definition of Point Source.

For purposes of the Federal Water Pollution Control Act, the term "point source" includes a landfill leachate collection system."]

(15) The term "biological monitoring" shall mean the determination of the effects on aquatic life, including accumulation of pollutants in tissue, in receiving waters due to the discharge of pollutants (A) by techniques and procedures, including sampling of organisms representative of appropriate levels of the food chain appropriate to the volume and the physical, chemical, and biological characteristics of the effluent, and (B) at appropriate frequencies and locations.

(16) The term "discharge" when used without qualification includes a discharge of a pollutant, and a discharge of pollutants.

(17) The term "schedule of compliance" means a schedule of remedial measures including an enforceable sequence of actions or operations leading to compliance with an effluent limitation, other limitation, prohibition, or standard.

(18) The term "industrial user" means those industries identified in the Standard Industrial Classification Manual, Bureau of the Budget, 1967, as amended and supplemented, under the category "Division D -- Manufacturing" and such other classes of significant waste products as, by regulation, the Administrator deems appropriate.

(19) The term "pollution" means the man-made or man-induced alteration of the chemical, physical, biological and radiological integrity of water.

Sec. 503. Water Pollution Control Advisory Board.

(a) (1) There is hereby established in the Environmental Protection Agency a Water Pollution Control Advisory Board, composed of the Administrator or his designee, who shall be Chairman, and nine members appointed by the President, none of whom shall be Federal officers or employees. The appointed members, having due regard for the purposes of this Act, shall be selected from among representatives of various State, interstate, and local governmental agencies, of public or private interests contributing to, affected by, or concerned with pollution, and of other public and private agencies, organizations, or groups demonstrating an active interest in the field of pollution prevention and control, as well as other individuals who are expert in this field,

(2) (A) Each member appointed by the President shall hold office for a term of three years, except that (i) any member appointed to fill a vacancy occurring prior to the expiration of the term for which his predecessor was

appointed shall be appointed for the remainder of such term, and (ii) the terms of office of the members first taking office after June 30, 1956, shall expire as follows: three at the end of one year after such date, three at the end of two years after such date, and three at the end of three years after such date, as designated by the President at the time of appointment, and (iii) the term of any member under the preceding provisions shall be extended until the date on which his successor's appointment is effective. None of the members appointed by the President shall be eligible for reappointment within one year after the end of his preceding term.

(B) The members of the Board who are not officers or employees of the United States, while attending conferences or meetings of the Board or while otherwise serving at the request of the Administrator, shall be entitled to receive compensation at a rate to be fixed by the Administrator, but not exceeding $100 per diem, including travel-time, and while away from their homes or regular places of business they may be allowed travel expenses, including per diem in lieu of subsistence, as authorized by law (5 U.S.C. 73b-2) for persons in the Government service employed intermittently.

(b) The Board shall advise, consult with, and make recommendations to the Administrator on matters of policy relating to the activities and functions of the Administrator under this Act.

(c) Such clerical and technical assistance as may be necessary to discharge the duties of the Board shall be provided from the personnel on the Environmental Protection Agency.

Sec. 504. Emergency Powers.

(a) Notwithstanding any other provision of this Act, the Administrator upon receipt of evidence that a pollution source or combination of sources is presenting an imminent and substantial endangerment to the health of persons or to the welfare of persons where such endangerment is to the livelihood of such persons, such as inability to market shellfish, may bring suit on behalf of the United States in the appropriate district court to immediately restrain any person causing or contributing to the alleged pollution to stop the discharge of pollutants causing or contributing to such pollution or to take such other action as may be necessary.

(b) [504(b) repealed by PL 96-510, Sec. 304(a)]

Sec. 505 Citizen Suits.

(a) Except as provided in subsection (b) of this section, and section 309(g)(6) any citizen may commence a civil action on his own behalf --

[Sec. 505(a) amended by PL 100-4]

(1) against any person (including (i) the United States, and (ii) any other governmental instrumentality or agency to the extent permitted by the Eleventh Amendment to the Constitution) who is alleged to be in violation of (A) an effluent standard of limitation under this Act or (B) an order issued by the Administrator or a State with respect to such a standard or limitation, or

(2) against the Administrator where there is alleged a failure of the Administrator to perform any act or duty under this Act which is not discretionary with the Administrator. The district courts shall have jurisdiction, without regard to the amount in controversy or the citizenship of the parties, to enforce such an effluent standard or limitation, or such an order, or to order the Administrator to perform such act or duty, as the case may be, and to apply any appropriate civil penalties under section 309(d) of this Act.

(b) No action may be commenced --

   (1) under subsection (a)(1) of this section --

      (A) prior to sixty days after the plaintiff has given notice of the alleged violation (i) to the Administrator, (ii) to the State in which the alleged violation occurs, and (iii) to any alleged violator of the standard, limitation, or order, or

      (B) if the Administrator or State has commenced and is diligently prosecuting a civil or criminal action in a court of the United States, or a State to require compliance with the standard, limitation, or order, but in any such action in a court of the United States any citizen may intervene as a matter of right.

   (2) under subsection (a)(2) of this section prior to sixty days after the plaintiff has given notice of such action to the Administrator. except that such action may be brought immediately after such notification in the case of an action under this section respecting a violation of sections 306 and 307(a) of this Act. Notice under this subsection shall be given in such manner as the Administrator shall prescribe by regulation.

(c) (1) Any action respecting a violation by a discharge source of an effluent standard or limitation or an order respecting such standard or limitation may be brought under this section only in the judicial district in which such source is located.

   (2) In such action under this section, the Administrator, if not a party, may intervene as a matter of right.

   (3) Protection of Interests of United States. -- Whenever any action is brought under this section in a court of the United States, the plaintiff shall serve a copy of the complaint on the Attorney General and the Administrator. No consent judgment shall be entered in an action in which the United States is not

a party prior to 45 days following the receipt of a copy of the proposed consent judgment by the Attorney General and the Administrator.

[Sec. 505(c)(3) added by PL 100-4]

(d) The court, in issuing any final order in any action brought pursuant to this section, may award costs of litigation (including reasonable attorney and expert witness fees) to any prevailing or substantially prevailing party, whenever the court determines such award is appropriate. The court may, if a temporary restraining order or preliminary injunction is sought, require the filing of a bond or equivalent security in accordance with the Federal Rules of Civil Procedure.

[Sec. 505(d) amended by PL 100-4]

(e) Nothing in this section shall restrict any right which any person (or class of persons) may have under any statute or common law to seek enforcement of any effluent standard or limitation or to seek any other relief (including relief against the Administrator or a State agency).

(f) For purposes of this section, the term "effluent standard or limitation under this Act" means (1) effective July 1, 1973, an unlawful act under subsection (a) of section 301 of this Act; (2) an effluent limitation or other limitation under section 301 or 302 of this Act; (3) standard of performance under section 306 of this Act; (3) prohibition, effluent standard or pretreatment standards under section 307 of this Act; (5) certification under section 401 of this Act; (6) a permit or condition thereof issued under section 402 of this Act, which is in effect under this Act (including a requirement applicable by reason of section 313 of this Act); or (7) a regulation under section 405(d) of this Act.

[Sec. 505(f) amended by PL 100-4]

(g) For the purposes of this section the term "citizen" means a person or persons having an interest which is or may be adversely affected.

(h) A Governor of a State may commence a civil action under subsection (a), without regard to the limitations of subsection (b) of this section, against the Administrator where there is alleged a failure of the Administrator to enforce an effluent standard or limitation under this Act the violation of which is occurring in another State and is causing an adverse effect on the public health or welfare in his State, or is causing a violation of any water quality requirement in his State.

Sec. 506. Appearance.

The Administrator shall request the Attorney General to appear and represent the United States in any civil or criminal action instituted under this Act to which the Administrator is a party. Unless the Attorney General notifies the Administrator within a reasonable time, that he will appear in a civil action, attorneys who are officers or employees of the Environmental Protection Agency shall appear and represent the United States in such action.

Sec. 507. Employee Protection.

(a) No person shall fire, or in any other way discriminate against, or cause to be fired or discriminated against, any employee or any authorized representative of employees by reason of the fact that such employee or representative has filed, instituted, or caused to be filed or instituted any proceeding under this Act, or has testified or is about to testify in any proceeding resulting from the administration or enforcement of the provisions of this Act.

(b) Any employee or a representative of employees who believes that he has been fired or otherwise discriminated against by any person in violation of subsection (a) of this section may, within thirty days after such alleged violation occurs, apply to the Secretary of Labor for a review of such firing or alleged discrimination. A copy of the application shall be sent to such person who shall be the respondent. Upon receipt of such application, the Secretary of Labor shall cause such investigation to be made as he deems appropriate. Such investigation shall provide an opportunity for a public hearing at the request of any party to such review to enable the parties to present information relating to such alleged violation. The parties shall be given written notice of the time and place of the hearing at least five days prior to the hearing. Any such hearing shall be of record and shall be subject to section 554 of title 5 of the United States Code. Upon receiving the report of such investigation, the Secretary of Labor shall make findings of fact. If he finds that such violation did occur, he shall issue a decision, incorporating an order therein and his bindings, requiring the party committing such violation to take such affirmative action to abate the violation as the Secretary of Labor deems appropriate, including, but not limited to, the rehiring or reinstatement of the employee or representative of employees to his former position with compensation. If he finds that there was no such violation, he shall issue an order denying the application. Such order issued by the Secretary of Labor under this subparagraph shall be subject to judicial review in the same manner as orders and decisions of the Administrator are subject to judicial review under this Act.

(c) Whenever an order is issued under this section to abate such violation, at the request of the applicant, a sum equal to the aggregate amount of all costs and expenses (including the attorney's fees), as determined by the Secretary of Labor, to have been reasonably incurred by the applicant for, or in connection with, the institution and prosecution of such proceedings, shall be assessed against the person committing such violation.

(d) This section shall have no application to any employee who, acting without direction from his employer (or his agent) deliberately violates any prohibition of effluent limitation or other limitation under section 301 or 302 of this Act, standards of performance under section 306 of this Act, effluent standard, prohibition or pretreatment standard under section 307 of this Act, or any other prohibition or limitation established under this Act.

(e) The Administrator shall conduct continuing evaluations of potential loss or shifts of employment which may result from the issuance of any effluent limitation or order under this Act, including, where appropriate, investigating threatened plant closures or reductions in employment allegedly resulting from such limitation or order. Any employee who is discharged or laid off, threatened with discharge or lay-off, or otherwise discriminated against by any person because of the alleged results of any effluent limitation or order issued under this Act, or any representative of such employee, may request the Administrator to conduct a full investigation of the matter. The Administrator shall thereupon investigate the matter and, at the request of any part, shall hold public hearings on not less than five days notice, and shall at such hearing require the parties, including the employer involved, to present information relating to the actual or potential effect of such limitation or order on employment and on any alleged discharge, layoff, or other discrimination and the detailed reasons or justification therefore. Any such hearing shall be of record and shall be subject to section 554 of title 5 of the United States Code, Upon receiving the report of such investigation, the Administrator shall make findings of fact as to the effect of such effluent limitation or order on employment and on the alleged discharge, lay-off, or discrimination and shall make such recommendations as he deems appropriate. Such report, findings, and recommendations shall be available to the public. Nothing in this subsection shall be construed to require or authorize the Administrator to modify or withdraw any effluent limitation or order issued under this Act.

Sec. 508. Federal Procurement

(a) No Federal agency may enter into any contract with any person, who has been convicted of any offense under section 309(c) of this Act, for the procurement of goods, materials, and services if such contract is to be performed at any facility at which the violation which gave rise to such conviction occurred, and if such facility is owned, leased, or supervised by such person. The prohibition in the preceding sentence shall continue until the Administrator certifies that the condition giving rise to such conviction has been corrected.

(b) The Administrator shall establish procedures to provide all Federal agencies with the notification necessary for the purposes of subsection (a) of this section.

(c) In order to implement the purposes and policy of this Act to protect and enhance the quality of the Nation's water, the President shall, not more than one hundred and eighty days after enactment of this Act, cause to be issued an order (1) requiring each Federal agency authorized to enter into contracts and each Federal agency which is empowered to extend Federal assistance by way of grant, loan, or contract to effectuate the purpose and policy of this Act in such contracting or assistance activities, and (2) setting forth procedures, sanctions, penalties, and such other provisions, as the President determines necessary to carry out such requirement.

(d) The President may exempt any contract, loan, or grant from all or part of the provisions of this section where he determines such exemption is necessary in the paramount interest of the United States and he shall notify the Congress of such exemption.

(e) The President shall annually report to the Congress on measures taken in compliance with the purpose and intent of this section, including, but not limited to, the progress and problems associated with such compliance.

Sec. 509. Administrative Procedure and Judicial Review.

(a) (1) For the purposes of obtaining information under section 305 of this Act, or carrying out section 507(e) of this act, the Administrator may issue subpoenas for the attendance and testimony of witnesses and production of relevant papers, books, and documents, and he may administer oaths. Except for effluent data, upon showing satisfactory to the Administrator that such papers, books, documents, or information or particular part thereof, if made public, would divulge trade secrets or secret processes, the Administrator shall consider such record, report, of information or particular portion thereof confidential in accordance with the purposes of section 1905 of title 18 of the United States Code, except that such paper, book, document, or information may be disclosed to other officers, employees, or authorized representatives of the United States concerned with carrying out this Act, or when relevant to any proceeding under this Act. Witnesses summoned shall be paid the same fees and mileage that are paid witnesses in the courts of the United States. In case of contumacy or refusal to obey a subpoena served upon any person under this subsection, the district court of the United States for any district in which such person is found or resides or transacts business, upon application by the United States and after notice to such person, shall have jurisdiction to issue an order requiring such person to appear and give testimony before the Administrator, to appear and produce papers, books and documents before the Administrator, or both, and any failure to obey such order of the court may be punished by such court as a contempt thereof.

(2) The district courts of the United States are authorized, upon application by the Administrator, to issue subpoenas for attendance and testimony of witnesses and the production of relevant papers, books, and documents, for purposes of obtaining information under sections 304(b) and (c) of this Act. Any papers, books, documents, or other information or part thereof, obtained by reason of such a subpoena shall be subject to the same requirements as are provided in paragraph (1) of this subsection.

(b) (1) Review of the Administrator's action (A) in promulgating any standard of performance under section 306, (B) in making any determination pursuant to section 306(b)(1)(C), (C) in promulgating any effluent standard, prohibition, or pretreatment standard under section 307, (D) in making any ·determination as to a State permit program submitted under section 402(b), (E) in approving or promulgating any effluent limitation or other limitation under sections 301, 302, 306, or 405[,] (F) in issuing or denying any permit under section 402, and (G) in promulgating any individual control strategy under section 304(1), may be had by any interested person in the Circuit Court of Appeals of the United States for the Federal judicial district in which such person resides or transacts business which is directly affected by such action upon application by such person. Any such application shall be made within 120 days from the date of such determination, approval, promulgation, issuance or denial, or after such date only if such application is based solely on grounds which arose after 120th day.

[Sec. 509(b)(1) amended by PL 100-4]

(2) Action of the Administrator with respect to which review could have been obtained under paragraph (1) of this subsection shall not be subject to judicial review in any civil or criminal proceeding for enforcement.

(3) Venue. --

[Sec. 509(b)(3) added by PL 100-4]

(A) Selection Procedure. -- If applications for review of the same agency action have been filed under paragraph (1) of this subsection in 2 or more Circuit Courts of Appeals of the United States and the Administrator has received written notice of the filing of one or more applications within 30 days or less after receiving written notice of the filing of the first application, then the Administrator shall promptly advise in writing the Administrative Office of the United States Courts that applications have been filed in 2 or more Circuit Courts of Appeals of the United States, and shall identify each court for which he has written notice that such applications have been filed within 30 days or less of receiving written notice of the filing of the first such application. Pursuant to a system of random selection devised for this purpose, the Administrative Office thereupon shall, within 3 business days of receiving such written notice from the Administrator, select the court in which the record shall be filed from among those identified by the Administrator. Upon notification of such selection, the Administrator shall promptly file the record in such court. For the purpose of review of agency action which has previously been remanded to the Administrator, the record shall be filed in the Circuit Court of Appeals of the United States which remanded such action.

(B) Administrator Provisions. -- Where applications have been filed under paragraph (1) of this subsection in two or more Circuit Courts of Appeals of the United States with respect to the same agency action and the record has been filed in one of such courts pursuant to subparagraph (A), the other courts in which such applications have been filed shall promptly transfer such applications to the Circuit Court of Appeals of the United States in which the record has been filed. Pending selection of a court pursuant to subparagraph (A), any court in which an application has been filed under paragraph (1) of this subsection may postpone the effective date of the agency action until 15 days after the Administrative Office has selected the court in which the record shall be filed.

(C) Transfers. -- Any court in which an application with respect to any agency action has been filed under paragraph (1) of this subsection, including any court selected pursuant to subparagraph (A), may transfer such application to any other Circuit Court of Appeals of the United States for the convenience of the parties or otherwise in the interest of justice.

(4) Award of Fees. -- In any judicial proceeding under this subsection, the court may award costs of litigation (including reasonable attorney and expert witness fees) to any prevailing or substantially prevailing party whenever it determines that such award is appropriate.

[Sec. 509(b)(4) added by PL 100-4]

(c) In any judicial proceeding brought under subsection (b) of this section in which review is sought of a determination under this Act required to be made on the record after notice and opportunity for hearing, if any party applies to the court for leave to adduce additional evidence, and shows to the satisfaction of the court that such additional evidence is material and that there were reasonable grounds for the failure to adduce such evidence in the proceeding before the Administrator, the court may order such additional evidence (and evidence in rebuttal thereof) to be taken before the Administrator in such manner and upon such terms and conditions as the court may deem proper. The Administrator may modify his findings as to the facts, or make new findings, by reason of the additional evidence so taken and he shall file such modified or new findings, and his recommendation, if any, for the modification or setting aside of his original determination, with the return of such additional evidence.

Sec. 510. State Authority

Except as expressly provided in this Act, nothing in this Act shall (1) preclude or deny the right of any State or political subdivision thereof or interstate agency to adopt or enforce (A) any standard or limitation respecting discharges of pollutants, or (B) any requirement respecting control or abatement of pollution; except that if an effluent limitation, or other limitation, effluent standard, prohibition, pretreatment standard, or standard of performance is in effect under this Act, such State or political subdivision or interstate agency may not adopt or enforce any effluent limitation, or other limitation, effluent standard, prohibition, pretreatment standard, or standard of performance which is less stringent than the effluent limitation, or other limitation, effluent standard, prohibition, pretreatment standard, or standard of performance under this Act; or (2) be construed as imparing or in any manner affecting any right or jurisdiction of the States with respect to the waters (including boundary waters) of such States.

Sec. 511. Other Affected Authority

(a) This act shall not be construed as (1) limiting the authority or functions of any officer or agency of the United States under any other law or regulation not inconsistent with this Act; (2) affecting or impairing the authority of the Secretary of the Army (A) to maintain navigation or (B) under the Act of March 3, 1899 (30 Stat. 1112); except that any permit issued under section 404 of this Act shall be conclusive as to the effect on water quality of any discharge resulting from any activity subject to section 10 of the Act of March 3, 1899, or (3) affecting or impairing the provisions of any treaty of the United States.

(b) Discharges of pollutants into the navigable waters subject to the Rivers and Harbors Act of 1910 (36 Sta. 593; 33 U.S.C. 421) and the Supervisory Harbors Act of 1888 (25 Stat 209; 33 U.S.C. 441-451b) shall be regulated pursuant to this Act, and not subject to such Act of 1910 and the Act of 1888 except as to effect on navigation and anchorage.

(c) (1) Except for the provision of Federal financial assistance for the purpose of assisting the construction of publicly owned treatment works as authorized by section 201 of this Act, and the issuance of a permit under section 402 of this Act for the discharge of any pollutant by a new source as defined in section 306 of this Act, no action of the Administrator taken pursuant to this Act shall be deemed a major Federal action significantly affecting the quality of the human environment within the meaning of the National Environmental Policy Act of 1969 (83 Stat. 852); and

(2) Nothing in the National Environmental Policy Act of 1969 (83 Stat. 852) shall be deemed to --

(A) authorize any Federal agency authorized to license or permit the conduct of any activity which may result in the discharge of a pollutant into the navigable waters to review any effluent limitation or other requirement established pursuant to this Act or the adequacy of any certification under section 401 of this Act; or

(B) authorize any such agency to impose, as a condition precedent to the issuance of any license or permit, any effluent limitation other than any such limitation established pursuant to this Act.

(d) Notwithstanding this Act or any other provision of law, the Administrator (1) shall not require any State to consider in the development of the ranking in order of priority of needs for the construction of treatment works (as defined in title II of this Act), any water pollution control agreement which may have been entered into between the United States and any other nation, and (2) shall not consider any such agreement in the approval of any such priority ranking.

Sec. 512. Separability

If any provision of this Act, or the application of any provision of this Act to any person or circumstance, is held invalid, the application of such provision to other persons or circumstances, and the remainder of this Act, shall not be affected thereby.

Sec. 513. Labor Standards.

The Administrator shall take such action as may be necessary to insure that all laborers and mechanics employed by contractors or subcontractors on treatment works for which grants are made under this Act shall be paid wages at rates not less than those prevailing for the same type of work on similar construction in the immediate locality, as determined by the Secretary of Labor, in accordance with the Act of March 3, 1931, as amended, known as the Davis-Bacon Act (46 Stat. 1494; 40 U.S.C., sec. 276a through 276a-5). The Secretary of Labor shall have, with respect to the labor standard specified in this subsection, the authority and functions set forth in Reorganization Plan Numbered 14 of 1950 (15 F.R. 3176) and section 2 of the Act of June 13, 1934, as amended (48 Stat. 948; 40 U.S.C. 276c).

Sec. 514. Public Health Agency Coordination.

The permitting agency under section 402 shall assist the applicant for a permit under such section in coordinating the requirements of this Act with those of the appropriate public health agencies.

Sec. 515. Effluent Standard and Water Quality Information Advisory Committee.

(a) (1) There is established an Effluent Standards and Water Quality Information Advisory Committee, which shall be composed of a Chairman and eight members who shall be appointed by the Administrator within sixty days after the date of enactment of this Act.

(2) All members of the Committee shall be selected from the scientific community, qualified by education, training, and experience to provide, assess, and evaluate scientific and technical information on effluent standards and limitations.

(3) Members of the Committee shall serve for a term of four years, and may be reappointed.

(b) (1) No later than one hundred and eight days prior to the date on which the Administrator is required to publish any proposed regulations required by section 304(b) of this Act, any proposed standard of performance for new sources required by section 306 of this Act, or any proposed toxic effluent standard required by section 307 of this Act, he shall transmit to the Committee a notice of intent to propose such regulations. The Chairman of the Committee within ten days after receipt of such notice may publish a notice of a public hearing by the Committee, to be held within thirty days.

(2) No later than one hundred and twenty days after receipt of such notice, the Committee shall transmit to the Administrator such scientific and technical information as is in its possession, including that presented at any public hearing, related to the subject matter contained in such notice.

(3) Information so transmitted to the Administrator shall constitute a part of the administrative record and comments on any proposed regulations or standard as information to be considered with other comments and information in making any final determinations.

(4) In preparing information for transmittal, the Committee shall avail itself of the technical and scientific services of any Federal agency, including the United States Geological Survey and any national environmental laboratories which may be established.

(c) (1) The Committee shall appoint and prescribe the duties of a Secretary, and such legal counsel as it deems necessary to exercise and fulfill its powers and responsibilities. The compensation of all employees appointed by the Committee shall be fixed in accordance with chapter 51 and subchapter III of chapter 53 of title V of the United States Code.

(2) Members of the Committee shall be entitled to receive compensation at a rate to be fixed by the President but not in excess of the maximum rate of pay for GS-18, as provided in the General Schedule under section 5332 of title V of the United States Code.

(d) Five members of the Committee shall constitute a quorum, and official actions of the Committee shall be taken only on the affirmative vote of at least five members. A special panel composed of one or more members upon order of the Committee shall conduct any hearing authorized by this section and submit the transcript of such hearing to the entire Committee for its action thereon.

(e) The Committee is authorized to make such rules as are necessary for the orderly transaction of its business.

Sec. 515. Reports to Congress

(a) Within ninety days folling the convening of each session of Congress, the Administrator shall submit to the Congress a report, in addition to any other report required by this Act, on measures taken toward implementing the objective of this Act, including, but not limited to, (1) the progress and problems associated with developing comprehensive plans under section 102 of this Act, area-wide plans under section 208 of this Act, basin plans under section 209 of this Act, and plans under section 303(e) of this Act; (2) a summary of actions taken and results achieved in the field of water pollution control research, experiments, studies, and related matters by the Administrator and other Federal grants or contracts;

(3) the progress and problems associated with the development of effluent limitations and recommended control techniques; (4) the status of State program plans for development and enforcement of water quality requirements; (5) the identification and status of enforcement actions pending or completed under such Act during the preceding year; (6) the status of State, interstate, and local pollution control programs established pursuant to, and assisted by, this Act; (7) a summary of the results of the survey required to be taken under section 210 of this Act; (8) his activities including recommendations under sections 109 through 111 of this Act; and (9) all reports and recommendations made by the Water Pollution Control Advisory Board.

(b) (1) The Administrator, in cooperation with the States, including water pollution control agencies and other water pollution control planning agencies, shall make (A) a detailed estimate of the cost of carrying out the provisions of this Act; (B) a detailed estimate, biennially revised, of the cost of construction of all needed publicly owned treatment works in all of the States and of the cost of construction of all needed publicly owned treatment works in each of the States; (C) a comprehensive study of the economic impact of affected units of government of the cost of installation of treatment facilities; and (D) a comprehensive analysis of the national requirements for and the cost of treating municipal, industrial, and other effluent to attain the water quality objectives as established by this Act or applicable State law. The Administrator shall submit such detailed estimate and such comprehensive study of such cost to the Congress no later than February 10, of each odd-numbered year. Whenever the Administrator pursuant to this subsection requests and receives an estimate of cost from a State, he shall furnish copies of such estimate together with such detailed estimate to Congress.

[Section 25 of PL 97-117 provides:

"Sec. 25. **Needs Survey**.

The Administrator of the Environmental Protection Agency shall submit to the Congress, not later than December 31, 1982, a report containing the detailed estimates, comprehensive study, and comprehensive analysis required by section 516(b) of the Federal Water Pollution Control Act, including an estimate of the total cost and the amount of Federal funds necessary for the construction of needed publicly owned treatment facilities. Such report shall be prepared in the same manner as is required by such section and shall reflect the changes made in the Federal water pollution control program by this Act and the amendments made by this Act. In preparing this report, the Administrator shall give emphasis to the effects of the amendment made by section 2(a) of this Act in addressing water quality needs adequately and appropriately."]

(2) Notwithstanding the second sentence of paragraph (1) of this subsection, the Administrator shall make a preliminary detailed estimate called for by subparagraph (B) of such paragraph and shall submit such preliminary detailed estimate to the Congress no later than September 3, 1974. The Administrator shall

require each State to prepare an estimate of cost for such State, and shall utilize the survey form EPA-1, O.M.B. No. 158-R0017, prepared for the 1973 detailed estimate, except that such estimate shall include all costs of compliance with section 201(g)(2)(A) of this Act and water quality standards established pursuant to section 303 of this Act, and all costs of treatment works as defined in section 212(2), including all eligible costs of constructing sewage collection systems and correcting excessive infiltration or inflow and all eligible costs of correcting combined storm and sanitary sewer problems and treating storm water flows. The survey form shall be distributed by the Administrator to each State no later than January 31, 1974.

(c) The Administrator shall submit to the Congress by October 1, 1978, a report on the status of combined sewer overflows in municipal treatment works operations. The report shall include (1) the status of any projects funded under this Act to address combined sewer overflows, (2) a listing by State of combined sewer overflow needs identified in the 1977 State priority listings, (3) an estimate for each applicable municipality of the number of years necessary, assuming an annual authorization and appropriation for the construction grants program of $5,000,000,000 to correct combined sewer overflow problems, (4) an analysis using representative municipalities faced with major combined sewer overflow needs, of the annual discharges of pollutants from overflows in comparison to treated effluent discharges, (5) an analysis of the technological alternatives available to municipalities to correct major combined sewer overflow problems, and (6) any recommendations of the Administrator for legislation to address the problem of combined sewer overflows, including whether a separate authorization and grant program should be established by the Congress to address combined sewer overflows.

(d) The Administrator shall submit to the Congress by October 1, 1978, a report on the status of the use of municipal secondary effluent and sludge for 'agricultural and other purposes that utilize the nutrient value of treated wastewater effluent. The report shall include (1) a summary of results of research and development programs, grants, and contracts carried out by the Environmental Protection Agency pursuant to sections 104 and 105 of this Act, regarding alternatives to disposal, landfill, or incineration of secondary effluent of sludge, (2) an estimate of the amount of sludge generated by public treatment works and its disposition, including an estimate of annual energy costs of incinerated sludge, (3) an analysis of current technologies for the utilization, reprocessing, and other uses of sludge to utilize the nutrient value of sludge, (4) legal, institutional, public health, economic, and other impediments to the greater utilization of treated sludge, and (5) any recommendations of the Administrator for legislation to encourage or require the expanded utilization of sludge for agricultural and other purposes. In carrying out this subsection, the Administrator shall consult with, and use the services of the Tennessee Valley Authority and other departments, agencies and instrumentalities of the United States, to the extent it is appropriate to do so.

(e) The Administrator, in cooperation with the States, including water pollution control agencies, and other water pollution control planning agencies, and water supply and water resources agencies of the States and the United States shall submit to Congress, within two years of the date of enactment of this section, a report with recommendations for legislation on a program to require coordination between water supply and wastewater control plans as a condition to grants for construction of treatment works under this Act. No such report shall be submitted except after opportunity for public hearings on such proposed report.

[Section 516(f) has not been enacted.]

(g) State Revolving Fund Report. --

(1) In General. -- Not later than February 10, 1990, the Administrator shall submit to Congress a report on the financial status and operations of water pollution control revolving funds established by the States under title VI of this Act. The Administrator shall prepare such report in cooperation with the States, including water pollution control agencies and other water pollution control planning and financing agencies.

(2) Contents. -- The report under this subsection shall also include the following:

(A) an inventory of the facilities that are in significant noncompliance with the enforceable requirements of this Act;

(B) an estimate of the cost of construction necessary to bring such facilities into compliance with such requirements;

(C) an assessment of the availability of sources of funds for financing such needed construction, including an estimate of the amount of funds available for providing assistance for such construction through September 30, 1999, from the water pollution control revolving funds established by the States under title VI of this Act;

(D) an assessment of the operations, loan portfolio, and loan conditions of such revolving funds;

(E) an assessment of the effect on user charges of the assistance provided by such revolving funds compared to the assistance provided with funds appropriated pursuant to section 207 of this Act; and

(F) an assessment of the efficiency of the operation and maintenance of treatment works constructed with assistance provided by such revolving funds compared to the efficiency of the operation and maintenance of treatment works constructed with assistance provided under section 201 of this Act.

[Sec. 516(g) added by PL 100-4]

Sec. 517. General Authorization.

There are authorized to be appropriated to carry out this Act, other than sections 104, 105, 106(a), 107, 108, 112, 113, 114, 115, 206, 207, 208(f) and (h), 209, 304, 311(c), (d), (i), (1), and (k), 314, 315, and 317, $250,000,000 for the fiscal year ending June 30, 1973, $300,000,000 for the fiscal year ending June 30, 1974, $350,000,000 for the fiscal year ending June 30, 1975, $100,000,000 for the fiscal year ending September 30, 1977, $150,000, 000 for the fiscal year ending September 30, 1978, $150,000,000 for the fiscal year ending September 30, 1979, $150,000,000 for the fiscal year ending September 30, 1980, $150,000,000 for the fiscal year ending September 30, 1981, $161,000,000 for the fiscal year ending September 30, 1982, such sums as may be necessary for fiscal years 1983 through 1985, and $135,000,000 per fiscal year for each of the fiscal years 1986 through 1990.

(Sec. 517 amended by PL 96-483; PL 100-4)

Sec. 518.   Indian Tribes.

[New Sec. 518 added by PL 100-4]

(a) Policy. -- Nothing in this section shall be construed to affect the application of section 101(g) of this Act, and all of the provisions of this section shall be carried out in accordance with the provisions of such section 101(g). Indian tribes shall be treated as States for purposes of such section 101(g).

(b) Assessment of Sewage Treatment Needs; Report. -- The Administrator, in cooperation with the Director of the Indian Health Service, shall assess the need for sewage treatment works to serve Indian tribes, the degree to which such needs will be met through funds allotted to States under Section 205 of this Act and priority lists under section 216 of this Act, and any obstacles which prevent such needs from being met. Not later than one year after the date of the enactment of this section, the Administrator shall submit a report to Congress on the assessment under this subsection, along with recommendations specifying (1) how the Administrator intends to provide assistance to Indian tribes to develop waste treatment management plans and to construct treatment works under this Act, and (2) methods by which the participation in and administration of programs under this Act by Indian tribes can be maximized.

(c) Reservation of Funds. -- The Administrator shall reserve each fiscal year beginning after September 30, 1986, before allotments to the States under section 205(e), one-half of one percent of the sums appropriated under section 207. Sums reserved under this subsection shall be available only for grants for the development of waste treatment management plans and for the construction of sewage treatment works to serve Indian tribes.

(d) Cooperative Agreements. -- In order to ensure the consistent implementation of the requirements of this Act, an Indian tribe and the State or States in which the lands of such tribe are located may enter into cooperative agreement, subject to the review and approval

of the Administrator, to jointly plan and administer the
requirements of this Act.

(e) Treatment as States. -- The Administrator is authorized to
treat an Indian tribe as a State for purposes of title II and
sections 104, 106, 303, 305, 308, 309, 314, 319, 401, and 404 of
this Act to the degree necessary to carry out the objectives of this
section, but only if --

(1) the Indian tribe has a governing body carrying out
substantial governmental duties and powers;

(2) the functions to be exercised by the Indian tribe pertain to
the management and protection of water resources which are held
by an Indian tribe, held by the United States in trust for
Indians, held by a member of an Indian tribe if such property
interest is subject to a trust restriction on alienation, or
otherwise within the borders of an Indian reservation; and

(3) the Indian tribe is reasonably expected to be capable, in
the Administrator's judgment, of carrying out the functions to
be exercised in a manner consistent with the terms and purposes
of this Act and of all applicable regulations.

Such treatment as a State may include the direct provision of funds
reserved under subsection (c) to the governing bodies of Indian
tribes, and the determination of priorities by Indian tribes, where
not determined by the Administrator in cooperation with the Director
of the Indian Health Service. The Administrator, in cooperation
with the Director of Indian Health Service, is authorized to make
grants under title II of this Act in an amount not to exceed 100
percent of the cost of a project. Not later than 18 months after
the date of the enactment of this section, the Administrator shall,
in consultation with Indian tribes, promulgate final regulations
which specify how Indian tribes shall be treated as States for
purposes of this Act. The Administrator shall, in promulgating such
regulations, consult affected States sharing common water bodies and
provide a mechanism for the resolution of any unreasonable
consequences that may arise as a result of differing water quality
standards that may be set by States and Indian tribes located on
common bodies of water. Such mechanism shall provide for explicit
consideration of relevant factors including, but not limited to, the
effects of differing water quality permit requirements on upstream
and downstream dischargers, economic impacts, and present and
historical uses and quality of the waters subject to such standards.
Such mechanism should provide for the avoidance of such unreasonable
consequences in a manner consistent with the objective of this Act.

(f) Grants for Nonpoint Source Programs. -- The Administrator shall
make grants to an Indian tribe under section 319 of this Act as
though such tribe was a State. Not more than one-third of one
percent of the amount appropriated for any fiscal year under section
319 may be used to make grants under this subsection. In addition
to the requirements of section 319, an Indian tribe shall be
required to meet the requirements of paragraphs (1), (2), and (3) of
subsection (d) of this section in order to receive such a grant.

(g) Alaska Native Organizations. -- No provision of this Act shall be construed to --

(1) grant, enlarge, or diminish, or in any way affect the scope of the governmental authority, if any, of any Alaska Native organization, including any federally-recognized tribe, traditional Alaska Native council, or Native Council organized pursuant to the Act of June 18, 1934 (48 Stat. 987), over lands or persons in Alaska;

(2) create or validate any assertion by such organization or any form of governmental authority over lands or persons in Alaska; or

(3) in any way affect any assertion that Indian country, as defined in section 1151 or title 18, United States Code, exists or does not exist in Alaska.

(h) Definitions. -- For purposes of this section, the term --

(1) "Federal Indian reservation" means all land within the limits of any Indian reservation under the jurisdiction of the United States Government, notwithstanding the issuance of any patent, and including rights-of-way running through the reservation; and

(2) "Indian tribe" means any Indian tribe, band, group, or community recognized by the Secretary of the Interior and exercising governmental authority over a Federal Indian reservation.

Sec. 519. Short Title.

This Act may be cited as the "Federal Water Pollution Control Act" (commonly referred to as the Clean Water Act).

[Former Sec. 518 redesignated as 519 by PL 100-4]

TITLE VI -- STATE WATER POLLUTION CONTROL REVOLVING FUNDS

[Title VI added by PL 100-4]

Sec. 601. Grants to States for Establishment of Revolving Funds.

(a) General Authority. -- Subject to the provisions of this title, the Administrator shall make capitalization grants to each State for the purpose of establishing a water pollution control revolving fund for providing assistance (1) for construction of treatment works (as defined in section 212 of this Act) which are publicly owned, (2) for implementing a management program under section 319, and (3) for developing and implementing a conservation and management plan under section 320.

(b) Schedule of Grant Payments. -- The Administrator and each State shall jointly establish a schedule of payments under which the Administrator will pay to the State the amount of each grant to be made to the State under this title. Such schedule shall be based on the State's intended use plan under section 606(c) of this Act, except that --

(1) such payments shall be made in quarterly installments, and

(2) such payments shall be made as expeditiously as possible, but in no event later than the earlier of --

(A) 8 quarters after the date such funds were obligated by the State, or

(B) 12 quarters after the date such funds were allocated to the State.

Sec. 602. Capitalization Grant Agreements.

(a) General Rule. -- To receive a capitalization grant with funds made available under this title and section 205(m) of this Act, a State shall enter into an agreement with the Administrator which shall include but not be limited to the specifications set forth in subsection (b) of this section.

(b) Specific Requirements. -- The Administrator shall enter into an agreement under this section with a State only after the State has established to the satisfaction of the Administrator that --

(1) the State will accept grant payments with funds to be made available under this title and section 205(m) of this Act in accordance with a payment schedule established jointly by the Administrator under section 601(b) of this Act and will deposit all such payments in the water pollution control revolving fund established by the State in accordance with this title;

(2) the State will deposit in the fund from State moneys an amount equal to at least 20 percent of the total amount of all capitalization grants which will be made to the State with funds to be made available under this title and section 205(m) of this

Act on or before the date on which each quarterly grant payment will be made to the State under this title;

(3) the State will enter into binding commitments to provide assistance in accordance with the requirements of this title in an amount equal to 120 percent of the amount of each such grant payment within 1 year after the receipt of such grant payment;

(4) all funds in the fund will be expended in an expeditious and timely manner;

(5) all funds in the fund as a result of capitalization grants under this title and section 205(m) of this Act will be used to assure maintenance of progress, as determined by the Governor of the State, toward compliance with enforceable deadlines, goals, and requirements of this Act, including the municipal compliance deadline;

(6) treatment works eligible under section 603(c)(1) of this Act which will be constructed in whole or in part before fiscal year 1995 with funds directly made available by capitalization grants under this title and section 205(m) of this Act will meet the requirements of, or otherwise be treated (as determined by the Governor of the State) under sections 201(b), 201(g)(1), 201(g)(2), 201(g)(3), 201(g)(5), 201(g)(6), 201(n)(1), 201(o), 204(a)(1), 204(a)(2), 204(b)(1), 204(d)(2), 211, 218, 511(c)(1), and 513 of this Act in the same manner as treatment works constructed with assistance under title II of this Act;

(7) in addition to complying with the requirements of this title, the State will commit or expend each quarterly grant payment which it will receive under this title in accordance with laws and procedures applicable to the commitment or expenditure of revenues of the State;

(8) in carrying out the requirements of section 606 of this Act, the State will use accounting, audit, and fiscal procedures conforming to generally accepted government accounting standards;

(9) the State will require as a condition of making a loan or providing other assistance, as described in section 603(d) of this Act, from the fund that the recipient of such assistance will maintain project accounts in accordance with generally accepted government accounting standards and

(10) the State will make annual reports to the Administrator on the actual use of funds in accordance with section 606(d) of this Act.

Sec. 603. Water Pollution Control Revolving Loan Funds.

(a) Requirements for Obligation of Grant Funds. -- Before a State may receive a capitalization grant with funds made available under this title and section 205(m) of this Act, the State shall first establish a water pollution control revolving fund which complies with the requirements of this section.

(b) Administration. -- Each State water pollution control revolving fund may be administered by an instrumentality of the State with such powers and limitations as may be required to operate such fund in accordance with the requirements and objectives of this Act.

(c) Projects Eligible for Assistance. -- The amounts of funds available to each State water pollution control revolving fund shall be used only for providing financial assistance (1) to any municipality intermunicipal, interstate, or State agency for construction of publicly owned treatment works (as defined in section 212 of this Act), (2) for the implementation of a management program established under section 319 of this Act, and (3) for development and implementation of a conservation and management plan under section 320 of this Act. The fund shall be established, maintained, and credited with repayments, and the fund balance shall be available in perpetuity for providing such financial assistance.

(d) Types of Assistance. -- Except as otherwise limited by State law, a water pollution control revolving fund of a State under this section may be used only --

   (1) to make loans, on the condition that --

      (A) such loans are made at or below market interest rates, including interest free loans, at terms not to exceed 20 years;

      (B) annual principal and interest payments will commence not later than 1 year after completion of any project and all loans will be fully amortized not later than 20 years after project completion;

      (C) the recipient of a loan will establish a dedicated source of revenue for repayment of loans; and

      (D) the fund will be credited with all payments of principal and interest on all loans;

   (2) to buy or refinance the debt obligation of municipalities and intermunicipal and interstate agencies within the State at or below market rates, where such debt obligations were incurred after March 7, 1985;

   (3) to guarantee, or purchase insurance for, local obligations where such action would improve credit market access or reduce interest rates;

   (4) as a source of revenue or security for the payment of principal and interest on revenue or general obligation bonds issued by the State if the proceeds of the sale of such bonds will be deposited in the fund;

   (5) to provide loan guarantees for similar revolving funds established by municipalities or intermunicipal agencies;

   (6) to earn interest on fund accounts; and

(7) for the reasonable costs of administering the fund and conducting activities under this title, except that such amounts shall not exceed 4 percent of all grant awards to such fund under this title.

(e) Limitation to Prevent Double Benefits. -- If a State makes, from its water pollution revolving fund, a loan which will finance the cost of facility planning and the preparation of plans, specifications, estimates for construction of publicly owned treatment works, the State shall ensure that if the recipient of such loan receives a grant under section 201(g) of this Act for construction of such treatment works and an allowance under section 201(1)(1) of this Act for non-Federal funds expended for such planning and preparation, such recipient will promptly repay such loan to the extent of such allowance.

(f) Consistency With Planning Requirements. -- A State may provide financial assistance from its water pollution control revolving fund only with respect to a project which is consistent with plans, if any, developed under sections 205(j), 208, 303(e), 319, and 320 of this Act.

(g) Priority List Requirement. -- The State may provide financial assistance from its water pollution control revolving fund only with respect to a project for construction of a treatment works described in subsection (c)(1) if such project is on the State's priority list under section 216 of this Act. Such assistance may be provided regardless of the rank of such project on such list.

(h) Eligibility of Non-Federal Share of Construction Grant Projects. -- A State water pollution control revolving fund may provide assistance (other than under subsection (d)(1) of this section) to a municipality or intermunicipal or interstate agency with respect to the non-Federal share of the costs of a treatment works project for which such municipality or agencyis receiving assistance from the Administrator under any other authority only if such assistance is necessary to allow such project to proceed.

Sec. 604. Allotment of Funds.

(a) Formula. -- Sums authorized to be appropriated to carry out this section for each of fiscal years 1989 and 1990 shall be allotted by the Administrator in accordance with section 205(c) of this Act.

(b) Reservation of Funds for Planning. -- Each State shall reserve each fiscal year 1 percent of the sums allotted to such State under this section for such fiscal year, or $100,000, whichever amount is greater, to carry out planning under section 205(j) and 303(e) of this Act.

(c) Allotment Period. --

(1) Period of Availability for Grant Award. -- Sums allotted to a State under this section for a fiscal year shall be available for obligation by the State during the fiscal year for which sums are authorized and during the following fiscal year.

(2) Reallotment of Unobligated Funds. -- The amount of any allotment not obligated by the State by the last day of the 2-year period of availability established by paragraph (1) shall be immediately reallotted the Administrator on the basis of the same ratio as is applicable to sums allotted under title II of this Act for the second fiscal year of such 2-year period. None of the funds reallotted by the Administrator shall be reallotted to any State which has not obligated all sums allotted to such State in the first fiscal year of such 2-year period.

Sec. 605. Correction Action.

(a) Notification of Noncompliance. -- If the Administrator determines that a State has not complied with its agreement with the Administrator under section 602 of this Act or any other requirement of this title, the Administrator shall notify the State of such noncompliance and the necessary corrective action.

(b) Withholding of Payments. -- If a State does not take corrective action within 60 days after the date a State receives notification of such action under subsection (a), the Administrator shall withhold additional payments to the State until the Administrator is satisfied that the State has taken the necessary corrective action.

(c) Reallotment of Withheld Payments. -- If the Administrator is not satisfied that adequate corrective actions have been taken by the State within 12 months after the State is notified of such actions under subsection (a), the payments withheld from the State by the Administrator under subsection (b) shall be made available for reallotment in accordance with the most recent formula for allotment of funds under this title.

Sec. 606. Audits, Reports, and Fiscal Controls: Intended Use Plan.

(a) Fiscal Control and Auditing Procedure. -- Each State electing to establish a water pollution control revolving fund under this title shall establish fiscal controls and accounting procedures sufficient to assure proper accounting during appropriate accounting periods for --

(1) payments received by the fund;

(2) disbursements made by the fund; and

(3) fund balances at the beginning and end of the accounting period.

(b) Annual Federal Audits. -- The Administrator shall, at least on an annual basis, conduct or require each State to have independently conducted reviews and audits as may be deemed necessary or appropriate by the Administrator to carry out the objectives of this section. Audits of the use of funds deposited in the water pollution revolving fund established by such State shall be conducted in accordance with the auditing procedures of the General Accounting Office, including chapter 75 of title 31, United States Code.

(c) Intended Use Plan. -- After providing for public comment and review, each State shall annually prepare a plan identifying the intended uses of the amounts available to its water pollution control revolving fund. Such intended use plan shall include, but not be limited to --

(1) a list of those projects for construction of publicly owned treatment works on the State's priority list developed pursuant to section 216 of this Act and a list of activities eligible for assistance under sections 319 and 320 of this Act;

(2) a description of the short- and long-term goals and objectives of its water pollution control revolving fund;

(3) information on the activities to be supported, including a description of project categories, discharge requirements under titles III and IV of this Act, terms of financial assistance, and communities served;

(4) assurances and specific proposals for meeting the requirements of paragraphs (3), (4), (5), and (6) of section 602(b) of this Act; and

(5) the criteria and method established for the distribution of funds.

(d) Annual Report. -- Beginning the first fiscal year after the receipt of payments under this title, the State shall provide an annual report to the Administrator describing how the State has met the goals and objectives for the previous fiscal year as identified in the plan prepared for the previous fiscal year pursuant to subsection (c) including identification of loan recipients, loan amounts, and loan terms and similar details on other forms of financial assistance provided from the water pollution control revolving fund.

(e) Annual Federal Oversight Review. -- The Administrator shall conduct an annual oversight review of each State plan prepared under subsection (d), each State report prepared under subsection (d), and other such materials as are considered necessary and appropriate in carrying out the purposes of this title. After reasonable notice by the Administrator to the State or the recipient of a loan from water pollution control revolving fund, the State or loan recipient shall make available to the Administrator such records as the Administrator reasonably requires to review and determine compliance with this title.

(f) Applicability of Title II Provisions. -- Except to the extent provided in this title, the provisions of Title II shall not apply to grants under this title.

Sec. 607. Authorization of Appropriations.

There is authorized to be appropriated to carry out the purposes of this title the following sums:

(1) $1,200,000,000 per fiscal year for each of fiscal years 1989 and 1990;

(2) $2,400,000,000 for fiscal year 1991;

(3) $1,800,000,000 for fiscal year 1992;

(4) $1,200,000,000 for fiscal year 1993; and

(5) $600,000,000 for fiscal year 1994.

APPENDIX A -- SHORT-TERM PRECURSORS TO THE 1972 ACT

Sec. 3. Authorizations for Fiscal Year 1972

(a) There is authorized to be appropriated for the fiscal year ending June 30, 1972, not to exceed $11,000,000 for the purpose of carrying out section 5(n) (other than for salaries and related expenses) of the Federal Water Pollution Control Act as it existed immediately prior to the date of the enactment of the Federal Water Pollution Control Act Amendments of 1972.

(b) There is hereby authorized to be appropriated for the fiscal year ending June 30, 1972, not to exceed $350,000,000 for the purpose of making grants under section 8 of the Federal Water Pollution Control Act as it existed immediately prior to the date of the enactment of the Federal Water Pollution Control Act Amendments of 1972.

(c) The Federal share of all grants made under section 8 of the Federal Water Pollution Control Act as it existed immediately prior to the date of enactment of the Federal Water Pollution Control Act Amendments of 1972 from sums herein and heretofore authorized for the fiscal year ending June 30, 1972, shall be that authorized by section 202 of such Act as established by the Federal Water Pollution Control Act Amendments of 1972.

(d) Sums authorized by this section shall be in addition to any amounts heretofore authorized for such fiscal year for sections 5(n) and 8 of the Federal Water Pollution Control Act as it existed immediately prior to the date of enactmenet of the Federal Water Pollution Control Act Amendments of 1972.

Sec. 4. Savings Provision.

(a) No suit, action, or other proceeding lawfully commenced by or against the Administrator or any other officer or employee of the United States in his official capacity or in relation to the discharge of his official duties under the Federal Water Pollution Control Act as in effect immediately prior to the date of enactment of this Act shall abate by reason of the taking effect of the amendment made by section 2 of this Act. The court may, on its own motion or that of any party made at any time within twelve months after such taking effect, allow the same to be maintained by or against the Administrator or such officer or employee.

(b) All rules, regulations, orders, determinations, contracts, certifications, authorizations, delegations, or other actions duly issued, made, or taken by or pursuant to the Federal Water Pollution Control Act as in effect immediately prior to the date of enactment of this Act, and pertaining to any functions, powers, requirements, and duties under the Federal Water Pollution Control Act as in effect immediately prior to the date of enactment of this Act, shall continue in full force and effect after the date of enactment of this Act, until modified or rescinded in accordance with the Federal Water Pollution Control Act as amended by this Act.

(c) The Federal Water Pollution Control Act as in effect immediately prior to the date of enactment of this Act shall remain applicable to all grants made from funds authorized for the fiscal year ending June 30, 1972, and prior fiscal years, including any increases in the monetary amount of any such grant which may be paid from authorizations for fiscal years beginning after June 30, 1972, except as specifically, otherwise provided in section 202 of the Federal Water Pollution Control Act as amended by this Act and in subsection (c) of section 3 of this Act.

Sec. 5. Oversight Study.

In order to assist the Congress in the conduct of oversight responsibilities the Comptroller General of the United States shall conduct a study and review of the research, pilot, and demonstration programs related to prevention and control of water pollution, including waste treatment and disposal techniques, which are conducted, supported, or assisted by any agency of the Federal Government pursuant to any Federal law or regulation and assess conflicts between, and the coordination and efficacy of, such programs, and make a report to the Congress thereon by October 1, 1973.

Sec. 6. International Trade Study.

(a) The Secretary of Commerce, in cooperation with other interested Federal agencies and with representatives of industry and the public, shall undertake immediately an investigation and study to determine:

(1) the extent to which pollution abatement and control programs will be imposed on, or voluntarily undertaken by, United States manufacturers in the near future and the probable short- and long-range effects of the costs of such programs (computed to the greatest extent practicable on an industry-by-industry basis) on (A) the production costs of such domestic manufacturers, and (B) the market prices of the goods produced by them;

(2) the probable extent to which pollution abatement and control programs will be implemented in foreign industrial nations in the near future and the extent to which the production costs (computed to the greatest extent practicable on an industry-by-industry basis) of foreign manufacturers will be affected by the costs of such programs;

(3) the probable competitive advantage which any article manufactured in a foreign nation will likely have in relation to a comparable article made in the United States if that foreign nation --

(A) does not require its manufacturers to implement pollution abatement and control programs.

(B) requires a lesser degree of pollution abatement and control in its programs, or

(C) in any way reimburses or otherwise subsidizes its manufacturers for the costs of such program;

(4) alternative means by which any competitive advantage accruing to the products of any foreign nation as a result of any factor described in paragraph (3) may be (A) accurately and quickly determined, and (B) equalized, for example, by the imposition of a surcharge or duty, on a foreign product in an amount necessary to compensate for such advantage; and

(5) the impact, if any, which the imposition of a compensating tariff of other equalizing measure may have in encouraging foreign nations to implement pollution and abatement control programs.

(b) The Secretary shall make an initial report to the President and Congress within six months after the date of enactment of this section of the results of the study and investigation carried out pursuant to this section and shall make additional reports thereafter at such times as he deems appropriate taking into account the development of relevant data, but not less than once every twelve months.

Sec. 7. International Agreements.

The President shall undertake to enter into international agreements to apply uniform standards of performance for the control of the discharge and emission of pollutants from new sources, uniform controls over the discharge and emission of toxic pollutants, and uniform controls over the discharge of pollutants into the ocean. For this purpose the President shall negotiate multilateral treaties, conventions, resolutions, or other agreements, and formulate, present, or support proposals at the United Nations and other appropriate international forums.

Sec. 8 Loans to Small Business Concerns for Water Pollution Control Facility

(a) Section 7 of the Small Business Act is amended by inserting at the end thereof a new subsection as follows:

"(g)(1) The Administration also is empowered to make loans (either directly or in cooperation with banks or other lenders through agreements to participate on an immediate or deferred basis) to assist any small business concern in affecting additions to or alternations in the equipment, facilities (including the construction of pretreatment facilities and interceptor sewers), or methods of operation of such concern to meet water pollution control requirements established under the Federal Water Pollution Control Act, if the Administration determines that such concern is likely to suffer substantial economic injury without assistance under this subsection.

"(2) Any such loan --

"(A) shall be made in accordance with provisions applicable to loans made pursuant to subsection (b)(5) of this section, except as otherwise provided in this subsection;

"(B) shall be made only if the applicant furnishes the Administration with a statement in writing from the Environmental Protection Agency, or, if appropriate, the State, that such additions or alterations are necessary and adequate to comply with requirements established under the Federal Water Pollution Control Act.

"(3) The Administrator of the Environmental Protection Agency shall, as soon as practicable after the date of enactment of the Federal Water Pollution Control Act Amendments of 1972 and not later than one hundred and eighty days thereafter, promulgate regulations establishing uniform rules for the issuance of statements for the purpose of paragraph (2)(B) of this subsection.

"(4) There is authorized to be appropriated to the disaster loan fund established pursuant to section 4(c) of this Act not to exceed $800,000,000 solely for the purpose of carrying out this subsection."

(b) Section 4(c)(1)(A) of the Small Business Act is amended by striking out "and 7(c)(2)" and inserting in lieu thereof "7(c)(2), and 7(g)".

Sec. 9. Environmental Court.

The President, acting through the Attorney General, shall make a full and complete investigation and study of the feasibility of establishing a separate court, or court system, having jurisdiction over environmental matters and shall report the results of such investigation and study together with his recommendations to Congress not later than one year after the date of enactment of this Act.

Sec. 10. National Policies and Goals Study.

The President shall make a full and complete investigation and study of all of the national policies and goals established by law for the purpose of determining what the relationship should be between these policies and goals, taking into account the resources of the Nation. He shall report the results of such investigation and study together with his recommendations to Congress not later than two years after the date of enactment of this Act. There is authorized to be appropriated not to exceed $5,000,000 to carry out the purposes of this section.

Sec. 11. Efficiency Study.

The President shall conduct a full and complete investigation and study of ways and means of utilizing in the most effective manner all of the various resources, facilities, and personnel of the Federal Government in order most efficiently to carry out the objective of the Federal Water Pollution Control Act. He shall

utilize in conducting such investigation and study, the General
Accounting Office. He shall report the results of such
investigation and study together with his recommendations to
Congress not later than two hundred and seventy days after the date
of enactment of this Act.

Sec. 12. Environmental Financing.

(a) This section may be cited as the "Environmental Financing Act of
1972".

(b) There is hereby created a body corporate to be known as the
Environmental Financing Authority, which shall have succession until
dissolved by Act of Congress. The Authority shall be subject to the
general supervision and direction of the Secretary of the Treasury.
The Authority shall be instrumentality of the United States
Government and shall maintain such offices as may be necessary or
appropriate in the conduct of its business.

(c) The purpose of this section is to assure that inability to
borrow necessary funds on reasonable terms does not prevent any
State of local public body from carrying out any project for
construction of waste treatment works determined eligible for
assistance pursuant to subsection (e) of this section.

(d) (1) The Authority shall have a Board of Directors consisting of
five persons, one of whom shall be the Secretary of the Treasury
or his designee as Chairman of the Board, and four of whom shall
be appointed by the President from among the officers or
employees of the Authority or of any department or agency of the
United States Government.

(2) The Board of Directors shall meet at the call of its
Chairman. The Board shall determine the general policies which
shall govern the operations of the Authority. The Chairman of
the Board shall select and effect the appointment of qualified
persons to fill the offices as may be provided for in the
bylaws, with such executive functions, powers, and duties as may
be prescribed by the bylaws or by the Board of Directors, and
such persons shall be the executive officers of the Authority
and shall discharge all such executive functions, powers, and
duties. The members of the Board, as such, shall not receive
compensation for their services.

(e) (1) Until July 1, 1975, the Authority is authorized to make
commitments to purchase, and to purchase on terms and conditions
determined by the Authority, any obligation or participation
therein which is issued by the State or local public body to
finance the non-Federal share of the cost of any project for the
construction of waste treatment works which the Administrator of
the Environmental Protection Agency has determined to be
eligible for Federal financial assistance under the Federal
Water Pollution Control Act.

(2) No commitment shall be entered into, and no purchase shall
be made, unless the Administrator of the Environmental
Protection Agency (A) has certified that the public body is

unable to obtain on reasonable terms sufficient credit to
finance it actual needs; (B) has approved the project as
eligible under the Federal Water Pollution Control Act; and (C)
has agreed to guarantee timely payment of principal and interest
on the obligation. The Administrator is authorized to guarantee
such timely payments and to issue regulations as he deems
necessary and proper to protect such guarantees. Appropriations
are hereby authorized to be made to the Administrator in such
sums as are necessary to make payments under such guarantees,
and such payments are authorized to made from such
appropriations.

(3) No purchase shall be made of obligations issued to finance
projects, the permanent financing of which occurred prior to the
enactment of this section.

(4) Any purchase by the Authority shall be upon such terms and
conditions as to yield a return on a rate determined by the
Secretary of the Treasury taking into consideration (A) the
current average yield on outstanding marketable obligations of
the United States of comparable maturity or in its stead
whenever the Authority has sufficient of its own long-term
obligations outstanding, the current average yield on
outstanding obligations of the Authority of comparable maturity;
and (B) the market yields on municipal bonds.

(5) The Authority is authorized to charge fees for its
commitments and other services adequate to cover all expenses
and to provide for the accumulation of reasonable contingency
reserves and such fees shall be included in the aggregate
project costs.

(f) To provide initial capital to the Authority the Secretary of the
Treasury is authorized to advance the funds necessary for this
purpose. Each such advance shall be upon such terms and conditions
as to yield a return at a rate not less than a rate determined by
the Secretary of the Treasury taking into consideration the current
average yield on outstanding marketable obligations of the United
State of comparable maturities. Interest payments on such advances
may be deferred, at the discretion of the Secretary, but any such
deferred payments shall themselves bear interest at the rate
specified in this section. There is authorized to be appropriated
not to exceed $100,000,000, which shall be available for the
purposes of this subsection.

(g) (1) The Authority is authorized, with approval of the Secretary
of the Treasury, to issue and have outstanding obligations
having such maturities and bearing such rate or rates of
interest as may be determined by the Authority. Such
obligations may be redeemable at the option of the Authority
before maturity in such manner as may be stipulated therein.

(2) As authorized in appropriation Acts, and such authorizations
may be without fiscal year limitation, the Secretary of the
Treasury may in his discretion purchase or agree to purchase any
obligations issued pursuant to paragraph (1) of this subsection,
and for such purpose the Secretary of the Treasury is authorized

to use as a public debt transaction the proceeds of the sale of any securities hereafter issued under the Second Liberty Bond Act, as now or hereafter in force, and the purposes for which securities may be issued under the Second Liberty Bond Act as now or hereafter in force, are extended to include such purchases. Each purchase of obligations by the Secretary of the Treasury under this subsection shall be upon such terms and conditions as to yield a return at a rate not less than a rate determined by the Secretary of the Treasury, taking into consideration the current average yield on outstanding marketable obligations of the United States of comparable maturities. The Secretary of the Treasury may sell, upon such terms and conditions and at such price or prices as he shall determine, any of the obligations acquired by him under this paragraph. All purchases and sales by the Secretary of the Treasury of such obligations under this paragraph shall be treated as public debt transactions of the United States.

(h) The Secretary of the Treasury is authorized and directed to make annual payments to the Authority in such amounts as are necessary to equal the amount by which the dollar amount of interest expense accrued by the Authority on account of its obligations exceeds the dollar amount of interest income accrued by the Authority on account of obligations purchased by it pursuant to subsection (e) of this section.

(i) The Authority shall have power --

(1) to sue and be sued, complain and defend, in its corporate name;

(2) to adopt, alter, and use a corporate seal, which shall be judicially noticed;

(3) to adopt, amend, and repeal bylaws, rules, and regulations as may be necessary for the conduct of its business;

(4) to conduct its business, carry on its operations, and have offices and exercise the powers granted by this section in any State without regard to any qualification or similar statute in any State;

(5) to lease, purchase, or otherwise acquire, own, hold, improve, use, or otherwise deal in and with any property, real, personal, or mixed, or any interest therein, wherever situated;

(6) to accept gifts or donations of services, or of property, real, personal, or mixed, tangible or intangible, in aid of any of the purposes of the Authority;

(7) to sell, convey, mortgage, pledge, lease, exchange, and otherwise dispose of its property and assets;

(8) to appoint such officers, attorneys, employees, and agents as may be required, to define their duties, to fix and to pay such compensation for their services as may be determined,

subject to the civil service and classification laws, to require bonds for them and pay the premium thereof; and

(9) to enter into contracts, to execute instruments, to incur liabilities, and to do all things as are necessary or incidental to the proper management of its affairs and the proper conduct of its business.

(j) The Authority, its property, its franchise, capital, reserves, surplus, security holdings, and other funds, and its income shall be exempt from all taxation now or hereafter imposed by the United States or by any State of local taxing authority; except that (A) any real property and any tangible personal property of the Authority shall be subject to Federal, State, and local taxation to the same extent according to its value as other such property is taxed, and (B) any and all obligations issued by the Authority shall be subject both as to principal and interest to Federal, State, and local taxation to the same extent as the obligations of private corporations are taxed.

(k) All obligations issued by the Authority shall be lawful investments, and may be accepted as security for all fiduciary, trust, and public funds, the investment or deposit of which shall be under authority or control of the United States or of any officer or officers thereof. All obligations issued by the Authority pursuant to this section shall be deemed to be exempt securities within the meaning of laws administered by the Securities and Exchange Commisison, to the same extent as securities which are issued by the United States.

(1) In order to furnish obligations for delivery by the Authority, the Secretary of the Treasury is authorized to prepare such obligations in such form as the Authority may approve, such obligations when prepared to be held in the Treasury subject to delivery upon order by the Authority. The engraved plats, dies, bed pieces, and so forth, executed in connection therewith, shall remain in the custody of the Secretary of the Treasury. The Authority shall reimburse the Secretary of the Treasury for any expenditures made in the preparation, custody, and delivery of such obligations.

(m) The Authority shall, as soon as practicable after the end of each fiscal year, transmit to the President and the Congress an annual report of its operations and activities.

(n) The sixth sentence of the seventh paragraph of section 5136 of the Revised Statutes, as amended (12 U.S.C.), is amended by inserting "or obligations of the Environmental Financing Authority" immediately after "or obligations, participations, or other instruments of or issued by the Federal National Mortgage Association or the Government National Mortgage Association".

(o) The budget and audit provisions of the Government Corporation Control Act (31 U.S.C. 846) shall be applicable to the Environmental Financing Authority in the same manner as they are applied to the wholly owned Government corporations.

(p) Section 3689 of the Revised Statutes, as amended (31 U.S.C. 711), is further amended by adding a new paragraph following the last paragraph appropriating moneys for the purposes under the Treasury Department to read as follows: "Payment to the Environmental Financing Authority: For payment to the Environmental Financing Authority under subsection (h) of the Environmental Financing Act of 1972."

Sec. 13. Sex Discrimination.

No person in the United States shall on the ground of sex be excluded from participation in, be denied the benefits of, or be subjected to discrimination under any program or activity receiving Federal assistance under this Act, the Federal Water Pollution Control Act, or the Environmental Financing Act. This section shall be enforced through agency provisions and rules similar to those already established, with respect to racial and other discrimination, under title VI of the Civil Rights Act of 1964. However, this remedy is not exclusive and will not prejudice or cut off any other legal remedies available to a discriminate.

APPENDIX B -- STAND-ALONE SECTIONS OF PL 95-217, THE 1977 ACT

[The following sections do not amend the Federal Water Pollution Control Act, but they are new parts of the Clean Water Act of 1977 (PL 95-217), and the section numbers refer to that Act.]

Sec. 73. Existing Guidelines.

Within 90 days after the date of enactment of this Act, the Administrator shall review every effluent guideline promulgated prior to the date of enactment of this Act which is final or interim final (other than those applicable to industrial categories listed in table 2 of Committee Print Numbered 95-30 of the Committee on Public Works and Transportation of the House of Representatives) and which applies to those pollutants identified pursuant to section 304(a) of the Federal Water Pollution Control Act. The Administrator shall review every guideline applicable to industrial categories listed in such table 2 on or before July 1, 1980. Upon completion of each such review the Administrator is authorized to make such adjustments in any such guidelines as may be necessary to carry out section 304(b)(4) of such Act. The Administrator shall publish the results of each such review, including, with respect to each such guideline, the determination to adjust or not to adjust such guideline. Any such determination by the Administrator shall be final except that if, on judicial review in accordance with section 509 of such Act, it is determined that the Administrator either did not comply with the requirements of this section or the determination of the Administrator was based on arbitrary and capricious action in applying section 304(b)(4) of such Act to such guideline, the Administrator shall make a further review and redetermination of any such guideline.

Sec. 74. Seafood Processing Study.

The Administrator of the Environmental Protection Agency shall conduct a study to examine the geographical, hydrological, and biological characteristics of marine waters to determine the effects of seafood processes which dispose of untreated natural wastes into such waters. In addition, such study shall examine technologies which may be used in such processes to facilitate the use of the nutrients in these wastes or to reduce the discharge of such wastes into the marine environment. The results of such study shall be submitted to Congress not later than January 1, 1979.

Sec. 75. Cost Recovery Study.

(a) The Administrator of the Environmental Protection Agency (hereafter in this section referred to as the "Administrator") shall study the efficiency of, and the need for, the payment by industrial users of any treatment works of that portion of the cost of construction of such treatment works (as determined by the Administrator) which is allocable to the treatment of industrial wastes to the extent attributable to the Federal share of the cost of construction. Such study shall include, but not be limited to, an analysis of the impact of such a system of payment upon rural communities and on industries in economically distressed areas or areas of high unemployment. No later than the last day of the twelfth month which begins after the date of enactment of this section, the Administrator shall submit a report to the Congress seting forth the results of such study.

(b) [Sec. 75(b) repealed by PL 96-483]

(c) for purposes of this section, the terms "industrial user" and "treatment works" have the same meaning given such terms in the Federal Water Pollution Control Act.

(d) [Sec. 75(d) repealed by PL 96-483]

Sec. 76. Lake Chelan Delegation.

The Secretary of the Army, acting through the Chief of Engineers, is authorized to delegate to the State of Washington upon its request all or any part of those functions vested in such Secretary by section 404 of the Federal Water Pollution Control Act and by sections 9, 10, and 13 of the Act of March 3, 1899, relating to Lake Chelan, Washington, if the Secretary determines (1) that such State has the authority, responsibility, and capability to carry out such functions, and (2) that such delegation is in the public interest. Such delegation shall be subject to such terms and conditions as the Secretary deems necessary, including, but not limited to, suspension and revocation for cause of such delegation.

Sec. 77. Secondary Treatment Facility Site.

The Administrator of the Environmental Protection Agency shall reimburse the city of Boston, Massachusetts, an amount equal to 75 per centum, but not to exceed $15,000,000, of the cost of constructing a modern correctional detention facility on a site in such city, on condition that such city convey to the Commonwealth of Massachusetts all of its right, title, and interest in and to that real property owned by such city on Deer Island which is the site of the existing correctional detention facility for use by such Commonwealth as the site for a publicly owned treatment works providing secondary treatment. There is authorized to be appropriated $15,000,000 to carry out the purposes of this section.

Sec. 78. Total Treatment System Funding.

Notwithstanding any other provision of law, in any case where the Administrator of the Environmental Protection Agency finds that the total of all grants made under section 201 of the Federal Water Pollution Control Act for the same treatment works exceeds the actual construction costs for such treatment works (as defined in that Act) such excess amount shall be a grant of the Federal share (as defined in that Act) of the cost of construction of a sewage collection system if -- (1) such sewage collection system was constructed as part of the same total treatment system as the treatment works for which such section 201 grants were approved, and (2) an application for assistance for the construction of such sewage collection system was filed in accordance with section 702 of the Housing and Urban Development Act of 1965 (42 U.S.C. 3102) before all such section 201 grants were made and such 702 grant

could not be approved due to lack of funding under such section 702.
The total of all grants for sewage collection systems made under
this section shall not exceed $2,800,000.

APPENDIX C -- SECTION 26 OF PL 97-117, THE 1981 ACT

[Section 26 of PL 97-117, the "Municipal Wastewater Treatment Construction Grant Amendments of 1981," did not amend the Act but made certain recommendations regarding consent agreements reached prior to enactment of PL 97-117. The text of that section follows:]

Sec. 26. Judicial Notice.

It is the sense of Congress that judicial notice should be taken of this Act and of the amendments to the Federal Water Pollution Control Act made by this Act, including reduced authorization levels under section 207 of such Act, and that the parties to Federal consent decrees establishing a deadline, schedule, or timetable for the construction of publicly owned treatment works are encouraged to reexamine the provisions of such consent decrees and, where required by equity, to make appropriate adjustments in such provisions.")

APPENDIX D -- LIST OF PRIORITY POLLUTANTS REFERRED TO IN SECTION 307

[Section 307(a)(1) of the Act refers to the list of toxic pollutants published in Table 1 of Committee Print Number 95-30 of the House Committee of Public Works and Transportation. Following is the text of Table 1:]

TABLE 1. -- SECTION 307 -- TOXIC POLLUTANTS

Acenaphthene
Acrolein
Acrylonitrile
Aldrin/Dieldrin
Antimony and compounds*
Arsenic and compounds
Asbestos
Benzene
Benzidine
Beryllium and compounds
Cadmium and compounds
Carbon tetrachloride
Chlordane (technical mixture and metabolites)
Chlorinated benzenes (other than dichlorobenzenes)
Chlorinated ethanes (including 1,2-dichloroethane,
    1,1,1-trichloroethane, and hexachloroethane)
Chloroalkyl ethers (chloromethyl, chloroethyl, and
    mixed ethers)
Chlorinated naphthalene
Chlorinated phenols (other than those listed elsewhere;
    includes trichlorophenols and chlorinated cresols)
Chloroform
2-chlorophenol
Chromium and compounds
Copper and compounds
Cyanides
DDT and metabolites
Dichlorobenzenes (u,2-, 1,3-, and 1,4-dichlorobenzenes)
Dichlorobenzidine
Dichloroethylenes (1,1- and 1,2-dichloroethylene)
2,4-dichlorophenol
Dichloropropane and dichloropropene
2,4-dimethylphenol
Dinitrotoluene
Diphenylhydrazine
Endosulfan and metabolites
Endrin and metabolites
Ethylbenzene
Fluoranthene
Haloethers (other than those listed elsewhere; includes
    chlorophenylphenyl ethers, bromophenylphenyl ether,
    bis(dischloroisopropyl) ether, bis-(chloroethoxy)
    methane and polychlorinated diphenyl ethers)
Halomethanes (other than those listed elsewhere; includes
    methylene chlorid methylchloride, methylbromide,
    bromide, bromoform, dichlorobromomethane,

trichlorofluoromethane, dichlorodifluoromethane)
Heptachlor and metabolites
Hexachlorobutadiene
Hexachlorocyclohexane (all isomers)
Hexachlorocyclopentadiene
Isophorone
Lead and compounds
Mercury and compounds
Naphthalene
Nickel and compounds
Nitrobenzene
Nitrophenols (Including 2,4-dinitrophenol) dinitrocresol)
Nitrosamines
Pentachlorophenol
Phenol
Phthalate esters
Polychlorinated biphenyls (PCSs)
Polynuclear aromatic hydrocarbons (including benzanthracenes,
     benzopyrenes, benzofluoranthene, chrysenes,
     dibenzanthracenes, and indenopyrenes)
Selenium and compounds
Silver and compounds
2,3,7,8-Tetrachlorodibenzo-p-dioxin (TCDD)
Tetrachloroethylene
Thallium and compounds
Toluene
Toxaphene
Trichloroethylene
Vinyl chloride
Zinc and compounds

---

* The term "compounds" shall include organic and inorganic
compounds.

APPENDIX E -- STAND-ALONE SECTIONS OF PL 100-4, THE 1987 ACT

[The following sections do not amend the Clean Water Act, but are
new provisions of the Water Quality Act of 1987 (PL 100-4), and the
section numbers refer to that Act.]

Sec. 317. **National Estuary Program.**

(a) Purposes and Policies. --

   (1) Findings. -- Congress finds and declares that --

      (A) the Nation's estuaries are of great importance for fish
      and wildlife resources and recreation and economic
      opportunity;

      (B) maintaining the health and ecological integrity of these
      estuaries is in the national interest;

      (C) increasing coastal population, development, and other
      direct and indirect uses of these estuaries threaten their
      health and ecological integrity;

      (D) long-term planning and management will contribute to the
      continued productivity of these areas, and will maximize
      their utility to the Nation; and

      (E) better coordination among Federal and State programs
      affecting estuaries will increase the effectiveness and
      efficiency of the national effort to protect, preserve, and
      restore these areas.

   (2) Purposes. -- The purposes of this section are to --

      (A) identify nationally significant estuaries that are
      threatened by pollution, development, or overuse;

      (B) promote comprehensive planning for, and conservation and
      management of, nationally significant estuaries;

      (C) encourage the preparation of management plans for
      estuaries of national significance; and

      (D) enhance the coordination of estuarine research.

Sec. 318. **Unconsolidated Quaternary Aquifer.**

Notwithstanding any other provision of law, no person may --

   (1) locate or authorize the location of a landfill, surface
   impoundment, waste pile, injection well, or land treatment
   facility over the Unconsolidated Quaternary Aquifer, or the
   recharge zone or streamflow source zone of such aquifer, in the
   Rockaway River Basin, New Jersey (as such aquifer and zones are

described in the Federal Register, January 24, 1984, pages 2946-2948); or

(2) place or authorize the placement of solid waste in a landfill, surface impoundment, waste pile, injection well, or land treatment facility over such aquifer or zone. This section may be enforced under sections 309(a) and (b) of the Federal Water Pollution Control Act. For purposes of section 309(c) of such Act, a violation of this section shall be considered a violation of section 301 of the Federal Water Pollution Control Act.

Sec. 407. Log Transfer Facilities.

(a) Agreement. -- The Administrator and Secretary of the Army shall enter into an agreement regarding coordination of permitting for log transfer facilities to designate a lead agency to process permits required under section 402 and 404 of the Federal Water Pollution Control Act, where both such sections apply, for discharges associated with the construction and operation of log transfer facilities. The Administrator and Secretary are authorized to act in accordance with the terms of such agreement to assure that, to the maximum extent practicable, duplication, needless paperwork and delay in the issuance of permits, and inequitable enforcement between and among facilities in different States, shall be eliminated.

(b) Applications and Permits Before October 22, 1985. -- Where both of sections 402 and 404 of the Federal Water Pollution Control Act apply, log transfer facilities which have received a permit under section 404 of such Act before October 22, 1985, shall not be required to submit a new application for a permit under section 402 of such Act. If the Administrator determines that the terms of a permit issued on or before October 22, 1985, under section 404 of such Act satisfies the applicable requirements of sections 301, 302, 306, 307, 308, and 403 of such Act, a separate application for a permit under section 402 of such Act shall not thereafter be required. In any case where the Administrator demonstrates, after an opportunity for a hearing, that the terms of a permit issued on or before October 22, 1985, under section 404 of such Act do not satisfy the applicable requirements of sections 301, 302, 306, 307, 308, and 403 of such Act, modifications to the existing permit under section 404 of such Act to incorporate such applicable requirements shall be issued by the Administrator as an alternative to issuance of a separate new permit under section 402 of such Act.

(c) Log Transfer Facility Defined. -- For the purposes of this section, the term "log transfer facility" means a facility which is constructed in whole or in part in waters of the United States and which is utilized for the purpose of transferring commercially harvested logs to or from a vessel or log raft, including the formation of a log raft.

Sec. 508. Special Provisions Regarding Certain Dumping Sites.

(a) Finding. -- The Congress finds that the New York Bight Apex is no longer a suitable location for the ocean dumping of municipal sludge.

Sec. 509. Ocean Discharge Research Projects.

(a) In General. -- Notwithstanding any other provision of law, the Administrator is authorized to issue a research permit to the Orange County, California, sanitation Districts for the discharge of preconditioned municipal sewage sludge into the ocean for the purpose of enabling research to be conducted in assessing and analyzing the effects of disposing of sewage sludge by pipeline into ocean waters --

> (1) if the Administrator is satisfied that such local governmental agency is actively pursuing long-term land-based options for the handling of its sludge with special emphasis on remote disposal alternatives set forth in 1980 LA/OMA sludge management project and on reuse of sludge or use of recycled sludge; and

> (2) if the Administrator determines that there is no likelihood of an unacceptable adverse effect on the environment as a result of issuance of such permit and that such permit would meet the requirements of paragraph (2) of section 301(h) of the Federal Water Pollution Control Act, as amended by this Act, and of the sentences following the first sentence of such section if such permit were being issued under such section.

(b) Permit Terms. --

> (1) Period. -- The permit for the discharge of sludge shall be for a period of 5 years commencing on the date of such discharge and shall not be extended or renewed.

> (2) Monitoring. -- Such permit shall provide for monitoring (including whole effluent monitoring) of permitted discharges and other discharges into the ocean in the same area and the effects of such discharges (including cumulative effects) in conformance with requirements established by the Administrator, after consultation with appropriate Federal and State agencies, and for the reporting of such monitoring to Congress and the Administrator every 6 months.

> (3) Volume of Discharge. -- Such permit shall provide that the volume of such local agency's sludge disposal of by such experimental pipeline shall be no more than one and one-half times that being disposed of by such remote disposal and alternatives for the reuse of sludge and the use of recycled sludge. In no event shall the agency dispose of more than 50 percent of its sludge by the pipeline.

> (4) Termination. -- The permit shall provide for termination of the permit if the Administrator determines that the disposal of sewage sludge is resulting in an unacceptable adverse impact on

fish, shellfish, and wildlife. The Administrator may terminate a permit issued under this section if the Administrator determines that there has been a decline in ambient water quality of the receiving waters during the period of the permit even if a direct cause and effect relationship cannot be shown. If the effluent from a source with a permit issued under this section is contributing to a decline in ambient water quality of the receiving waters, the Administrator shall terminate such permit.

(c) Limitation on Precedent. -- The facts and circumstances described in subsection (a) present a unique situation which will not establish a precedent for the relaxation of the requirements of the Federal Water Pollution Control Act applicable to similarly situated discharges.

(d) Report. -- Such districts shall report the results of the program and an analysis of such program to Congress under this section not later than four and one-half years after issuance of the permit.

Sec. 510. San Diego, California.

(a) Purpose. -- The purpose of this section is to protect the economy, public health, environment, surface water and public beaches, and water quality of the city of San Diego, California, and surrounding areas, which are endangered and are being polluted by raw sewage emanating from the city of Tijuana, Mexico.

(b) Construction Grants. -- Upon approval of the necessary plans and specifications, the Administrator is authorized to make grants to the Secretary of State, acting through the American Section of the International Boundary and Water Commission (hereinafter in this section referred to as the "Commission"), or any other Federal agency or any other appropriate commission or entity designated by the President. Such grants shall be for construction of a project consisting of --

   (1) defensive treatment works to protect the residents of the city of San Diego, California, and surrounding areas from pollution resulting from any inadequacies or breakdowns in wastewater treatment works and systems in Mexico; and

   (2) treatment works in the city of San Diego, California, to provide primary or more advanced treatment of municipal sewage and industrial waste from Mexico, including the city of Tijuana, Mexico.

(c) Limitation on Grants. -- Notwithstanding subsection (b), the Administrator may make grants for construction of treatment works described in subsection (b)(2) only if, after public notice and comment, the Administrator determines that treatment works in Mexico, in conjunction with any defensive treatment works constructed under this or any other Act, are not sufficient to protect the residents of the city of San Diego, California, and surrounding areas from water pollution originating in Mexico.

(d) Operation and Maintenance. -- The Commission or such other agency, commission, or entity as may be designated under subsection (b) is authorized to operate and maintain any treatment works constructed under subsection (b) in order to accomplish the purposes of this section.

(e) Approval of Plans. -- Any treatment works for which a grant is made under this section shall be constructed in accordance with plans developed by the Commission or such other agency, commission, or entity as may be designated under subsection (b), in consultation with the city of San Diego, and approved by the Administrator to meet the construction standards which would be applicable if such treatment works were being constructed under title II of the Federal Water Pollution Control Act.

(f) Federal Share. -- Construction of the treatment works under subsection (b) shall be at full Federal expense less any costs paid by the Government of Mexico as a result of agreements negotiated with the United States.

(g) Ocean Outfall Permit. -- Notwithstanding section 301(j) of the Federal Water Pollution Control Act, upon application of the city of San Diego, California, the Administrator may issue a permit under section 301(h) of such Act which modifies the requirements of section 301(b)(1)(B) of such Act to permit the discharge of pollutants for any ocean outfall constructed with Federal assistance under this section if the Administrator finds that issuing such permit is in the best interests of achieving the goals and requirements of such Act. The Administrator may waive the requirements of section 301(b)(5) of such Act with respect to the issuance of such permit if the Administrator finds that such waiver is in the best interests of achieving the goals and requirements of such Act.

(h) Treatment of San Diego Sewage. -- If any treatment works constructed pursuant to this section becomes no longer necessary to provide protection from pollution originating in Mexico, the city of San Diego, California, may use such treatment works to treat municipal and individual waste originating in the city of San Diego and surrounding areas if the city of San Diego enters into a binding agreement with the Administrator to pay to the United States 45 percent of the costs incurred in the construction of such treatment works.

(i) Definitions. -- For purposes of this section, the terms "construction" and "treatment works" have the meanings such terms have under section 212 of the Federal Water Pollution Control Act.

(j) Authorization of Appropriations. -- There is authorized to be appropriated for fiscal years beginning after September 30, 1986, such sums as may be necessary to the Administrator to make grants under this section and such sums as may be necessary to the Commission or such other agency, commission, or entity as the President may designate under subsection (b), to carry out this section.

Sec. 511. Limitation on Discharge of Raw Sewage by New York City.

(a) In General. --

(1) North River Plant. -- If the wastewater treatment plant identified in the consent decree as the North River plant has not achieved advanced preliminary treatment as required under the terms of the consent decree by August 1, 1986, the city of New York shall not discharge raw sewage from the drainage area of such plant (as defined in the consent decree) into navigable waters after such date in an amount which is greater for any 30-day period than an amount equal to 30 times the average daily amount of raw sewage discharged from such drainage area during the 12-month period ending on the earlier of the date on which such plant becomes operational or March 15, 1896 (as determined by the Administrator), except as provided in subsection (b).

(2) Red Hook Plant. -- If the wastewater treatment plant identified in the consent decree as the Red Hook plant has not achieved advanced preliminary treatment as required under the terms of the consent decree by August 1, 1987, the city of New York shall not discharge raw sewage from the drainage area of such plant (as defined in the consent decree) into navigable waters after such date in an amount which is greater for any 30-day period than an amount equal to 30 times the average daily amount of raw sewage discharged from such drainage area during the 12-month period ending on the earlier of the date on which such plant becomes operational or March 15, 1987 (as determined by the Administrator), except as provided in subsection (b).

(b) Waivers. --

(1) Interruption of Plant Operation. -- In the event of any significant interruption in the operation of the North River plant or the Red Hook plant caused by an event described in subparagraph (A), (B), or (C) of paragraph (5) occurring after the applicable deadline established under subsection (a), the Administrator shall waive the limitation of subsection (a) with respect to such plant, but only to such extent and for such limited period of time as may be reasonably necessary for the city of New York to resume operation of such plant.

(2) Increased Precipitation. -- In the event that the volume of precipitation occurring after the applicable deadline established under subsection (a) causes the discharge of raw sewage to exceed the limitation under subsection (a), the Administrator shall waive the limitation of subsection (a) with respect to either or both such plants, but only to such extent and for such limited period of time as the Administrator determines to be necessary to take into account the increased discharge caused by such volume of precipitation.

(3) Variations in Certain North River Drainage Area Discharges. -- In the event that an increase in discharges from the North River drainage area constituting a violation of subsection (a)(1) is due to a random or seasonal variation, and that any

sewer hookup occurring, or permit for a sewer hookup granted, after July 31, 1986, is not responsible for such violation, the Administrator shall waive the limitation of subsection (a)(1), but only to such extent and for such limited period of time as the Administrator determines to be reasonably necessary to take into account such random or seasonal variation.

(4) Variations in Certain Red Hook Drainage Area Discharges. -- In the event that an increase in discharges from the Red Hook drainage area constituting a violation of subsection (a)(2) is due to a random or seasonal variation, and that any sewer hookup occurring, or permit for a sewer hookup granted, after July 31, 1987, is not responsible for such violation, the Administrator shall waive the limitation of subsection (a)(2), but only to such extent and for such limited period of time as the Administrator determines to be reasonably necessary to take into account such random or seasonal variation.

(5) Circumstances Beyond City's Control. -- The Administrator shall extend either deadline under paragraph (1) or (2) of subsection (a) to such extent and for such limited period of time as may be reasonably required to take into account any --

(A) act of war,

(B) unanticipated grave natural disaster or other natural phenomenon of an exceptional, inevitable, and irresistible character, the effects of which could not have been prevented or avoided by the exercise of due care or foresight, or

(C) other circumstances beyond the control of the city of New York, except such circumstances shall not include (i) the unavailability of Federal funds under section 201 of the Federal Water Pollution Control Act, (ii) the unavailability of funds from the city of New York or the State of New York, or (iii) a policy decision made by the city of New York or the State of New York to delay the achievement of advanced preliminary treatment at the North River plant or Red Hook plant beyond the applicable deadline set forth in subsection (a).

(c) Penalties. -- Except as otherwise provided in subsection (b), any violation of subsection (a) shall be considered to be a violation of section 301 of the Federal Water Pollution Control Act, and all provisions of such Act relating to violations of such section 301 shall apply.

(d) Consent Decree Defined. -- For purposes of this section, the term "consent decree" means the consent decree entered into by the Environmental Protection Agency, the city of New York, and the State of New York, on December 30, 1982, relating to construction and operation of the North River and Red Hook wastewater treatment plants.

(e) Cooperation. -- The Administrator shall work with the city of New York to eliminate the discharge of raw sewage by such city at the earliest practicable date.

(f) Savings Clause. -- Nothing in this section shall be construed as modifying the terms of the consent decree.

(g) Sense of Congress. -- It is the sense of Congress that the Administrator should not agree to any further modification of the consent decree with respect to the schedule for achieving advanced preliminary treatment.

(h) Termination Dates. --

    (1) North River Plant. -- The provisions of this section shall remain in effect with respect to the North River drainage area until such time as the North River plant has achieved advanced preliminary treatment (as defined in the consent decree) for a period of six consecutive months.

    (2) Red Hook Plant. -- The provisions of this section shall remain in effect with respect to the Red Hook drainage area until such time as the Red Hook plant has achieved advanced preliminary treatment (as defined in the consent decree) for a period of six consective months.

(i) Monitoring Activities. -- The Administrator shall promptly establish and carry out a program within available funds to implement the monitoring activities which may be required under subsection (a).

(j) Establishment of Methodologies. -- The Administrator shall establish the methodologies, data base, and any other information required for making determinations under subsection (b) --

    (1) for the North River drainage area (as defined in the consent decree) by July 31, 1986, unless the requirements of subsection (h)(1) have been satisfied, and

    (2) for the Red Hook drainage area (as defined by the consent decree) by July 31, 1987, unless the requirements of subsection (h)(2) have been satisfied.

(k) Violations. -- In carrying out this section, if the Administrator finds that a violation of subsection (a) has occurred, the Administrator shall also determine, within 30 days after such finding, whether a provision of subsection (b) applies. If the Administrator requires information from the city of New York in order to determine whether a provision of subsection (b) applies, the Administrator shall request such information. If the city of New York does not supply the information requested by the Administrator, the Administrator shall determine that subsection (b) does not apply. The City of New York shall be responsible only for such expenses as are necessary to provide such requested information. Enforcement action pursuant to subsection (c) shall be commenced at the end of such 30 days unless a provision of subsection (b) applies.

Sec. 512. Oakwood Beach and Red Hook Projects, New York.

(a) Relocation of Natural Gas Facilities. -- Notwithstanding any provision of the Federal Water Pollution Control Act, the Administrator shall pay, to the extent provided in appropriation Acts, in the same proportion as the Federal share of other project costs, all expenses for the relocation of factilities for the distribution of natural gas with respect to the entire wastewater treatment works known as the Oakwood Beach (EPA Grant Numbered 360392) and Red Hook (EPA Grant Numbered 360394) projects, New York.

(b) Authorization of Appropriations. -- There is authorized to be appropriated for fiscal years beginning after September 30, 1986, not to exceed $7,000,000 to carry out this section.

Sec. 513. Boston Harbor and Adjacent Waters.

(a) Grants. -- The Administrator shall make grants to the Massachusetts Water Resource Authority for purposes of --

(1) assessing the principal factors having an adverse effect on the environmental quality of Boston Harbor and its adjacent waters;

(2) developing and implementing a management program to improve the water quality of such Harbor and waters; and

(3) constructing necessary waste water treatment works for providing secondary treatment for the areas served by such authority.

(b) Federal Share. -- The Federal share of projects described in subsection (a) shall not exceed 75 percent of the cost of construction thereof.

(c) Emergency Improvements. -- The Administrator is authorized and directed to make grants to the Massachusetts Water Resource Authority for a project to undertake emergency improvements at the Deer Island Waste Water Treatment Plant in Boston, Massachusetts. The Federal share of such project shall not exceed 75 percent of the cost of carrying out such improvements.

(d) Authorization of Appropriations. -- There is authorized to be appropriated $100,000,000 to carry out this section for fiscal years beginning after September 30, 1986, to remain available until expended. Such sums shall be in addition to and not in lieu of any other amounts authorized to be appropriated under title II of the Federal Water Pollution Control Act.

Sec. 514. Wastewater Reclamation Demonstration.

(a) Authority to Make Grants. -- The Administrator is authorized to make a grant to the San Diego Water Reclamation Agency, California, to demonstrate and field test for public use innovative processes which advance the technology of wastewater reclamation and which promote the use of reclaimed watewater.

(b) Federal Share. -- The Federal share of grants made under this section shall be 85 percent of the costs of conducting such demonstration and field test.

(c) Authorization of Appropriations. -- There is authorized to be appropriated not to exceed $2,000,000 to carry out this section for fiscal years beginning after September 30, 1986.

Sec. 515. Des Moines, Iowa.

(a) Grant. -- The Administrator is authorized to make a grant to the city of Des Moines, Iowa, for construction of the Central Sewage Treatment Plant component of the Des Moines, Iowa, metropolitan area project. The Federal share of such project shall be 75 percent of the cost of construction.

(b) Authorization of Appropriations. -- There is authorized to be appropriated to carry out this section not to exceed $50,000,000 for fiscal years beginning after September 30, 1986. Such sums shall be in addition to and not in lieu of any other amounts authorized to be appropriated under title II of the Federal Water Pollution Control Act.

Sec. 516. Study of De Minimis Discharges.

(a) Study. -- The Administrator shall conduct a study of discharges of pollutants into the navigable waters and their regulation under the Federal Water Pollution Control Act to determine whether or not there are discharges of pollutants into such waters in amounts which, in terms of volume, concentration, and type of pollutant, are not significant and to determine the most effective and appropriate methods of regulating any such discharges.

(b) Report. -- Not later than 1 year after the date of the enactment of this Act, the Administrator shall submit to the Committee on Public Works and Transportation of the House of Representatives and the Committee on Environment and Public Works of the Senate a report on the results of such study along with recommendations and findings concerning the most effective and appropriate methods of regulating any discharges of pollutants into the navigable waters in amounts which the Administrator determines under such study to be not significant.

Sec. 519. Study of Pretreatment of Toxic Pollutants.

(a) Study. -- The Administrator shall study --

(1) the adequacy of data on environmental impacts of toxic industrial pollutants discharged from publicly owned treatment works;

(2) the extent to which secondary treatment at publicly owned treatment works removes toxic pollutants;

(3) the capability of publicly owned treatment works to revise pretreatment requirements under section 307(b)(1) of the Federal Water Pollution Control Act;

(4) possible alternative regulatory strategies for protecting the operations of publicly owned treatment works from industrial discharges, and shall evaluate the extent to which each such strategy identified may be expected to achieve the goals of this Act;

(5) for each such alternative regulatory strategy, the extent to which removal of toxic pollutants by publicly owned treatment works results in contamination of sewage sludge and the extent to which pretreatment requirements may prevent such contamination or improve the ability of publicly owned treatment works to comply with sewage sludge criteria developed under section 405 of the Federal Water Pollution Control Act; and

(6) the adequacy of Federal, State, and local resources to establish, implement, and enforce multiple pretreatment limits for toxic pollutants for each such alternative strategy.

(b) Report. -- Not later than 4 years after the date of the enactment of this Act, the Administrator shall submit a report on the results of such study along with recommendations for improving effectiveness of pretreatment requirements to the Committee on Public Works and Transportation of the House of Representatives and the Committee on Environment and Public Works of the Senate.

Sec. 520. Studies of Water Pollution Problems in Aquifers.

(a) Studies. -- The Administrator, in conjunction with State and local agencies and after providing an opportunity for full public participation, shall conduct studies for the purpose of identifying existing and potential point and nonpoint sources of pollution, and of identifying measures and practices necessary to control such sources of pollution, in the following groundwater systems and aquifers:

(1) the groundwater system of the Upper Santa Cruz Basin and the Avra-Altar Basin of Pima, Pinal, and Santa Cruz Counties, Arizona;

(2) the Spokane-Rathdrum Valley Aquifer, Washington and Idaho;

(3) the Nassau and Suffolk Counties Aquifer, New York;

(4) the Whidbey Island Aquifer, Washington;

(5) the Unconsolidated Quaternary Aquifer, Rockaway River area, New Jersey;

(6) contaminated ground water under Litchfield, Hartford, Fairfield, Tolland, and New Haven counties, Connecticut; and

(7) the Sparta Aquifer, Arkansas.

(b) Reports. -- Not later than 2 years after the date of the enactment of this Act, the Administrator shall submit to Congress a report on the studies conducted under this section.

(c) Authorization of Appropriations. -- There is authorized to be appropriated $7,000,000 for fiscal years beginning after September 30, 1986, to carry out this section.

Sec. 521. Great Lakes Consumptive Use Study.

(a) Study of Consumptive Uses. -- In recognition of the serious impacts on the Great Lakes environment that may occur as a result of increased consumption of Great Lakes water, including loss of wetlands and reduction of fish spawning and habitat areas, as well as serious economic losses to vital Great Lakes industries, and in recognition of the national goal to provide environmental protection and preservation of our natural resources while allowing for continued economic growth, the Secretary of the Army in cooperation with the Administrator, other interested departments, agencies, and instrumentalities of the United States, and the eight Great Lakes States, is authorized to conduct a study of the effects of Great Lakes water consumption on economic growth and environmental quality in the Great Lakes region and of control measures that can be implemented to reduce the quantity of water consumed.

(b) Matters Included. -- The study authorized by this section shall at a minimum include the following:

(1) a review of the methodologies used to forecast Great Lakes consumptive uses, including an analysis of the sensitivity of key variables affecting such uses;

(2) an analysis of the effect that enforcement of provisions of the Federal Water Pollution Control Act relating to thermal discharges has had on consumption of Great Lakes water;

(3) an analysis of the effect of laws, regulations, and national policy objectives on consumptive uses of Great Lakes water used in manufacturing;

(4) an analysis of the associated environmental impacts and of the economic effects on industry and other interests in the Great Lakes region associated with individual consumptive use control strategies; and

(5) a summary discussion containing recommendations for methods of controlling consumptive uses which methods maximize benefits to the Great Lakes ecosystem and also provide for continued full economic growth for consuming industries as well as other industries which depend on the use of Great Lakes water.

(c) Great Lakes States Defined. -- For purposes of this section, the "Great Lakes States" means Minnesota, Wisconsin, Illinois, Ohio, Michigan, Indiana, Pennsylvania, and New York.

(d) Authorization of Appropriations. -- There is authorized to be appropriated for fiscal years beginning after September 30, 1986, $750,000 to carry out this section. Sums appropriated under this section shall remain available until expended.

Sec. 522. Sulfide Corrosion Study.

(a) Study. -- The Administrator shall conduct a study of the corrosive effects of sulfides in collection and treatment systems, the extent to which the uniform imposition of categorical pretreatment standards will exacerbate such effects, and the range of available options to deal with such effects.

(b) Consultation. -- The study required by this section shall be conducted in consultation with the Los Angeles City and County sanitation agencies.

(c) Report. -- Not later than 1 year after the date of the enactment of this Act, the Administrator shall submit a report on the results of the study, together with recommendations for measures to reduce the corrosion of treatment works, to the Committee on Public Works and Transportation of the House of Representatives and the Committee on Environment and Public Works of the Senate.

(d) Authorization of Appropriations. -- There is authorized to be appropriated $1,000,000 to carry out this section for fiscal years beginning after September 30, 1986.

Sec. 523. Study of Rainfall Induced Infiltration Into Sewer
           Systems.

(a) Study. -- The Administrator shall study problems associated with rainfall induced infiltration into wastewater treatment sewer systems. As part of such study, the Administrator shall study appropriate methods of regulating rainfall induced infiltration into the sewer system of the East Bay Municipal Utility District, California.

(b) Report. -- Not later than one year after the date of the enactment of this Act, the Administrator shall submit to Congress a report on the results of such study, along with recommendations on reasonable methods to reduce such infiltration.

Sec. 524. Dam Water Quality Study.

The Administrator, in cooperation with interested States and Federal agencies, shall study and monitor the effects on the quality of navigable waters attributable to the impoundment of water by dams. The results of such study shall be submitted to Congress not later than December 31, 1987.

Sec. 525. Study of Pollution in Lake Pend Oreille, Idaho.

The Administrator shall conduct a comprehensive study of the sources of pollution in Lake Pend Oreille, Idaho, and the Clark Fork River and its tributaries, Idaho, Montana, and Washington, for the purpose of identifying the sources of such pollution. In conducting such study, the Administrator shall consider existing studies, surveys, and test results concerning such pollution. The Administrator shall report to Congress the findings and recommendations concerning the study conducted under this section.